1983
SEASON
THE COMPLETE HANDBOOK OF
PRO HOCKEY

SHORELINE JR. SEC.

1983 SEASON

THE COMPLETE HANDBOOK OF
PRO HOCKEY

EDITED BY ZANDER HOLLANDER

A SIGNET BOOK

NEW AMERICAN LIBRARY

TIMES MIRROR

ACKNOWLEDGMENTS

Can the Devils find happiness in the New Jersey Meadowlands? Will the Islanders drink from the Cup for the fourth straight time? Will Wayne Gretzky make it as a movie star? Stay tuned for the ongoing serial that lends intrigue to the 1982-83 season. All that is certain is that this marks the 12th edition of THE COMPLETE HANDBOOK OF PRO HOCKEY, for which we acknowledge the efforts of contributing editor Eric Compton, Pat Calabria, Hugh Delano, Frank Orr, John Herbert, Tim Moriarty, Jeff Shermack, Mark Ruskie, Howard Blatt, Phyllis Hollander, Steve Wisniewski, Rich Rossiter, Rodger Gottlieb, Beri Greenwald, Dot Gordineer, Pat Murphy, Judie Marks and the NHL team publicity directors.

Zander Hollander

PHOTO CREDITS: Cover—Paul Bereswill; back cover—Bruce Bennett. Inside photos—Bruce Bennett, Hockey Hall of Fame, Rich Pilling, Robert Shaver, Sutter Collection, Gordon Waldock, UPI and the NHL teams.

SIGNET, SIGNET CLASSICS, MENTOR, PLUME, MERIDIAN AND NAL BOOKS
are published by The New American Library Inc. 1633 Broadway
New York, New York 10019

First Printing, October 1982

1 2 3 4 5 6 7 8 9

PRINTED IN THE UNITED STATES OF AMERICA

CONTENTS

Editor's Note: The material herein includes trades and rosters up to final printing deadline.

How Mike Bossy Became Lord Stanley's King

By PAT CALABRIA

He's tall and lean, wears a bright smile and is as popular for his homespun politeness as he is for the immense talents he brings to the game. He's a young hero in a sport where the newest stars still have pimples and only wisps of beards. He's mature beyond his 25 years. He's rich beyond his wildest imagination. He's even kind to children.

If it seems that there is nothing that exceeds Mike Bossy's grasp, he would be the first to concur. And that, in fact, is his greatest attribute. "I always think I can do something more," he said. Of course, he usually does.

He scores goals by the bushel, wins awards and trophies by the gross and inspires admiration by the ton. He is frank to the point of being blunt and he is friendly to the point of being charming, but Bossy hardly ever is so noticeable as he is when he is wagging his stick over his shoulder, begging for the puck and then whistling it past a flabbergasted goalie.

Wayne Gretzky may have commanded all the attention of the 1981-82 hockey season, but it was Bossy who commanded the team which commanded the National Hockey League by winning its third straight Stanley Cup. That was the appropriate ending to a season Bossy enjoyed from start to finish because of the blend of eye-opening personal accomplishment and overwhelming team success.

His 147 points were second only to Gretzky's record-shattering 212 and were the fourth-highest total ever registered. He was Team Canada's MVP in the Canada Cup, the all-star MVP and

On the road and at home, Pat Calabria of Newsday *enjoys a close relationship with Mike Bossy.*

Mike Bossy scores OT goal vs. Vancouver in Game 1, 1982.

the MVP and the hero in the playoffs, especially in the four-game final sweep of the Vancouver Canucks. He did all that with skill and grace and determination. And he did it with the burden of past playoff disappointments and failures eating away at him.

"People never let me forget some things," he said. "I wouldn't let myself forget them either. I knew I still had some things to prove and I wanted to prove them very badly."

Turn back the clock. Bossy's rookie season, 1977-78. He scores a rookie-record 53 goals. He enters the playoffs with a head of steam. The Islanders are ousted—stunned, actually—by the Toronto Maple Leafs in the Stanley Cup quarterfinals and Bossy is given the "choke" collar after he succumbs to vicious checking. He is beaten and intimidated.

One year later, Bossy scores 69 goals, the Islanders are the

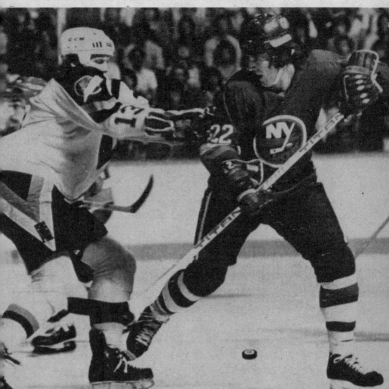

Bossy's passing froze Canuck defenders in 1982 Cup action.

best team in the land and Bossy is held to one goal as the Islanders again are upset, this time in the semifinals, by the rival New York Rangers—a bitter, wrenching, galling defeat. The "choke" collar tightens around Bossy's neck. He stews privately and publicly, dodges the media, becomes temperamental.

"Looking back, I know I didn't handle things like I wished I could have," Bossy said. "It's a matter of maturity. If the same thing happened to me again, I have to think I wouldn't react like that anymore. You have to take into consideration some things. Like '78, I had never been in the playoffs before. I had a good year, but the playoffs were a whole new experience for me. It was intimidating, and the Maple Leafs were intimidating, too. I'm not ashamed to admit that."

The confession is just another shred of evidence in Bossy's growing stature as a leader who sets examples by his forthright facing of the issues. When hockey violence became an issue, Bossy was virtually alone in declaring he would never drop his gloves to fight. The posture earned him taunts from opponents, but Bossy never wavered. He is among the few players who truly would appreciate the Lady Byng Trophy, an award which still has eluded him.

Few other achievements have. He has been Rookie of the Year, the Conn Smythe winner and a first-team all-star at right wing. But Bossy never felt he made his mark until the Islanders won their first Stanley Cup in 1980. Bossy made his contributions in big ways and in small ones.

Of course, he scored his goals, but it was the psychological triumphs which were just as important. Mel Bridgman, then the feisty center of the Philadelphia Flyers, was assigned to pester the gentle Bossy, throw him off his game and bully him. Bossy knew that was Bridgman's assignment and he wouldn't crumble.

Bossy would skate to the bench between whistles and Bridgman would deliberately stand in his path, trying to force Bossy to go around him. It was not unlike Robin Hood and Little John meeting on the log above the river. Bossy wouldn't back down.

"I knew I couldn't," he said. "I couldn't because that's what everyone expected me to do."

So, the first time, Bossy skated right into Bridgman and a scuffle ensued. Bossy emerged from it with a black eye, but clearly he was the victor in a more important sense. He kept skating into Bridgman and soon the Flyers tired of trying to upset Bossy. It wasn't long before Bossy and Bridgman passed each other without incident, and it wasn't Bossy who gave way.

"I'll never forget that," Bossy said. "In its own way, I think it was important for me. I had to let him know I was there. I wasn't going to fight, but I wasn't going to move for him, either. And I didn't."

Bossy used the experience to his advantage. He set a playoff record 35 points the following season when the Islanders repeated and he again was crucial when the Islanders completed their hat trick last season. His seven goals in the final series tied Jean Beliveau's record, which was set in a five-game final 26 years before. More than that, he once more did it against a team which tried to rattle him.

Bossy was checked by Tiger Williams, the outrageous Vancouver left wing and an old adversary. Williams was on the Toronto team that upset the Islanders in '78 and he has never liked Bossy's method of playing the game. Ignoring Bossy's development into a fine all-around player, Williams tried to stick Bossy with an old tag earlier in the finals.

"Defense?" Williams bristled, when asked about Bossy's pesty forechecking. "He doesn't know how to spell the word."

A rather disputable point, to be sure. But even Williams would not dispute what Bossy can do with the puck. Bossy scored three goals in the opener of the finals, getting the game-tying goal with less than five minutes left in regulation and the game-winner with just two seconds left in overtime. He did it with typical Bossy aplomb.

He intercepted a pass from Harold Snepsts and without wasting a second, took two strides toward the net and flicked a shot past goalie Richard Brodeur. "He's probably the only one who could have scored that goal," Snepsts marveled later.

Bossy also scored the second, essential goal in a 3-0 victory over Vancouver in Game 3. He did it shoveling three straight shots at Brodeur, the last one as he flipped it into the air, parallel to the ground, with nothing touching the ice beneath him except his outstretched stick. From that position, Bossy still managed to pull the puck from his backhand to his forehead and ease a shot past astonished defenseman Colin Campbell, who had rushed to guard the open net.

"I couldn't believe it," Campbell said. "There was maybe an inch between me and the post. I swear, he knew that and put the puck in sideways. Tell me, who else could have scored that goal, who?"

That Bossy did it after again taking a pounding from Williams merely displayed his unshakable confidence. He added two more goals in the finale, including one moments after Williams, the willing villian, had rubbed his glove across Bossy's face. Bossy never even acknowledged that Williams was there.

"I wouldn't," he said. "It must have been frustrating to him knowing that he wasn't frustrating me."

It had taken Bossy years to get to that point, but once climbed, the mountain was his. After winning the MVP award, even Williams had to throw down his sword at Bossy's feet. "He's unbelievable," Williams said. "If they can get him on my team, I'll pay part of his salary."

That would cost plenty. Bossy makes $600,000—more than any other Islander and more than any other player in the league with the exception of Gretzky. Clearly, he has earned that king's ransom. His triumph is as personal as it is profound.

All the while, he let others say that a victory over the Canucks was a victory over the clutch-and-grab mayhem of which coach Roger Neilson was the architect. Bossy was the only player on either finalist to complete the playoffs without a penalty. Bossy always did wear the white hat, and now it fits him perfectly.

"I'm proud of the way I play hockey," he said. "I'm damn proud of the way I performed under the circumstances. People still talk about 1978. I'd been living with that. Everyone said I was scared. That I wasn't tough. I wasn't going into this series and letting everything I worked for get washed away in one game by one guy. I would not let that happen."

Bossy is bold and self-assured and that's what makes him great, too. Quiet off the ice, he becomes a demon on it—hungry, persistent, dominant. He has a way for getting what he wants even when it appears he can't get it. Two years ago, when he was seeking the mark of 50 goals in 50 games, he went down to the last four minutes of his 50th game needing two goals. He got the two goals.

In the first-round playoff series against Pittsburgh last season, Bossy was hobbled by ligament damage in his left knee, an injury that would slow him throughout the playoffs. He played one period of the first game and scored a goal. He played one period of the second game and scored a goal.

And again he resisted the taunts of opponents who hoped to throw him offstride and dupe him into the penalty box. Bossy takes the strong-arm tactics coolly. He laughed at the recollection and the reminder that his wife Lucie thinks he takes too much.

"She wonders why I put up with that," Bossy said. "She thinks I should get involved more than I do. But that's the way she is. She gets mad at me sometimes because of the way I play. She's the fighter in the family. If she was a hockey player, she'd fight."

Lucie Bossy and the couple's three-year-old daughter, Josianne, have helped Bossy mature, too. He no longer is the frightened, skinny teenager out of juniors who wept to his new bride over the telephone at training camp. Bossy had never been away from home and it hurt.

"I had a roommate who spoke French, so I'd walk down the street so he couldn't hear what I was saying," said Bossy, whose household is French-speaking. "I didn't want him to hear me saying how badly I wanted to come home. A lot of nights, I had tears in my eyes."

Now Bossy is a family man, having moved from an apartment on Long Island to more permanent quarters in a luxury condominium on Nassau County's fabulous North Shore. That's part of the maturing process, too.

"Like, Bossy Nystrom, he's a true Islander," Bossy said of his teammate who wed a Long Island girl and is identified with the team more than any other player. "I'm getting there. I'm out of my apartment. I couldn't fix it up because it wasn't mine. I couldn't sit in the backyard on a nice day because we didn't have a backyard. Now we have neighbors for the first time and that's nice. People who we've gotten to know, people to say hello to and have dinner with. Now I have my home. I have something that's mine."

And he has his reputation along with the rest of the Islanders. They are the first NHL team based in an American city to win three straight championships. Only two other franchises have ever produced that many consecutive Stanley Cups—the charter franchises of Toronto and Montreal. The Islanders have been certified a dynasty and the team isn't through yet. Neither is Bossy.

He is known as a great playoff player only three years after being condemned as a playoff bust. He has three overtime goals and only two players—Nystrom and Maurice Richard—have more. He's done almost everything he's wanted to do, not bad for a player ignored in the 1977 amateur draft until the Islanders selected him 15th, after six other right wings had already been taken.

He had the reputation as a prima donna and one-way player and even Bossy concedes he had much improving to do when he first joined the team. He remembers going through a forechecking drill one day and coach Al Arbour pointing out where the forwards ought to be positioned and how they should rotate.

"I didn't have a clue as to what he was talking about," Bossy said.

But Arbour made him work and Bossy willingly toiled at the thankless task of playing defense. His scoring never suffered. Bossy even believes it may have been enhanced by it, with his defense helping to cause giveaways that led to goals. For example, the pass he intercepted from Snepsts. Or the way he hounded the Vancouver defense to earn himself three shots in a row and a tantalizing goal.

No wonder the Canuck fans made Bossy the prime target of the message in their banners at Pacific Coliseum. "Break Bossy's Legs," one pleaded. To Bossy, it was the supreme compliment.

Another compliment was the Smythe Trophy, which he wanted to win badly. It confirmed his greatness as an individual and also as a teammate. While Bossy once was looked upon as an appendage to Bryan Trottier, the Islanders' great center, they are now considered equals. Indeed, a major reason why Trottier enjoyed his first 50-goal season was Bossy's dramatic improvement and

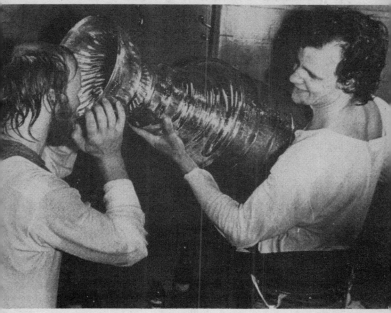

Butch Goring (left) and Stefan Persson savor third Cup.

confidence in handling the puck. Not only did Bossy have 64 goals, but he also had 83 assists.

More importantly, he had the unqualified respect of everyone, Tiger Williams included, by the time the playoffs ended. Bossy appreciated that, but he appreciated the saeson more. It was, after all, his finest season.

"I'll play the way I want," he said. "I'm glad it worked. I remember the years when it didn't. But that was a while ago. I'm not the same person."

He's a better person.

WAYNE GRETZKY'S LIFE AT THE TOP

By JOHN HERBERT

What's it really like to be Wayne Douglas Gretzky, hockey player, Edmonton Oilers, National Hockey League?

What's it like on top?

It's dining with presidents and prime ministers; meeting rock stars and movie stars; one more press conference; one more round of autographs; one more charity function; one more TV appearance; floods of compliments in print (and inevitably a critic or two); one more request prefaced with "I just need five minutes," or one more business opportunity.

It's studio portraits to send out to Hollywood stars at Christmas and having your portrait painted by LeRoy Neiman—who only paints the legends of sports. It's having a major sports complex in hometown Brantford renamed in your honor.

It's having a girlfriend and 500 marriage proposals (to say nothing of propositions); your own company (Merak Investments Ltd.); your own western clothing store (expensive, he says); your own lawyer, accountant, marketing staff, agent; another trophy; one more personal appearance; one more complimentary plane ticket; trying through it all to maintain family ties . . . and just plain playing NHL hockey.

Playing hockey.

That's what he does best. That's what put him on top. For that, he's paid the best: $1 million a season.

John Herbert, hockey writer for The Free Press *in London, Ontario, and a close friend of Wayne Gretzky's, spent 10 days in Edmonton for this closeup of the Oiler superstar. It appeared in a special 32-page section last April and is reprinted with the permission of* The Free Press.

Wayne Gretzky tosses puck from his 200th point (vs. Flames).

Life at the top . . .

It's hardly ever having a moment to yourself unless it's out on the ice where nobody seems to be able to catch you. Even then, some, such as Boston Bruin Steve Kasper, try to take away your privacy by shadowing you the way a puppy tags along with his master.

Gretzky . . . the master.

At 21 years of age, No. 99 has proven it with flabbergasting records of 92 goals and 120 assists for 212 points—standards of hockey excellence which may never be equalled. Last season he scored 28 more goals than anyone else (Mike Bossy of the New York Islanders), 27 more assists than anyone else (Peter Stastny of the Quebec Nordiques) and 66 more total points than anyone else (Bossy).

Life at the top . . .
What's it really like?
What does he mean to kids?

Adulation. Green garbage bags jammed full of mail each week.

Thousands of letters from kids who adore Gretzky the way Gretzky once idolized Gordie Howe. It's kids . . . and that's what it's all about.

Kids from Finland, USSR, Czechoslovakia, Sweden, United States or Canada. They propose marriage. They tell him whom to marry. They ask for autographs and pictures. They invite him to their homes. They are four-year-old boys. They are 79-year-old grandmothers. Sophie Moss, the mother of Wayne's girlfriend, Vicki, answers 200 letters a day. She can't keep up.

Some excerpts:

Dear Wayne:

I like you a lot. Hope you win the scoring race. Are you and Vicki getting married? I watch you all the time. I have a brother Jason, a hamster Snowball, my dad Jack, my mom Flo. I think you are cute. I am nine years old. My birthdate is October 13, 1972. Please write to me!!!!

Andre. Age 9

Zau Wayne:

You are number 1. And superstar. I collect superstars' photographs. I have Trottier, Dionne, Holmgren, Williams, Dryden, Lafleur, Nystrom, Callighen, Gainey, Babych, Clarke, Sittler, Federko, Barber—all original signatures. But your photograph and original signature be king.

Thomas. Age 15. Finland

Wayne Gretzky:

You are fastly becoming my idol, so keep on scoring

Mark. Age 11. Illinois

Dear Mr. Gretzky:

I am Czech and I am a big hockey fan. Be so kind and send me please photos with your autograph and if is possible some little souvenir for me. Something.

Lubos. Age 18. Czechoslovakia

Wayne:

This letter is to invite you and a few of your friends to come to Corner Brook, Newfoundland, to do some fishing. My family has a cabin.

Heidi, Corner Brook, Newfoundland

Dear Wayne:

Once again you are a great hockey player. May you have good health to keep it up and carry on. One thing bothers me. You are from Ukrainian background but a true Canadian. I hope and pray you pick a Canadian girl with a Ukrainian background. So many are beautiful girls. Why not give one a chance for a good and happy life?

Unsigned

What's it like meeting other celebrities or the prime minister or the U.S. President?

Roommate Kevin Lowe says Gretzky is like a little boy around movie stars, almost as excited as the people who ask him for an autograph. Missing Johnny Carson's Tonight Show when Wayne's flight was grounded in Toronto by bad weather was a heartbreak . . . the only big one of the season. In the spring, after the playoffs, he hoped to tape the show.

Who wouldn't be excited lunching with Pierre Trudeau? But he was only one of four players with class enough not to snub the prime minister the day following the Canada Cup setback. Or, having your name on the lips of President Reagan during the NFL All-Star luncheon in Washington: "Rumor has it, Wayne, Washington has been trying to get you. I asked what Edmonton is getting in return and they told me two first-round draft picks and the state of Texas."

The celebrity list grows every day: Trudeau, Reagan, Paul Anka, Billy Joel, Neiman, David Hartman, Terry Bradshaw, Jamie Farr, Rod Stewart . . .

Mike Barnett, a friend and business adviser in Western Canada for Sierra Sports Group (Gus Badali), recalled a time this season when "Stewart's people" called and asked Gretzky, for publicity purposes, to present Stewart with an Oilers' sweater.

"This is Wayne's town," Barnett said. "You present something to Wayne."

Stewart got his sweater. In return, he wore it during the concert.

How is Gretzky around ordinary people?

Arnold Anderson's story says it best.

The sports director at CKPC Radio in Brantford shares the same Jan. 26 birthdate. Every Jan. 26, Gretzky calls to wish him happy birthday.

"It's a refreshing side of him to me that's legitimate," Anderson said. "It's really nice of him. He doesn't do it for effect. This year he called for me at home and the station but we were up north for an Alexanders' (junior A) game."

Anderson said Gretzky also called the day after 132 persons

came to a new conference in Toronto last season. Anderson said Gretzky wanted to assure him he'd still be available even though the Oilers had cut off personal interviews for the rest of the season.

Barnett said Gretzky takes it on himself to visit the unfortunate.

"We were in Vancouver and I remember making a notation. I read in the paper about a skier from an acrobatic team who was in the hospital, paralyzed from an accident. The next day I was telling Wayne about it, and how he should go to the hospital to see him. He said he had already visited him."

What's it like being Gretzky's roommate?

Kevin Lowe's nickname is "Vicious" but he and Gretzky are compatible, as bachelors go.

Lowe, 21, is a defenseman from Lachute, Que., and has shared an apartment with Gretzky for the past three years.

Gretzky was billeted in an Edmonton home his first pro season in the World Hockey Association. When Lowe joined the club the following season from the Quebec Remparts, the pair got together. Last season they moved into a split-level penthouse downtown.

One of the attractions was the view of a ravine and the North Saskatchewan River twisting through the city when they moved into the apartment in June.

"A week later two cranes come out of nowhere," Lowe said. Three high-rises now block much of the view.

Lowe's the cook. Gretzky's the bottle washer and all-round housekeeper. Keeping the apartment spic and span is always a problem for bachelors. They do their best. They hired a woman to clean up once a week.

"You've got to, even though we're cleaning it," Gretzky said. "You know guys. We don't get behind the furniture."

The apartment suggests the prosperity of the young hockey stars. They have all the latest in kitchen appliances such as a microwave oven and fridge with an ice-cube and water dispenser on the door. There is a hearty supply of pirogi, hotdogs, milk and pop—not much else. Obviously, they enjoy dining out or sharing home-cooked meals at the homes of married players. The dining-room table, like the living-room furniture, is top of the line. Andy Warhol prints hang on the walls beside Neiman prints.

The phone bill runs $400 (per roomie) a month.

Fights? Never.

"In three years we've never had an altercation," Lowe said. "When we get mad, we both sense it and leave."

"Yeah, we're doing good that way," Gretzky said.

If there's anything that ticks Lowe off it's all the telephone calls (for Gretzky) and trips to the corner store for everyday requirements such as bread and milk. Gretzky's "excuse" is it'll

Teammates embrace Gretzky after record-breaking 77th goal.

mean one more round of autographs.

"He has nothing but sports on his mind," Lowe says. "He reads a lot of sports magazines. He devours statistics. He can instantly tell you George Brett's batting average.

"When he goes to the movies he generally looks for comedies."

What's it like going to McDonald's for a burger?

Mission impossible.

Wayne and Vicki do it anyway. They refuse the drive-thru. They go in and sit down like normal folks.

"Eat first, sign later," he insists.

First, that Big Mac he loves, then the autographs. That's the Gretzky rule. All the autographs which follow are a stiff price, but sometimes the McDonald's staff throws in an extra McDonald's contest puzzle piece.

What's it like playing and working alongside The Great Gretzky?

Veteran Garry Unger: "Gordie Howe was my idol. He always will be. You always have an image of a person in your mind until you meet him. For me, it was Gordie Howe. Then I met him, played with him, skied with him. To me, he was far above any person I ever met.

"I saw Gordie play from 36 to 40. I always said I wanted to see him play in his prime. I'm getting my reward now.

"No matter what anybody accomplishes in hockey, it's how they handle it as a human being. I think with Wayne . . . it's him off the ice as a guy, a person, that to me is more important than any record.

"If he scores 50 next year and we win the Cup, I'm sure he'll feel better than if he scored 100 this year and we didn't win the Cup."

Assistant coach Billy Harris: "His unselfish play—I'll remember what he did before he got No. 77 (to break Phil Esposito's regular-season goal-scoring record). It's the first period. (Jari) Kurri and Gretzky go down on a two-on-one. Wayne dumps a pass to Kurri for an easy goal. Wayne felt Kurri was in a better place to score. I'll always remember Wayne had the opportunity to score and he passed. It's the last thing the goalie (Don Edwards) expected him to do.

"If Wayne was a selfish hockey player, he'd score 150 goals a year. Maybe I'm exaggerating. Maybe 125."

Captain Lee Fogolin: "He's the greatest player in the world. What's so special to me is that he's a great guy. He's an unselfish person. He doesn't make anybody feel less than him."

Winger Pat Hughes: "People say he can't skate. That's crap," said the player who scored the goal on Gretzky's historic 200th point last season.

Winger Dave Hunter: "What everybody should say is he's a great team man. He's such a good guy off the ice. Some guys who are superstars and big scorers are not like that. Every game you get chills watching him.

"You know what he really wants? It's got to be the Stanley Cup. That would be his biggest accomplishment. He really does want that more than anything else. I know. I've played four years with him."

Radio broadcaster Rod Phillips: A flaw? "He can't block shots. Why worry about defense when you're the best offensive player in the world? You don't make the best piano player in the world into a bass fiddler."

Maurice (Rocket) Richard says: "He's a natural scorer, just like I was. He's moving all the time and it seems the players trying to check him can't catch him. He would have been the best scorer in the league (in the 1950s.)"

What riles Gretzky?

Hamilton television personality Dick Beddoes; New York writer Stan Fischler; the Not-So-Great Gretzky fans; critics who claim he can't skate; a magazine which followed him and demanded much of his time for three solid weeks shooting pictures, then published just one print.

One of the magazine's requests required him to pose in full hockey gear in temperature of 40 below on a lake outside Edmonton. One of Beddoes' favorite potshots is that Gretzky would be a fourth-string center on Toronto teams of the 1950s and 1960s. Fischler says Gretzky is an impostor in comparison with the Rocket because he is skating in a world without hitting or defense.

"Those two guys just don't seem to like me, but they have their rights and opinions. Mr. Beddoes and Mr. Fischler cut me up as a person. That's when I look at the distance to second place (in scoring). That makes me think, 'If I'm that bad, what's it make them?'

"I'm caught in circumstances I don't want to be caught in. I'm being compared with Howie Morenz, Gordie Howe, Bobby Orr, Maurice Richard and others. I'm not saying I'm better. Every era it changes. Maybe ten years ago I couldn't play. This style I can play.

"It's not my fault I play in this era."

What pleases him away from the rink?

Vicki Moss tops the list. Pirogi and macaroni five days a week. Interviews—he often stands for 45 minutes after a game, his skates not yet unlaced, answering questions. Baseball.

Vicki, from Edmonton and a family of 13, sings professionally.

Celebrity! Wayne mugs with Goldie Hawn and Burt Reynolds.

They have been dating for 2½ years.

Baseball is his second love. While he played lacrosse and took boxing lessons for two years as a kid, baseball was his other game. He pitched in the Junior Inter-County League for Brantford before the Oilers and Badali put the clamps on him. George Brett and Reggie Jackson are his baseball idols. Gretzky was in a quandary recently because a letter, requesting an autographed picture, came to his business office signed George Brett. The way it was worded, Gretzky thought the request might have been a fake. He wanted it checked out quietly to avoid embarrassment on both sides. He prides his California Angels' jacket like a little boy who takes his baseball glove to bed. Gretzky leaves his jacket over the banister post at the foot of the stairs.

The thought of dropping in on a ball game in Edmonton (Triple A) or on the Blue Jays in Toronto appeals to Gretzky. He has also realized this season he just can't be a normal baseball fan and sit in the regular seats, enjoying ball-park franks and a beverage. He's scheming to figure out a way to see the Blue Jays play.

What's it like to be one of the other Gretzkys?

For Kim Gretzky, 19, it means a new name. She will be Kim

Smith just to avoid the fuss, attention and notoriety attached to her last name when she moves to Edmonton to take a job at a day-care center.

For Keith, 15, it means instant recognition because of the 7-Up TV commercials, jeering from fans because he wears red and white skates, long autograph sessions after playing games for the touring Slapshot Live team. He played minor midget last season in Brantford for Canning Lumber Cougars, scoring more than 50 goals.

Younger brothers Brent, 12, and Glen, 10, are cast in a much lower profile lifestyle—for now. Glen, however, when featured on a W5 television program near the end of the season, said he wants to be a pro hockey player and be better than Wayne.

For father Walter, it means a four-week leave from his job as a Bell Canada serviceman. The pressure was getting to him, the demands on his time as a celebrity father, the demands to give equal attention and time to his other children. Before taking time off, Walter said he was "shaking" and sleeping only two hours a night. He says he's feeling much better now.

For mom, Phyllis, it's lots of hockey arenas as she dedicates herself to the other children, the way she did when Wayne was younger.

Kim was in Edmonton for a week late last season and got her first taste of Gretzkymania. She said she had no idea her brother was such a big star and was quite taken by the mob scene at the airport when hundreds of children showed up for a Gretzky poster competition to welcome the team back from a 21-day road trip. By the end of her stay, she became accustomed to the autograph-hunters, cameras, interviews, celebrities and everything that was happening around her big brother. She was anxious to come back—to live.

Wayne says Keith is good enough to try junior A next season, hinting it might be for a team outside of Brantford. Walter says Keith is staying in Brantford.

Keith says Wayne hasn't changed much. He said they have a normal relationship—and fight.

"A couple of summers ago my sister and I got into an argument," Keith said. "I wanted her to drive me someplace. He came in and saw me pushing my sister. He pushed me, got me into a headlock and threw me down.

"He's the same old brother to me. He moved away when he was 14 and he's always been away. I only see him two or three times a year."

The family remains in the modest bungalow despite efforts by Wayne for them to move into a new home.

"Wayne keeps hoping," Walter said. "I indicated one day we would move to keep him happy. One day, maybe. I like it where I am. This home's mine. It's paid for."

What does Wayne Gretzky think of his record season?

He says the important thing is the Oilers are winners. "That's what hockey's all about."

Financially, the season is a gold mine to be tapped.

There's the new $1-million-a-year-contract stretched over 15 years and the shopping center Oilers' owner Peter Pocklington tossed in to sweeten the pot. Pocklington has also unloaded his Westown automobile dealership in Edmonton, helping free Gretzky from a long-term commitment to Ford products in his previous contract.

There's the U.S. exposure and endorsements which will provide an additional $500,000 (after expenses) in 1982. His name is or will be lined to Bic razors and pens, 7-Up, Titan sticks, Daoust skates, Joffa equipment, automobiles, appliances, a line of clothing, thermos containers, book binders, sweaters and watches.

"What it also means to me, let's face it, is national television exposure in the U.S.," he said. "That opens the doors to a lot of things. The Paul Anka show I've already done and a few acting parts. Things like that lead to more endorsements. We haven't before stepped into the U.S. much, except with 7-Up.

"There are opportunities to do things. Movie offers."

Gretzky's marketing man, Mike Barnett, says the phones have been ringing off the hook. He says he has been working from 8 a.m. until after dark every day on endorsement deals with major U.S. companies since Gretzky won the Sporting News Man-of-the-Year award in January. The U.S. companies ask only if Gretzky is available, seldom inquiring about the price.

Barnett is not only Gretzky's business partner, but he is also a friend who acts as a buffer against intrusions on Gretzky's private world. Barnett also helps keep Gretzky out of awkward situations before they can develop. In one instance, a bar owner tried to cash in on the Gretzky name. He took on a new partner—Steve Gretzky, no relation—and renamed the place "Gretzkys" with the house specialty price at 99 cents. Barnett heard about it and started legal action to stop it.

What's it's like to be a star?

It means being told by dad you can do better.

"A year ago I had 164 points (NHL record) and everybody was congratulating me," Gretzky said. "I got home and dad says I should have had 175. That's the family thinking, whether it is school or sports. I've been taught you can always do better by parents, coaches and teachers."

When Gretzky ended a six-game slump late in the season with goals No. 83 and 84, he called home.

"My little brother (Brent) comes on the phone and says, 'You've finally found the pipes again.'"

Being a star means seeing a giant poster of you—naked from the waist up—hanging behind an interviewer at a recruiting session in Toronto to lure young nurses to the promises of Western Canada.

It means picking up major magazines and seeing your face on the covers. It's walking down the street in any city and seeing all the kids wearing jerseys with your name and No. 99 on the back.

It's instant recognition.

"Sure there's a price to pay . . . but it is nice," he said. "It makes your life more hectic, but it's all worth it."

He goes shopping on Monday afternoons at the local Red Rooster Supermarket because that's the quietest day. He pays his bills by mail. He had a section blocked off at a local restaurant where he often goes with teammates and Vicki for dinner after games. When he goes out downtown, he goes to the quiet places.

He remembers names and faces. His phone bill suggests he keeps in touch with the family back home. One of those calls was on Dec. 30, minutes after a five-goal game against Philadelphia broke a 65-year record. The goals gave him 50 in 39 games, wiping out a record of 50 goals in 50 games shared by the Rocket and Bossy.

"There aren't many 21-year-olds who'd take the time right away to call home," father Walter said. "That phone call . . . well, to Phyllis and me, it was somebody handing us a million dollars. Tax free."

What can he can do for an encore next season?

One hundred goals?

"It leaves me something for next year, doesn't it?" he said.

"Actually, I scored a lot more goals than I ever thought I could. Bossy . . . he's more of a natural scorer than me. He knows where to be around the net and has a quick release on his shot.

Gretzky wants to be more consistent next season. "I can start a little better. I want to bear down on the power play. I don't score that many on it. I would like to be a more consistent scorer. I've been a bunch scorer. Next year I don't want to go six games without a goal.

"If I can improve on those, I'll be a better player."

What's does he want to do after hockey?

He's not sure but acting is a strong possibility. "I may feel out parts. Myabe that's the field for me. I like the media side, too.

Commentary. Gus (Badali) and Mike (Barnett) will have some business adventures for me. Maybe I'll just go to Phoenix and lie in the sun."

He will know when to quit.

"People keep saying you go until you stop enjoying it. How many guys do you read who say that? You never stop enjoying the game. That's like the guys who get 90 points when they're 23 and when they're 28, they get 65. They say, 'Well, now I'm more of an all-round player.' That's just a crutch.

"When I can't put the puck in the net I'll pay my dues (retire). I might be 29. Maybe 35. I'll know. The bottom line is I get paid to score goals."

What's it like for him in Edmonton?

He loves it. He spent most of the summer there with a side trip to the Soviet Union for a documentary film with Soviet hockey star Vladislav Tretiak.

Yes, he gets recognized. Yes, he signs autographs.

But, Gretzky says, it's not half as bad as walking down the street in Toronto or Montreal. That, he admits, is next to impossible. He says people in Edmonton seem to keep their distance more, respecting his privacy.

"My first year here someone from the East was saying it's too bad I'm in Edmonton and not the East because there's no media or endorsements. As it turned out, Edmonton is the greatest city I could play in. It's smaller (approximately 700,000) and I get some privacy."

Endorsements? How could he handle more?

The Oilers hung up a "No personal interviews" sign in St. Louis on Jan. 16, but it wasn't an attempt by Gretzky to duck the swarms of media. It was the club's idea, to say "no" for Gretzky. In Toronto, the Oilers called a special news conference after receiving 132 requests for exclusive interviews. There were 125 reporters jammed into a special room in Buffalo the night he broke Esposito's 76-goal record.

The policy also covered the Oilers at home, even though the demand for his time in Edmonton was not as heavy because of the cost factor of getting there. Team public relations director Bill Tuele said there are still 50 requests a day for either interviews or personal appearances.

What's it like to sign Gretzky's paychecks?

Oilers' owner Peter Pocklington, who began as a fast-buck artist transporting old cars from the West for resale in the East while still a teenager attending Medway High School in Arva, just loves The Kid. His wife, Eva, has jokingly said he loves The Kid more than her.

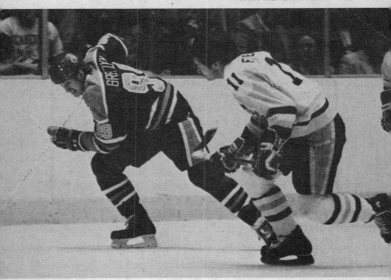

This was on a record-setting night against Pittsburgh in 1981.

Few realize Gretzky almost became a Winnipeg Jet.

Gretzky started his professional career as a 17-year-old with the Indianapolis Racers, a club that was owned by Nelson Skalbania. Early in the season, Skalbania ran into financial difficulties and decided to "sell" Gretzky to keep afloat. On a flight with Jets' president Michael Gobutny, Skalbania suggested a game of backgammon to settle the haggling over Gretzky. Gobutny, the story goes, didn't play backgammon. Exit Jets. Enter Oilers.

Skalbania's friend, Pocklington, quickly settled on a deal to bring Gretzky to Edmonton.

Gretzky's first pro contract for four years plus a three-year option contract was bumped by Pocklington to run through 1999 and then was renegotiated early this season, his fourth as a pro. "Gus (Badali) was right," Gretzky says, reflecting on the very first contract which would have expired at the end of this season. "He said four years would be the right time to sign another."

Pocklington said one of his thrills, over and above all the goals, has been watching Gretzky grow and mature.

"He's gone from a boy, to a young man, to a man this year," he said.

Where does Gretzky go after games?

He slides behind the wheel of his new, brown Lincoln—he has a black Ferrari back home in Brantford—and heads to the The Grinder (restaurant), to nightclubs where Vicki sings, out with the boys to the Sports Page lounge, over to visit friends or just back to the apartment to relax.

Gretzky spends about two hours in the dressing room fiddling and fussing before finally hitting the road. There's a certain routine to follow: the interviews, shower, whirlpool and some ping pong. Usually, there are kids Pocklington has brought into the room. Always, Gretzky is the one they search out and find.

What's it like to be assigned to follow Wayne Gretzky for 10 days?

It's Cloud Nine!

He cooks a steak for you in his apartment; invites you to tag along just about everywhere he goes; takes you into off-limits places in the dressing room; chauffeurs you about town in his Lincoln; takes you to his business office; to Vicki's brother's house to shoot pool and talk hockey over Chinese food; to the clubs where Vicki sings; to restaurants and lounges after games . . .

With an advance warning to no private interviews and no posed pictures, friend or no friend, it looked like a tough assignment.

But Gretzky hadn't changed despite all the pressure.

He stepped off a plane from a 21-day road trip and spotted me in the crowd.

"What are you doing here?" I tell him. "Don't worry, I'll help with anything you need. You've got my number? See you at practice tomorrow morning."

The red carpet treatment . . .

Hooking up with Gretzky is a chance to observe what goes on around him and see how his lifestyle has changed. But he can also tell good stories, such as the night of his embarrassing fall during a between-periods goal-scoring competition with Dino Ciccarelli of the Knights before a capacity London Gardens crowd. Ciccarelli won.

Walter Gretzky has a deep respect for London Knights' general manager Bill Long for something that happened the same evening, Gretzky's last visit to London as a member of the Sault Ste. Marie Greyhounds. Long waited 25 minutes outside the Sault dressing room until Gretzky has showered, dressed and finished with the media. When he came out, Long extended his hand to Gretzky to thank him for participating in the contest and for his contribution to the Ontario Hockey League.

"Hell of a kid. Never seen anyone like him who can handle everything the way he has and still be a regular guy," Long said.

"I'll always admire the man," Walter said of Long.

Gretzky memories . . .

There was the night at the Grinder. The first night. You remember not having time to feel uncomfortable because Gretzky introduces you to everyone . . . Laurie Boschman was there. Lowe, Kim Gretzky, Barnett, Vicki, and Wayne round out the table.

There was that night at the home of Vicki's brother, Jim Moss and his wife Laurie. The pool game. "Saturday Night Fever" was playing on television. The girls slid into the TV room. The guys, as always, gathered to talk hockey. Gretzky talked about watching his brother Keith play. He talked about the Oilers' attempts to acquire Rob Ramage from Colorado. He talked about Dave Semenko. Earlier that night Semenko had tried to get into a fight with Tiger Williams of Vancouver. Tiger had called Semenko a big goof in the Hockey News.

"I just reminded Sammy (Semenko) about it in the dressing room (before the game)," Gretzky recalled.

During the game, Gretzky said he reminded Williams.

The response?

"Bleep, bleep you prima donna."

You remember the night he ripped his trousers, catching them on an edge of the ping-pong table, and his quick retort," No wonder, they're Team Canada pants." He left the Coliseum in a sweat suit, heading to his apartment to change before going downtown to hear Vicki open a two-week singing stand at a supper club. Vicki just finished her show as Gretzky walked into the club. The next night he got there in time to take in the show.

Or riding in Gretzky's car after a game and being trailed by another with three occupants; how he shook the vehicle, gripping the wheel the way he would his hockey stick to make some unexpected moves in traffic.

You remember most the final day and the pregame meal at his apartment, him saying only two other publications had been allowed to shoot pictures there—none before at the new penthouse. You feel good. Lowe cooks the spaghetti he will share with Free Press photographer Sam McLeod. Gretzky cooks a huge steak for us. The week was complete. Gretzky calls a cab.

"See you tonight," Gretzky said as he picked up a copy of the afternoon newspaper from his doorstep before closing the door.

You know what you remember most?

Sure . . . the records, the way he played the game in 1981-82, the media clustered around after games and the autograph scenes . . . but something more important.

He's still the same nice kid I met five years ago.

Considering everything he's done in the past five years, that says a lot about The Great Gretzky.

Bobby Carpenter
and
The Young Americans

By HUGH DELANO

An American couple from New Jersey took their 12-year-old son to one of Canada's leading summer hockey camps in 1971 and was surprised but gratified to find almost two dozen boys from the United States enrolled for instruction along with predominantly Canadian youngsters.

After the boys had been registered and assigned to their cabins in a picturesque wooded area near a crystal-clear lake in Ontario, the American couple found themselves sharing morning coffee with a Canadian couple. The Americans told how hockey interest was growing in the United States, how more young boys were learning how to skate and play hockey at newly built ice rinks in the cities and suburbs, how youth leagues were forming and how many high schools now had hockey teams.

"That's nice," the Canadian mother said politely. "But, of course, we've always had rinks and skating, and our boys have always learned how to play the game when they were little more than toddlers. Remember, hockey is our game, Canada's game, not an American's game."

True. Hockey is Canada's game. It always has been and always will be. But try telling Bobby Carpenter of Peabody, Mass., Neal Broten of Roseau, Minn., Nick Fotiu of Staten Island, N.Y., or Joe Mullen from the sidewalks of New York City that Americans can't compete with Canadians in hockey. Try telling it to Robbie Ftorek of Needham, Mass. Try telling it to Herb Brooks and Craig Patrick and the members of their 1980 United States Olympic team which beat the Russians and won a gold medal at Lake Placid.

And, if you have a sense of hockey's history, try to convince

Hugh Delano casts a veteran's eye on hockey's youth movement as a sportswriter for the New York Post.

The day in 1981 when Bobby Carpenter signed with Capitals.

Frank Brimsek of Eveleth, Minn., Cecil Dillon of Toledo, Ohio, Pete Babando of Braeburn, Pa., Bill Moe of Danvers, Mass., or Tommy Williams of Duluth, Minn., that, as Americans, they had no business playing hockey.

American-born and American-trained hockey players, relegated to a minority role in the sport for many years, now are making their greatest breakthrough in both numbers and prominence in the highest level of hockey—the NHL.

An American playing in the NHL, especially playing well, used to be a rarity, a novelty, a quirk of fate. Thirty years ago there were only three Americans playing in the NHL. Twenty years ago there still were only three. Fourteen years ago there were only six. Ten years ago there were only 15. Five years ago the ranks of Americans in the NHL had climbed to 37.

Consider what happened last season in the NHL: there were 71 Americans playing in the NHL...the most in NHL history. Of the 21 teams in the NHL, only the Calgary Flames failed to have an American player in their lineup at one time or another. The New York Rangers had the most Americans, 12; the Minnesota North Stars used 10 players born in the United States. The St. Louis Blues, Hartford Whalers and Colorado Rockies each used seven American players. Additionally, the Americanization of the NHL found two teams with American-born coaches and general managers: Brooks, who went from U.S. Olympic team "Miracle on Ice" fame to coaching the Rangers, is from St. Paul, Minn., and Patrick, the Rangers' general manager, was born in Detroit. Larry Pleau, Hartford's general manager, is from Lynn, Mass., and made the breakthrough as a player in 1969 with the Montreal Canadians. The Whalers' assistant coach, John Cunniff, is from Boston.

"I think you're going to see more Americans playing in the NHL in the years ahead," said Boston Bruins' General Manager Harry Sinden. "American boys can see now they have an opportunity to make a good career out of playing hockey, an opportunity that wasn't there in the past. What Bobby Carpenter accomplished should be a great incentive to other good young American hockey players."

Carpenter spent his formative years in the sport in a hotbed of hockey—the New England area. He starred at St. John's Prep in Danvers, Mass., acclaimed as the best American high school hockey player. Hartford wanted to draft him. So did most NHL teams. The Washington Capitals selected him as their first draft choice in 1981. He was the third player chosen in the draft, the highest draft selection ever of an American.

The smooth, graceful, 6-0, 185-pound Carpenter was only 17 when he was drafted. By 18 he was playing regularly, either at center or left wing, with Washington, earning a $200,000 salary as the first U.S. high school player to go directly to the NHL. He already was battle-hardened, having played in international tournaments in Europe.

"It was something no other American ever had the chance to do," said Carpenter. "Even if I failed, I could say I tried to do it."

Carpenter never came close to failure. As an 18-year-old, he scored 32 goals, 35 assists, 67 points in his first season as a professional in the NHL, scoring four goals in one game.

"Bobby Carpenter has a tremendous career ahead of him, a chance for greatness," said Brooks. "He has everything he needs to be great. So does Neal Broten."

Herb Brooks coached North Stars' Neal Broten at U. of Minn.

Brooks can't help being partial to the 23-year-old Broten. He coached him at the University of Minnesota after watching him star for Roseau High School in Minnesota's outstanding high school hockey competition. Broten played for Brooks' 1980 gold medal U.S. Olympic team. His brother, Aaron Broten, played for the Colorado Rockies last season.

Broten scored 38 goals and added 59 assists for 97 points in his rookie season with the Minnesota North Stars, becoming the highest-scoring American player in NHL history. He's one of 10 members of Brooks' 1980 U.S. Olympic team making his mark

Ranger Mark Pavelich: Free agent to rookie record-holder.

in the NHL. Others are the Winnipeg's Dave Christian; the North Stars' Steve Christoff; the Rangers' Mark Pavelich, Dave Silk and Rob McClanahan; Mark Johnson, traded by the Pittsburgh Penguins to the North Stars; Ken Morrow of the New York Islanders; Mike Ramsey of the Buffalo Sabres, and Colorado Rockies' goaltender Steve Janaszak. Jim Craig, the U.S. Olympic team's goaltending hero, played in the NHL briefly in 1979–80 and 1980–81 but was relegated to the minor leagues last season.

The Minnesota-born Pavelich had a remarkable first season in

A rarity is New York-born Nick Fotiu, a Ranger favorite.

the NHL with the Rangers, setting a team rookie scoring record with 33 goals, 43 assists, 76 points. He did it as a walk-on, a free agent other teams overlooked, believing he lacked the size and stamina to play in the NHL.

While Neal Broten and Carpenter established themselves as potential American-born NHL superstars, Christian and Christoff had their second successive successful NHL seasons. Minnesota-born Reed Larson strengthened his status as one of the league's best defensemen for the Detroit Red Wings.

If awards were given for true grit in reaching the NHL as American players, they would go to two New York products—the Rangers' Fotiu and the Blues' Mullen. Unlike most of the American players in the NHL who either played college hockey or were talented enough to play junior hockey in Canada, Fotiu and Mullen developed in youth leagues in the United States. Mullen did, however, attend Boston College, gaining All-America honors. But he never was drafted by an NHL team.

Fotiu, easily the most popular Ranger because of his vigorous style of play, grew up in Staten Island and became a Ranger fan but didn't learn to skate until he was 15. He used to ride the subways at midnight to a rink in Coney Island so he could skate. He played in the Metropolitan Junior Hockey League, organized by the Rangers.

"I'd go to Madison Square Garden as a kid, sit in the cheap seats, watch the Rangers play and dream that someday I could play in the NHL," said Fotiu, who started in the World Hockey Association in 1974 and reached the NHL two years later. "Everybody said I was crazy, an American kid, from New York, with no chance of making it to the NHL. But I kept dreaming about it and I wouldn't give up trying."

Mullen had an exceptional rookie season as a right wing with the Blues, scoring 25 goals and 59 points in only 45 games. "He was our best player," said Emile Francis, the Blues' president, general manager and coach, who helped form the junior league in which Fotiu and Mullen played, and encouraged American boys they had a chance to play in the NHL.

Mullen played roller hockey in the streets or playgrounds near the old Madison Square Garden, a tough part of New York City known as Hell's Kitchen. "It wasn't until I was around 10 that I started playing on ice at a little rink in West New York, N.J.," said the Blues' rookie.

A St. Louis teammate, Jim Paves, from Long Island, played in the Metropolitan Junior Hockey League, too. The New York-area youth league has sent seven to the NHL in the last 10 years: Chris Ahrens (North Stars); Fotiu; Richie Hansen, a kid from the Bronx who has played for the Islanders and Blues; Mullen; Paul Skidmore, a Blues' goalie from Long Island, Pavese and Val James. James, born in Florida but raised on Long Island, played briefly for the Buffalo Sabres last season. In addition to being an American, James is only the ninth black player to play in the NHL, and the first American-born black player.

Another graduate of the New York Metropolitan League could be playing in the NHL this season: Bob Francis, son of the Blues' Francis. The younger Francis was born in Canada, but learned his hockey playing on Long Island when his father was general manager and coach of the Rangers. He led the Central League in scoring last season and is a rookie center with Calgary this season.

There are several reasons why more American-born players are in the NHL, the Rangers' Brooks notes.

"There's been a big breakthrough for American kids in hockey in the last 10 to 15 years," he said. "Now there are 21 teams. Before there were only six. The Olympic exposure helped. More colleges are into hockey and the level of training and coaching is excellent. We develop great athletes in baseball, football and basketball in this country; no reason why it can't help in hockey."

It is happening.

"We're selling hockey in a North American market and we need all the good American players we can get," said Sinden. "We need to have American-born players who can become stars. We need them badly for the good of the game. We haven't had enough of them. We can't just look to Canada anymore for all our players. The league has expanded for six to 21 teams but Canada is still only producing about the same number of quality players now as when the NHL had six teams."

Francis doesn't see the increase in American players in a Canadian game as a hinderance; he sees it helping the sport grow.

"Basically, most of our players will still come out of Canada because more kids play hockey there than in the United States," said Francis. "But hockey is better organized in the United States now than it used to be, largely through the amateur programs. We're finally developing some really good American players."

Francis and Winnipeg GM John Ferguson were among the first to recognize the need for Americanization in the mid-1970s. So was Scotty Bowman, Buffalo's general manager, who chose Minnesota's Ramsey as his first draft choice in 1979.

Throughout the 1950s, '60s and early '70s, when only a few Americans played in the NHL, there were occasional stories of resentment and lack of respect toward American players by some of the dominant Canadian players.

"That doesn't exist any more," said the Rangers' John Davidson, a Canadian. "Oh, maybe there might be occasional kidding and teasing but the guys from the States in the league now number quite a few and we know they're good hockey players. I think most Canadians would rather see Americans in the NHL than too many guys coming over from Europe. I don't look at it as a Canada-United States thing; I tend to look at it as a North America thing.

"Besides, our countries are so much alike. Most of the teams in the NHL are in the United States. More American players help the structure and promoting of the game. American players in the league help create interest for American fans. Personally, I think a lot of the college-trained American players have received better coaching than some Canadian kids get in junior hockey. No question, the Americans in the league have probably raised the average intelligence and level of education of players in hockey."

There's sometimes good-natured kidding between American and Canadian teammates.

"If one of my Canadian buddies starts kidding around, I just start saying, 'U.S.A.!'" joked Massachusetts-born Ranger goalie Stave Baker, alluding to the U.S.A.'s 1980 Olympic Gold Medal.

"When the U.S. beat the Russians and won the gold medal in the Olympics, I think I felt as proud as any American guy on our club," said the Rangers' Dave Maloney, a Canadian.

When the Rangers acquired another American player last season (Rob McClanahan), Eddie Johnstone and Steve Vickers joked about it. "We Canadians better start sticking together," joked John-stone to Vickers. "We're becoming a minority in hockey."

Ron Andrews, the former NHL director of information, re-members how few Americans were in hockey when he joined the league in 1963.

"The only two I remember are Tommy Williams and Carl Wetzel," said Andrews.

Wetzel, from Detroit, played briefly as a goaltender. Williams was the first American-born player to have a successful and lengthy career in the NHL. He played for the 1960 U.S. Olympic team and entered the NHL in 1961 with Boston. In a career lasting until 1976, he scored 161 goals and 430 points in 663 games with the Bruins, North Stars, California Seals and Washington.

"There were only a couple of us Americans then," recalled Williams.

One of them was Detroit-born Charlie Burns, who played from 1958 to 1973 in the NHL and later coached the North Stars briefly. "The problem then was American kids didn't have the chance to learn to play hockey the way the kids did in Canada," said Wil-liams.

The Rangers' Robbie Ftorek is one of the senior American-born players in length of service in the NHL today. Like Carpenter, Ftorek was a scholastic star in Massachusetts. He entered the NHL with Detroit in 1972 and starred for several years in the WHA, where he was named MVP, before returning to the NHL. Bobby Sheehan, also a Massachusetts product, made his NHL debut with the Montreal Canadiens in 1969–70 and still was playing last season.

Other Americans before the big breakthrough included Detroit-born Doug Roberts, Minnesota-born Henry Boucha, Craig and Glenn Patrick and Larry Pleau. Other Americans in the not-too-distant past included Stan Gilbertson, Gerry O'Flaherty, Fred Ahearn, Pete Lopresti and Mike Christie, a Texan by birth.

Mention of the name Curt Bennett, who played mostly with Atlanta through the 1970s, usually stirs debate. A 34-goal-scorer one season, Bennett was born in Canada but raised from boyhood in Cranston, R.I., played at Brown University, was an American citizen and played for Team USA in the Canada Cup. The United States Hockey Hall of Fame refers to him as an "American de-veloped" player because of his birth in Canada.

Conversely, the Rangers' Ed Hospodar was born in Ohio of Canadian parents, spent most of his youth in Canada but, tech-nically, may be categorized as an American-born player.

Several prominent American-born players distinguished them-selves in the NHL in the 1920s, 1930s and 1940s. Cecil Dillon was an all-star with the Rangers. Frank Brimsek was a six-time all-star as a goaltender and twice won the Vezina Trophy as the league's best goalie, spending most of his career with Boston from 1938 to 1950. Pete Babando was a solid player from 1947 to 1953 with Boston, Detroit, Chicago and the Rangers. Sam Lopresti, whose son later played goal in the NHL, was a prominent goalie in the 1940s. He was from Eveleth, Minn., home of John Mariucci, a Black Hawks' defenseman from 1940 to 1948.

Billy Burch, from Yonkers, N.Y., won the Hart Trophy as MVP in 1925 while playing for the New York Americans. Taffy Abel, a defenseman from Michigan, was the first American-born player to perform for a Stanley Cup championship team. He was a member of the Rangers' Cup champions of 1928. The next year Myles Lane of Melrose, Mass., who later became a New York State Supreme Court Judge, was a member of Boston's Stanley Cup championship team.

Elwin (Doc) Romnes (Minnesota) starred in the NHL from 1930 to 1940. He was a member of Chicago's Stanley Cup champion team in 1938, which, remarkably, had eight American-born players, including Carl Voss of Chelsea, Mass., who in 1950 became the NHL's first referee-in-chief. Coaching the Blacks Hawks' Cup victory was Bill Stewart of Fitchburg, Mass., who became well known as a major league baseball umpire. His goaltender, Mike Karakas, was from Aurora, Minn., played in the NHL from 1935 to 1946 and gained all-star stature. Carl (Cully) Dahlstrom of Minneapolis played for the 1938 Black Hawks. Cliff (Fido) Purpur, from Grand Forks, N.D., played in the NHL from 1934 to 1945. Massachusetts' Bill Moe is remembered as a Ranger defenseman from 1944 to 1949.

Americans have even made their mark as officials in the Canadian-dominated sport. New Yorker Bill Chadwick still holds the record for service as an NHL referee, officiating 778 regular-season and 105 playoff games from 1941 to 1955. Today there are eight referees and linesmen with American birth certificates on the rolls of the NHL: referees Bob Henry of Detroit and Mike Noeth of Boston; linesmen Bob Luther, Roger Gilbertson and Ron Foyt, all from Minnesota, Kevin Collins and Paul Flaherty, both Massachusetts-born, and Gordon Broseker, born in Baltimore, Md.

The NHL still is dominated by Canadian players but don't let anyone tell you Americans haven't made a significant contribution. And with the coming of the young Americans, the letters U.S.A. now carry more impact than ever before in the NHL.

(Note: The Americans' records follow.)

AMERICANS' 1981-82 NHL RECORDS

BOSTON

PLAYER	HOME STATE	GP	G	A	P	PM	PLAYOFFS			
Tom Fergus	Illinois	61	15	24	39	12	6	3	0	3	0
Mike O'Connell	Illinois	80	5	34	39	75	11	2	2	4	20
Mike Milbury	Massachusetts	51	2	10	12	71	11	0	4	4	6

BUFFALO

PLAYER	HOME STATE	GP	G	A	P	PM	PLAYOFFS			
Mike Ramsey	Minnesota	80	7	23	30	56	4	1	1	2	14
Richie Dunn	Massachusetts	72	7	19	26	73	4	0	1	1	0
Val James	Florida	7	0	0	0	16	3	0	0	0	0
Jim Walsh	Virginia	4	0	1	1	4	0	0	0	0	0

CHICAGO

PLAYER	HOME STATE	GP	G	A	P	PM	PLAYOFFS			
Dave Feamster	Michigan	29	0	2	2	29	15	2	4	6	53

COLORADO

PLAYER	HOME STATE	GP	G	A	P	PM
Bob Miller	Massachusetts	56	11	20	31	27
Aaron Broten	Minnesota	58	15	24	39	6
Joe Micheletti	Minnesota	41	5	17	22	32
Jack Hughes	Massachusetts	8	0	0	0	13

DETROIT

PLAYER	HOME STATE	GP	G	A	P	PM
Reed Larson	Minnesota	80	21	39	60	112

EDMONTON

PLAYER	HOME STATE	GP	G	A	P	PM	PLAYOFFS			
Lee Fogolin	Illinois	80	4	25	29	154	5	1	1	2	14
Don Jackson	Minnesota	8	0	0	0	18	0	0	0	0	0

HARTFORD

PLAYER	HOME STATE	GP	G	A	P	PM
Mark Howe	Michigan	76	8	45	53	18
Warren Miller	Minnesota	74	10	12	22	68
Russ Anderson	Minnesota	56	1	4	5	183
Marty Howe	Michigan	13	0	4	4	2
Mike Fidler	Massachusetts	2	0	1	1	0
Jeff Brownschidle	New York	3	0	1	1	2
Mike McDougal	Michigan	3	0	0	0	0

LOS ANGELES

PLAYER	HOME STATE	GP	G	A	P	PM	PLAYOFFS			
Steve Jensen	Minnesota	45	8	19	27	19
Alan Hangsleben	Minnesota	35	3	7	10	84
*Rick Chartraw	Pennsylvania	33	2	8	10	56	10	0	2	2	10
Bob Sheehan	Massachusetts	4	0	0	0	2

*Chartraw born in Venezuela; American citizen raised in Pennsylvania.

MINNESOTA

PLAYER	HOME STATE	GP	G	A	P	PM	PLAYOFFS			
Neal Broten	Minnesota	73	38	59	97	42	4	0	2	2	0
Steve Christoff	Minnesota	69	26	30	56	14	2	0	0	0	2
Gordie Roberts	Michigan	79	4	30	34	119	4	0	3	3	25
Mark Johnson	Wisconsin	56	12	13	25	40	4	2	0	2	0
Mike Eaves	Colorado	25	11	10	21	0
Jack Carlson	Minnesota	57	8	4	12	103	1	0	0	0	15
Bill Nyrop	Wash., D.C.	42	4	8	12	35	2	0	0	0	0
Gary Sargent	Minnesota	15	0	5	5	18
Mike Antonovich	Minnesota	2	0	0	0	0

PLAYER	HOME STATE	GP	G	A	P	PM	PLAYOFFS				

MONTREAL

PLAYER	HOME STATE	GP	G	A	P	PM					
*Rod Langway	Massachusetts	66	5	34	39	116	5	0	3	3	18
Chris Nilan	Massachusetts	49	7	4	11	204	5	1	1	2	22
Jeff Brubaker	Maryland	3	0	1	1	32	2	0	0	0	27

*Langway born in Taiwan; American citizen raised in Massachusetts.

NEW YORK ISLANDERS

Dave Langevin	Minnesota	73	1	20	21	82	19	2	4	6	16
Ken Morrow	Michigan	75	1	18	19	56	19	0	4	4	8

NEW YORK RANGERS

Mark Pavelich	Minnesota	79	33	43	76	67	6	1	5	6	0
Robbie Ftorek	Massachusetts	49	9	33	42	28	10	7	4	11	11
Dave Silk	Massachusetts	64	15	20	35	39	9	2	4	6	4
Nick Fotiu	New York	70	8	10	18	151	10	0	2	2	6
Rob McClanahan	Minnesota	39	5	12	17	21	10	2	5	7	2
Dean Talafous	Minnesota	29	6	7	13	8					
Ed Hospodar	Ohio	41	3	8	11	152					
Tom Younghans	Minnesota	50	4	5	9	17	2	0	0	0	0
Gary Burns	Massachusetts	0	0	0	0	0	4	0	0	0	4

PHILADELPHIA

Paul Holmgren	Minnesota	41	9	22	31	183	4	1	2	3	6
Tom Gorence	Minnesota	66	5	8	13	8	3	0	0	0	0
Gary Morrison	Michigan	7	0	0	0	2					

QUEBEC

Jere Gillis	Oregon	38	5	10	15	16					

ST. LOUIS

Joe Mullen	New York	45	25	34	59	4	10	7	11	18	4
Jack Brownschidle	New York	80	5	33	38	26	8	0	0	2	14
Rick Wilson	California	48	3	18	21	24	9	0	3	3	4
Bill Baker	Minnesota	49	3	8	11	67	4	0	0	0	0
Jim Pavese	New York	42	2	9	11	101	4	0	3	3	2
Richie Hansen	New York	2	0	2	2	0					

TORONTO

Jim Korn	Minnesota	70	2	10	12	148					

VANCOUVER

Curt Fraser	Ohio	79	28	39	67	175	17	3	7	10	98

WASHINGTON

Bobby Carpenter	Massachusetts	80	32	35	67	69					
Lee Norwood	California	28	7	10	17	117					
Tom Rowe	Massachusetts	27	5	1	6	54					

WINNIPEG

Dave Christian	Minnesota	80	25	51	76	28	4	0	1	1	2
Moe Mantha	Ohio	25	0	12	12	28	4	1	3	4	16

GOALTENDERS
COLORADO

PLAYER	HOME STATE	GP	RECORD	AVG.	PLAYOFFS
Steve Janaszak	Minnesota	2	0-1-0	7.80	

MONTREAL

Mark Holden	Massachusetts	1	0-0-0	0.00	

NEW YORK RANGERS

Steve Baker	Massachusetts	6	1-5-0	6.04	
John Vanbiesbrouck	Michigan	1	1-0-0	1.00	

ST. LOUIS

Paul Skidmore	New York	2	1-1-0	3.00	

TOP PERFORMANCES
BY AMERICAN-BORN PLAYERS

MOST GOALS ONE SEASON—Neal Broten, Minnesota, 1981-82 (38); Mark Pavelich, New York Rangers, 1981-82 (33); Bobby Carpenter, Washington, 1981-82 (32); Tom Rowe, Washington, 1978-79 (31); Paul Holmgren, Philadelphia, 1979-80 (30).

MOST ASSISTS ONE SEASON—Neal Broten, Minnesota, 1981-82 (59); Mark Howe, Hartford, 1979-80 (56); Dave Christian, Winnipeg, 1981-82 (51); Reed Larson, Detroit, 1978-79 (49); Robbie Ftorek, Quebec, 1980-81 (49).

MOST POINTS ONE SEASON—Neal Broten, Minnesota, 1981-82 (97); Mark Howe, Hartford, 1979-80 (80); Mark Pavelich, New York Rangers, 1981-82 (76); Dave Christian, Winnipeg, 1981-82 (76); Robbie Ftorek, Quebec, 1980-81 (73); Dave Christian, Winnipeg, 1980-81 (71).

MOST POINTS BY A DEFENSEMAN ONE SEASON—Reed Larson, Detroit, 1978-79 (67).

MOST GOALS BY A DEFENSEMAN ONE SEASON—Reed Larson, Detroit, 1980-81 (27).

MOST SHUTOUTS BY A GOALTENDER ONE SEASON—Frank Brimsek, Boston, 1938-39 (10). Mike Karakas, Chicago, 1935-36 (9).

BEST GOALS-AGAINST AVERAGE BY A GOALTENDER ONE SEASON—Brimsek, Boston, 1938-39 (1.60); Mike Karakas, Chicago, 1935-36 (1.91).

Minnesota-born Frankie Brimsek is in Hall of Fame.

THE SIX SENSATIONAL SUTTERS

By TIM MORIARTY

They walk into the IGA supermarket in their hometown of Viking, Alberta, where their mother works part-time at a checkout counter, and heads turn and people murmur. They produce the same head turning and whispers when they enter a bar or restaurant on Long Island or in Chicago or St. Louis—their main centers of employment.

They are the Sutter brothers—hockey's first family.

If they were a circus act, they would be billed as "the daring, death-defying, dynamic Sutters."

If they were a vaudeville act, they would be billed as "the eager, energetic, exciting Sutters."

But in hockey circles they are recognized simply as The Sutters. No adjectives, just respect. You learn to respect the Sutters or you wind up with a fat lip, mister.

The Sutter Brothers. It has a certain ring, doesn't it? A little like the James Brothers. Lock up the wife and the kids and the horses. Here come the Sutters.

There were four of them playing in the National Hockey League last season—two with the Stanley Cup champion Islanders. And two more—identical twins, no less—were among the graduating amateurs picked in the first round of the June draft.

Without further adieu, step up and meet the Sutter Brothers:

Brian Sutter, left wing, St. Louis Blues. Age: 26. The first brother to reach the NHL. Was only 23 when he became the youngest team captain in the Blues' history. Scored only nine

---

Tim Moriarty, longtime hockey writer for Long Island's Newsday, visited the Sutter homestead in southern Alberta.

Sutters with Cup: (l. to r.) Duane, Ron, Dad, Richie, Brent.

goals in his first full season with St. Louis in 1977-78, but had a career-high 41 the following season. Totaled 39 goals and 74 points last season and led the team in penalty minutes (239). Nickname: Sudsy. Disposition: feisty.

Darryl Sutter, left wing, Chicago Black Hawks. Age: 24. Took a circuitous route to the NHL. Was the Hawks' 11th pick (179th overall) in the 1978 draft and spent the following season playing in Japan. Scored 40 goals for the Hawks during the 1980-81 season, a club record for a rookie. Missed 40 games with a shoulder separation last season and his goal production dropped to 23. Nickname: None. Disposition: feisty.

Duane Sutter, right wing, New York Islanders. Age: 22. Picked in the first round (17th overall) in the 1979 draft. Promoted to the Islanders two months into the 1979-80 season, scored 15 goals in 56 games, and contributed a key goal in the Isles' Cup-clinching game against the Flyers. Knee surgery caused him to miss 55 games in 1980-81, but he came back last season to help the Isles win their third straight Cup. Nickname: Dog. Disposition: feisty.

Brent Sutter, center, New York Islanders. Age: 20. Followed Duane's route to the NHL. Also a first-round (17th overall) pick in the 1980 draft. Put in an additional year of junior A hockey before joining the Islanders midway through last season. Played on the same line with Duane and totaled 21 goals and 114 penalty

Rich Sutter (left) was drafted by Penguins, Ron by Flyers.

minutes in 43 games. Nickname: Pookie. Disposition: feisty.

Richie Sutter, right wing, drafted by the Pittsburgh Penguins. Age: 18. Had 34 goals and 213 penalty minutes with Lethbridge of the Western Hockey League last season. Nickname: Twin. Disposition: feisty.

Ron Sutter, center, drafted by the Philadelphia Flyers. Age: 18. Played on the same line with twin Richie at Lethbridge. Had 31 goals and 174 penalty minutes. Nickname: Twin. Disposition: feisty.

Blues' Brian (Sudsy) Sutter was first in family to make NHL.

There is another Sutter brother who has no major-league ambitions—not as a player anyway. He is Gary, the oldest at 27 who played Tier Two amateur hockey before turning to coaching. He coached a Tier Two team in Calgary last season.

The Sutters, who have no sisters, grew up on a 640-acre farm nine miles outside Viking in east central Alberta. It is a working farm of wheat and oats, pigs and cattle, fruits and vegetables. And presiding over things are the parents, Grace and Louie Sutter. They produced and cultivated their brood of boys under regulations

Brent Sutter became an Islander during the 1981-82 season.

stricter than the rules of hockey.

Duane Sutter recently recalled his adolescent days on the farm. "It was strict, all right, and hectic. Dad spent most of his time planting crops, but he was tough when he had to be. And mother was always there to lay down the law, too...We used to help her with the dishes and do all those odd jobs and chores a girl

Duane Sutter has played on all three Islander Cup teams.

would do if we had a sister."

He offered another memory of Viking and the farm. "Mom and Dad were great fans, of course," Duane said. "Once the chores were done, they would have two radios and the TV tuned to games. They still do that. Sometime Dad would climb into the truck in the yard and listen to a game there because the reception was better on the truck radio. Mother would have the radio and TV on in the house. Yeah, it was hectic."

Brian Sutter has a different memory of his youth. He remembers brawling with his brothers. "Going out to catch the school bus, we'd have five fights before getting to the end of the road. I can remember some good ones. No broken bones, but lots of bloody noses."

Brent Sutter claims Duane got the nickname "Dog" after losing a childhood fight to Brian. "He came home yipping like a dog," Brent said. Duane, who denies the allegation, admits he was quick to defend Brent. "I jumped in a lot of times because I figured it was my duty," Duane said. "Maybe I looked over him too much. Now I've learned he can handle himself, so I say, 'Hey, Pookie, do it.' And he does it."

Competitiveness is a Sutter hallmark. So is determination. Somebody once pointed out that a Sutter skates and works like a mule. It's not a flattering appraisal, but it's reasonably accurate. Every Sutter digs and checks in the corners and will take a hit instead of giving up the puck. They are not fancy skaters—Ron is perhaps the best of a poor lot—but they are indefatigable.

When Duane joined the Islanders, general manager Bill Torrey said, "He's not going to win any Sonja Henie awards for skating, but he gets there. And when he gets the puck, he won't throw it away."

The Sutters also are extremely unselfish. Brian proved that to his St. Louis teammates last season. "That guy gives away more goals," said defenseman Gerry Hart. "He finished the season with 39, but I'm sure he had five or six more that he wouldn't claim. And it cost him a couple of thousand dollars because he had a bonus (clause in his contract) for 40 goals. But that's the kind of player Brian is."

That's the kind of player the Sutters are. They will fight at the drop of a glove, but they also display considerable compassion. Bob Bourne has played with and against the Sutters and offered this observation: "They all have a burning desire to win," the Islanders' winger said. "But they have something else that's important. They have a lot of character. Some are quiet and some do a lot of yapping, but they all have character."

Some NHL fans are anticipating the day when two of the brothers square off and spar in a game. Brian and Darryl came close while scuffling for a puck in a playoff game. Darryl was out of position at the time and Brian looked him in the eye and whispered, "Get back on your wing." That was all.

During Duane's first season with the Islanders, he and Brian shoved each other after colliding at mid-ice in a game at the Nassau

Coliseum, but nothing developed. "You know why?" an Islander said. "Everybody in that family fears Brian. They're scared to death of him."

Said Duane: "Brian is the most hard-nosed one in the family. Some guys underestimate him because he's not big. But he's strong and wiry. He doesn't lose many fights."

The Sutters remind some old-timers of the Richard brothers, but only two Richards made the NHL—Maurice and Henri—and both battled their way into the Hall of Fame. Other Hall of Fame brother pairs include Doug and Max Bentley and Frank and George Boucher. The Bouchers held the record for most brothers who played in the NHL—Frank, George, Billy and Bob—until the Sutters came along.

It is hockey night in Lethbridge, a small city of almost 40,000 inhabitants in southern Alberta and approximately 50 miles from the northern boundary of Montana. The Lethbridge Broncos are entertaining the Brandon Wheat Kings in a Western League game in the Sportsplex, a modernistic, 5,500-seat arena on the outskirts of Lethbridge. It is here that the Sutters—all the Sutters—polished their skills as amateurs in an extremely rough-and-tumble environment.

Jimmy Devellano, the Islanders' assistant general manager and director of scouting, is in the crowd of 2,931 for this late-season game last February. He had made a side trip from Calgary to check on the progress of the twins, and was disappointed to learn that Richie had been scratched from the Broncos' lineup because of an aching back.

Ron Sutter is playing, though. And how! Early in the second period, he is backchecking in the Brandon zone when he slams Bill Vince of the Wheat Kings against the sideboards with such force that Vince drops his stick. Ron skates away with a grin on his thin face. "He's a Sutter, all right," Devellano says. He is grinning, too.

On his next shift, Ron is wide with a shot, circles the net and bodychecks Darrell Mulvenna of the Wheat Kings. Richie is seated in the stands, keeping track of "hits" on a lined scoring pad. "That was Ron's 14th takeout of the game," Richie points out. "Not bad, eh?"

Margaret Ross is watching the action from a seat in the lower stands across the ice from the Lethbridge bench. She and her husband, Stubb, who operates a commuter airline, provided comfortable living quarters for the Sutters in the basement of their Lethbridge home.

"All six stayed with us while they played in Lethbridge," Mrs.

Ross said. "They're all well mannered. Their parents did a good job bringing up those boys. They're also well disciplined. We had a birthday party for the twins in December and they really enjoyed themselves. Just a few beers and something to eat and they were happy."

Ron Sutter is listed as half an inch taller and two pounds heavier than 5-11, 164-pound Richie. The twins have the same hairstyle, the same angular face and aquiline nose, the same voice inflection, the same easygoing personality. Even their teammates have had problems telling them apart.

"When one twin is too busy to pick up the phone, the other fills in for him," Mrs. Ross discloses. "Hardly anybody can tell the difference."

The comely, friendly landlady was also disappointed that Richie's sore back prevented him from playing. "They are twice as effective when they play together," she said. "Richard is the roughest and a great crowd favorite, but I think Ron is going to become the best of the lot."

Richie would not disagree with that. "Ron is a better two-way player than me," he said. "He's a little smarter with the puck and makes better plays. He's also a smoother skater. But I don't think he's as aggressive as me."

Now the game is over and Ron Sutter is not happy. He had one assist but failed to score a goal as the Broncos lost to the Wheat Kings, 6-3. "We should have beaten those guys," Ron said. "We would have, too, if Rich was able to play."

John Chapman, the Lethbridge coach, also is unhappy. However, he warms up when discussing the Sutter twins. He calls them "the Magpies," but with reverence. "Those kids come from a great family," Chapman said. "They're winners and they have a great desire to succeed. They will, too. They know where they're going and they know how to get there."

Later, the twins sit in a side room next to the coach's office and recall those days when they played floor hockey with their older brothers in a hay loft on the farm. "We started playing in the loft when we were about six or seven years old," Rich said. "Ron and I were the youngest so they put us in the net and fired tennis balls at us. We didn't have goalie gloves, so we used baseball gloves. A lot of slashing went on and it seemed we never finished a game without a fight breaking out."

When Ron Sutter noticed the Stanley Cup championship ring Devellano was wearing, he exclaimed: "That's a beauty. I'd like to have one like that."

Devellano smiled benignly. "You'll have one someday, son." he said. "I'm sure of it."

It is the day after the Islanders won their third straight Stanley Cup. Louie and Grace Sutter, who had attended the final game in Vancouver, arrived back in Viking by mid-afternoon. Less than an hour later, Louie Sutter was out in the fields, planting oats. The Sutter parents never infringe on each other's territory. The fields belong to Louie Sutter, the kitchen belongs to Grace Sutter.

The Sutter kitchen is the center of the farmhouse, both by design and as a matter of convenience. It is there that Grace works when she is not behind a cash register at the local supermarket.

Darryl Sutter of the Black Hawks played in Japan in 1978-79.

She took the part-time job after the boys grew out of adolescence because, as she explains, "It gives me a feeling of independence. Besides, I work only four days a week and it still gives me time to look after the family."

So Grace goes about her kitchen chores while preparing dinner for her husband and discussing her sons. She recalls those days when the boys opposed each other in minor hockey leagues around Viking. "We'd be riding home and the boys would get in a hassle and I'd tell them, 'Children, that game ended on the ice. I don't want you carrying it into the car or into the house.' Most of the time they'd obey me and shut up."

Like most boys, the Sutters had hefty appetites when they were growing up. They would pile into the kitchen after a game, aching for sustenance. "It's a good thing we always grew our own food," Grace said. "We've always had a large vegetable garden and a big kitchen table to pile it on. The boys were heavy eaters. They still are. Lots of steaks and gravy and potatoes. And, of course, they always wanted to top off the meals with lots of desserts."

When the Sutters oppose each other in NHL games, their mother encounters problems. "I pray that they don't get hurt," she said. "Then I root for a tie."

In discussing the dispositions of her sons, Grace is cautious. "Richard is sorta bubbly and I guess Duane is the most easy-going one," she said. "The quietest? Well, it might be Darryl. We always got along well. When he was home, he'd help in the yard or in the garden. He'd go about his own business and if he felt like talking, well, we'd talk."

Asked to pick the best player among her sons, Grace is coy. And charming. "Oh, I can't do that," she said. "Darryl, though, is a real opportunist. He scores goals that nobody else could score. Even when he's falling or is down on the ice, he scores."

Like Mike Bossy?

"Oh, my, yes," Grace Sutter said.

Louie Sutter completes his day's chores at dusk, has supper, then discusses everything from the weather to hockey to the Russians.

"We had a very late spring," he said. "Had some snow only two weeks ago. But lately it's been dry as hell. Still, it's better than rain. Can't work when it rains."

Two years ago, a national magazine (Sports Illustrated) ran a feature story on the Sutters that irked the boys' father. "Too much bullshit," Louie said. He also was annoyed when a writer suggested that "the father's biggest dream is to have a son playing for the Montreal Canadiens."

Louie said: "That was bullshit, too. Somebody told the writer that as a gag. Hell, I don't like the Canadiens. I even pull for the Russians when they play the Canadiens."

Most of the Sutters inherited the speech patterns of their father. Plus the use of an occasional expletive. However, the cursing is restricted to barnyard terms and never becomes intolerable.

Louie chuckles when asked about John Sutter—a great, great uncle of the current crop—who discovered gold at his California sawmill in 1848. The great Gold Rush ensued. Sutter was eventually swindled out of his holdings and was bankrupt by 1852.

"They tell me all that stuff about John Sutter is true, but I have no way of knowing it," Louie said.

Asked if he inherited any of that gold from the Sutter sawmill, Louie chuckles again. "Hell, no," he said.

Having six hockey playing sons had not affected Louie Sutter's life to any great degree, nor has it established him as a celebrity in Viking. He still has to pay the same price for farm equipment at local stores. "And sometimes they charge me more," he said.

But the Sutters are celebrities, of course, and they attract the normal amount of telephone calls—some from admirers, some from cranks, some from screwballs. "We get a lot of calls from Edmonton fans, and they're not pleasant," Grace said. "I guess it's one of the things you have to live with. We haven't had to change our phone number yet, but the boys had to. They only keep their numbers for four or five months, but even when they're unlisted, they seem to leak out.

"Even here on the farm we get nasty calls. It's really ignorance, I guess, the things they say. We usually know what they want, though. They want to be nasty. There's strange people all over the world."

One caller to the Sutter farmhouse once suggested that if he were an NHL general manager he would give Louie and Grace an all-expenses paid trip to Hawaii and hope they would produce more hockey-playing sons. The suggestion did not annoy 51-year-old Louie. "Hell, let 'em have fun with those jokes," he said. "I don't mind."

Ma and Pa Sutter can boast about what they have produced so far—a record First Family.

"I'm proud about that," Louie Sutter said.

He should be.

INSIDE THE NHL

**By PAT CALABRIA, HUGH DELANO
and FRANK ORR**

PREDICTED ORDER OF FINISH

Adams	Patrick	Norris	Smythe
Boston	Islanders	Minnesota	Edmonton
Quebec	Rangers	St. Louis	Winnipeg
Montreal	Philadelphia	Chicago	Vancouver
Buffalo	Pittsburgh	Toronto	Los Angeles
Hartford	Washington	Detroit	Calgary
	New Jersey		

Stanley Cup: New York Islanders

   The National Hockey League is fiddling with geography again. For the 1982-83 season, the Rockies are in the East, a nifty feat, and Winnipeg now is in the West.

   One season into a total realignment of the league's divisions, a system that worked fairly well, the NHL was forced to make changes.

   The Colorado Rockies died. Cynics can claim that team has been dead since its 1974 birth as the Kansas City Scouts. The team was sold and moved to New Jersey, where it will be located in the Brendan Byrne Arena in the Meadowlands complex.

   The team will play in the Patrick Division with the New York

---

Frank Orr of the Toronto Star *wrote the Norris and Smythe divisions, Pat Calabria of Long Island's* Newsday *did the Adams and Hugh Delano of the New York* Post *covered the Patrick. Orr deliberated with Calabria and Delano before writing the introduction, and somehow they agreed on the same 1982-83 champion.*

Islanders and Rangers, Philadelphia Flyers, Pittsburgh Penguins and Washington Capitals.

Boosted by some financial benefits, the Winnipeg Jets abandoned the Norris Division and switched to the Smythe sector which they share with the Los Angeles Kings, Vancouver Canucks, Calgary Flames and Wayne Gretzky (a.k.a. Edmonton Oilers).

Now, the NHL, which lost approximately $20 million last season, has high hopes that its arrangement of teams will have a few trouble-free years to establish gate-boosting rivalries. Parity, of course, is a pipe-dream world because as long as there are sports leagues, good and bad teams will exist.

However, the NHL did have a much more competitive product in the 1981-82 season than at any time in the past decade. The influx of talented young players into the league, spurred by the drafting of players as young as 18, gave clubs a chance to improve quickly and several did.

The league now has three good divisions—the Adams, Patrick and Smythe—and a fourth, the Norris, that lost an exciting attraction in the peppy, young Jets.

The Norris teams averaged 69.6 points last season and three clubs—Minnesota North Stars, St. Louis Blues and Chicago Black Hawks—are extremely competitive. However, the presence of the sad-sack Detroit Red Wings and Toronto Maple Leafs drag it down.

The Jets will make the Smythe sector (81.2 average) a good one that should supply extremely entertaining, offensive hockey. The Oilers, Kings and Jets are teams that like to play wide-open while the grinder Canucks, who wrote the big success story of the playoffs by advancing to the final, and Calgary Flames should be strong, too.

The Hartford Whalers did improve last season but they're in a tough Adams Division (88-point average) that includes the Boston Bruins, Buffalo Sabres, Montreal Canadiens and Quebec Nordiques, four clubs that have intense rivalries.

The New York Islanders, seeking their fourth consecutive Stanley Cup and having a good chance to get it, lead the Patrick Division (81-point average), where the competition is torrid, especially with the Rangers and Flyers. The Caps and Penguins compete for the fourth playoff spot while the New Jersey club faces a long first season in the East.

The consensus from here: another Cup for the Islanders.

BOSTON BRUINS

TEAM DIRECTORY: Pres.-Gov.: Paul A. Mooney; GM: Harry Sinden; Asst. GM: Tom Johnson; Dir. Pub. Rel.: Nate Greenberg; Coach: Gerry Cheevers. Home ice: Boston Garden (14,597; 195' × 83'). Colors: Gold, black and white. Training camp: Danvers, Mass.

SCOUTING REPORT

OFFENSE: Just a few years ago the Bruins were about as up-to-date as a butter churner. While the rest of the NHL was looking for speed and imagination, the Bruins continued to slog up and down the ice in the fashion that earned them the nickname, "The Lunchpail Crew." All that's changed.

The Bruins still check tirelessly, make no mistake about that. But coach Gerry Cheevers has adapted very nicely to the trend to swiftness and has the bodies to blend quickness and strength. As a result, the Bruins' attack no longer is one-dimensional and the offense again is one of the most feared in the league.

No one typifies the revitalized Bruins better than Rick Middleton, who led the team with 51 goals and 94 points while winning the Lady Byng Trophy for gentlemanly play. Middleton may very well be the best one-on-one player in the league and is easily Boston's biggest threat. He is helped by a squad of young, vigorous players. While such veterans as Terry O'Reilly and Stan Jonathan still are around, they have given way to the fresh-faced players. Steve Kasper, who scored 20 goals while winning the Frank Selke Trophy as the best defensive forward, is a gem along with center Barry Pederson, who had an excellent rookie season, scoring 92 points. Keith Crowder chipped in with 23 goals.

To a cast like that, add Normand Leveille, who had a tough time adjusting as a rookie last season, but still managed 14 goals in 65 games. He could be a big surprise this season. There also is Peter McNab, the dependable center. But the Bruins' real strength is the way they mix their abilities and tailor them to the kind of game being played. They can score or check or scratch out a victory, even when they aren't playing well.

Last season's upset in the Adams Division playoffs aside, the Bruins have an explosive team that just may be ready to ignite. The fans in Boston will get a bang out of that.

DEFENSE: The Bruins have long been respected as a team which plays tough, aggressive defense, but that reputation was dented in the playoffs. Yet the Bruins allowed only 285 goals last season,

Wayne Cashman is the best 37-year-old player in the NHL.

fourth in the league, and they can't help but be improved this season. The big—really big—reason is draft choice Gord Kluzak, the first choice overall in the amateur draft. Kluzak is 6-4, 220, and looks like he could reach from one end of Boston's cramped rink to the other. Maybe he really can.

Kluzak is one of the best defenseman to come out of junior hockey the last few years, according to anyone who has seen him play. If Kluzak is as dominant as he looks, the Bruins will make things easier on their goaltenders. While Boston surrendered Brad McCrimmon in the trade for Pete Peeters, Ray Bourque is around and coming off an all-star season. Brad Park has considered retirement, however, so the Bruins need players such as Mike Milbury and Larry Melnyk to fill the void. Mike O'Connell is steady and smart.

The Bruins also appear to have gone a long way toward settling a muddled goalie situation. By obtaining Peeters, a terrible grouch, the Bruins may not have improved their popularity, but their goaltending should be better. Peeters will duel with either Rogie Vachon or Mike Moffat.

BRUIN ROSTER

No.	Player	Pos.	Hgt.	Wgt.	Born	1981-82	G	A	Pts.	PIM
	Dave Barr	C	6-1	185	11-30-60/Edmonton, Alta.	Boston	0	0	0	0
						Erie	18	48	66	29
7	Raymond Bourque	D	5-11	197	12-28-60/Montreal, Que.	Boston	17	49	66	51
12	Wayne Cashman	LW	6-2	208	6-24-45/Kingston, Ont.	Boston	12	31	43	59
32	Bruce Crowder	RW	6-0	180	3-25-57/Essex, Ont.	Erie	6	6	12	6
						Boston	16	11	27	31
18	Keith Crowder	RW	6-0	190	1-6-59/Windsor, Ont.	Boston	23	21	44	101
28	Tom Fergus	C	6-0	179	6-16-62/Chicago, Ill.	Boston	15	24	39	12
14	Mike Gillis	RW-C	6-2	190	12-1-58/Toronto, Ont.	Boston	9	8	17	54
23	Randy Hillier	D	6-0	178	3-30-60/Toronto, Ont.	Boston	0	8	8	29
						Erie	6	13	19	52
17	Stan Jonathan	LW	5-8	175	5-9-55/Brantford, Ont.	Boston	6	17	23	57
11	Steve Kasper	LW	5-8	159	9-28-61/Montreal, Que.	Boston	20	31	51	72
	Gord Kluzak	D	6-4	220	3-6-64/Climax, Sask.	Billings	9	24	33	110
25	Mike Krushelynski	C	6-2	200	4-27-60/Montreal, Que.	Boston	3	3	6	2
						Erie	31	52	83	44
19	Normand Leveille	LW	5-10	175	1-10-63/Montreal, Que.	Boston	14	19	33	49
	Craig MacTavish	C	6-0	185	8-15-58/London, Ont.	Boston	0	1	1	0
						Erie	24	30	54	47
8	Peter McNab	C	6-3	203	5-8-52/Vancouver, B.C.	Boston	36	40	76	19
33	Larry Melnyk	D	6-0	181	2-21-60/New Westminster, B.C.	Boston	0	8	8	84
						Erie	0	3	3	36
16	Rick Middleton	RW	5-11	170	12-4-53/Toronto, Ont.	Boston	51	43	94	12
26	Mike Milbury	D	6-1	202	6-17-52/Brighton, Mass.	Boston	2	10	12	71
	Doug Morrison	C	5-11	185	2-1-60/Vancouver, B.C.	Boston	0	0	0	0
						Erie	24	36	60	31
20	Mike O'Connell	D	5-9	180	11-25-55/Chicago, Ill.	Boston	5	34	39	75
24	Terry O'Reilly	RW	6-1	195	6-7-51/Oshawa, Ont.	Boston	22	30	52	213
	Brad Palmer	LW-RW	6-0	180	9-14-61/Duncan, B.C.	Minnesota	22	23	45	18
22	Brad Park	D	6-0	200	7-6-48/Toronto, Ont.	Boston	14	42	56	82
10	Barry Pederson	C	5-11	171	3-13-61/Big River, Sask.	Boston	44	48	92	53
6	Dick Redmond	D	5-11	175	8-14-49/Kirkland Lake, Ont.	Boston	0	0	0	0
						Erie	8	13	21	14

No.	Player	Pos.	Hgt.	Wgt.	Born	1981-82	GP	GA	SO	Avg.
31	Marco Baron	G	5-11	179	4-8-59/Montreal, Que.	Boston	44	144	1	3.44
						Erie	2	8	0	4.03
30	Jim Craig	G	6-1	190	5-3-57/N. Easton, Mass.	Erie	13	57	0	4.61
	Mike Moffat	G	5-10	165	2-4-62/Galt, Ont.	Boston	2	6	0	3.00
	Pete Peeters	G	6-0	170	8-1-57/Edmonton, Alta.	Philadelphia	44	160	0	3.71
1	Rogatien Vachon	G	5-8	160	9-8-45/Palmarolle, Que.	Boston	38	132	1	3.66

OUTLOOK: The Bruins have slowly been rebuilt and now the team that looked like it was ready to crumble appears strong. There is no doubt that the Bruins will be a contender this season. The doubt is whether they can endure a rigorous playoff format. There is a nice blend of youth and experience which has made the team fresher and better. It may even make the Bruins winners again.

BRUIN PROFILES

PETER McNAB 30 6-3 203   Forward
It's Peter, not Pete... Solid all-around center who will always find a way to put puck in net... Not speedy, but knows how to score... Scored overtime goal in sixth game that prolonged quarterfinal series against Quebec... Bright, friendly and articulate... Was first Bruin ever awarded a penalty shot in playoffs, against Minnesota in 1981... One of most quotable players around... Born May 8, 1952, in Vancouver... Father Max is former GM of Washington and brother Dave a former scout for Capitals... Grew up in southern California and attended Denver University on baseball scholarship... Starred in college on NCAA hockey championship team... Wife Diana edited the Bruins' family cookbook.

Year	Club	GP	G	A	Pts.
1973-74	Buffalo	22	3	6	9
1974-75	Buffalo	53	22	21	43
1975-76	Buffalo	79	24	32	56
1976-77	Boston	80	38	48	86
1977-78	Boston	79	41	39	80
1978-79	Boston	76	35	45	80
1979-80	Boston	74	40	38	78
1980-81	Boston	80	37	46	83
1981-82	Boston	80	36	40	76
	Totals	623	276	315	591

RAY BOURQUE 21 5-11 197   Defenseman
One of the leading young blueliners in league... Has excellent puck control and is a magnificent passer... Rifle shot makes him extremely dangerous on power plays... "The most gifted player since Bobby Orr," says GM Harry Sinden... Born Dec. 28, 1960, in Montreal... Was only fifth defenseman in history to win Calder

Trophy as best rookie in 1980 . . . Set a rookie defenseman record of 65 points . . . Was first non-goalie to win Calder and berth on first all-star team . . . Was sorely missed in last two games of losing playoff series to Quebec last season when he fractured his left wrist . . . Supremely confident from his first shift in league . . . Hits hards when he has to.

Year	Club	GP	G	A	Pts.
1979-80	Boston	80	17	48	65
1980-81	Boston	67	27	29	56
1981-82	Boston	65	17	49	66
	Totals	212	61	126	187

RICK MIDDLETON 28 5-11 170   Forward

Tricky Rick . . . Supreme one-on-one player who is dangerous with the puck or without it . . . Fluid skater and accurate shooter . . . Plays power plays, kills penalties and does everything well . . . Has lightning-quick speed and tremendous acceleration . . . Last season led Bruins in goals, points, power plays goals (19) and game-winning goals (9) . . . A perennial Lady Byng candidate who had only 12 penalty minutes . . . Born Dec. 4, 1953, in Toronto . . . Has led club in scoring four straight years . . . Was the prize in one of the most lopsided trades ever, the Bruins acquiring him from Rangers for Ken Hodge in 1976 . . . It's been called the worst trade Rangers ever made and also the best the Bruins ever made . . . A born skater who has tremendous balance.

Year	Club	GP	G	A	Pts.
1974-75	New York R.	47	22	18	40
1975-76	New York R.	77	24	26	50
1976-77	Boston	72	20	22	42
1977-78	Boston	79	25	35	60
1978-79	Boston	71	38	48	86
1979-80	Boston	80	40	52	92
1980-81	Boston	80	44	59	103
1981-82	Boston	75	51	43	94
	Totals	581	264	303	567

TERRY O'REILLY 31 6-1 195   Forward

Solid right wing and solid left hook . . . Fierce competitor who isn't afraid to drop his gloves . . . Suspended for first 10 games this season after punching referee Andy Van Hellemond in last playoff game . . . Off the ice, he's a charmer . . . Delightful wit and remarkable attitude . . . Broods only when he thinks he's let down teammates . . . Disappointing playoff has led him to think about retirement . . . Plays hard and has the scars to prove it . . . Born June 7, 1951, in Niagara Falls, Ont. . . . Loves to work in the corners . . . Is only Bruin ever to lead club in both scoring and penalty minutes . . . Was victim of memorable three-fight battle with Clark Gillies in 1980 quarterfinals . . . Got into a fight in the first game his wife ever saw him play.

Year	Club	GP	G	A	Pts.
1971-72	Boston	1	1	0	1
1972-73	Boston	72	5	22	27
1973-74	Boston	76	11	24	35
1974-75	Boston	68	15	20	35
1975-76	Boston	80	23	27	50
1976-77	Boston	79	14	41	55
1977-78	Boston	77	29	61	90
1978-79	Boston	80	26	51	77
1979-80	Boston	71	19	42	61
1980-81	Boston	77	8	35	43
1981-82	Boston	70	22	30	52
	Totals	751	173	353	526

STEVE KASPER 21 5-8 159   Forward

Kasper the ghost . . . You don't see him, but he's there . . . Mr. Defense . . . Last year's winner of Frank Selke Trophy awarded to outstanding defensive forward . . . Nicknamed "The Shadow" . . . How can you stop Wayne Gretzky? Only The Shadow knows . . . Highlight of his brief career has been playing great defense on Gretzky . . . Not only held Gretzky without a point in one game last season, but even scored a goal himself . . . Born Sept. 28, 1961, in Montreal . . . Talented passer who has high level of enthusiasm . . . Scored the 11,000th goal in club history . . . Consistently plays excellent defense against outstanding centers in league . . . Made team as dark-horse candidate three years ago and has been regular ever since.

Year	Club	GP	G	A	Pts.
1980-81	Boston	76	21	35	56
1981-82	Boston	73	20	31	51
	Totals	149	41	66	107

BRAD PARK 34 6-0 200 Defenseman

Central Park . . . Central to Bruins' defense . . . Central to team's spirit . . . Central to team's victories . . . One of great blueliners of all time . . . Has overcome several knee operations to remain solid player . . . Also is a gentleman . . . Had terrific season in twilight of career last season . . . Scored eight power-play goals and anchored young defense . . . Has been considering retirement . . . Born July 6, 1948, in Toronto . . . Seven times an all-star . . . Will always be remembered as one of the principals in most earthshaking trade in league history, acquired from Rangers with Jean Ratelle for Phil Esposito and Carol Vadnais in 1976.

Year	Club	GP	G	A	Pts.
1968-69	New York R.	54	3	23	26
1969-70	New York R.	60	11	26	37
1970-71	New York R.	68	7	37	44
1971-72	New York R.	75	24	49	73
1972-73	New York R.	52	10	43	53
1973-74	New York R.	78	25	57	82
1974-75	New York R.	65	13	44	57
1975-76	N.Y.R.-Boston	56	18	41	59
1976-77	Boston	77	12	55	67
1977-78	Boston	80	22	57	79
1978-79	Boston	40	7	32	39
1979-80	Boston	32	5	16	21
1980-81	Boston	78	14	52	66
1981-82	Boston	75	14	42	56
	Totals	890	185	574	759

MIKE O'CONNELL 26 5-9 180 Defenseman

Iron Mike . . . Small, but determined . . . Able and ready . . . Good on ice, good in the dressing room . . . Very intelligent . . . Avid reader . . . Soft-spoken, interesting guy who is full of opinions . . . Played on Team USA in 1981 Canada Cup . . . Helps steady defense with coolness and experience . . . Can also score or make assist when it's needed . . . Born Nov. 25, 1955, in Chicago but actually grew up in Boston and was raised a Bruins fan . . . Oddity is, he began career with Black Hawks . . . Traded for Al Secord in 1981 and because of trade that year he led all NHL players in games played with 82 . . . Son of Tommy O'Connell, former Chicago Bears quarterback.

Year	Club	GP	G	A	Pts.
1977-78	Chicago	6	1	1	2
1978-79	Chicago	48	4	22	26
1979-80	Chicago	78	8	22	30
1980-81	Chi.-Bost.	82	15	38	53
1981-82	Boston	80	5	34	39
	Totals	294	33	117	150

ROGIE VACHON 37 5-7 165   Goaltender

No longer the great one, but still does the job... Probably highest-paid goalie ever, with contract worth $380,000 a season... Two years ago he logged the highest number of minutes by a Bruin goalie in five years... In 17th on all-time shutout list... Has played for three Stanley Cup winners and shared Vezina Trophy while in Montreal... Voted MVP of Canada Cup series in 1976... Born Sept. 8, 1945, in Palmorolle, Que.... Game is slipping, but enthusiasm isn't... Still produced 19 victories last season... One of smallest goalies to play in NHL... A former first-team all-star with Los Angeles.

Year	Club	GP	GA	SO	Avg.
1966-67	Montreal	19	47	1	2.48
1967-68	Montreal	39	92	4	2.48
1968-69	Montreal	36	98	2	2.87
1969-70	Montreal	64	162	4	2.63
1970-71	Montreal	47	118	2	2.64
1971-72	Mont.-L.A.	29	111	0	4.15
1972-73	Los Angeles	53	148	4	2.85
1973-74	Los Angeles	65	175	5	2.80
1974-75	Los Angeles	54	121	6	2.24
1975-76	Los Angeles	51	160	5	3.14
1976-77	Los Angeles	68	184	8	2.72
1977-78	Los Angeles	70	196	4	2.86
1978-79	Detroit	50	189	0	3.90
1979-80	Detroit	59	209	4	3.61
1980-81	Boston	53	168	1	3.34
1981-82	Boston	38	132	1	3.66
	Totals	795	2310	51	2.99

BARRY PEDERSON 21 5-11 171   Forward

Emerged as leading contender for Rookie of the Year honors after finishing second on club in scoring... Was only fifth rookie in NHL history to reach 40-goal plateau... Shattered club rookie record for most goals, easily bettering 52-year-old mark of 26 held by Roy Conacher...Also set club rookie point record of 65, formerly held by Ray Bourque...Born March 13, 1961, in Big River, Sask....Terrific young center...Notched power-play goal on just second shift in first NHL game...Played for Memorial Cup finalist Victoria after being returned to juniors two years ago and scored hat trick in playoffs.

Year	Club	GP	G	A	Pts.
1980-81	Boston	9	1	4	5
1981-82	Boston	80	44	48	92
	Totals	89	45	52	97

WAYNE CASHMAN 37 6-2 208   Forward

Captain Crunch...Hits hard, gets hit hard and never quits... Someday he'll get tired...Is fourth on all-time Bruin scoring list behind John Bucyk, Phil Esposito and Bobby Orr...Only one of two remaining players along with Don Marcotte from Stanley Cup winners of 1970 and '72...A leader on the ice and off it...Has lost some of his scoring touch, but is still valuable...Does terrific work in corners...Doesn't fight like he used to, but doesn't have to...Born June 24, 1945, in Kingston, Ont....Also called "Cash"...Appropriate nickname for a money player...Spends off-ice hours at horse stables he owns.

Year	Club	GP	G	A	Pts.
1964-65	Boston	1	0	0	0
1967-68	Boston	12	0	4	4
1968-69	Boston	51	8	23	31
1969-70	Boston	70	9	26	35
1970-71	Boston	77	21	58	79
1971-72	Boston	74	23	29	52
1972-73	Boston	76	29	39	68
1973-74	Boston	78	30	59	89
1974-75	Boston	42	11	22	33
1975-76	Boston	80	28	43	71
1976-77	Boston	65	15	37	52
1977-78	Boston	76	24	38	62
1978-79	Boston	75	27	40	67
1979-80	Boston	44	11	21	32
1980-81	Boston	77	25	35	60
1981-82	Boston	64	12	31	43
	Totals	962	273	505	778

Lady Byng winner Rick Middleton scored 94 points last year.

COACH GERRY CHEEVERS: Did outstanding job in second season to silence critics who said he couldn't coach former pals... Good at motivating players... Has changed Bruins' style from bump-and-grind to run-and-gun... Adjusts nicely to trends and styles of opponents... Guided Bruins to second-place finish in Adams Division before losing in division finals to Quebec... One of few goalies to coach an NHL team... Still called "Cheesy" by old mates... Born Dec. 7, 1940, in St. Catharines, Ont.... Outstanding sense of humor... Terribly popular in Boston area... A horse owner who always likes to go to the track... One of best playoff goalies in history... Still doesn't like to wear neckties... Says the briefcase he carries is for his underwear.

GREATEST CENTER

He owned the city of Boston, pronounced "Bah-ston," the way he owned a seat at the 4B's Pub or, more accurately, the way he owned a square of ice in front of the net that became known as his personal kingdom. Phil Esposito was not fast or bold or graceful. But he was big—6-2 and 205 pounds—and he was smart. And he knew how to score goals. So many, in fact, that Phil Esposito rewrote the record books, became one of the leading scorers of his generation and remains one of the leading scorers in the history of the National Hockey League.

He was a good center still far from blossoming when the Chicago Black Hawks made what will go down as one of the most one-sided trades ever, dealing Esposito to the Bruins in 1967 along with Ken Hodge and Fred Stanfield for Pit Martin, Gilles Marotte and Jack Norris. Three years later, Esposito scored an amazing 76 goals in 78 games and totaled 152 points; both records stood until a pimpled youngster named Wayne Gretzky began his own assault two years ago. When Gretzky scored his 77th goal last season en route to 92, Esposito was there to applaud the achievement.

Like Gretzky, Esposito was far ahead of most of his contemporaries. He scored 60 goals or more four times in five seasons. He scored 120 points or more five straight seasons. And when the Bruins made the shocking decision to trade Esposito to the New York Rangers in 1976, Esposito kept gunning. He scored more than 30 goals four consecutive seasons in New York and helped take the Rangers to the Stanley Cup finals in 1979. By the time he retired in the middle of the 1980-81 season, Esposito had racked up 1,590 points, second only to Gordie Howe's 1,850, and 717 goals, second only to Howe's 801 in the NHL. In many ways, though, Esposito was second to no one.

ALL-TIME BRUIN LEADERS

GOALS: Phil Esposito, 76, 1970-71
ASSISTS: Bobby Orr, 102, 1970-71
POINTS: Phil Esposito, 152, 1970-71
SHUTOUTS: Hal Winkler, 15, 1927-28

BUFFALO SABRES

TEAM DIRECTORY: Pres.: Seymour Knox III; Dir. Hockey Operations and GM-Coach: Scotty Bowman; Asst. Coaches: Jim Roberts and Nick Polano; Dir. Pub. Rel.: Gerry Helper. Home ice: Memorial Auditorium (16,433; 196′ × 85′). Colors: Blue, white and gold. Training camp: Lake Placid, N.Y., Buffalo, N.Y.

SCOUTING REPORT

OFFENSE: One of the least inventive and least exciting teams until recently, the Sabres are trying hard to overhaul their image as losers. Save for a semifinal berth three years ago, Buffalo has

Gil Perreault has over 1,000 points in his NHL career.

been a playoff bust. A lack of consistent scoring has been the major reason. So Scotty Bowman has begun to overhaul his team. The Sabres were one of the most active teams over the summer and the result is the Sabres had three first-round draft picks and five selections in the first 30.

But the players most likely to help Buffalo are already there. Gil Perreault came off the disabled list to score 31 goals in 62 games. He still is the center of attention and the biggest gate attraction in the Aud. But now the Sabres will have a full season of Mike Foligno, the right wing who came in the midseason trade with Detroit. Foligno is one of the most coveted forwards in the league and should boost the Sabres' production from 307 goals, which was better than only one other team in the Adams Division (lowly Hartford).

Also around for the full term will be center Dale McCourt, who came along with Foligno. McCourt hasn't been quite the player he was supposed to be when the Red Wings once made him the first player selected in the draft, but he gives the Sabres depth behind Perreault, not an insignificant addition.

Beyond that, the Sabres are nameless and faceless but do have some hard workers. Ric Seiling is a good, all-around player and Yvon Lambert was of surprising help last season. But Tony McKegney needs to improve and Craig Ramsay isn't the Ramsay of old, although he still tries as hard as ever.

DEFENSE: That's the encouraging word. The Sabres ranked third in defense behind only Montreal and the Islanders, and the Sabres can't help but get better. They had the fourth selection in the amateur draft and chose Phil Housley of South St. Paul High School in Minnesota. Housley may or may not be ready to help the team. If he is ready, even Willie Sutton wouldn't be able to crack the Sabres' defense.

The reputations won't scare anybody and there is a lack of mobility, but the Sabres have size and strength. Lindy Ruff is a bruising checker and Larry Playfair and Bill Hajt are solid. The one Sabre on defense who knows how to handle the puck is John Van Boxmeer, coming off one of his finest seasons. Van Boxmeer had 54 assists, possesses a booming shot and skates well. One surprise could be Bob Hess, who has bounced around for years but once had enough talent to be a first-round draft in St. Louis.

Bowman has his reputation as a wheeler-dealer and has done nothing to change the thinking. After trading Bob Sauve in midseason, who would have thought that Sauve would somehow wind up back in Buffalo as the No. 1 goalie? He has. Sauve became

SABRE ROSTER

No.	Player	Pos.	Hgt.	Wgt.	Born	1981-82	G	A	Pts.	PIM
	Dave Andreychuk	C	6-3	195	9-29-63/Hamilton, Ont.	Oshawa	58	43	101	71
	Randy Cunneyworth	C	6-0	177	5-10-61/Etobichoke, Ont.	Rochester	12	15	27	86
						Buffalo	2	4	6	47
	Paul Cyr	LW	5-11	185	10-31-63/St. Alberni, B.C.	Victoria	52	56	108	167
	Jeff Eatough	RW	5-9	168	6-2-63/Toronto, Ont.	Buffalo	0	0	0	0
						Cornwall	53	37	90	180
	Ron Fischer	D	6-2	195	4-12-59/Merritt, B.C.	Buffalo	0	7	7	6
						Rochester	12	15	27	86
17	Mike Foligno	RW	6-2	190	1-29-59/Sudbury, Ont.	Det.-Buff.	33	44	77	177
24	Bill Hajt	D	6-3	215	11-18-51/Borden, Sask.	Buffalo	2	9	11	44
	Gilles Hamel	RW	6-0	183	12-15-57/Asbestos, Que.	Buffalo	2	7	9	2
						Rochester	31	44	75	55
23	Bob Hess	D-RW	5-11	175	5-19-55/Edmonton, Alta.	Buffalo	0	8	8	14
						Rochester	6	11	17	10
	Phil Housley	D	5-10	180	3-9-64/St. Paul, Minn.	S. St. Paul H.S.	38	41	79	24
15	Yvon Lambert	LW	6-2	190	5-20-50/Drummondville, Que.	Buffalo	25	39	64	38
7	Dale McCourt	C	5-10	185	1-26-57/Sudbury, Ont.	Det.-Buff.	33	36	69	18
8	Tony McKegney	LW	6-1	198	2-15-58/Sarnia, Ont.	Buffalo	23	29	52	41
	Sean McKenna	C	6-0	186	3-17-62/Asbestos, Que.	Sherbrooke	57	33	90	29
						Buffalo	0	1	1	2
	Mike Moller	RW	6-0	189	6-16-62/Red Deer, Alta.	Buffalo	0	0	0	0
						Lethbridge	41	81	122	38
25	Bob Mongrain	C	5-10	165	8-31-59/LaBarre, Que.	Rochester	37	37	74	45
						Buffalo	6	4	10	6
	Steve Patrick	RW	6-3	206	2-4-61/Winnipeg, Man.	Buffalo	8	8	16	64
						Rochester	11	9	20	15
11	Gil Perreault	C	6-0	202	11-13-50/Victoriaville, Que.	Buffalo	31	42	73	40
20	Brent Peterson	C	6-0	190	2-15-58/Calgary, Alta.	Det.-Buff.	10	5	15	49
27	Larry Playfair	D	6-4	201	6-23-58/Ft. St. James, B.C.	Buffalo	6	10	16	258
10	Craig Ramsey	RW	5-10		3-17-51/Toronto, Ont.	Buffalo	16	35	51	8
5	Mike Ramsey	D	6-3	190	12-3-60/Minneapolis, Minn.	Buffalo	7	23	30	56
22	Lindy Ruff	D	6-2	190	2-17-60/Warburg, Alta.	Buffalo	16	32	48	194
12	Andre Savard	C	6-1	185	2-9-53/Temiskaming, Que.	Buffalo	18	20	38	24
21	J. F. Sauve	C	5-6	175	1-23-60/St. Genevieve, Que.	Buffalo	19	36	55	46
						Rochester	5	8	13	4
16	Ric Seiling	RW	6-1	178	12-15-57/Elmira, Ont.	Buffalo	22	25	47	58
	Dean Turner	D	6-2	215	6-22-58/Dearborn, Mich.	Rochester	8	46	54	155
5	John Van Boxmeer	D	6-1	192	8-13-52/Petrolia, Ont.	Buffalo	14	54	68	62

No.	Player	Pos.	Hgt.	Wgt.	Born	1981-82	GP	GA	SO	Avg.
	Jacques Cloutier	G	5-7	154	1-3-60/Noranda, Que.	Buffalo	7	13	0	2.51
						Rochester	23	64	0	2.81
30	Paul Harrison	G	6-1	175	2-11-55/Timmins, Ont.	Pitt.-Buff.	19	78	0	5.06
	Jari Paavola	G	5-8	167	3-18-60/Finland	Rochester	3	12	0	5.11
28	Bob Sauve	G	5-8	165	6-17-55/St. Genevieve, Que.	Buff.-Det.	55	200	0	3.84

a free agent, was not offered a contract by Detroit and re-signed with the Sabres. That allowed Bowman to deal Don Edwards, a fine goalie, to Calgary in a complex deal for four draft choices. Sauve will be backed up by Jacques Cloutier, who played seven games for the Sabres last season and is supposed to be a real comer.

OUTLOOK: The Sabres will be better, but may not have a better record. It's their misfortune to be in the Adams Division, where just a few points could make the difference between first place and fourth place. The offense isn't good enough, the defense is and the goaltending probably is somewhere in between. And that's about where the Sabres will wind up. Somewhere in between.

SABRE PROFILES

GILBERT PERREAULT 31 6-0 202   Forward
Passed the 1,000-point mark last season... Missed 18 games due to knee injury suffered in Canada Cup... Has gotten second wind after nearly being traded three years ago... Sleek and quick and easily one of the most exciting players around... A big breakaway threat... Once hailed as the second coming of Jean Beliveau... Was first draft pick in club history... Won Calder Trophy in 1970-71... Born Nov. 13, 1950, in Victoriaville, Que.... Past winner of Lady Byng Trophy (1973) and twice a second-team all-star... Has rounded into an adequate defensive player... Selected to Challenge Cup team that played against Soviets in 1979... Holds 10 team records, including seven-point game in 1976... Last remaining member of French Connection line that also included Rich Martin and Rene Robert.

Year	Club	GP	G	A	Pts.
1970-71	Buffalo	78	38	34	72
1971-72	Buffalo	76	26	48	74
1972-73	Buffalo	78	28	60	88
1973-74	Buffalo	55	18	33	51
1974-75	Buffalo	68	39	57	96
1975-76	Buffalo	80	44	69	113
1976-77	Buffalo	80	39	56	95
1977-78	Buffalo	79	41	48	89
1978-79	Buffalo	79	27	58	85
1979-80	Buffalo	80	40	66	106
1980-81	Buffalo	56	20	39	59
1981-82	Buffalo	62	31	42	73
	Totals	871	391	610	1001

DALE McCOURT 25 5-10 185   Forward

Centerpiece in one of the biggest trades in NHL history...Dealt by Detroit along with Brent Peterson and Mike Foligno for Jim Schoenfeld, Danny Gare and Bob Suave last Dec....Consistent, heady center who gets points...Created controversy three years ago when he challenged his being awarded to Los Angeles as compensation for Detroit signing Rogie Vachon...Stayed with team while matter was settled in court...Was first player selected in 1977 draft on basis of outstanding junior career...Born Jan. 26, 1957, in Falconbridge, Ont....Scored 20 goals in 52 games with Sabres after trade...Seemed to recapture some of enthusiasm that had faded with Red Wings...A player you can build a team around when his head is on straight.

Year	Club	GP	G	A	Pts.
1977-78	Detroit	76	33	39	72
1978-79	Detroit	79	28	43	71
1979-80	Detroit	80	30	51	81
1980-81	Detroit	80	30	56	86
1981-82	Det.-Buff.	78	33	36	69
	Totals	393	154	225	379

JOHN VAN BOXMEER 29 6-1 192   Defenseman

"Boxy"...Quick, hard-shooting blueliner involved in one of team's most controversial trades...Acquired from Colorado for fading hero Rene Robert...Trade reunited him with GM Scotty Bowman, his former coach in Montreal...Has shrugged off injuries to have fine career...Named to Wales Conference all-star team last season...Holds every single-season scoring mark by a Buffalo defenseman...Was first defenseman ever to lead club in assists when he scored 51 in 1980–81...Came within one assist of duplicating feat last season...Contributed seven power-play goals...Born Nov. 20, 1952, in Petrolia, Ont....Stronger than he looks...Wicked shot makes him especially dangerous from the point...Very popular with knowledgeable Buffalo fans.

Year	Club	GP	G	A	Pts.
1973-74	Montreal	20	1	4	5
1974-75	Montreal	9	0	2	2
1975-76	Montreal	46	6	11	17
1976-77	Mont.-Colo.	45	2	12	14
1977-78	Colorado	80	12	42	54
1978-79	Colorado	76	9	34	43
1979-80	Buffalo	80	11	40	51
1980-81	Buffalo	80	18	51	69
1981-82	Buffalo	69	14	54	68
	Totals	505	73	250	323

CRAIG RAMSAY 31 5-10 176   Forward

"Rammer"... Steady, unexciting, quietly effective center who is particularly good at the small stuff... Excellent on faceoffs... Has been one of league's best penalty-killers for years... Never out of the lineup... Plays hurt or tired... Has appeared in 721 consecutive regular-season games, the second longest streak in NHL history behind only Garry Unger's 914... But holds the record for consecutive games played with one team... Has not missed a game since March 27, 1973... Born March 17, 1951, in Weston, Ont.... Third on team's all-time scoring list behind only Gil Perreault and Richard Martin... Has eye-opening total of 24 career shorthanded goals, two last season... Was finalist in balloting for Bill Masterton Trophy last season.

Year	Club	GP	G	A	Pts.
1971-72	Buffalo	57	6	10	16
1972-73	Buffalo	76	11	17	28
1973-74	Buffalo	78	20	26	46
1974-75	Buffalo	80	26	38	64
1975-76	Buffalo	80	22	49	71
1976-77	Buffalo	80	20	41	61
1977-78	Buffalo	80	28	43	71
1978-79	Buffalo	80	26	31	57
1979-80	Buffalo	80	21	39	60
1980-81	Buffalo	80	24	35	69
1981-82	Buffalo	80	16	35	51
	Totals	851	220	364	584

BOB SAUVE 27 5-8 165   Goaltender

Back in Buffalo... Spent parts of six seasons with Sabres before trade to Detroit early last season... Apparently he went to Motor City as a loan, though, because he immediately went back to Sabres in June... Lost only once in 12 decisions and had fine 2.76 goals-against average in Buffalo last year... Suffered with hapless Red Wings, though, and fell to 11-25-4 with a 4.19 average... Shared Vezina Trophy with Don Edwards in 1979-80 as he had 2.36 average in regular season... Sabres' trade of Edwards this past summer will mean more net time for Sauve... Buffalo's No. 1 pick in 1975 amateur draft... Born June 17, 1955, in Ste. Genevieve, Quebec... Brother Jean Francis Sauve was 19-goal scorer for Sabres last season.

Year	Club	GP	GA	SO	Avg.
1976-77	Buffalo	4	11	0	3.55
1977-78	Buffalo	11	20	0	2.50
1978-79	Buffalo	29	100	0	3.73
1979-80	Buffalo	32	74	4	2.36
1980-81	Buffalo	35	111	2	3.17
1981-82	Buff.-Det.	55	200	0	3.84
	Totals	166	516	6	3.30

RIC SEILING 24 6-1 178   Forward

Enthusiastic, hard-working right winger who knows how to play at both ends of the ice . . . Sidelined by injuries for 23 games last season but still managed to score at least 20 goals for fourth straight year . . . Had three game-winners . . . Not flashy but gets the job done . . . Strong checker and very durable . . . Brother Rod was longtime defenseman for Rangers . . . Rod introduced him once in Ranger dressing room, predicting he'd outdo older brother . . . He has . . . Was first-round pick in 1977 . . . Born Dec. 15, 1957, in Elmira, Ont. . . . Involved in family's harness horse business . . . Noticeable by curly head of hair . . . Brother Don also is a former hockey player . . . Popular with fans because of his nonstop style of mucking for puck in the corners.

Year	Club	GP	G	A	Pts.
1977-78	Buffalo	80	19	19	38
1978-79	Buffalo	78	20	22	42
1979-80	Buffalo	80	25	35	60
1980-81	Buffalo	74	30	27	57
1981-82	Buffalo	57	22	25	47
	Totals	369	116	128	244

MIKE FOLIGNO 23 6-2 190   Forward

One of the leading young right wings around . . . Tremendous natural talent . . . Helps himself even more with tireless work along boards, in the corners and around the net . . . Was one of Detroit's most hailed draft choices in generations . . . Did nothing to disappoint team . . . Was reluctantly part of blockbuster deal that sent Dale McCourt and Brent Peterson to Sabres in return for Jim Schoenfeld, Danny Gare and Bob Sauve . . . Born Jan. 29, 1959, in Sudbury, Ont. . . . Strong skater who has powerful shot . . . Extremely tough . . . Totaled 177 penalty minutes, including 149 in only 56 games with the Sabres...Was coveted by every team in the league...A player who can lift a franchise all by himself.

Year	Club	GP	G	A	Pts.
1979-80	Detroit	80	36	35	71
1980-81	Detroit	80	28	35	63
1981-82	Det.-Buff.	82	33	44	77
	Totals	242	97	114	211

TONY McKEGNEY 24 6-1 198   Forward

Very quiet...Very solid...Very steady...Doesn't score a lot...Doesn't check a lot...Doesn't get a lot of penalties...Just does his job and does it well...Not a strong skater and that hurts him...Lacks a really good scoring touch...Still a good man to have around...One of six Blacks in the NHL and was only the third in nearly 20 years when he joined the league...Raised by adoptive white parents...Born Feb. 15, 1958, in Montreal ...Adoptive father was member of Canadian Air Force who was saddened by orphans he saw during World War II...He adopted Tony and several other children...One of the best left wings in the corners...Durable...Failed to play entire season for first time in three years.

Year	Club	GP	G	A	Pts.
1978-79	Buffalo	52	8	14	22
1979-80	Buffalo	80	23	29	52
1980-81	Buffalo	80	37	32	69
1981-82	Buffalo	73	23	29	52
	Totals	285	91	104	195

YVON LAMBERT 32 6-0 190   Forward

Career revived under old coach Scotty Bowman, his mentor when they shared Stanley Cups...Waw claimed in intraleague draft at start of the season and turned into big bargain...Led team with 14 power-play goals...Also had four game-winning scores...Big, strong left wing...Is especially tough in playoffs...Once finished fourth in scoring on a championship Canadiens team...

Doesn't fight anymore because no one dares challenge him... Was one of great Montreal steals when team plucked him in league draft from Detroit... Born May 20, 1950, in Drummondville, Que.... Grew up on farm and didn't get first pair of skates until he was 14 years old... Hitchhiked 13 miles to play hockey... The oldest of eight children.

Year	Club	GP	G	A	Pts.
1972-73	Montreal	1	0	0	0
1973-74	Montreal	60	6	10	16
1974-75	Montreal	80	32	35	67
1975-76	Montreal	80	32	35	67
1976-77	Montreal	79	24	28	52
1977-78	Montreal	77	18	22	40
1978-79	Montreal	79	26	40	66
1979-80	Montreal	77	21	32	53
1980-81	Montreal	73	22	32	54
1981-82	Buffalo	77	25	39	64
	Totals	683	206	273	479

ANDRE SAVARD 29 6-1 185   Forward

Tough little guy who always comes to play... Underrated as good two-way forward... Will score a big goal or make a big defensive play... Will try, try and try again... Biggest problem is consistency... Will be up for two weeks and down for three... Was first pick of Boston Bruins in 1973 but was acquired as compensation for Bruins' signing of free agent Peter McNab... Has been sent to minors but always comes back... Was groomed as penalty killer, eventually succeeding Don Luce... Does all the little things well—faceoffs, defense, backchecking... Born Sept. 2, 1953, in Temiscaming, Que.... Never quits... Showed up at camp two years ago without a job and was in starting lineup opening night.

Year	Club	GP	G	A	Pts.
1973-74	Boston	72	16	14	30
1974-75	Boston	77	19	25	44
1975-76	Boston	79	17	23	40
1976-77	Buffalo	80	25	35	60
1977-78	Buffalo	80	19	20	39
1978-79	Buffalo	65	18	22	40
1979-80	Buffalo	33	3	10	13
1980-81	Buffalo	79	31	43	74
1981-82	Buffalo	62	18	20	38
	Totals	627	166	212	378

COACH SCOTT BOWMAN: Temperamental, tough and abrasive...Also smart, shrewd and successful...One of the leading coaches in the history of the game...A real innovator...But call him Scott, not Scotty...Real name is William but no one calls him that...Can't give up the reins...Promised to stick only to general manager's chores after returning to bench early last season but relieved assistant Jim Roberts in last month...Planned to come back again this season...Couldn't prevent first-round ouster in playoffs, but again won respect of players...They either love him or hate him...Born Sept. 18, 1933, in Montreal...Fulfilled lifelong dream by coaching Canadiens...Led team to four straight Stanley Cups, including two sweeps in final round...Has 607 career victories, second only to Dick Irvin's 690...Doesn't tolerate mistakes in fundamentals...Was coach of Team Canada squad that lost to Soviets last season...Known best for his tight collars that seem to squeeze his neck.

GREATEST CENTER

Few players can match the skill Gilbert Perreault has. Few can match the excitement he generates. Probably none can match the misfortune that has blemished, but not stopped, his fabulous career. Appropriately, he was the first player ever drafted by the fledgling Buffalo Sabres and he quickly became the centerpiece of the young franchise.

Swift and shifty, Perreault was the glue to the famed "French Connection" line that took the Sabres to the Stanley Cup finals in only their fifth season. Rick Martin and Rene Robert have long since departed, but Perreault has survived injuries, slumps and purges to remain the Sabres' most gifted player. He is the only player in club history to exceed the 1,000-point mark. He holds team records for games (871), goals (391) and assists (610). He has won the Calder Trophy as Rookie of the Year, the Lady Byng Trophy for sportsmanship and twice been named to NHL squads that took on the Soviets in the Challenge Cup and Canada Cup. Even last season, when he missed 18 games because of a fractured ankle, Perreault still led the Sabres with 31 goals—the seventh time in his 11 seasons he has topped the 30-goal mark.

Perhaps the greatest attribute ever paid Perreault was the time he was compared to Jean Beliveau, the great Montreal center of another generation. The comparison was made by none other than

Beliveau himself. In time, no doubt, there will be another young, swift center on the Sabres and he will inspire comparisons to Perreault. That's a nice thought.

ALL-TIME SABRE LEADERS

GOALS: Danny Gare, 56, 1979-80
ASSISTS: Gil Perreault, 69, 1975-76
POINTS: Gil Perreault, 113, 1975-76
SHUTOUTS: Don Edwards, 5, 1977-78

Steady Ric Seiling has had four 20-goal seasons.

CALGARY FLAMES

TEAM DIRECTORY: President/GM: Cliff Fletcher; Asst. GM: David Poile; Dir. Player Personnel: Al MacNeil; Dir. Pub Rel.: Al Coates; Coach: Bob Johnson. Home ice: Calgary Corral (7,223; 200' x 85'). Colors: Red, white and gold. Training camp: Calgary, Alberta.

SCOUTING REPORT

OFFENSE: There was little wrong with the Flames' attack in 1981-82 even though center Kent Nilsson, a 131-point producer a year earlier, missed half the season with injuries.

The emergence of sophomores Jim Peplinski and Kevin Lavallee as 30-goal scorers took up the slack and Mel Bridgman and Lanny McDonald, good veterans added in deals after the season started, were solid producers.

New coach Bob Johnson doesn't inherit a powerhouse attack but there's sufficient talent to build a solid one.

Nilsson had 55 points in the 41 games he played and when he's sound, the fleet Swede is superb offensively. Bridgman (33 goals, 87 points) was a defensive player with the Philadelphia Flyers and blossomed when placed in an attacking role. McDonald, a premier gunner, had 40 goals and Guy Chouinard had 80 points in 64 games.

Steve Christoff, a U.S. Olympic hero acquired from Minnesota, has good scoring potential if he can stay healthy. Peplinski and Lavallee, a pair of hard-working kids, should maintain last season's level.

There's attack from the back, too. Pekka Rautakallio (68 points) and Paul Reinhart (61) are good rushing defensemen.

In U.S. college hockey, Johnson's Wisconsin U. teams were noted for their potent power plays and the Flames have the material to construct a good one.

DEFENSE: The Flames' big offseason acquisition was goalie Don Edwards from the Buffalo Sabres. Pat Riggin and Rejean Lemelin simply failed to give the club consistent work last season and Edwards, if anything, is reliable and steady. His 2.90 career average in six NHL seasons is a dandy.

Competition for jobs on the Flames' backline will be keen, especially if Bill Nyrop, who joined the team in the Christoff trade with Minnesota, reports to Calgary. Nyrop had led the world in "thinking about playing" through three years of retirement from Montreal until he joined the North Stars last season.

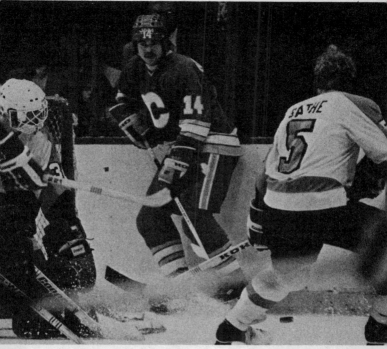

Kent Nilsson scored 26 goals in only 41 games last year.

Nyrop, Richie Dunn, added from Buffalo, and rookie Allan McInness are new candidates. Rautakallio, Reinhart and Phil Russell are the veterans and two kids who earned jobs last season—Steve Konroyd and Charles Bourgeois—give Johnson plenty to choose from.

OUTLOOK: Johnson brings an impressive record over a long haul in U.S. college hockey. In handling Team USA in the 1981 Canada Cup tournament, he impressed the NHL players.

The Flames had floundered with a cast of players in Atlanta and when they advanced to the semifinals in 1981, it appeared they had arrived as a respectable team. But they sagged again in 1981-82 and GM Cliff Fletcher launched a housecleaning, a job he continued during the summer.

The club will present a vastly changed face this season, starting with coach Johnson. Look for a big improvement.

FLAME ROSTER

No.	Player	Pos.	Hgt.	Wgt.	Born	1981-82	G	A	Pts.	PIM
2	Charles Bourgeois	D	6-4	205	11-11-59/Moncton, N.B.	Oklahoma City	2	2	4	17
						Calgary	2	13	15	112
26	Mel Bridgman	C	6-0	190	4-28-55/Victoria, B.C.	Phil.-Calgary	33	54	87	141
16	Guy Chouinard	C	5-11	182	12-20-56/Quebec, Que.	Calgary	23	57	80	12
	Steve Christoff	LW-C	6-1	180	1-23-58/Richfield, Minn.	Minnesota	26	30	56	14
10	Bill Clement	C	6-1	190	12-20-50/Buckingham, Que.	Calgary	4	12	16	28
12	Denis Cyr	RW	5-11	180	2-4-61/Montreal, Que.	Oklahoma City	10	4	14	16
						Calgary	12	10	22	13
	Richie Dunn	D	6-0	192	5-12-57/Boston, Mass.	Buffalo	7	19	26	73
	Mike Dwyer	LW	5-11	172	9-16-57/Brampton, Ont.	Calgary	0	2	2	0
						Oklahoma City	9	21	30	35
	Bruce Eakin	C	5-10	185	9-29-62/Winnipeg, Man.	Calgary	0	0	0	0
						Oklahoma City	0	3	3	0
						Saskatoon	42	125	167	120
8	Kari Eloranta	D	6-2	200	4-29-56/Lahti, Fin.	Oklahoma City	3	27	30	31
						Cal.-St. L.	1	12	13	20
	Bobby Francis	C	5-9	180	12-5-58/N. Battleford, Sask.	Oklahoma City	48	66	114	76
17	Jamie Hislop	RW	5-10	180	1-20-54/Sarnia, Ont.	Calgary	16	25	41	35
	Bill Hobbins	C	5-11	190	4-13-60/Edmonton, Alta.	Oklahoma City	13	15	28	28
	Steve Konroyd	D	6-1	195	2-10-61/Scarborough, Ont.	Calgary	3	14	17	78
						Oklahoma City	2	3	5	15
21	Dan Labraaten	LW	6-0	185	6-9-51/Arvika, Swe.	Calgary	10	12	22	6
15	Kevin Levalee	LW	5-8	180	9-16-61/Sudbury, Ont.	Calgary	32	29	61	30
	Alex MacInnis	D	6-1	185	7-11-63/Inverness, N.S.	Calgary	0	0	0	0
						Kitchener	25	50	75	145
	Gary McAdam	RW	5-11	175	12-31-55/Smith Falls, Ont.	Dallas	10	10	20	14
						Calgary	12	15	27	18
9	Lanny McDonald	RW	6-0	190	2-16-53/Hanna, Alta.	Col.-Calgary	40	42	82	57
	Alex McKendry	RW	6-4	200	11-21-56/Midland, Ont.	Oklahoma City	27	59	86	163
14	Kent Nilsson	C	6-1	185	8-31-56/Nyasham, Swe.	Calgary	26	29	55	8
	Bill Nyrop	D	6-2	205	7-23-52/Washington, D.C.	Minnesota	4	8	12	35
24	Jim Peplinski	RW	6-2	201	10-24-60/Renfrew, Ont.	Calgary	30	37	67	115
23	Paul Reinhart	D	5-11	216	1-8-60/Kitchener, Ont.	Calgary	13	48	61	17
	Pat Ribble	D	6-4	210	4-26-54/Leamington, Ont.	Wash.-Calgary	1	2	3	16
						Oklahoma City	1	9	10	44
3	Phil Russell	D	6-1	195	7-21-52/Edmonton, Alta.	Calgary	4	25	29	110
	Randy Turnbull	D	6-0	185	2-7-62/Bentley, Alta.	Calgary	0	0	0	2
						Portland	5	19	24	430
	Rick Vasko	D	6-0	185	12-1-57/St. Catherine's, Ont.	Oklahoma City	9	32	41	92
	Howard Walker	D	6-0	205	8-5-58/Grand Prairie, Alta.	Washington	0	2	2	26
						Hershey	3	4	7	62
22	Gord Wappel	D	6-2	204	7-26-58/Regina, Sask.	Calgary	0	1	1	6
						Oklahoma City	6	13	19	52

							GP	GA	SO	Avg.
	Hardy Astrom	G	6-0	170	3-29-51/Skelleftea, Swe.	Oklahoma City	35	154	0	4.84
	Tim Bernhardt	G	5-9	159	4-19-58/Sarnia, Ont.	Rochester	29	95	0	3.59
						Oklahoma City	10	45	0	5.13
	Don Edwards	G	5-9	160	9-28-55/Hamilton, Ont.	Buffalo	62	205	0	3.51
31	Rejean Lemelin	G	5-11	160	11-19-54/Sherbrooke, Que.	Calgary	34	135	0	4.34

FLAME PROFILES

MEL BRIDGMAN 27 6-0 190   Forward

Trade to Flames from Philadelphia early in 1981-82 season changed emphasis in career...With Flyers, he was defensive specialist, assigned to check top centers...Flames allowed him to be offensive player and he had best season with 33 goals, 54 assists...Tough, hard-nosed type who handles the puck well, checks strongly and is a hard hitter...Born Apr. 28, 1955, in Trenton, Ont....Played junior hockey with Victoria Cougars...First player selected in 1975 amateur draft...Had six solid years with Flyers...Traded to Flames in October, 1981, for defenseman Brad Marsh...Enjoys playing the stock market.

Year	Club	GP	G	A	Pts.
1975-76	Philadelphia	80	23	27	50
1976-77	Philadelphia	70	19	38	57
1977-78	Philadelphia	76	16	32	48
1978-79	Philadelphia	76	24	35	59
1979-80	Philadelphia	74	16	31	47
1980-81	Philadelphia	77	14	37	51
1981-82	Phil.-Calg.	72	33	54	87
	Totals	525	145	254	399

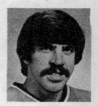

LANNY McDONALD 29 6-0 190   Forward

Big Mac...One of NHL's most consistent shooters in past nine seasons, with 319 goals...Owns a superb shot, is a strong checker and hard worker...Joined Flames early in 1981-82 season from Colorado in exchange for Bob MacMillan and Don Lever...Had fifth 40-goal season last year...Born Feb. 16, 1953, in Hanna, Alta....Junior star with Medecine Hat Tigers...First-round draft choice of Toronto in 1973...Became very popular player with Leafs, then was dealt to Colorado with Joel Quenneville in controversial 1979 deal for Wilf Paiement and Pat Hickey...Splendid team player...Among best at delivering clean, open-ice bodycheck.

Year	Club	GP	G	A	Pts.
1973-74	Toronto	70	14	16	30
1974-75	Toronto	64	17	27	44
1975-76	Toronto	75	37	56	93
1976-77	Toronto	80	46	44	90
1977-78	Toronto	74	47	40	87
1978-79	Toronto	79	43	42	85
1979-80	Tor.-Col.	81	40	35	75
1980-81	Colorado	80	35	46	81
1981-82	Col.-Calg.	71	40	42	82
	Totals	674	319	348	667

GUY CHOUINARD 26 5-11 182   **Forward**
Plagued by injuries the past two seasons...When sound, he is a splendid attacker, swift, excellent scorer and playmaker...Had 50 goals, 107 points in Atlanta in 1978-79...Produced 80 points in 64 games last season...Born Oct. 20, 1956, in Quebec City...Flames' first-round draft pick in 1974...Rookie of Year in Central League in 1974-75, and again in the American League the next season...Drafted at 18, an eight-year pro although only 26...One of the NHL's best power-play workers, he scored 13 of 23 goals in that situation last season.

Year	Club	GP	G	A	Pts.
1974-75	Atlanta	5	0	0	0
1975-76	Atlanta	4	0	2	2
1976-77	Atlanta	80	17	33	50
1977-78	Atlanta	73	28	30	58
1978-79	Atlanta	80	50	57	107
1979-80	Atlanta	76	31	46	77
1980-81	Calgary	52	31	52	83
1981-82	Calgary	64	23	57	80
	Totals	434	180	277	457

PEKKA RAUTAKALLIO 28 5-11 185   **Defenseman**
Excellent 1981-82 play made him an all-star candidate...Top puckhandler and rusher, solid defensively...Had best offensive season with 17 goals, 68 points...Played in 1982 All-Star Game...Born July 25, 1953, in Pori, Finland...Starred with Finnish national junior team, then spent two seasons in WHA with Phoenix Roadrunners...Returned to Finland for two seasons with Assat club...Signed by Flames in 1979...Played for Finnish national team in Canada Cup tournaments in 1976 and 1981...Deeply involved in fitness programs and is extremely strong.

Year	Club	GP	G	A	Pts.
1979-80	Atlanta	79	5	25	30
1980-81	Calgary	76	11	45	56
1981-82	Calgary	80	17	51	68
	Totals	235	33	121	154

JIM PEPLINSKI 22 6-2 201   **Forward**
Big, strong, hard-working two-way center...Second NHL season was a good one with 30 goals, 67 points...Not fast or fancy but

aggressive and intelligent... Gung-ho team player... Born Oct. 24, 1960, in Renfrew, Ont.... Junior star with Toronto Marlboros (101 points in 1979-80)... Fourth-round draft pick in 1979... Can play all three forward positions but used mainly at center... Solid rookie season with 38 points when used mainly in defensive role... Friendly, outgoing attitude and quick wit makes him popular with media.

Year	Club	GP	G	A	Pts.
1980-81	Calgary	80	13	25	38
1981-82	Calgary	74	30	37	67
	Totals	154	43	62	105

KEVIN LAVALLEE 21 5-8 180   Forward

Young player on the verge of stardom... Scored 32 goals in 1981-82, his second NHL season... Ambitious, quick, possessor of a deadly shot... Short but very strong... Born Sept. 16, 1961, in Sudbury, Ont.... Spent two seasons with Brantford Alexanders, scoring 65 goals, 135 points in 1979-80... A second-round pick in 1980 draft... Strong camp earned him big-league job when club had him ticketed for return to junior hockey... Nicknamed "Eddie Munster"... Has potential to be a 50-goal scorer... Owns an especially quick move off the wing.

Year	Club	GP	G	A	Pts.
1980-81	Calgary	77	15	20	35
1981-82	Calgary	75	32	29	61
	Totals	152	47	49	96

PAUL REINHART 22 5-11 216   Defenseman

Premier talent but, like many Flames, had below-form season in 1981-82... Big, strong, fast, with excellent offensive skills... Improving as defensive player... Logged much time as a center in junior hockey... Had 61 points last season... Born Jan. 8, 1960, in Kitchener, Ont.... Spent four seasons with Kitchener Rangers . . . Had 129 points in 1978-79 junior season, divided between center and backline . . . First-round draft pick in 1979 . . . Trained with Canadian Olympic team but opted for pro contract . . . Member of Team Canada in 1981 Canada Cup tournament . . . Spends summers working on family dairy farm near Kitchener.

Year	Club	GP	G	A	Pts.
1979-80	Atlanta	79	9	38	47
1980-81	Calgary	74	18	49	67
1981-82	Calgary	62	13	48	61
	Totals	215	40	135	175

KENT NILSSON 26 6-1 185   **Forward**

His absence with a shoulder problem and team's first-half woes was more than coincidence . . . At top of any list of offensive players in NHL . . . Among league's fastest skaters, splendid stickhandler and playmaker, awesome shot . . . Big season in 1980-81 with 49 goals, 131 points . . . Played only 41 games last term but produced 26 goals, 55 points . . . Born Aug. 31, 1956, in Nynashamn, Sweden . . . Had two 107-point seasons with Winnipeg Jets in WHA . . . Reclaimed by Flames in 1979 expansion draft . . . Top pointman on power play . . . Holds most club scoring records.

Year	Club	GP	G	A	Pts.
1977-78	Winnipeg (WHA)	80	42	65	107
1978-79	Winnipeg (WHA)	78	39	68	107
1979-80	Atlanta	80	40	53	93
1980-81	Calgary	80	49	82	131
1981-82	Calgary	41	26	29	55
	Totals	359	196	297	493

DON EDWARDS 27 5-9 165   **Goaltender**

High-quality goalie, acquired by Flames from Buffalo Sabres with defenseman Richie Dunn for draft choices in June 1982 . . . His 2.90 career average is among the best of active goalies . . . Standup style, strong technically, superb reflexes and fine catching hand . . . Born Sept. 28, 1955, in Hamilton, Ont. . . . Had splendid junior record with Kitchener Rangers...Claimed by Sabres on sixth round of 1975 amateur draft...Spent one season in the minors, then took over Sabres' top job...Has 14 career shutouts...Excellent golfer.

Year	Club	GP	G	A	Pts.
1976-77	Buffalo	25	62	2	2.51
1977-78	Buffalo	72	185	2	2.64
1978-79	Buffalo	54	159	2	3.02
1979-80	Buffalo	49	125	2	2.57
1980-81	Buffalo	45	133	3	2.96
1981-82	Buffalo	62	205	0	3.51
	Totals	307	869	14	2.90

STEVE CHRISTOFF 24 6-1 180   Forward

Traded to the Flames in June 1982 with Bill Nyrop by Minnesota in exchange for Willi Plett...Has fought injuries in first two NHL seasons...Very fast skater with good shot, has potential to be a 40-goal scorer...Had 26 goals in 56 games in 1980-81, 26 in 69 last season...Born Jan. 23, 1958, in Springfield, Ill....High school star in Richfield, Minn....Majored in geography, led team in scoring at University of Minnesota for two seasons...Important member of victorious U.S. Olympic team in 1980...Tends to score in streaks.

Year	Club	GP	G	A	Pts.
1979-80	Minnesota	20	8	7	15
1980-81	Minnesota	56	26	13	39
1981-82	Minnesota	69	26	30	56
	Totals	145	60	50	110

COACH BOB JOHNSON: Most successful coach in U.S. college hockey...Head coach of the University of Wisconsin Badgers for 15 seasons...Compiled a 332-164-22 won-lost-tied record...Won three NCAA championships and lost 1982 final to North Dakota...Coached Team USA to good success in 1981 Canada Cup tournament...Has coached U.S. entry in world championships twice, including

1982...Was tenured professor in Wisconsin physical education department...Decision to take NHL job was thus a difficult one...Creative, innovative coach, excellent student of the game and its trends...Surprised Team USA pros with "Crazy Capers", tumbling exercises at end of workouts...Born March 4, 1931, in Minneapolis...Son Mark was a member of the 1980 U.S. Olympic team...Son Pete played on Wisconsin's 1981 NCAA champs...Noted for strong power play in college hockey...Had turned down several NHL offers before taking Flame job.

GREATEST CENTER

Many NHL people feel that Tom Lysiak never lived up to the immense promise he demonstrated as a junior with the Medicine Hat Tigers. However, Lysiak, who was traded to the Chicago Black Hawks by the then Atlanta Flames in 1979, has had a solid big league career and rates as the best center the franchise ever has owned.

In 445 games with the Flames in Atlanta, Lysiak scored 155 goals and 276 assists for 431 points and was a strong defensive worker. He has continued his solid play with the Black Hawks.

Lysiak has strong competition for the No. 1 spot on the Flame center list. Guy Chouinard, who produced 107 points in 1978-79, has counted 457 points in his time with the team. The best single season by a Flame center was the 131 points by Kent Nilsson in 1980-81.

But for all-around achievement, Lysiak gets the nod as the best man-in-the-middle.

ALL-TIME FLAME LEADERS

GOALS: Guy Chouinard, 50, 1978-79
ASSISTS: Kent Nilsson, 82, 1980-81
POINTS: Kent Nilsson, 131, 1980-81
SHUTOUTS: Dan Bouchard, 5, 1973-74
                 Phil Myre, 5, 1974-75

CHICAGO BLACK HAWKS

TEAM DIRECTORY: Chairman: Arthur M. Wirtz; Pres.: William W. Wirtz; VP: Arthur M. Wirtz, Jr.; VP: Tommy Ivan; GM: Bob Pulford; Dir. Pub. Rel.: Don Murphy; Coach: Orval Tessier. Home ice: Chicago Stadium (17,300; 188' x 85'). Colors: Red, black and white. Training camp: Chicago.

SCOUTING REPORT

OFFENSE: Center Denis Savard is one of the most talented and exciting attackers to arrive on the NHL scene in many years. Ultra-quick, very slick, a master stickhandler and playmaker, Savard makes things happen. He had 119 points in the season and added

Doug Wilson scored 85 points and won the Norris Trophy.

11 goals and 18 points in 15 playoff matches to lead the Hawk advance to the conference final.

There's able support for Savard. Defenseman Doug Wilson was the NHL's best, producing 39 goals and 85 points. Up front, Tom Lysiak (32 goals, 82 points), Al Secord (44 goals), Darryl Sutter (23 in 40 games) Grant Mulvey (30), Tim Higgins, Rich Preston and Terry Ruskowski supply a sound offense.

The Hawks' first pick in the entry draft, center Ken Yaremchuk from the Portland juniors, is compared to Savard, a swift, exciting attacker. He produced 264 points in two seasons, including 157 in 1981-82. However, he's only 18 and the Hawks could figure another season of junior hockey is needed. Yaremchuk himself has stated that he feels he's not ready for the NHL.

New coach Orval Tessier, a fabled minor league scorer, takes over a team that has no problems scoring goals.

DEFENSE: Preventing scores is not a Hawk strong point. Only the Los Angeles Kings and Toronto Maple Leafs surrendered more goals than the Hawks' 363.

When GM Bob Pulford took over the coaching post, he immediately went to work on the team's defensive play and improvement in that area was the big reason for a strong finish and good playoff.

Tessier is a no-nonsense disciplinarian whose junior and minor pro teams were strong defensively. How well he convinces the Hawks to check will determine the team's fate.

Goaltending is a spot where the Hawks must be concerned. Tony Esposito is 39 and in 1981-82, his 4.52 average in 52 games was by far the worst of his distinguished career. There were a few nights when he looked like a goalie who had lost it, although he did redeem himself in the playoffs. Backup Murray Bannerman is untested as a main man and there's little else in the chain.

Wilson heads a defense of some quality. He's the NHL's workhorse, logging as much ice time as any player and thriving on the load.

Keith Brown and Bob Murray, both of whom missed large chunks of the season with injuries, are good ones. There's promise in Dave Feamster, Jerome Dupont and Doug Crossman, experience from Dave Hutchison and Greg Fox.

Look for Tessier to carry on the Pulford pattern on disciplined defensive play.

OUTLOOK: With Savard and Wilson, the Hawks generate excitement that's been missing from Chicago Stadium, along with large numbers of fans, for a few seasons. The Hawks have the

BLACK HAWK ROSTER

No.	Player	Pos.	Hgt.	Wgt.	Born	1981-82	G	A	Pts.	PIM
	Bruno Baseotto	RW	5-10	180	3-24-60/Calgary, Alta.	Fort Wayne	28	31	59	38
						New Brunswick	0	0	0	0
	Louis Begin	LW	6-0	195	2-6-60/St. Lambert, Que.	New Brunswick	34	37	71	12
25	Keith Brown	D	6-1	192	5-6-60/Cornerbrook, Nfld.	Chicago	4	20	24	26
29	Ted Kerr	LW	6-1	192	3-25-55/Windsor, Ont.	Chicago	12	18	30	120
23	Doug Crossman	D	6-2½	180	6-13-60/Peterborough, Ont.	Chicago	12	8	40	24
	Jerome Dupont	D	6-3	190	2-21-62/Ottawa, Ont.	Chicago	0	4	4	51
	Dave Feamster	D	5-11	180	9-10-58/Detroit, Mich.	Chicago	0	2	2	29
						New Brunswick	6	30	36	69
2	Greg Fox	D	6-2	190	8-12-53/Port McNeil, B.C.	Chicago	2	19	21	137
14	Bill Gardner	C	6-0	175	3-19-60/Toronto, Ont.	Chicago	8	15	23	20
15	Tim Higgins	RW	6-1	185	2-7-58/Ottawa, Ont.	Chicago	20	30	50	85
5	Dave Hutchison	D	6-3	215	5-2-52/London, Ont.	Chicago	5	18	23	246
10	Reg Kerr	LW	5-9	175	10-16-57/Oxbow, Sask.	Chicago	11	28	39	39
	Steve Larmer	RW	5-10	185	6-16-61/Peterborough, Ont.	Chicago	0	0	0	0
						New Brunswick	38	44	82	46
31	Steve Ludzik	C	5-11	170	4-3-61/Toronto, Ont.	Chicago	2	1	3	2
						New Brunswick	21	41	62	142
12	Tom Lysiak	C	6-1	196	4-22-53/High Prairie, Alta.	Chicago	32	40	82	84
11	John Marks	LW-D	6-2	185	3-22-48/Winnipeg, Man.	Chicago	1	0	1	7
						Indianapolis	6	20	26	73
17	Peter Marsh	RW	6-1	175	12-21-56/Halifax, N.S.	Chicago	10	18	28	47
22	Grant Mulvey	RW	6-4	202	9-17-56/Sudbury, Ont.	Chicago	30	19	49	141
6	Bob Murray	D	5-10	183	11-26-54/Kingston, Ont.	Chicago	8	22	30	48
	Troy Murray	C	5-11	180	7-31-62/ —	Chicago	0	0	0	0
						U. N.Dakota	13	17	30	
	Jack O'Callahan	D	6-1	185	7-24-57/Charleston, Mass.	New Brunswick	15	33	48	130
26	Rick Paterson	C	5-9	187	2-10-58/Kingston, Ont.	Chicago	4	7	11	8
						New Brunswick	8	16	24	45
16	Rich Preston	RW	5-11	185	5-22-52/Regina, Sask.	Chicago	15	28	43	30
	Florent Robidoux	LW	6-2	172	5-5-60/Cypress River, Man.	Chicago	1	2	3	0
						New Brunswick	31	35	66	200
8	Terry Ruskowski	C	5-9	170	12-31-54/Prince Albert, Sask.	Chicago	7	30	37	120
18	Denis Savard	C	5-10	167	2-2-61/Pt. Gatineau, Que.	Chicago	32	87	119	82
20	Al Secord	LW	6-1	205	9-20-58/Sudbury, Ont.	Chicago	44	31	75	303
7	Glen Sharpley	LW-C	6-0	188	9-6-56/York, Ont.	Chicago	9	7	16	11
	Brian Shaw	RW	6-1	190	5-20-62/Edmonton, Alta.	Portland	56	76	132	193
	Sean Simpson	C	6-0	185	5-4-60/Clemsboro, Eng.	New Brunswick	19	16	35	4
27	Darryl Sutter	C	5-11	175	8-19-58/Viking, Alta.	Chicago	23	12	35	31
	Tony Tanti	C	5-10	180	9-7-63/Toronto, Ont.	Chicago	0	0	0	0
						Oshawa	62	64	126	138
24	Doug Wilson	D	6-1	187	7-5-57/Ottawa, Ont.	Chicago	39	46	85	54
	Ken Yaremchuk	C	5-11	185	1-1-64/Edmonton, Alta.	Portland	58	99	157	181
28	Miles Zaharko	D	6-0	197	4-30-57/Mannville, Alta.	Chicago	1	2	3	18
						New Brunswick	6	12	18	50

No.	Player	Pos.	Hgt.	Wgt.	Born		GP	GA	SO	Avg.
30	Murray Bannerman	G	5-11	184	4-27-57/Ft. Frances, Ont.	Chicago	29	116	1	4.17
35	Tony Esposito	G	5-11	185	4-23-44/Sault Ste. Marie, Ont.	Chicago	52	231	1	4.52
	Bob Janecyk	G	6-1	180	5-18-57/Chicago, Ill.	New Brunswick	53	153	2	2.85
	Jim Ralph	G	5-9	165	5-13-62/Sault Ste. Marie, Ont.	Ottawa	56	185	0	3.45
	Warren Skorodenski	G	5-9	158	3-22-60/Winnipeg, Man.	Chicago	1	5	0	5.00
						New Brunswick	28	70	3	2.55

material to be well above .500 if they have solid, consistent goaltending.

Tessier has been a winner everywhere he's coached and the string shouldn't be snapped now.

BLACK HAWK PROFILES

TONY ESPOSITO 39 5-11 185   Goaltender

Had worst season of 13-year career with 4.52 average in 52 games...But 2.80 lifetime average is among the best...Played strongly in playoffs to help team to conference final...Leads active goalies with 74 career shutouts...Master of the much-duplicated "butterfly" style of goaltending...Born April 23, 1943, in Sault Ste. Marie, Ont....Brother of scoring great Phil Esposito...Has degree in business from Michigan Tech, where he played college hockey...Started NHL career with Canadiens and was claimed by Hawks in 1969 intra-league draft...Won Calder Trophy as top rookie in 1969-70, when he had 2.17 average and 15 shutouts...A five time all-star...President of NHL Players' Association.

Year	Club	GP	G	A	Pts.
1968-69	Montreal	13	34	2	2.73
1969-70	Chicago	63	136	15	2.17
1970-71	Chicago	57	126	6	2.27
1971-72	Chicago	48	82	9	1.76
1972-73	Chicago	56	140	4	2.51
1973-74	Chicago	70	141	10	2.04
1974-75	Chicago	71	193	6	2.74
1975-76	Chicago	68	198	4	2.97
1976-77	Chicago	69	234	2	3.45
1977-78	Chicago	64	168	5	2.63
1978-79	Chicago	63	206	4	3.27
1979-80	Chicago	69	205	6	2.97
1980-81	Chicago	66	246	0	3.75
1981-82	Chicago	52	231	1	4.52
	Totals	829	2340	74	2.86

TIM HIGGINS 24 6-1 185   Forward

Has seemed on the verge of breakthrough to stardom for three seasons but has yet to take the big step...Big, strong, good skater and puckhandler...Had 20 goals and 50 points in 1981-82 but seems capable of much more...Good defensive play, though, makes him an asset...Born Feb. 7, 1958, in Ottawa...Good junior with Ottawa 67s on high-scoring line with Bobby Smith and Steve Payne of Minnesota . . . First-round pick in 1978 entry draft . . . Hawks use him both on right wing and at center.

Year	Club	GP	G	A	Pts.
1978-79	Chicago	36	7	16	23
1979-80	Chicago	74	13	12	25
1980-81	Chicago	78	24	35	59
1981-82	Chicago	74	20	30	50
	Totals	262	64	93	157

TOM LYSIAK 29 6-1 196   **Forward**
Had probably best season in good NHL career in 1981-82 . . . Counted 32 goals, 82 points, and added 15 points in 15 playoff games . . . Never has quite lived up to expectations of his super junior play . . . Strong skater and playmaker, excellent skater, good penalty-killer and effective on the power play . . . Born April 22, 1953, in High Prairie, Alta. . . . Teamed with Lanny McDonald on Medecine Hat Tigers to terrorize junior hockey . . . First-round draft pick of Atlanta Flames in 1973 . . . Joined the Hawks in big eight-player trade in 1979 . . . Lives on a farm in rural Georgia in the offseason.

Year	Club	GP	G	A	Pts.
1973-74	Atlanta	77	19	45	64
1974-75	Atlanta	77	25	52	77
1975-76	Atlanta	80	31	51	82
1976-77	Atlanta	79	30	51	81
1977-78	Atlanta	80	27	42	69
1978-79	Atl.-Chi.	66	23	45	68
1979-80	Chicago	77	26	43	69
1980-81	Chicago	72	21	55	76
1981-82	Chicago	71	32	50	82
	Totals	679	234	434	668

BOB MURRAY 27 5-10 183   **Defenseman**
Missed close to half the 1981-82 season with a knee injury . . . Returned to be key man in playoff success . . . Slowly matured into front-line player . . . Excellent rusher, strong puckhandler with a good shot . . . Had best offensive season in 1980-81 with 60 points . . . Born Nov. 26, 1954, in Kingston, Ont. . . . Played junior hockey with Cornwall Royals . . . Third-round choice in 1974 draft . . . Spent one good season in CHL before becoming a Hawk

regular in 1975-76...Goalies claim he has one of the hardest shots in NHL.

Year	Club	GP	G	A	Pts.
1975-76	Chicago	64	1	2	3
1976-77	Chicago	77	10	11	21
1977-78	Chicago	70	14	17	31
1978-79	Chicago	79	19	32	51
1979-80	Chicago	74	16	34	50
1980-81	Chicago	77	13	47	60
1981-82	Chicago	45	8	22	30
	Totals	486	81	165	246

GRANT MULVEY 26 6-3 202　　　　　　　**Forward**

In his ninth NHL season although he's only 26...Joined the Hawks at 18 in 1974-75...Scored 30 goals in 1981-82...Appeared to have made step to stardom in 1979-80 when he had 39 scores...Broken arm forced him to miss most of 1980-81 season...Tabbed as future superstar when Hawks drafted him...A solid, competent NHL winger...Born Sept. 17, 1956, in Sudbury, Ont....Played one season of junior hockey with Calgary Centennials...Was one of the first 17-year olds claimed by NHL club in draft...First-round choice in 1974.

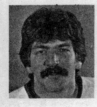

Year	Club	GP	G	A	Pts.
1974-75	Chicago	74	7	4	11
1975-76	Chicago	64	11	17	28
1976-77	Chicago	80	10	14	24
1977-78	Chicago	78	14	24	38
1978-79	Chicago	80	19	15	34
1979-80	Chicago	80	39	26	65
1980-81	Chicago	42	18	14	32
1981-82	Chicago	73	30	19	49
	Totals	571	148	133	281

RICH PRESTON 30 5-11 185　　　　　　　**Forward**

Solid, two-way player who's backbone of team with consistent work...His 15 goals, 43 points don't measure value to team because he's excellent penalty-killer and he often shadows opposition's big shooters...Born May 22, 1952, in Regina, Sask....Played college hockey at Denver University...Spent four seasons with Houston and one with Winnipeg in WHA ...Reclaimed by Hawks for 1979 expansion draft...Scored 31 goals in 1979-80...Missed half of 1980-81 term with a knee injury...Good banjo player.

Year	Club	GP	G	A	Pts.
1974-75	Houston (WHA)	78	20	21	41
1975-76	Houston (WHA)	77	22	33	55
1976-77	Houston (WHA)	80	38	41	79
1977-78	Houston (WHA)	73	25	25	50
1978-79	Winnipeg (WHA)	80	28	32	60
1979-80	Chicago	80	31	30	61
1980-81	Chicago	47	7	14	21
1981-82	Chicago	75	15	28	43
	Totals	590	186	224	410

DENIS SAVARD 21 5-10 167   Forward

The NHL's newest superstar...Exciting, ultra-swift center whose great offensive skills lift fans out of their seats...Marvelous stick-handler and playmaker, all executed at high speed...After good 75-point rookie season in 1980-81, he exploded with 119 points last season...Led march to conference final with 11 goals, 18 points in 15 playoff matches...Born Feb. 4, 1961, in Pt. Gatineau, Que....Big junior star with Montreal team, scoring 181 points in final season...First-round draft choice in 1980...Important to Hawk franchise as a box-office attraction.

Year	Club	GP	G	A	Pts.
1980-81	Chicago	76	28	47	75
1981-82	Chicago	80	32	87	119
	Totals	156	60	134	194

AL SECORD 24 6-1 205   Forward

Blossomed as a shooter in 1981-82 when he scored 44 goals...Previous best season was 23 scores...One of the NHL's strongest, toughest players...Has dabbled in boxing, hopes to fight some amateur bouts...Probably best fist fighter in NHL...Teams well with Denis Savard...Benefitting from Savard's playmaking, he provides protection for little center...Born March 3, 1958, in Sudbury, Ont....Played junior hockey with Sudbury Wolves...First-round choice of Boston in 1978 draft...Traded to Hawks in 1980 for defenseman Mike

O'Connell... Needs only four goals to crack 100 barrier in NHL career.

Year	Club	GP	G	A	Pts.
1978-79	Boston	71	16	7	23
1979-80	Boston	77	23	16	39
1980-81	Bos.-Chi.	59	13	12	25
1981-82	Chicago	80	44	31	75
	Totals	287	96	66	162

DARRYL SUTTER 24 5-11 175   **Forward**

Cut from the mold of the Viking, Alta., family that has sent four brothers to the NHL (Bryan of St. Louis, Brent and Duane of the Islanders) to the NHL and has two more (Rich, Ron) on the way... Tough, hard-nosed and determined... Became third NHL rookie to score 40 goals when he hit that figure in 1980-81 season... A knee injury restricted him to 40 games last season but he still managed 23 goals... Born Aug. 19, 1958, in Viking, Alta.... Played junior hockey with Lethbridge Broncos... Eleventh-round draft pick (No. 179) in 1978 draft... Top rookie in AHL in 1979-80 with New Brunswick Hawks.

Year	Club	GP	G	A	Pts.
1979-80	Chicago	8	2	0	2
1980-81	Chicago	76	40	22	62
1981-82	Chicago	40	23	12	35
	Totals	124	65	34	99

DOUG WILSON 25 6-1 187   **Defenseman**

Superb season in 1981-82 for splendid player... Led Hawk backline men in scoring with 85 points, logged as much ice time as any player in NHL... Runaway winner in Norris Trophy balloting ... Developed defensive skills in early seasons, then slowly used fine offensive ability... Strong, swift skater and good puckhandler with a splendid shot... Born July 5, 1957, in Ottawa... Played junior hockey with Ottawa 67s... First-round selection in 1977 draft... Brother of former Canadien and King Murray

Wilson . . . Superb in Hawks' march to conference final in playoffs with 13 points in 15 games.

Year	Club	GP	G	A	Pts.
1977-78	Chicago	77	14	20	34
1978-79	Chicago	56	5	21	26
1979-80	Chicago	73	12	49	61
1980-81	Chicago	76	12	39	51
1981-82	Chicago	76	39	46	85
	Totals	358	82	175	257

COACH ORVAL TESSIER: A big puzzle is that he hasn't been granted an NHL coaching post long before this . . . A winner many times at several levels of hockey . . . Coached New Brunswick Hawks to the American League title in 1981-82 . . . Earlier had great success coaching junior hockey with the Quebec Remparts, Cornwall Royals and Kitchener Rangers . . . Known as a stern disciplinarian and a good teacher of hockey fundamentals . . . Also was general manager of several teams . . . Born June 3, 1933, in Cornwall, Ont. . . . Played junior hockey with Kitchener Greenshirts and Barrie Flyers . . . A fabled scorer in minor pro hockey . . . Played only 59 games in the NHL with Montreal Canadiens and Boston Bruins . . . Had 15 seasons in the minors, scoring more than 50 goals in four seasons . . . Won MVP awards in Quebec and Eastern pro leagues . . . Finished career with Portland in old Western League in the mid-1960s.

GREATEST CENTER

Stan Mikita's credentials not only make him a shoo-in as the greatest center the Black Hawks have had in their history. They place him high on the list of greatest players, centers or otherwise, who have played the game.

In 22 seasons in Chicago, Mikita played 1,394 games, scored 541 goals, 926 assists, had 150 points in the playoffs, earned six first and two second all-star team selections and won the Hart Trophy as MVP and Lady Byng Trophy twice each.

Mikita was born in Czechoslovakia and, at a young age, a visiting uncle and aunt from Canada took him home with them because his parents wanted him to avoid the suppression of his homeland. He became a junior star with the St. Catharines, Ont., TeePees, turned pro with the Hawks in 1958 and embarked on an illustrious career.

Tough, smart, a magician with the puck, superb on faceoffs— name it and Mikita had it.

ALL-TIME BLACK HAWK LEADERS

GOALS: Bobby Hull, 58, 1968-69
ASSISTS: Denis Savard, 87, 1981-82
POINTS: Denis Savard, 119, 1981-82
SHUTOUTS: Tony Esposito, 15, 1969-70

DETROIT RED WINGS

TEAM DIRECTORY: Owner: Michael Illich; GM: Jim Devellano; Dir. Pub. Rel.: Budd Lynch; Coach and Asst. GM: Nick Polano. Home ice: Joe Louis Arena (19,275; 200′ x 85′). Training camp: Port Huron, Mich.

SCOUTING REPORT

OFFENSE: The Red Wings engineered an unusual deal last season when they peddled the young heart of their attack, Dale

Danny Gare averages nearly a point per game for Wings.

McCourt and Mike Foligno, to Buffalo for veterans Danny Gare, Derek Smith and Jim Schoenfeld.

Thus, the team's new owner, pizza baron James Illich, takes over a club with little attacking sting and few attackers with much promise.

The Wings' best young forwards are good but far from great. Rookie Mark Osborne was the team's leading scorer with 26 goals and 67 points. Mike Blaisdell had 23 goals and John Ogrodnick, a solid winger, had 28.

Gare, a solid 40-goal-plus scorer throughout his career, had only 20 and Smith managed nine. Defenseman Reed Larson was the team's No. 2 scorer with 60 points.

The Wings' first-round draft pick, center Murray Craven, 18, didn't set the junior ranks on fire. He had a modest 35-46-81 point total for Medicine Hat Tigers.

The Wings desperately need Gare, 28, to be healthy, hungry and back in the 40-goal category.

DEFENSE: The Wings haven't shared in the bonanza of good, young defensemen who have entered the NHL in recent years. As a result, their backline is mostly veterans who could be an adequate corps if the team had disciplined checking from the forwards and strong goaltending. Thus, the backline struggles much of the time.

The defense does handle and move the puck fairly well. Larson (60 points), Willie Huber (45) and Greg Smith (32) can launch and participate in attacks. They face a problem with the Wings, though: there's not much attack to launch.

Schoenfeld is a fine old defensive backliner and John Barrett is solid.

Had the Wings been able to sign goalie Bob Sauve, who came to Detroit in the big deal, they would have had good protection at an important position. But they couldn't get together on a contract and he returned to the Sabres. Now the Wings' goaltending, like just about everything on the roster, is iffy. There's veteran Gilles Gilbert, youngsters Corrado Micalef and Greg Stefan.

OUTLOOK: Once a proud, dominant NHL franchise, the Wings have earned playoff spots twice in 16 seasons. Bruce Norris could do the NHL a big favor now that he's sold the Wings and is out of the league. He could write a book on the mistakes an owner can make because he's made 'em all.

The team is in a good hockey town and a .500 team that provides a little entertainment would fill Joe Louis Arena with good fans. The new ownership's only hope is a long-range plan of reconstruction.

It won't be easy.

RED WING ROSTER

No.	Player	Pos.	Hgt.	Wgt.	Born	1981-82	G	A	Pts.	PIM
3	John Barrett	D	6-1	210	7-1-58/Ottawa, Ont.	Detroit	1	12	13	93
21	Mike Blaisdell	RW	6-1	169	1-18-60/Regina, Sask.	Detroit	23	32	55	48
	Boris Fistric	D	6-3	220	9-15-60/Edmonton, Alta.	Kalamazoo	7	28	35	397
17	Jody Gage	RW-LW	5-11	182	11-29-59/Toronto, Ont.	Detroit	9	9	18	2
						Adirondack	21	20	41	21
	Danny Gare	RW	5-9	175	5-14-54/Nelson, B.C.	Buff.-Detroit	20	24	44	99
7	Willie Huber	D	6-5	228	1-15-58/Strasskirchen, W. Ger.	Detroit	15	30	45	98
	Earl Ingarfield	LW	5-11	165	1-30-59/New York, N.Y.	Adirondack	24	19	43	86
22	Greg Joly	D	6-1	185	5-30-54/Calgary, Alta.	Detroit	1	5	6	30
						Adirondack	3	22	25	59
16	Mark Kirton	C	5-10	175	2-3-58/Toronto, Ont.	Detroit	14	28	42	62
	Kelly Kisio	RW	5-9	170	9-18-59/Peace River, Alta.	Dallas	62	39	101	59
28	Reed Larson	D	6-0	188	7-30-56/Minneapolis, Minn.	Detroit	21	39	60	112
	Mark Lofthouse	RW	6-1	190	4-21-57/New Westminster, B.C.	Detroit	3	4	7	13
						Adirondack	33	38	71	75
	Claude Loiselle	C	5-11	170	5-29-63/Ottawa, Ont.	Detroit	1	0	1	2
						Windsor	36	73	109	192
	Peter Mahovlich	C	6-5	210	10-10-46/Timmins, Ont.	Adirondack	22	45	67	66
11	Walt McKechnie	C	6-2	190	6-19-47/London, Ont.	Detroit	18	37	55	35
	Perry Miller	D	6-1	194	6-24-52/Winnipeg, Man.	Adirondack	13	31	44	121
14	Don Murdoch	RW	5-11	178	10-25-56/Cranbrook, B.C.	Detroit	9	13	22	23
						Adirondack	10	13	23	24
20	Vaclav Nedomansky	C	6-1	210	3-14-44/Redonia, Czech.	Detroit	12	28	40	22
12	Ted Nolan	RW	6-0	185	4-7-58/Sault Ste. Marie, Ont.	Detroit	4	13	17	45
						Adirondack	12	18	30	81
	Mark Osborne	LW	6-1	185	8-13-61/Toronto, Ont.	Detroit	26	41	67	61
25	John Ogrodnick	RW	6-0	190	6-20-59/Edmonton, Alta.	Detroit	28	26	54	28
	Joe Patterson	LW-C	6-1	208	6-25-60/Calgary, Alta.	Adirondack	22	27	49	22
2	Jim Schoenfeld	D	6-2	208	9-4-52/Galt, Ont.	Buff.-Detroit	8	11	19	99
27	Brad Smith	C	6-1	195	4-13-58/Windsor, Ont.	Detroit	2	0	2	80
						Adirondack	10	5	15	126
24	Derek Smith	C	5-11	177	7-31-54/Quebec, Que.	Buff.-Det.	9	15	24	12
5	Greg Smith	D	6-0	195	7-8-55/Ponoka, Alta.	Detroit	10	22	32	79
19	Eric Vail	LW	6-2	210	9-16-53/Schumacher, Ont.	Oklahoma City	0	3	3	0
						Cal.-Detroit	14	15	29	35
						Adirondack	3	4	7	0
15	Paul Woods	C	5-10	175	4-12-55/Milton, Ont.	Detroit	10	17	27	48

No.	Player	Pos.	Hgt.	Wgt.	Born		GP	GA	SO	Avg.
1	Gilles Gilbert	G	6-0	175	3-21-49/St. Espirit, Que.	Detroit	27	105	0	4.26
	Claude Legris	G	5-9	160	6-11-56/Verdun, Que.	Detroit	1	0	0	0.00
						Springfield	18	71	0	4.25
	Larry Lozinski	G	5-11	175	3-11-58/Hudson Bay, Sask.	Adirondack	55	175	1	3.27
30	Corrado Micalef	G	5-8	175	4-20-61/ —	Adirondack	1	0	0	0.00
						Kalamazoo	20	91	1	4.76
						Detroit	18	63	0	4.67

RED WING PROFILES

MARK OSBORNE 21 6-1 185   **Forward**

Unheralded skater who had impressive rookie season...One of the few bright spots on disaster team...Wings' top scorer with 26 goals, 41 assists...Good skater, strong playmaker, solid defensively...Member of Team Canada for 1982 world championships in Finland...Born Aug. 13, 1961, in Toronto...Played junior hockey with Niagara Falls Flyers...Was modest scorer (39 goals in final season) but had 21 points in 12 playoff games...Drafted by Wings in 1979...On a talent-poor team, he's one of the future hopes.

Year	Club	GP	G	A	Pts.
1981-82	Detroit	80	26	41	67

REED LARSON 26 6-0 188   **Defenseman**

Perhaps the fastest skater among NHL defensemen...One of highest offensive producers with 311 points in past five seasons...Free-wheeling puck-carrier with devastating shot feared by goalies...Has expressed frustration at toiling with non-contender throughout career...Born July 30, 1956, in Minneapolis...Claimed by Wings on second round of 1976 draft from University of Minnesota...Had 14-game tryout with team late in 1976-77 season after college suspension over fighting incident...Member of Team USA in 1981 world tournament, 1981 Canada Cup.

Year	Club	GP	G	A	Pts.
1976-77	Detroit	14	0	1	1
1977-78	Detroit	75	19	41	60
1978-79	Detroit	79	18	49	67
1979-80	Detroit	80	22	44	66
1980-81	Detroit	78	27	31	58
1981-82	Detroit	80	21	39	60
	Totals	406	107	205	312

MIKE BLAISDELL 22 6-1 169   **Forward**

Solid NHL player in second pro season...Scored 23 goals, 55 points, played well defensively...Good skater with scoring touch...Spent most of 1980-81 with Adirondack Wings in AHL...Born Jan. 18, 1960, in Moose Jaw, Sask....Spent a year of U.S. college hockey at University of Wisconsin, then returned to junior ranks with Regina Pats...Scored 71 goals in 1979-80 with Pats...Claimed by Wings on first round of 1980 entry draft...Wings are certain that he'll live up to junior scoring promise in the NHL.

Year	Club	GP	G	A	Pts.
1980-81	Detroit	32	3	6	9
1981-82	Detroit	80	23	32	55
	Totals	112	26	38	64

JOHN OGRODNICK 23 6-0 190   Forward

Prime prospect who had so-so season in 1981-82 after 35 goals, 70 points in previous season...Sagged to 28 goals, 54 points and play lacked excellence of big season...Big, hard-striding, physical winger with strong shot...Born June 20, 1959, in Ottawa ...Played junior hockey with New Westminster Bruins...Member of two Canadian junior championship teams...Fourth-round draft pick in 1979...Divided rookie pro season between Wings and minors...Member of Team Canada in 1981 world championships.

Year	Club	GP	G	A	Pts.
1979-80	Detroit	41	8	24	32
1980-81	Detroit	80	35	35	70
1981-82	Detroit	80	28	26	54
	Totals	301	71	85	156

WILLIE HUBER 24 6-5 228   Defenseman

Gigantic, surprisingly agile, always seems capable of much more than he delivers...Could still be key man if some stability established in team...Good puckhandler and skater for man his size...Has produced 49 and 45 points in past two seasons...Born Jan. 15, 1958, in Strasskirchen, Germany...Family migrated to Canada when he was an infant...Played junior hockey in Hamilton...Wings' first-round draft choice in 1978...Spent time in minors in first two pro seasons... Played in 1978 world junior championships and 1981 world championships in Stockholm.

Year	Club	GP	G	A	Pts.
1978-79	Detroit	68	7	24	31
1979-80	Detroit	76	17	23	40
1980-81	Detroit	80	15	34	49
1981-82	Detroit	74	15	30	45
	Totals	298	54	111	165

DANNY GARE 28 5-9 175   Forward

High quality veteran acquired by Wings from Buffalo in 1981 trade with Derek Smith and Bob Sauve for Mike Foligno, Dale McCourt and Brent Peterson... Had worst season in eight in NHL with 20 goals, 44 points in 59 games... Quick, abrasive, gung-ho winger with big shot... Had 260 goals in seven seasons with Sabres... Born in Nelson, B.C., on May 14, 1954... Played junior with Calgary Centennials... Sabres' second-round draft pick in 1974... Had two 50-goal years with Sabres... Still burns for success, can be leader of Red Wing rebirth.

Year	Club	GP	G	A	Pts.
1974-75	Buffalo	78	31	31	62
1975-76	Buffalo	79	50	23	73
1976-77	Buffalo	35	11	15	26
1977-78	Buffalo	69	39	38	77
1978-79	Buffalo	71	27	40	67
1979-80	Buffalo	76	56	33	89
1980-81	Buffalo	73	46	39	85
1981-82	Buff.-Det.	59	20	24	44
	Totals	540	280	243	523

GREG SMITH 27 6-0 195   Defenseman

Useful journeyman backliner, tough on defense, good offensively... Joined Wings with Don Murdoch in 1981 trade from Minnesota for Detroit's first-round draft pick... Good skater, aggressive, handles and moves puck well... Born July 8, 1955, in Ponoka, Alta.... Spent three years at Colorado College... After two seasons with old Cleveland Barons, he became a North Star when teams merged in 1978... Fourth-round draft pick in 1975... Member of Team Canada in 1979 world championships ... Had requested trade from Stars because of differences with management.

Year	Club	GP	G	A	Pts.
1975-76	California	1	0	1	1
1976-77	Cleveland	74	9	17	26
1977-78	Cleveland	80	7	30	37
1978-79	Minnesota	80	5	27	32
1979-80	Minnesota	55	5	13	18
1980-81	Minnesota	74	5	21	26
1981-82	Detroit	69	10	22	32
	Totals	433	41	131	172

JIM SCHOENFELD 30 6-2 208   Defenseman

First-rate veteran, among NHL's best backliners for past decade ... Became a Wing in blockbuster trade which saw Schoenfeld, Danny Gare, Derek Smith and Bob Sauve go to Detroit from Buffalo for Dale McCourt, Mike Foligno and Brent Peterson ... Big, quick, smart on the ice ... Battled injuries through much of career ... Perhaps NHL's best at blocking shots ... Born Sept. 4, 1952, in Galt, Ont. ... Played junior hockey with London, Hamilton and Niagara Falls ... First-round draft pick in 1972 ... Key man in Sabres' climb from expansion team to contender ... Deeply involved in charity work.

Year	Club	GP	G	A	Pts.
1972-73	Buffalo	66	4	15	19
1973-74	Buffalo	28	1	8	9
1974-75	Buffalo	68	1	19	20
1975-76	Buffalo	56	2	22	24
1976-77	Buffalo	65	7	25	32
1977-78	Buffalo	60	2	20	22
1978-79	Buffalo	46	8	17	25
1979-80	Buffalo	77	9	27	36
1980-81	Buffalo	71	8	25	33
1981-82	Buff.-Det.	52	8	11	19
	Totals	589	50	189	239

MARK KIRTON 24 5-10 175   Forward

Effective two-way worker ... Fine penalty-killer, he can shut down the opposition's big shooters ... Has totalled 32 goals, 41 assists in two years ... Joined Red Wings in 1980 from Toronto in trade for goalie Jim Rutherford ... Excellent skater who knows what to do when he doesn't have the puck ... Born Feb. 3, 1958, in Regina, Sask. ... Grew up in Toronto where he was an excellent age-group soccer player in addition to hockey...Played junior hockey with Peterborough Petes...Toronto's third-round draft pick in 1978...Spent two seasons in AHL before trade to Wings.

Year	Club	GP	G	A	Pts.
1979-80	Toronto	2	1	0	1
1980-81	Tor.-Det.	61	18	13	31
1981-82	Detroit	74	14	28	42
	Totals	137	33	41	74

DEREK SMITH 28 5-11 177   **Forward**
Swift, slick center who had off year in 1981-82...Scored only nine goals after getting 45 in previous two seasons...Went from Buffalo to Red Wings in huge six-player trade...Had split four seasons between Sabres and minors before blossoming as solid big leaguer...Born July 31, 1954, in Quebec City...Sabres' tenth-round draft pick in 1974...Scored 30 goals twice in AHL...Arrived in NHL with 14 goals in 43 games in 1978-79...Wings are counting heavily on his regaining top form.

Year	Club	GP	G	A	Pts.
1976-77	Buffalo	5	0	0	0
1977-78	Buffalo	36	3	3	6
1978-79	Buffalo	43	14	12	26
1979-80	Buffalo	79	24	39	63
1980-81	Buffalo	69	21	43	64
1981-82	Buff.-Det.	61	9	15	24
	Totals	293	71	112	183

COACH NICK POLANO: Named coach in August, Nick brings an impressive set of credentials to his first head-coaching role in the NHL...The Hockey News' Minor-League Executive of the Year in 1980-81, he coached the Erie Blades in the EHL beginning in 1975-76 and was general manager and coach in his last three seasons (championships each time) prior to joining the Buffalo Sabres as an assistant coach last year...Twice the EHL's Coach of the Year...Was a minor-league defenseman for 15 years, mostly in the AHL with Baltimore, Hershey and Providence...Born in Sudbury, Ont., on March 25, 1941.

GREATEST CENTER

Fats! That's the nickname Alex Delvecchio carried throughout his distinguished hockey career because he looked more like the tenth man on a church league softball team than one of the greatest centers in NHL history. At 6 feet and 195 pounds, the nickname was appropriate.

Delvecchio, however, was deceptively fast, not blindingly quick but the possessor of sufficient speed. One spot where he was extremely fast was in his head because Delvecchio was extremely smart and creative. He was a master at controlling the pace of the game, slowing the tempo to lull opponents into slumber, then popping a quick play that caught them by surprise.

In 24 NHL seasons, Delvecchio played 1,549 games, scoring 456 goals and 825 assists for 1281 points. He had 104 points in 121 playoff games.

Throughout most of his career, Delvecchio worked with Gordie Howe on his right flank and they were one of the most effective combos ever to play the game.

ALL-TIME RED WING LEADERS

GOALS: Mickey Redmond, 52, 1972-73
ASSISTS: Marcel Dionne, 74, 1974-75
POINTS: Marcel Dionne, 121, 1974-75
SHUTOUTS: Terry Sawchuk, 12, 1951-52, 1954-55
    Glenn Hall, 12, 1955-56

EDMONTON OILERS

TEAM DIRECTORY: Owner: Peter Pocklington; VP/GM/Coach: Glen Sather; Dir. Pub. Rel.: Bill Tuele. Home ice: Northlands Coliseum (17,490; 200′ x 85′). Colors: Royal blue, orange and white.

SCOUTING REPORT

OFFENSE: Awesome! If the Oilers, who scored an NHL record 417 goals, had Wayne Gretzky and a group of Latvian dwarfs, their attack would be strong enough to get the job done.

But while No. 99 is the most productive attacking machine the

Grant Fuhr wasn't beaten often in his rookie season.

NHL has ever seen, the Oilers have a large cast of shooters and more on the way.

All Gretzky did was score 92 goals and 212 points and to say he's productive is the same as saying that Dolly Parton is stacked. Whether he can duplicate it matters not. The Kid's workload could be eased slightly this season as coach Glen Sather wants to have him as fresh as possible for the playoffs.

Glenn Anderson (38 goals, 105 points), Mark Messier (50, 88), Jari Kurri (32, 86) and Dave Lumley (32 goals) all are excellent young gunners.

Pat Hughes and Laurie Boschman, acquired late last season from Toronto, are tough, two-way workers and big Dave Semenko, Gretzky's bodyguard, adds muscle.

Two splendid prospects—center Marc Habscheid and winger Todd Strueby—had big seasons in junior hockey and should earn jobs. The Oilers also added Jaroslav Pouzar, 31, a splendid veteran of the Czechoslovakian national team.

Paul Coffey, despite a late sag, led all defensemen with 89 points and Risto Siltanen had 63 points.

The ingredients are all there for a devastating attack, although the production could dip as the club makes the necessary defensive improvement.

DEFENSE: The Oilers' aim appears to be a duplication of the Montreal Canadiens' approach when they dominated the NHL in the 1970s and led the league in both attack and defense. That requires a puck-control game and quick exits from their own zone. Maturity by a young club is needed to make that a reality.

Grant Fuhr, as a 19-year-old, had a superb rookie season with a 3.31 average in 48 games to earn second all-star team honors. He's just a brilliant young netminder with an unlimited future. Ron Low is a useful veteran in the backup role and Andy Moog, 22, a hero in the 1981 playoffs, had a fine 2.99 average in 40 Central League games.

Despite Coffey's slump, he remains a brilliant young defenseman and Kevin Lowe, 23, had a fine year and is an excellent defensive player. Siltanen is a good one, too, and veterans Lee Fogolin and Gary Lariviere supply stability.

Part of the young forwards' growing up will include improved defensive work.

OUTLOOK: The fact that the Oilers were ousted in the first playoff line tends to obscure the extraordinary season they had and the amazing progress the team has made in three NHL seasons. General manager-coach Glen Sather has assembled a remarkable

OILER ROSTER

No.	Player	Pos.	Hgt.	Wgt.	Born	1981-82	G	A	Pts.	PIM
9	Glenn Anderson	RW	5-11	175	10-2-60/Vancouver, B.C.	Edmonton	38	67	105	71
	Todd Bidner	LW	6-2	205	7-5-61/Petrolia, Ont.	Washington	2	1	3	7
						Hershey	6	12	18	28
						Wichita	2	9	11	17
19	Ken Berry	LW	5-9	173	6-21-60/New	Wichita	28	29	57	70
					Westminster, B.C.	Edmonton	2	3	5	9
	John Blum	D	6-3	205	10-8-59/Detroit, Mich.	Wichita	8	33	41	247
	Laurie Boschman	C	6-0	185	6-4-60/Kerrobert, Man.	Tor.-Edmon.	11	22	33	187
15	Curt Brackenbury	RW	5-10	190	1-31-52/Kapuskasing, Que.	Edmonton	0	2	2	12
						Wichita	11	27	38	99
7	Paul Coffey	D	6-1	185	6-1-61/Weston, Ont.	Edmonton	29	60	89	106
	Ed Cooper	LW	5-10	188	8-28-60/Loon Lake, Sask.	Colorado	1	0	1	0
						Ft.W.-Wich.	13	29	42	26
	Peter Driscoll	LW	6-0	190	10-27-54/Kingston, Ont.	Wichita	25	29	54	229
2	Lee Fogolin	D	6-0	200	2-7-55/Chicago, Ill.	Edmonton	4	25	29	154
23	Mike Forbes	D	6-2	200	9-20-57/Brampton, Ont.	Edmonton	1	7	8	26
						Wichita	4	28	32	94
99	Wayne Gretzky	C	5-11	170	1-26-61/Brantford, Ont.	Edmonton	92	120	212	26
	Mark Habscheid	C	5-11	169	3-1-63/Swift Current, Sask.	Edmonton	1	3	4	2
						Saskatoon	64	87	151	
10	Matti Hagman	C	6-1	184	9-21-56/Helsinki	Edmonton	21	38	59	18
22	Charlie Huddy	D	5-11	203	6-2-59/Oshawa, Ont.	Edmonton	4	11	15	48
						Wichita	7	19	26	51
16	Pat Hughes	RW	6-1	185	3-25-55/Toronto, Ont.	Edmonton	24	22	46	99
12	Dave Hunter	LW	5-11	195	1-1-58/Petrolia, Ont.	Edmonton	16	22	38	63
	Don Jackson	D	6-2	210	9-2-56/Minneapolis, Minn.	Edmonton	0	0	0	18
						Wichita	7	37	44	116
17	Jari Kurri	LW	6-1	185	5-18-60/Helsinki	Edmonton	32	54	86	32
6	Gary Lariviere	D	6-0	190	12-6-54/St. Catherine's, Ont.	Edmonton	1	21	22	41
4	Kevin Lowe	D	6-2	197	4-15-59/Hawksbury, Ont.	Edmonton	9	31	40	63
20	Dave Lumley	C	6-0	185	9-1-54/Toronto, Ont.	Edmonton	32	42	74	96
11	Mark Messier	LW	6-1	190	1-18-61/Edmonton, Alta.	Edmonton	50	38	88	119
	Paul Mulvey	LW	6-4	219	9-27-58/Sudbury, Ont.	Pitt.-LA	1	14	15	126
						New Haven	3	3	6	65
	Lance Nethery	C	6-0	185	5-23-57/Toronto, Ont.	Rang.-Edm.	0	2	2	2
						Springfield	5	5	10	0
						Wichita	35	32	67	46
	Jim Playfair	D	6-3	186	5-22-64/Vanderhoof, B.C.	Portland	4	13	17	121
24	Tom Roulston	C	6-1	185	11-20-57/Winnipeg, Man.	Edmonton	11	3	14	22
						Wichita	22	28	50	46
27	Dave Semenko	LW	6-3	210	7-12-57/Winnipeg, Man.	Edmonton	12	12	24	194
8	Risto Siltanen	D	5-8	185	10-31-58/Mantta, Fin.	Edmonton	15	48	63	24
	Todd Strueby	C	6-2	189	6-15-63/Lanigan, Sask.	Edmonton	0	0	0	0
						Saskatoon	60	58	118	160
	Mike Toal	C	6-0	170	3-23-59/Red Deer, Alta.	Wichita	15	15	30	14
77	Garry Unger	C	5-11	170	12-7-47/Edmonton, Alta.	Edmonton	7	13	20	69

No.	Player	Pos.	Hgt.	Wgt.	Born	1981-82	GP	GA	SO	Avg.
1	Grant Fuhr	G	5-10	181	9-28-62/Spruce Grove, Alta.	Edmonton	48	157	0	3.31
	Gord Garbutt	G	5-8	170	11-7-58/Oakville, Ont.	Wichita	31	118	1	3.98
30	Ron Low	G	6-1	205	6-21-50/Bertle, Man.	Edmonton	29	100	0	3.86
35	Andy Moog	G	5-8	165	2-18-60/Princeton, B.C.	Edmonton	8	32	0	4.81
						Wichita	40	119	1	2.99

collection of young talent and there appears to be no way the Oilers can miss a long stay at the top.

However, no team has made it yet without growing pains and how much the Oilers learned from the playoff defeat will determine how far they advance in the spring of 1983.

OILER PROFILES

WAYNE GRETZKY 21 5-11 170   **Forward**

Figures like a career total: 92 goals, 120 assists, 212 points...Career? No, merely the 1981-82 season of the NHL's No. 1 star...The Great Gretzky had 50 goals in 39 games, too, for another record...Perhaps biggest gate attraction in history, attracting sellout crowds and hordes of media everywhere...Added more shooting to dazzling array of offensive skills...Born Jan. 26, 1961, in Brantford, Ont....Has earned wide publicity since he was ten years old...Highest paid player in the league; salary includes gradual ownership of shopping center...Nice guy, too, who handles incredible demands with grace and good humor...Has heavy list of endorsements...Credits teaching of his father, Walter, with development.

Year	Club	GP	G	A	Pts.
1978-79	Ind.-Edm. (WHA)	80	46	64	110
1979-80	Edmonton	79	51	86	137
1980-81	Edmonton	80	55	109	164
1981-82	Edmonton	80	92	120	212
	Totals	319	244	379	623

GLENN ANDERSON 22 5-11 175   **Forward**

Electrifying performer, ultra-fast, tough and skilled...Had 38 goals, 105 points in 1981-82...Very aggressive, plays as if he were much larger...Has a very relaxed approach to life, claims he would be just as happy being a salmon fisherman...Born Oct. 2, 1960, in Vancouver...Star in U.S. college hockey at University of Denver...Top player on Canadian Olympic team in 1980 Games at Lake Placid...Played on excellent line with Mark

Messier and Matti Hagman . . . Good penalty-killer . . . Headed for all-star status.

Year	Club	GP	G	A	Pts.
1980-81	Edmonton	58	30	23	53
1981-82	Edmonton	80	38	67	105
	Totals	138	68	90	158

PAUL COFFEY 21 6-1 185   Defenseman

Play tailed off at end of 1981-82 season but, overall, he had outstanding campaign . . . Led all NHL defensemen with 89 points . . . Superb skater and puckhandler with a big shot, and he's improving defensively . . . First-round draft pick in 1980 after 102-point season with Kitchener Rangers . . . Born June 1, 1961, in Weston, Ont. . . . Struggled through first half of rookie NHL season but finished strongly to lead team's playoff success in 1981 . . . Played in 1982 All-Star Game . . . Supplies a young team with important dimension of a rushing defenseman.

Year	Club	GP	G	A	Pts.
1980-81	Edmonton	74	9	23	32
1981-82	Edmonton	80	29	60	89
	Totals	154	38	83	121

MARK MESSIER 21 6-1 190   Forward

Blossomed into perhaps the NHL's best left winger with 50 goals . . . Swift, big, strong and belligerent . . . A four-year pro; he was in WHA at 17 out of Tier Two junior . . . Future is unlimited because he can do it all . . . Excellent penalty-killer, good checker . . . Born Jan. 18, 1961, in Edmonton . . . Played a season with Indianapolis and Cincinnati in WHA . . . Third-round pick in 1979 draft . . . Admits to not being serious enough about game in early stages...Can also play center...His father, Doug Messier, was a minor-league defenseman.

Year	Club	GP	G	A	Pts.
1978-79	Ind.-Cinn. (WHA)	52	1	10	11
1979-80	Edmonton	75	12	21	33
1980-81	Edmonton	72	23	40	63
1981-82	Edmonton	78	50	38	88
	Totals	277	86	109	195

JARI KURRI 22 6-1 185 **Forward**

Splendid young winger with skill in all areas of game...Played on a line with Wayne Gretzky and produced 32 goals, 86 points...Oiler assistant coach Bill Harris claims there are few better wingers in all areas of the ice...Improved defensive play immeasurably in first two NHL seasons...Born May 18, 1960, in Jokerit, Finland...Claimed in fourth round of 1980 draft...Other NHL teams believed he had signed two-year agreement to stay in Finland and passed on him...Oilers knew he hadn't signed deal and claimed him...Had solid rookie season in 1980-81 with 32 goals...Excellent skater...Played for Finland in 1981 Canada Cup tournament.

Year	Club	GP	G	A	Pts.
1980-81	Edmonton	75	32	43	75
1981-82	Edmonton	71	32	54	86
	Totals	146	64	97	161

GRANT FUHR 20 5-10 181 **Goaltender**

Outstanding rookie season...Had 3.31 goals-against average, 28-5-14 won-lost-tied record...Extraordinary reflexes, good technically, stand-up style...Great attitude because nothing seems to bother him...First black goalie in NHL history...Born Sept. 28, 1962, in Spruce Grove, Alta....Had offer of baseball contract from Montreal Expos...Rated as best junior goalie in past decade with Victoria Cougars...Had astounding 2.79 junior average in 59 games in 1980-81...First-round draft pick in

1980 . . . His acquisition completed Oiler cast of fine youngsters, with a potential all-star at every position.

Year	Club	GP	GA	SO	Avg.
1981-82	Edmonton	48	157	0	3.31

DAVE LUMLEY 28 6-0 185   Forward

Veteran pro who attained notoriety in 1981-82 season when he set record of goals in 12 consecutive games . . . Previous mark of ten was shared by Bobby Hull, Andy Bathgate and Mike Bossy . . . Useful, two-way player whose 32 goals and 74 points were highs of four-year pro career . . . Strong defensive player and a solid digger . . . Born Sept. 1, 1954, in Toronto . . . Played college hockey at University of New Hampshire . . . Was 199th player picked in 1974 draft . . . Spent two seasons in the minors at Nova Scotia . . . Claimed by Oilers in 1979 expansion draft . . . Good foot soldier on a team of fancy gunners.

Year	Club	GP	G	A	Pts.
1978-79	Montreal	3	0	0	0
1979-80	Edmonton	80	20	38	58
1980-81	Edmonton	53	7	9	16
1981-82	Edmonton	66	32	42	74
	Totals	202	59	89	148

KEVIN LOWE 23 6-2 197   Defenseman

Rated as Oilers' best defenseman in 1981-82 season . . . Defensive type who excels in own zone and at moving the puck . . . Solid offensively with 63 points and was a plus-46 . . . Good in short-handed situations . . . Born Apr. 15, 1959, in Hawksbury, Ont. . . . Was junior standout with Quebec Remparts, where he was high scorer (86 points in 1978-79) . . . First-round draft pick in 1979 . . . Scored Oilers' first goal in NHL . . . Excellent gourmet cook who frequently prepares lunch for his mates...Cool, poised performer who's already among league's best defenders.

Year	Club	GP	G	A	Pts.
1979-80	Edmonton	64	2	19	21
1980-81	Edmonton	79	10	24	34
1981-82	Edmonton	63	15	48	63
	Totals	206	27	91	118

LEE FOGOLIN 27 6-0 200   Defenseman

The team's captain and anchor...Solid, unspectacular, hard worker who's efficient defensively...His experience, poise and dedication are big assets to a young team...Eight-year veteran although he's only 27...Claimed by Buffalo Sabres at 18 in 1974 draft...Best player available in 1979 expansion draft...A puzzle that Sabres didn't protect him...Born Feb. 15, 1955, in Chicago ...Played junior hockey with Oshawa Generals...Only Oiler to play in all 240 games since club entered the NHL...Skilled woodworker who has built most of the furniture in his home...Father Lee was NHL defenseman with Chicago and Detroit.

Year	Club	GP	G	A	Pts.
1974-75	Buffalo	50	2	2	4
1975-76	Buffalo	58	0	9	9
1976-77	Buffalo	71	3	15	18
1977-78	Buffalo	76	0	23	23
1978-79	Buffalo	74	3	19	22
1979-80	Edmonton	80	5	10	15
1980-81	Edmonton	80	13	17	30
1981-82	Edmonton	80	4	25	29
	Totals	569	30	120	150

LAURIE BOSCHMAN 22 6-0 185   Forward

Joined team at trading deadline in deal with Toronto...Oilers feel he has potential to be front-line center...First-round draft choice in 1979, had three troubled seasons in Toronto...Had good rookie year with 48 points...Second season ruined by mononucleosis, then was criticized by Leaf owner Harold Ballard for Christian beliefs last season...Went to Oilers in deal for forwards Walt Poddubny and Phil Drouillard...Born June 4, 1960, in Major,

Sask.... Junior star with Brandon Wheat Kings... Not especially fast but solid scorer, strong defensively and aggressive.

Year	Club	GP	G	A	Pts.
1979-80	Toronto	80	16	32	48
1980-81	Toronto	53	14	19	33
1981-82	Tor.-Edm.	65	11	22	33
	Totals	198	41	73	114

COACH GLEN SATHER: Has full command of franchise as general manager and coach, also serves as team's alternate governor on NHL board... Has built one of the league's best organizations, especially in scouting talent... One of the most quoted executives who has a great deal of fun but is tough and a hard worker... Has talked of abandoning coaching job to concentrate on front office but obviously loves that side of the game... Born Sept. 2, 1943, in High River, Alta.... Played junior hockey in Edmonton and nine seasons in NHL with six different teams... Defensive specialist who scored 80 goals in 648 games... Joined Oilers in WHA as a player in 1977, moved into executive end of the game as assistant coach halfway through that season... Nicknamed "Slats"... Has done remarkable job of building club to contending status in three years... Concedes that having Gretzky was a good start in that direction.

GREATEST CENTER

Is there any doubt? Wayne Gretzky has played only three seasons in the NHL with the Oilers and his offensive totals—198 goals, 315 assists, 513 points—once were considered a more-than-adequate production for a ten-year career.

No player in NHL history has conducted an assault on the NHL's record book to equal Gretzky's. In the 1981-82 season, just about everything he did smashed another standard, 92 goals, including 50 in 39 games; 120 assists, 212 assists.

Gretzky became the NHL's No. 1 star and its biggest gate attraction. In every NHL city, a visit by the Oilers and The Kid last season meant capacity crowds and large hordes of media folks.

When he won his third consecutive Hart Trophy as the NHL's Most Valuable Player in 1981-82, Gretzky achieved another first. He became the only player ever to score a unanimous vote. He collected all 63 first-place ballots.

Not bad for a skinny lad from Brantford, Ont., who had his 21st birthday in January 1982.

ALL-TIME OILER LEADERS

GOALS: Wayne Gretzky, 92, 1981-82
ASSISTS: Wayne Gretzky, 120, 1981-82
POINTS: Wayne Gretzky, 212, 1981-82
SHUTOUTS: Eddie Mio, 1, 1978-80

Glenn Anderson scored 38 goals at age 21 last year.

HARTFORD WHALERS

TEAM DIRECTORY: Managing Gen. Partner: Howard Baldwin; Dir. Pub. Rel.: Bob Casey; Dir. Hockey Oper.: Larry Pleau; Coach: Larry Kish. Home ice: Hartford Civic Center (14,600; 200' × 85'). Colors: Green, blue and white.

SCOUTING REPORT

OFFENSE: It should first be established that Hartford does not have a whale of an offense. In these times of games in double figures and 90-goal scorers, the Whalers managed just 264 goals last season, better than only the forgettable Colorado Rockies. Hartford has only three dangerous scorers and even one of those, Pierre Larouche, is as dependable as a convertible in a hurricane. Blaine Stoughton scored 52 goals, a truly amazing figure considering there was hardly anybody else opponents had to worry about. Stoughton's ability to score with other teams keying on him is a remarkable achievement.

The third member of the Whalers' deadly trio is Ron Francis, who didn't even join the team until over 20 games had gone by. Once called up from juniors, Francis made everyone ask what he was doing there all along. He not only helped the offense, he generated it and controlled it.

Besides that, the Whalers will be lucky to get a handful of goals from the rest of their players. Doug Sulliman did get 29, but there are those who say they want to see him do it again. Sulliman is a marvelous player to have on a team, fresh and energetic and a good checker, but he can't be asked to do everything. Garry Howatt had one of the best seasons of his career after coming over from the Islanders, but he is beginning to slow down, although he does provide some badly-needed spark at the right moments. Unfortunately, he doesn't get much help.

DEFENSE: Only four teams gave up more than the 351 goals the Whalers allowed last season and Hartford is going to have its problems keeping the puck out of the net this season, too. There are big hitters in Chris Kotsopoulos and Jack McIlhargey and Russ Anderson, but the one, swift, mobile defenseman the team had suffered through a miserable season and has been the subject of trade rumors. That would be Mark Howe, once one of the best young defenseman around until he suffered a freak injury to his back that nearly ended his career. The Whalers don't own a dominant player, one who can control the puck or the pace of the game or riddle opponents with check after check.

That's too bad, because the Whalers do have a quality goalie in Greg Millen. He couldn't help but tire under the fusillade of shots he faced each night. Millen came to Hartford as a free agent, but he might be rethinking his decision after playing in 55 games. Without a proven backup, Millen again is likely to see a lot of playing time and also a lot of shots. If anything happens to him, the Whalers will be on the way to a 400-goal season.

OUTLOOK: Cloudy, with periods of thunderstorms. No sunshine all season. The Whalers have done little to improve themselves

Rookie Ron Francis celebrates one of his 25 goals.

WHALER ROSTER

No.	Player	Pos.	Hgt.	Wgt.	Born	1981-82	G	A	Pts.	PIM
7	Russ Anderson	D	6-3	210	2-12-55/Minneapolis, Minn.	Pitt.-Hart.	1	4	5	183
	Norm Barnes	D	6-0	190	8-24-53/Toronto, Ont.	Hartford	1	4	5	19
						Binghamton	4	17	21	58
	Jeff Brownschidle	D	6-2	205	—/Buffalo, N.Y.	Hartford	0	1	1	2
						Binghamton	4	23	27	24
12	Dan Bourbonnais	LW	5-11	180	3-6-62/Winnipeg, Man.	Hartford	3	9	12	11
11	Jordy Douglas	C	6-0	195	1-20-58/Winnipeg, Man.	Hartford	10	7	17	44
						Binghamton	0	0	0	0
4	Ron Francis	C	6-1	170	3-1-63/ —	Hartford	25	43	68	51
	Michel Galarneau	C	6-1	175	3-1-61/Montreal, Que.	Hartford	0	0	0	4
						Binghamton	15	17	32	52
	Don Gillen	RW	6-3	222	12-24-60/Edmonton, Alta.	Hartford	1	4	5	22
						Binghamton	20	11	31	100
8	Garry Howatt	LW	5-9	173	9-26-52/Grand Center, Alta.	Hartford	18	32	50	242
5	Mark Howe	D-RW	5-11	188	5-28-55/Detroit, Mich.	Hartford	8	45	53	18
18	Marty Howe	D	6-1	185	2-18-54/Detroit, Mich.	Hartford	0	4	4	2
						Binghamton	8	38	46	42
24	Chris Kotsopoulos	D	6-3	215	11-27-58/Toronto, Ont.	Hartford	13	20	33	147
28	Pierre Larouche	C	5-11	175	11-16-55/Teschereau, Que.	Mont.-Hart.	34	37	71	12
	Paul Lawless	LW	5-11	181	7-2-64/Scarborough, Ont.	Windsor	24	25	49	47
	Gilles Lupien	D	6-6	203	4-20-54/Lachute, Que.	Hartford	0	1	1	2
						Binghamton	8	20	28	284
	George Lyle	LW	6-2	210	11-24-53/W. Vancouver, B.C.	Det.-Hart.	3	14	17	13
33	Jack McIlhargey	D	6-1	190	3-7-52/Edmonton, Alta.	Hartford	1	5	6	60
	Mike McDougal	RW	6-2	205	4-30-58/Port Huron, Mich.	Hartford	0	0	0	0
						Binghamton	10	17	27	54
20	Rick Meagher	RW	5-10	175	11-4-53/Belleville, Ont.	Hartford	24	19	43	51
	Glenn Merkosky	C	5-10	175	8-4-60/Edmonton, Alta.	Hartford	0	0	0	2
						Binghamton	29	41	70	85
27	Warren Miller	RW	5-11	180	1-1-54/St. Paul, Minn.	Hartford	10	12	22	68
26	Don Nachbaur	C	6-1	183	1-30-59/Kitimat, B.C.	Hartford	5	21	26	117
10	Ray Neufeld	RW	6-3	215	4-15-59/St. Boniface, Man.	Hartford	4	3	7	4
						Binghamton	28	31	59	81
25	Mark Renaud	D	5-11	180	2-21-59/Windsor, Ont.	Hartford	1	17	18	39
						Binghamton	3	19	22	70
3	Paul Shmyr	D	5-11	175	1-28-46/Cutworth, Sask.	Hartford	1	11	12	134
	Stu Smith	D	6-1	185	3-17-60/Toronto, Ont.	Hartford	0	3	3	15
						Binghamton	4	21	25	121
21	Blaine Stoughton	RW	5-10	185	3-13-53/Gilbert Plaines, Man.	Hartford	52	39	91	57
22	Doug Sulliman	LW	5-9	195	8-29-59/Glace Bay, N.S.	Hartford	29	40	69	39
32	Mickey Volcan	D	6-0	190	3-3-62/Edmonton, Alta.	Hartford	1	5	6	29
						Binghamton	4	13	17	47
6	Blake Wesley	D	6-1	200	7-10-59/Red Deer, Alta.	Hartford	9	18	27	123

							GP	GA	SO	Avg.
	Ken Holland	G	5-8	164	11-10-55/Vernon, B.C.	Binghamton	46	133	2	2.92
30	Greg Millen	G	5-9	160	6-25-57/Toronto, Ont.	Hartford	55	229	0	4.29
	Michel Plasse	G	5-11	175	6-1-48/Montreal, Que.	Quebec	8	35	0	5.41
						Binghamton	8	32	0	4.32
31	Mike Veisor	G	5-8	158	7-25-52/Toronto, Ont.	Hartford	13	53	0	4.54
						Binghamton	22	67	1	3.09

and their surrendering of draft choices probably will hurt them in the long run. It hasn't even helped them in the short run. But they could make the playoffs this season if Buffalo falls into Lake Erie.

WHALER PROFILES

JORDY DOUGLAS 24 6-0 195   **Forward**

Speedy left wing with outstanding potential but nagged by injuries . . . Played in only 30 games last season because of shoulder separation suffered three weeks into the season in game at Edmonton . . . Missed final six weeks of previous season due to hairline fracture in left foot . . . Missed final two weeks of '79–80 and playoffs with broken bone in foot . . . Would be consistent 30-goal scorer if he could stay in one piece . . . Has outstanding shot and quick release that makes it doubly dangerous . . . Born Jan. 20, 1958, in Winnipeg . . . Active in many sports, including amateur basketball and charity softball . . . Also enjoys watching stock car races . . . Has filled in as disc jockey on Hartford radio station . . . Likeable and friendly.

Year	Club	GP	G	A	Pts.
1978-79	New England (WHA)	51	6	10	16
1979-80	Hartford	77	33	24	57
1980-81	Hartford	55	13	9	22
1981-82	Hartford	30	10	7	17
	Totals	213	62	50	112

RON FRANCIS 19 6-1 170   **Forward**

Rejoined club month into season after being returned to junior team . . . Didn't disappoint, scoring 12 power-play goals, second on the club only to Blaine Stoughton's 13 . . . Averaged 1.15 points a game and had a hand in remarkable 74 per cent of the team's goals that were scored while he was on the ice . . . Also led Whalers with four unassisted goals . . . Was underage draft in 1981 and the youngest player ever in club's training camp . . . Born March 1, 1963, in Sault Ste. Marie, Ont. . . . Played junior in his hometown, a center on the same club Wayne Gretzky once played for . . . Was leading the Ontario Hockey League with 47 points before his recall . . . Swift, with accurate shot . . . Supremely confident and has reason to be...Had four two-goal games, including one against Stanley Cup champion Islanders and another in Montreal.

Year	Club	GP	G	A	Pts.
1981-82	Hartford	59	25	43	68

CHRIS KOTSOPOULOS 23 6-3 215   Defenseman

"Kosty"...A Greek who earns his money...Tough, hard-nosed and hungry...Won trophy as club's best defenseman...Short on natural ability, but long on desire...Can let temper get the best of him...Supplied needed physical play to Whalers, finishing second among defensemen in penalty minutes...Acquired along with Doug Sulliman for in deal that sent Mike Rogers to Rangers...Born Nov. 27, 1958, in Toronto...Was toiling in American Hockey League when then-Ranger coach Fred Shero spotted him and gave him a chance to play...Cocky, but not quite as good as he thinks he is...His 147 penalty minutes were most by a Whaler defenseman since the team joined the NHL...Had five game-tying goals and three tie-breaking goals...Lives within walking distance of the Civic Center.

Year	Club	GP	G	A	Pts.
1980-81	New York R.	54	4	12	16
1981-82	Hartford	68	13	20	33
	Totals	122	17	32	49

RUSS ANDERSON 27 6-3 210   Defenseman

Big, strong and good at taking opponents out in front of the net...Called "The Enforcer" for good reason...No wonder he also played linebacker on football team in addition to hockey at University of Minnesota...Born Feb. 12, 1955, in Minneapolis ...Married Dorothy Benham, Miss America of 1976...Was second-round draft pick of Penguins...Established Penguin club record of nine penalties for 51 minutes in game against Edmonton,

Jan. 19, 1981...Obtained by Whalers last March for Rick MacLeish...Added needed bulk to a soft defense...Made immediate hit in more ways than one...A sleeper...Could be better than everyone thinks he is...Not a great skater, but doesn't have to be.

Year	Club	GP	G	A	Pts.
1976-77	Pittsburgh	66	2	11	13
1977-78	Pittsburgh	74	2	16	18
1978-79	Pittsburgh	72	3	13	16
1979-80	Pittsburgh	76	5	22	27
1980-81	Pittsburgh	34	3	14	17
1981-82	Pitt.-Hart.	56	1	4	5
	Totals	378	16	80	96

BLAINE STOUGHTON 29 5-10 185   Forward

Exciting scorer who thrives on fast-paced games...Is already third-leading scorer in Whaler history...Nicknamed "Stash" and has way of stashing goals...Deadly around the net...Deadly from outside...Once had 13-tie-breaking goals in one season...Led league last season with seven game-tying goals...Led club with 266 shots...Was on ice for 51 of team's 68 power-play goals...Led team with three hat tricks...Holds club record with 56 goals in one season...Scored first goal of a game seven times...Twelve times scored goals that brought Whalers to within one goal...Born March 13, 1953, in Gilbert Plains, Man....Has competed in arm-wrestling promotion in Las Vegas...Also likes tennis and golf...Once missed first month of season with contract dispute and still scored 43 goals.

Year	Club	GP	G	A	Pts.
1973-74	Pittsburgh	34	5	6	11
1974-75	Toronto	78	23	14	37
1975-76	Toronto	43	6	11	17
1976-77	Cincinnati (WHA)	81	52	52	104
1977-78	Cinc.-Ind. (WHA)	77	19	26	45
1978-79	Ind.-N.E. (WHA)	61	18	12	30
1979-80	Hartford	80	56	44	100
1980-81	Hartford	71	43	30	73
1981-82	Hartford	80	52	39	91
	Totals	605	274	234	508

PIERRE LAROUCHE 26 5-11 175   Forward

Lucky Pierre...Also unlucky Pierre...Outstanding natural goal-scorer who remains petulant and moody...Can score at will or slump at will... Had incredible 94 goals and 251 points for Sorel junior team... Was star at 19 with Pittsburgh and washed up at 23... Trade to Montreal revived career... Protest over ice time led to trade to Whalers in March, 1982... Born Nov. 16, 1955, in Taschereau, Que.... Remains one of the swiftest centers alive... Had 10 goals in nine-game stretch last season... Gave Whalers needed speed and experience down the middle... Just don't ask him to play defense... A child at heart... Once agreed to participate in "Win a Date with Pierre" contest in Pittsburgh.

Year	Club	GP	G	· A	Pts.
1974-75	Pittsburgh	79	31	37	68
1975-76	Pittsburgh	76	53	58	111
1976-77	Pittsburgh	65	29	34	63
1977-78	Pitt.-Mont.	64	23	37	60
1978-79	Montreal	36	9	13	22
1979-80	Montreal	73	50	41	91
1980-81	Montreal	61	25	28	53
1981-82	Mont.-Hart.	67	34	37	71
	Totals	521	254	285	539

DOUG SULLIMAN 23 5-9 195   Forward

Sully... Actually, real first name is Simon... Simon says check... Simon says work hard... Spunky player and bouncy skater... A pint-sized version of Ranger Don Maloney, a close friend and former junior teammate... Small but fearless... Born Aug. 29, 1959, in Glace Bay, N.S.... Acquired from Rangers in deal that sent Mike Rogers to New York October 2, 1981... Enjoyed best season of career while becoming favorite of Hartford fans... Can play either wing... Has All-American smile... Always said he could be a goal-scorer and has proved it... Kind of guy you'd like your daughter to marry.

Year	Club	GP	G	A	Pts.
1979-80	New York R.	31	4	7	11
1980-81	New York R.	32	4	1	5
1981-82	Hartford	77	29	40	69
	Totals	140	37	48	85

MARK HOWE 27 5-11 188   Defenseman

Quick and mobile with terrific shot... Especially dangerous from the point... One of the real quality blueliners in game... Doesn't hit too hard... Likes to skate instead... Played for Team USA in Canada Cup strictly as exercise to get into shape after being sidelined with injury the year before . . . Son of hockey great Gordie Howe, who became a Hartford teammate . . . Assisted on dad's last career goal in 1980 playoffs against Montreal . . . Born May 28, 1955, in Detroit . . . Struggled last season, missing 12 games with nagging injuries . . . Lucky to be still playing after suffering dangerous puncture wound in buttocks when he landed on sharp metal post-support in January, 1981 . . . Was member of silver medalist USA team at '72 Olympics at age 16 . . . Was member of Memorial Cup champion Toronto Marlboros a year later . . . Became first NHL defenseman to score two shorthanded goals in one period and the second to score three goals in one period.

Year	Club	GP	G	A	Pts.
1973-74	Houston (WHA)	76	38	41	79
1974-75	Houston (WHA)	74	36	40	76
1975-76	Houston (WHA)	72	39	37	76
1976-77	Houston (WHA)	57	23	52	75
1977-78	New England (WHA)	70	30	61	91
1978-79	New England (WHA)	77	42	65	107
1979-80	Hartford	74	24	56	80
1980-81	Hartford	63	19	46	65
1981-82	Hartford	76	8	45	53
	Totals	639	259	443	702

GREG MILLEN 25 6-9 160   Goaltender

Excellent young shotstopper who has never had benefit of solid defense . . . Played in 55 games last season, among highest in league for goalies . . . Still searching for consistency . . . Quick and agile and a student of the game . . . Willing to work hard . . . Born June 25, 1957, in Toronto . . . Signed as free agent before last season . . . Whalers thought enough of him to surrender Pat Boutette in compensation to Pittsburgh . . . A stand-up goalie who is good at handling the puck . . . Relaxes by playing the piano and drums . . . Once did a dance after stopping shot in playoffs . . . Had 25 of Pittsburgh's 30 wins his last season as Penguin.

Year	Club	GP	GA	SO	Avg.
1978-79	Pittsburgh	28	86	2	3.37
1979-80	Pittsburgh	44	157	2	3.64
1980-81	Pittsburgh	63	258	0	4.16
1981-82	Hartford	55	229	0	4.29
	Totals	190	730	4	3.97

GARRY HOWATT 30 5-9 173   **Forward**

Still the Toy Tiger...Reckless, feisty left wing who never quits...Literally puts punch into an offense...A good fighter but real asset is a voice in the dressing room...An obscure 10th-round draft pick who clawed his way onto expansion Islanders and stayed 10 years...Played on two Stanley Cup winners...Born Sept. 26, 1952, in Grand Center, Alta....Hometown rink is named for him...Requested trade to Hartford last season to gain more playing time...Of course led team in penalty minutes with career-high 242...Set rookie records with most penalty minutes without a misconduct (204) and most major penalties (30)...Total of 1,708 penalty minutes is seventh-highest in league history...A junior teammate of Whalers' Blaine Stoughton...Has overcome epilepsy in story that would make good Hollywood movie...Can be surprisingly soft off the ice.

Year	Club	GP	G	A	Pts.
1972-73	New York I.	8	0	1	1
1973-74	New York I.	78	6	11	17
1974-75	New York I.	77	18	30	48
1975-76	New York I.	80	21	13	34
1976-77	New York I.	70	13	15	28
1977-78	New York I.	61	7	12	19
1978-79	New York I.	75	16	12	28
1979-80	New York I.	77	8	11	19
1980-81	New York I.	70	4	15	19
1981-82	Hartford	80	18	32	50
	Totals	676	111	152	263

COACH LARRY KISH: Long-time minor-league coach who  raised eyebrows with outstanding jobs at every stop...Was All-American wing for Providence College, which he led to Eastern Intercollegiate championship in 1964...Spent eight years as coach of Mount St. Charles High School in Rhode Island...Made jump to minor-league hockey, where he coached Rhode Island Eagles, the Cape Cod Codders, the Sun Coast Suns and the Binghamton Dusters...Hired by Whalers in 1979, their first season in NHL...Became coach of franchise's top minor-league affiliate in Springfield, Mass. in American Hockey League...Moved back to Binghamton when Hartford struck working agreement with that city last season...Coached

Dusters to 46-28-6 record last season for Southern Division title of AHL and berth in finals against New Brunswick...Lost series, 4-1, but Kish still impressed observers with knowledge and technique...Born Dec. 11, 1941, in Welland, Ont....Said to have good rapport with players...Had coached such current Whalers as Jordy Douglas, Ray Neufeld and Mark Renaud when they were in minors...Was sought by major colleges and Philadelphia Flyers to coach Maine farm team before deciding to take Whalers' job...Replaces Larry Pleau, who remains solely as general manager.

Blaine Stoughton has averaged 50 goals in last three years.

GREATEST CENTER

He has a thick beard and an impish smile and most of all he has a head of steam that makes him exceedingly dangerous and one of the biggest little men in the league. Mike Rogers may be only 5-9, but you wouldn't know it the way he frightens hulking defensemen assigned the terrifying task of trying to stop him. Rogers is with the New York Rangers now, having been the principal player in a six-man deal that stunned and saddened the city of Hartford. For it was there, as a member of the Whalers, that Rogers first made his mark in the WHA and later had the last laugh at those who belittled those accomplishments.

In his first season in the NHL, all Rogers did was score 105 points. All he did in his second season was match it exactly. Rogers still holds or shares a truckload of Hartford scoring records—his 65 assists being especially noteworthy. He still leads the club in career assists (285) and career points (467). He became only the 10th player in history to notch back-to-back 100 point seasons and registered the longest point-scoring streak in the league two years ago, getting a goal or an assist in 18 straight games.

Not only is Rogers speedy, but his accurate shot and clever touch make him dangerous from anywhere on the ice, the mark of great players. Even great small players. No wonder the day that Rogers was traded to the Rangers, some loyal fans in Hartford threatened to cancel their season tickets. For the Whalers, Mike Rogers was always the center of attention.

ALL-TIME WHALER LEADERS

GOALS: Blaine Stoughton, 56, 1979-80
ASSISTS: Mark Howe, 65, 1978-79
           Mike Rogers, 65, 1980-81
POINTS: Mark Howe, 107, 1978-79
SHUTOUTS: Al Smith, 3, 1972-73
              Louis Levasseur, 3, 1977-78

LOS ANGELES KINGS

TEAM DIRECTORY: Chairman: Dr. Jerry Buss; Pres.: Lou Baumeister; GM: George Maguire; Dir. Pub. Rel.; Scott Carmichael; Coach: Don Perry. Home ice: The Forum (16,005; 200′ x 85′). Colors: Royal blue and gold. Training camp: Victoria, B.C., and Los Angeles.

SCOUTING REPORT

OFFENSE: The Kings' attack was strong late in the season and in the playoffs and the arrival of some kids and health to Charlie Simmer's leg was a big reason for it.

Kings' Triple Trouble: Line of Simmer, Taylor, Dionne.

Center Bernie Nicholls had 32 points in the concluding 22 games of the season; winger Darryl Evans, another late call-up, had 11 playoff points.

Twice a 50-goal shooter, Simmer struggled much of the schedule after breaking his leg late in the 1980-81 season. He was strong in the playoffs and starts the new season optimistically, joining Triple Crown Line mates Marcel Dionne (50 goals, 117 points) and Dave Taylor (39, 106) on one the league's premier attack units.

Jim Fox (68 points), Steve Bozek, who had 33 rookie goals, Greg Terrion, Dan Bonar, Doug Smith, Nicholls and Evans are youngsters who can give the team some depth.

Defensemen Larry Murphy (66 points) and Mark Hardy (45) supply some sting from the backline and draft pick Mike Heidt had 57 junior points to indicate some proficiency on the attack.

Scoring goals won't be a King problem. Once again, the club will be among the most entertaining offensive sides in the NHL.

DEFENSE: While scoring wasn't a King woe, preventing goals certainly was last season. The 369 goals they yielded placed them 20th among 21 teams.

Chubby, little goalie Mario Lessard has alternated good and bad seasons and 1982-83 should be a good one if the pattern continues.

Of course, it would be a big boost if Lessard can regain his form of 1980-81 when he led the NHL with 35 wins and had a 3.25 average in 64 games.

Backup Doug Keans isn't really the answer, either, and the Kings would like to make a trade for a veteran goalie.

Although he didn't have an especially good season, Murphy remains a prime young defenseman who should be an all-star. He's strong at the game's skills and can take a heavy workload.

Hardy, too, is young enough to improve and veterans Rick Chartraw, Dave Lewis and Jerry Korab are adequate big leaguers.

OUTLOOK: Coach Don Perry, who took over from Parker MacDonald late in the season and immediately earned a suspension, had enough time to establish that he's going to be the boss. The team executed his plan well enough to eliminate the Edmonton Oilers.

Perry is a coach who likes basic, fundamental execution and that's something the Kings need. They have the flair and flash to play shootout but to engineer any sort of a climb up the ladder, they simply must chop down that goals-against total.

With the Triple Crown Line and some promising offensive

KING ROSTER

No.	Player	Pos.	Hgt.	Wgt.	Born	1981-82	G	A	Pts.	PIM
	Blair Barnes	RW	5-11	190	9-21-60/Windsor, Ont.	Wichita	28	34	62	99
8	Danny Bonar	C	5-8	170	9-23-56/Deloraine, Man.	Los Angeles	13	23	36	111
26	Steve Bozek	C	5-11	170	11-26-60/Castlegar, BC	Los Angeles	33	23	56	68
27	Rick Chartraw	D-RW	6-2	210	7-13-54/Caracas, Ven.	Los Angeles	2	8	10	56
						New Haven	3	9	12	39
16	Marcel Dionne	C	5-8	185	8-3-51/Drummondville, Que.	Los Angeles	50	67	117	50
15	Darryl Evans	RW	5-8	176	1-12-61/Toronto, Ont.	Los Angeles	2	6	8	2
						New Haven	33	57	90	42
19	Jim Fox	RW	5-8	170	5-18-60/Coniston, Ont.	Los Angeles	30	38	68	23
	Glenn Goldup	RW	5-11	185	4-26-53/St. Catherine's, Ont.	Los Angeles	0	0	0	2
						New Haven	14	17	31	41
	Larry Goodenough	D	6-0	195	1-19-53/Toronto, Ont.	New Haven	3	27	30	60
	Scott Gruhl	LW	5-11	185	9-13-59/Port Colbourne, Ont.	New Haven	28	41	69	107
						Los Angeles	2	1	3	2
	Al Hangsleben	D-RW	6-1	195	2-22-53/Warroad, Minn.	Wash.-LA	3	7	10	84
						Hersh-NH	6	6	12	54
20	Mark Hardy	D	5-11	195	2-1-59/Semaden, Switz.	Los Angeles	6	39	45	130
	Warren Holmes	C	6-1	185	2-18-57/Beaton, Ont.	Los Angeles	0	2	2	0
						New Haven	27	28	55	29
12	Dean Hopkins	RW	6-1	205	6-6-59/Cobourg, Ont.	Los Angeles	2	13	15	102
22	Steve Jensen	LW	6-0	180	4-14-55/Minneapolis, Minn.	Los Angeles	8	19	27	19
						New Haven	5	8	13	4
4	Jerry Korab	D	6-2	215	9-15-48/Sault Ste. Marie, Ont.	Los Angeles	5	13	18	91
17	John Paul Kelly	LW	6-0	212	11-15-59/Edmonton, Alta.	Los Angeles	12	11	23	100
25	Dave Lewis	D	6-2	205	7-3-53/Kindersley, Sask.	Los Angeles	1	13	14	75
	Dave Morrison	RW	6-0	186	6-12-62/Thornton, Ont.	New Haven	0	0	0	2
						Los Angeles	0	0	0	0
5	Larry Murphy	D	6-1	210	3-8-61/Scarborough, Ont.	Los Angeles	22	44	66	95
7	Mike Murphy	RW	5-11	175	9-12-50/Toronto, Ont.	Los Angeles	5	10	15	20
9	Bernie Nicholls	C	6-0	185	6-24-61/Haliburton, Ont.	New Haven	41	30	71	31
						Los Angeles	14	18	32	27
6	Rob Palmer	D	5-11	190	9-10-56/Sarnia, Ont.	Los Angeles	0	2	2	0
						New Haven	2	23	25	22
11	Charlie Simmer	LW	6-3	210	3-20-54/Terrace Bay, Ont.	Los Angeles	15	24	39	42
2	Al Sims	D	6-0	182	4-18-53/Toronto, Ont.	Los Angeles	1	1	2	16
						New Haven	4	27	31	53
23	Doug Smith	C	5-11	178	5-17-63/Ottawa, Ont.	Los Angeles	16	14	30	64
21	Phil Sykes	LW	6-0	180	— /Dawson Creek, B.C.	U. North Dakota	20	11	31	
18	Dave Taylor	RW	6-0	195	12-4-55/Sudbury, Ont.	Los Angeles	39	67	106	130
14	Greg Terrion	C	6-0	190	5-2-60/Peterborough, Ont.	Los Angeles	15	22	37	23
3	Ian Turnbull	D	6-0	185	12-22-53/Montreal, Que.	Toronto-LA	11	17	28	89
						New Haven	1	7	8	4
24	Jay Wells	D	6-1	205	5-18-59/Paris, Ont.	Los Angeles	1	8	9	145

							GP	GA	SO	Avg.
	Mike Blake	G			— /	Saginaw	36	151	0	4.57
						Los Angeles	2	2	0	2.35
31	Doug Keans	G	5-7	174	1-7-58/Pembroke, Ont.	Los Angeles	31	103	0	4.30
						New Haven	13	33	2	2.89
1	Mario Lessard	G	5-9	177	6-25-54/East Broughton, Que.	Los Angeles	52	213	2	4.36
	Paul Pageau	G	5-9	160	10-1-59/Montreal, Que.	Saginaw	29	140	0	5.18

players, the Kings have sufficient attack. How well they fare will depend on how well Perry can convince them that the attack must spring from a sound defensive base.

KING PROFILES

MARCEL DIONNE 31 5-8 185   Forward
Among the NHL's elite stars for the past decade... Brilliant offensive player with all the skills... His 117 points last season marked the sixth time he's gone over 100 points; he now has 1,180 points in 11 years... Had best playoff with seven goals in ten games... Was strong player for Team Canada in 1981 Canada Cup tournament... Born Aug. 3, 1951, in Drummondville, Que.... Drafted by Detroit in 1971, spent four years with Red Wings, then became King as first big-name player to change teams as free agent... One of the NHL's quickest skaters with great acceleration... Nicknamed "Lou" because mates claim he resembles comedian Lou Costello... An outspoken critic of fighting and violence in hockey.

Year	Club	GP	G	A	Pts.
1971-72	Detroit	78	28	49	77
1972-73	Detroit	77	40	50	90
1973-74	Detroit	74	24	54	78
1974-75	Detroit	80	47	74	121
1975-76	Los Angeles	80	40	54	94
1976-77	Los Angeles	80	53	69	122
1977-78	Los Angeles	70	36	43	79
1978-79	Los Angeles	80	59	71	130
1979-80	Los Angeles	80	53	84	137
1980-81	Los Angeles	80	58	77	135
1981-82	Los Angeles	78	50	67	117
	Totals	857	488	692	1180

DAVE TAYLOR 26 6-0 195   Forward
Could be prototype for complete winger... Strong, aggressive, good scorer and playmaker (106 points in 1981-82), sound defensively, tough in corners... Teams well with center Dionne and winger Simmer on Triple Crown Line.... Born Dec. 4, 1955, at Levack, Ont.... Attended Clarkson College and was 210th player picked in 1975 draft after sophomore year... By his senior year, he added 30 pounds and led NCAA with 108 points... Three summers' work in mine in hometown convinced him to try hockey as a career... Doesn't have great speed but that's his only flaw.

Year	Club		GP	G	A	Pts.
1977-78	Los Angeles	....	64	22	21	43
1978-79	Los Angeles	....	78	43	48	91
1979-80	Los Angeles	....	61	37	53	90
1980-81	Los Angeles	....	72	47	65	112
1981-82	Los Angeles	....	78	39	67	106
	Totals	....	353	188	254	442

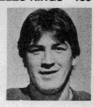

JIM FOX 22 5-8 170   Forward

Made a solid improvement in second NHL season...From 43 points as a rookie, he jumped to 30 goals, 68 points in 1981-82...Skilled offensive player, small but very quick...Had excellent junior career with Ottawa 67s, producing 396 points in three seasons...Won Ontario League scoring title in 1979-80 with 166 points in only 62 games...Born May 18, 1960, in Coniston, Ont....First-round draft pick in 1980...Part of youth movement that gives Kings a bright future.

Year	Club		GP	G	A	Pts.
1980-81	Los Angeles	....	71	18	25	43
1981-82	Los Angeles	....	77	30	38	68
	Totals	....	148	48	63	111

LARRY MURPHY 21 6-1 210   Defenseman

Exceptional young all-around backliner who appears headed for all-star status...Play slipped slightly in sophomore season after standout rookie term in 1980-81...Finished season strongly (22 goals, 66 points) and had good playoff...Has all the attributes to be a star: intelligence, size, offensive skill and defensive ability plus his good work as power-play pointman...Born Mar. 8, 1961, in Scarborough, Ont....Played on Canadian midget and junior championship teams...First-round draft pick (No. 4 overall) in 1980...Very important part of the team's future.

Year	Club		GP	G	A	Pts.
1980-81	Los Angeles	....	80	16	60	76
1981-82	Los Angeles	....	79	22	44	66
	Totals	....	159	38	104	142

CHARLIE SIMMER 28 6-3 210   Forward

Much of 1981-82 season was therapeutic, recovering from severely broken leg suffered in Toronto in March, 1981...Missed 30 games and was below par until late in the season...Good playoff work indicates complete recovery...Had been first all-star left winger in previous two seasons, scoring 56 goals in each...Born Mar. 20, 1954, in Terrace Bay, Ont....Spent five years between minors and NHL and was ready to give up on career...Called up during 1978–79 season, clicked immediately on line with Dionne and Taylor...Not fast but uses size and reach extremely well.

Year	Club	GP	G	A	Pts.
1974-75	California	35	8	13	21
1975-76	California	21	1	1	2
1976-77	Cleveland	24	2	0	2
1977-78	Los Angeles	3	0	0	0
1978-79	Los Angeles	38	21	27	48
1979-80	Los Angeles	64	56	45	101
1980-81	Los Angeles	65	56	49	105
1981-82	Los Angeles	50	15	24	39
	Totals	300	159	159	318

BERNIE NICHOLLS 21 6-0 185   Forward

Another good young prospect...Called up from minors late in 1981-82 season, produced 32 points in 22 games, added four goals in playoffs...Big, free-wheeling center with good attacking skills...Born June 24, 1961, in Haliburton, Ont....Was a fourth-round draft pick in 1980 from Kingston juniors...Returned to junior hockey for 1980-81 season and counted 152 points...With Greg Terrion and Doug Smith, gives Kings fine young centers...A future star.

Year	Club	GP	G	A	Pts.
1981-82	Los Angeles	22	14	18	32

DOUG SMITH 19 5-11 178   Forward

Second player picked in 1981 draft, he earned big-league spot at 18...Kings liked his aggressiveness and defensive ability to complement other centers...Played all 80 games as a rookie, producing 16 goals and 30 points...Showed good defensive skill, working as a penalty-killer and covering opposition's big shooters...Born May 17, 1963, in Ottawa, Ont....Played Major Junior hockey at 16 with Ottawa 67s...Counted 100 points in second season to become coveted draft choice...Kings' scout Wren Blair compares him to Bobby Clarke.

Year	Club		GP	G	A	Pts.
1981-82	Los Angeles	....	80	16	14	30

STEVE BOZEK 21 5-11 170   Forward

Excellent rookie season with 33 goals...Replaced injured Simmer on Triple Crown line with Dionne and Taylor for part of season...Very fast with a strong shot, which he unloads quickly...Another excellent youngster who should help move team to front ranks...Born Nov. 26, 1960, in Castlegar, B.C....Had outstanding college career at Northern Michigan University and was named an All-American twice...Counted 179 points in 85 games in last two college seasons...Third-round draft pick in 1980.

Year	Club		GP	G	A	Pts.
1981-82	Los Angeles	....	71	33	23	56

MARIO LESSARD 28 5-9 177   Goaltender

Has alternated good and bad seasons through NHL career...This should be a banner year for him...Earned second all-star team honors and led league in wins in 1980-81...Average skidded to 4.36 last season, although he redeemed himself with strong playoff work...Born June 25, 1954, in East Broughton, Que....Was 156th player picked in 1974 draft...One of 12 children...Served four-year apprenticeship in minors...Had outstanding rookie term in 1978-79 with 3.10 average in 49 games... Relies on quickness and reflexes.

Year	Club	GP	GA	SO	Avg.
1978-79	Los Angeles	49	148	4	3.10
1979-80	Los Angeles	50	185	0	3.91
1980-81	Los Angeles	64	203	2	3.25
1981-82	Los Angeles	52	213	2	4.36
	Totals	215	749	8	3.63

MARK HARDY 23 5-11 195   **Defenseman**

Has made rapid improvement in first three NHL seasons... Team's most consistent backliner in 1981–82... Upped point total to 45 and played sound defensive hockey... Strong skater with good speed... Second-round draft pick in 1979 from Montreal juniors... Born Feb. 1, 1959, in Semaden, Switzerland... Father played hockey in Europe... Mother was a member of England's figure skating team in the 1952 Olympics, placing seventh... Spent most of rookie season in minors.

Year	Club	GP	G	A	Pts.
1979-80	Los Angeles	15	0	1	1
1980-81	Los Angeles	77	5	20	25
1981-82	Los Angeles	77	6	39	45
	Totals	169	11	60	71

COACH DON PERRY: Replaced Parker MacDonald as Kings' coach late in season... Had served long apprenticeship as general manager and coach of minor-league teams, getting first chance in the NHL at 52... Was involved in widely-publicized incident with Paul Mulvey early in stay with Kings and was suspended for actions... Returned to job to inspire the team to strong finish and first-round playoff upset of heavily favored Edmonton Oilers...A strong believer in discipline and fundamentals...Most King players liked his tough approach...Was a fabled tough guy in his playing career in Old Eastern League...Operated several teams in Eastern and International Leagues...Was coaching Kings' American League farm team at New Haven when he was promoted to NHL post...Frank, outspoken type who quickly became a favorite with NHL writers.

GREATEST CENTER

Picking the best center in the history of the Kings produced a close race and, for a variety of reasons, perhaps a dead heat is the best verdict. Thus, two superb little men—Marcel Dionne and Robert (Butch) Goring—share the honors.

Goring joined the Kings in 1969, two seasons after the club joined the NHL, and was a mainstay until late in the 1980 season when he was traded to the New York Islanders, where he has helped that club win three consecutive Stanley Cups. In 736 games, he had 275 goals, 659 points and was one of the NHL's best penalty-killers.

Dionne was the first big-name free agent to change teams. He switched from the Detroit Red Wings to the Kings in 1975 and has been one of the NHL's premier attackers. Dionne has scored 349 goals and 814 points in 548 games since moving to California.

Dionne, 5-8, and Goring, 5-9, prove that there's a spot in hockey for the good little man.

ALL-TIME KING LEADERS

GOALS: Marcel Dionne, 59, 1978-79
ASSISTS: Marcel Dionne, 84, 1979-80
POINTS: Marcel Dionne, 137, 1979-80
SHUTOUTS: Rogatien Vachon, 8, 1976-77

MINNESOTA NORTH STARS

TEAM DIRECTORY: Chairman: George Gund III; Pres.: John Karr; GM: Lou Nanne; Dir. Hockey Info.: Dick Dillman; Coach: Glen Sonmor. Home ice: Met Center (15,184; 200′ x 85′). Colors: Green, white and gold. Training camp: Bloomington, Minn.

SCOUTING REPORT

OFFENSE: From the time he took command of the North Stars in 1978, GM Lou Nanne seemed to have an affection for finesse. The team's speed and attack carried it to the final in 1981 when it appeared the club had sufficient muscle to survive. But when the Chicago Black Hawks mugged the Stars into oblivion in the first playoff round in 1982, Nanne obviously changed his outlook.

Not that he's abandoned slick, talented players; the Stars have an abundance of that type. But Nanne did try to upgrade the team's foot soldiers. The main addition in that area was big Willi Plett, a grinding but not untalented winger, who was acquired from Calgary. When Willi is in the mood, he can smite just about any foe in the league.

Nanne then staged a "Bellows-hunt," sending two players to the Boston Bruins to guarantee that the Stars would draft winger Brian Bellows, the most publicized junior in years from the Kitchener Rangers. Bellows is 18 but going on 35, a mature, talented lad who carries a large "can't miss" tag.

The Stars have some splendid forwards—center Bobby Smith (43 goals, 114 points), sniper Dino Ciccarelli (55, 107), slick pivot Neal Broten (38, 97) and left winger Steve Payne (33, 77)—plus such competent performers as Al MacAdam, Mark Johnson, Anders Hakansson and Kent-Erik Anderson.

It will be a big boost if two good ones, Tom McCarthy and Tim Young, can play more than the 40 and 49 games they worked last season because of injuries.

DEFENSE: The Stars owned the sixth-best defensive mark in the NHL last season and were only two goals from fourth. They should be even better as their players mature.

Gilles Meloche had a dandy season in goal, a 3.47 average and 26 wins in 51 games. He's just a solid old pro. The rookie sensation of 1980-81, Don Beaupre, was hampered by injuries but at 21 remains an outstanding prospect, although he needs a good stretch to recapture the initial splash he made on the NHL.

Defenseman Craig Hartsburg is among the league's elite, sound

Steve Payne and Al MacAdam combined for 51 goals last year.

defensively and a fine rusher (77 points). Behind him, though, the cast is good but not exactly exceptional—Curt Giles, Gordie Roberts, Brad Maxwell and Fred Barrett. Ron Meighan is a kid with promise.

OUTLOOK: Coach Glen Sonmor is the NHL's champ of enthusiasm. Sometimes his gung-ho attitude behind the bench leads the players to ask him to cool it down a little. He's also a fine coach and with assistants J.P. Parise and Murray Oliver, the Stars have one of the best staffs in the league.

However, this is a "prove-it" season for the North Stars, for

NORTH STAR ROSTER

No.	Player	Pos.	Hgt.	Wgt.	Born	1981-82	G	A	Pts.	PIM
8	Kent-Erik Andersson	RW	6-2	185	5-24-51/Oresbro, Swe.	Minnesota	9	12	21	18
3	Fred Barrett	D	6-0	188	1-26-50/Ottawa, Ont.	Minnesota	1	15	16	89
	Brian Bellows	RW	5-11	194	9-1-64/St. Catherine's, Ont.	Kitchener	45	52	97	23
7	Neal Broten	RW	5-9	160	11-24-59/Roseau, Minn.	Minnesota	38	59	97	42
	Murray Brumwell	D	6-1	190	3-31-60/Calgary, Alta.	Minnesota	0	3	3	18
						Nashville	4	21	25	66
21	Jack Carlson	LW	6-3	200	8-23-54/Virginia, Minn.	Minnesota	8	4	12	103
	Steve Carlson	C	6-3	180	8-26-55/Virginia, Minn.	Nashville	23	39	62	63
20	Dino Ciccarelli	C	5-10	181	2-8-60/Sarnia, Ont.	Minnesota	55	52	107	138
28	Mike Eaves	C	5-10	180	6-10-56/Denver, Colo.	Minnesota	11	10	21	0
	Rob Flockhart	LW	6-0	185	2-6-56/Sicamous, B.C.	Nashville	27	30	57	98
2	Curt Giles	D	5-8	180	11-30-58/Humboldt, Sask.	Minnesota	3	12	15	87
16	Anders Hakansson	RW	6-2	192	4-27-56/Munkfors, Swe.	Minnesota	12	4	16	29
4	Craig Hartsburg	D	6-1	200	6-29-59/Stratford, Ont.	Minnesota	17	60	77	115
9	Mark Johnson	C	5-9	160	9-22-57/Madison, Wis.	Pitt.-Minn.	12	13	25	40
25	Al MacAdam	LW	6-0	180	3-6-52/Charlottetown, PEI	Minnesota	18	43	61	37
5	Brad Maxwell	D	6-2	192	7-7-57/Brandon, Man.	Minnesota	10	21	31	96
11	Tom McCarthy	LW	6-2	197	7-31-60/Toronto, Ont.	Minnesota	12	30	42	36
	Ron Meighan	D	6-3	184	5-26-63/Montreal, Que.	Minnesota	1	1	2	2
26	Steve Payne	LW	6-2	214	8-16-58/Toronto, Ont.	Minnesota	33	44	77	76
	Willi Plett	RW	6-3	211	6-7-55/Paraguay, S.A.	Calgary	21	36	57	288
	Dan Poulin	D	5-11	183	9-19-53/Robertsonville, Que.	Nashville	29	56	85	104
						Minnesota	1	1	2	2
10	Gordie Roberts	D	6-1	190	10-2-57/Detroit, Mich.	Minnesota	4	30	34	119
22	Gary Sargent	D	5-11	210	2-18-54/Bemidji, Minn.	Minnesota	0	5	5	18
15	Bobby Smith	C	6-4	212	2-12-58/North Sydney, N.S.	Minnesota	43	71	114	84
12	Ken Solheim	RW	6-2	203	3-27-61/Hythe, Alta.	Minnesota	4	5	9	4
						Nashville	23	18	41	40
17	Tim Young		6-1	190	2-22-55/Scarborough, Ont.	Minnesota	10	31	41	67

No.	Player	Pos.	Hgt.	Wgt.	Born	1981-82	GP	GA	SO	Avg.
33	Don Beaupre	G	5-8	149	9-19-61/Waterloo, Ont.	Minnesota	29	101	0	3.71
						Nashville	5	25	0	5.02
27	Gilles Meloche	G	5-9	186	7-12-50/Montreal, Que.	Minnesota	51	175	1	3.47
	Lindsay Middlebrook	G	5-7	170	9-7-55/Collingwood, Ont.	Minnesota	3	7	0	3.00
						Nashville	31	93	3	2.99
	Robbie Moore	G	5-5	155	5-3-54/Sarnia, Ont.	Nashville	39	159	0	4.33

Nanne, Sonmor and the players. The talent is there, seemingly in the right blend, to make a big run at a Stanley Cup.

The lack-of-maturity rationalization doesn't apply now and it's time for the Minnesota club to produce an Islanders' type of season with consistency, a solid stretch run to hit the playoffs in high gear. If it isn't there, a shake-up is needed.

NORTH STAR PROFILES

BOBBY SMITH 24 6-4 212   **Forward**
Made breakthrough to front ranks of NHL attackers in 1981-82 with 114 points... Agile skater with long stride... Excellent stickhandler and playmaker, improving goal scorer... Despite 250 points in first three seasons, he was regarded as disappointment, a view he scuttled last season... Born Feb. 12, 1958, in North Sydney, N.S.... Superb junior with Ottawa 67s and was Canada's junior player-of-the-year in 1977-78... First player chosen in 1978 entry draft... Excellent student who was accepted in medical school... From family of athletes; sister Mary was age-group tennis champ, brother Dan a college quarterback.

Year	Club	GP	G	A	Pts.
1978-79	Minnesota	80	30	44	74
1979-80	Minnesota	61	27	56	83
1980-81	Minnesota	78	29	64	93
1981-82	Minnesota	80	43	71	114
	Totals	299	129	235	364

DINO CICCARELLI 22 5-10 181   **Forward**
Flamboyant, cocky, best pure goal scorer to hit league since Mike Bossy... Scored rookie-record 14 goals in 1981 playoffs... Proved it was no fluke with 55-goal season in 1981-82... Very quick in offensive zone with a quickly released, deadly accurate shot... Born Feb. 8, 1960, in Sarnia, Ont.... High junior scorer with London Knights... Severe leg fracture that required insertion of steel rod threatened career... Wasn't claimed in entry draft, signed by North Stars as a free agent in 1979... Made complete recovery

although he has a foot-long scar on leg . . . Big favorite of Minnesota fans, who wave Dino The Dinosaur dolls.

Year	Club	GP	G	A	Pts.
1980-81	Minnesota	32	18	12	30
1981-82	Minnesota	76	55	52	107
	Totals	108	73	64	137

NEAL BROTEN 22 5-9 160   Forward

Slick, smooth and skilled . . . Among best NHL rookies in 1981-82 with 38 goals, 97 points—highest total ever by American-born player . . . Excellent skater, good defensively . . . Joined team for 1981 playoffs after outstanding college career at University of Minnesota . . . Starred for U.S. Olympic team in 1980 triumph . . . Born Nov. 29, 1959, in Roseau, Minn. . . . All-state high school player . . . Exceptional college career, top college player in U.S. in 1978-79 . . . Second-round draft pick in 1979 . . . Brother Aaron is with New Jersey . . . Scored in first NHL game . . . Future star with all-star potential.

Year	Club	GP	G	A	Pts.
1980-81	Minnesota	3	2	0	2
1981-82	Minnesota	73	38	59	97
	Totals	76	40	59	99

STEVE PAYNE 24 6-2 214   Forward

Big, fast winger with devastating shot but inconsistent in four NHL seasons . . . Had 42 goals in sophomore term, 30 and 33 in past two seasons . . . Outstanding in 1981 playoff success with 17 goals, 29 points in 19 games . . . Team would like him to be more aggressive and use size and strength . . . Born Aug. 16, 1958, in Toronto . . . Played junior hockey with Ottawa 67s on superb line with Star-mate Bobby Smith and Tim Higgins (Chicago) . . . Second-round draft pick (after Smith) in 1978 . . . Has the potential to be an all-star if he can find consistency . . . Nicknamed "Rooster".

Year	Club	GP	G	A	Pts.
1978-79	Minnesota	70	23	17	40
1979-80	Minnesota	80	42	43	85
1980-81	Minnesota	76	30	28	58
1981-82	Minnesota	74	33	44	77
	Totals	300	128	132	260

CRAIG HARTSBURG 23 6-1 200   Defenseman

High-quality player, key man in club's future . . . In front ranks of NHL defensemen in 1981-82 . . . Good rusher and puckhandler, produced 77 points last season . . . Fine defensive player, too . . . Born June 29, 1959, in Stratford, Ont. . . . Father Bill played minor pro hockey . . . Junior all-star with Sault Ste. Marie Greyhounds . . . Turned pro early with Birmingham Bulls of WHA . . . First-round pick (sixth overall) in 1979 entry draft . . . Member of Team Canada in 1981 Canada Cup tournament . . . Had 15 points in 1981 playoffs . . . Signed seven-year contract, longest ever granted by team.

Year	Club	GP	G	A	Pts.
1978-79	Birmingham (WHA)	77	9	40	49
1979-80	Minnesota	79	14	30	44
1980-81	Minnesota	74	13	30	43
1981-82	Minnesota	76	17	60	77
	Totals	306	53	160	213

TIM YOUNG 27 6-1 190   Forward

Broken ankle in offseason softball game made 1981-82 season partial writeoff . . . Missed 31 games, had 41 points in 49 matches he played . . . Solid big-league center with complete offensive skills, especially playmaking ability . . . Excellent power-play pointman . . . Set club record with 95 points in second season, 1976-77, broken by Bobby Smith last season . . . Born Feb. 22, 1955, in Scarborough, Ont. . . . Excellent junior with Ottawa

67s... First-round pick of Los Angeles Kings in 1975 draft, traded to Stars for second-round draft choice two weeks later... Team captain.

Year	Club	GP	G	A	Pts.
1975-76	Minnesota	63	18	33	51
1976-77	Minnesota	80	29	66	95
1977-78	Minnesota	78	23	35	58
1978-79	Minnesota	73	24	32	56
1979-80	Minnesota	77	31	43	74
1980-81	Minnesota	74	25	41	66
1981-82	Minnesota	49	10	31	41
	Totals	494	160	281	441

BRAD MAXWELL 25 6-2 192   Defenseman

Has battled injuries for past three seasons... Solid, long-striding rearguard when sound... Good on the attack, has excellent slap shot... Had 31 points in 51 games last season... Born July 8, 1957, in Brandon, Man.... Played junior hockey in New Westminster, B.C., as defensive partner of Rangers' Barry Beck... First-round draft choice in 1977... Had excellent 1981 playoff with 14 points... Fine golfer with a five handicap... Sister is married to Rick LaPointe of St. Louis.

Year	Club	GP	G	A	Pts.
1977-78	Minnesota	75	18	29	47
1978-79	Minnesota	70	9	28	37
1979-80	Minnesota	58	7	30	37
1980-81	Minnesota	27	3	13	16
1981-82	Minnesota	51	10	21	31
	Totals	281	47	121	168

GILLES MELOCHE 32 5-9 186   Goaltender

All-star candidate with outstanding 1981-82... In 51 games, he built 3.47 average and had 26 victories... Has been a front-line goalie through 12-season career, much of it with bad teams (California, Cleveland)... Stand-up style, good technique, excellent puckhandler... Joined Stars from Cleveland in 1978 merger of the teams... Born in Montreal on July 12, 1950... Played junior hockey in Sorel, Que.... Turned pro in Chicago chain, traded to California in 1971... Spent six seasons with Seals, later Barons, and faced enormous shot load . . . 1980 was first playoff year . . . Owns a restaurant in Montreal.

Year	Club	GP	GA	SO	Avg.
1970-71	Chicago	2	6	0	3.00
1971-72	California	56	173	4	3.32
1972-73	California	59	235	1	4.06
1973-74	California	47	198	1	4.24
1974-75	California	47	186	1	4.03
1975-76	California	41	140	1	3.44
1976-77	Cleveland	51	171	2	3.47
1977-78	Cleveland	54	195	1	3.77
1978-79	Minnesota	53	173	2	3.33
1979-80	Minnesota	54	160	1	3.06
1980-81	Minnesota	38	120	2	3.25
1981-82	Minnesota	51	175	1	3.47
	Totals	553	1932	17	3.59

WILLI PLETT 27 6-3 211   Forward

Acquired by North Stars to add some muscle in June, 1982, trade with Calgary for Steve Christoff and Bill Nyrop . . . Inconsistency had been the consistent factor of his career . . . Had best NHL season in 1980-81 with 38 goals and excelled in playoffs . . . Sagged to 21 goals last season . . . Big, tough, good skills and a strong shot . . . One of the league's most feared cornermen and fighters . . . Size and strength mean he's challenged only by the foolhardy . . . Born June 7, 1955, in Paraguay, South America . . . Won Calder Trophy as top rookie in 1976 when he scored 33 goals . . . Fourth-round draft pick in 1975 from St. Catharines juniors.

Year	Club	GP	G	A	Pts.
1975-76	Atlanta	4	0	0	0
1976-77	Atlanta	64	33	23	56
1977-78	Atlanta	78	22	21	43
1978-79	Atlanta	74	23	20	43
1979-80	Atlanta	76	13	19	32
1980-81	Calgary	78	38	30	68
1981-82	Calgary	78	21	36	57
	Totals	452	150	149	299

TOM McCARTHY 22 6-2 197   Forward

Bright prospect who has been hit by injuries in first three NHL seasons . . . Missed half 1981-82 season with wrist injury, had 42 points in 40 games he played . . . Big, strong winger with good shot and puckhandling skills . . . Born in Toronto on July 31,

1960 . . . Outstanding junior star with Oshawa Generals, second-leading scorer in Ontario league in 1978-79 . . . Was picked ahead of Wayne Gretzky in junior draft of 16-year-old players . . . North Stars' first-round pick in 1979 . . . Another young player who could lead club to the very top if he can avoid injuries.

Year	Club	GP	G	A	Pts.
1979-80	Minnesota	68	16	20	36
1980-81	Minnesota	62	23	25	48
1981-82	Minnesota	40	12	30	42
	Totals	170	51	75	126

COACH GLEN SONMOR: Mr. Enthusiasm . . . Gregarious, outgoing, outrageous . . . First-rate coach and motivator . . . Feels it's important to produce a team that entertains spectators, based on quick pace and offense . . . Born April 22, 1929, in Moose Jaw, Sask. . . . Raised in Hamilton, Ont., where he excelled in hockey, baseball, basketball, football and track and field . . . Good enough baseball pitcher to receive pro offers . . . Played junior hockey in Guelph, Ont., and Brandon, Man. . . . Played parts of two NHL seasons with New York Rangers and in AHL with Cleveland . . . Eye injury ended his career in 1955 . . . Took degree in physical education at University of Minnesota . . . Coached junior and pro hockey, then six seasons at U. of M. . . . Was both manager and coach of Minnesota Fighting Saints in WHA . . . Coached Birmingham Bulls in 1977-78 . . . Joined North Stars in 1978 as chief scout, took over coaching post early in 1978-79 season.

GREATEST CENTER

In selecting the "greatest" player in a team's history at any position, two factors must be considered—achievement and longevity. Thus, in the North Stars' case, the nod as greatest center goes to Tim Young over Bobby Smith and the reason is that Young has been on the scene a little longer.

Young joined the Stars in 1975 and has played 494 games, producing 160 goals, 281 assists for 441 points in that stretch. He held the team record of 95 points in a season until it was smashed by Smith's 114 points in 1981-82.

Young was claimed by the Los Angeles Kings in the 1975 entry draft, then traded to the North Stars two weeks later. He's an excellent stickhandler and playmaker, one of the NHL's best power-play point workers.

With 364 points in 299 games in four seasons, Smith seems destined to inherit the role as greatest center. But at this point, the edge goes to Young.

ALL-TIME NORTH STAR LEADERS

GOALS: Dino Ciccarelli, 55, 1981-82
ASSISTS: Bobby Smith, 71, 1981-82
POINTS: Bobby Smith, 114, 1981-82
SHUTOUTS: Cesare Maniago, 6, 1967-68

Fan favorite Dino Ciccarelli was a 55-goal man in 1981-82.

MONTREAL CANADIENS

TEAM DIRECTORY: Pres.: Morgan McCammon; Exec. VP-Man. Dir.: Irving Grundman; Dir. Pub. Rel.: Claude Mouton; Coach: Bob Berry. Home ice: Montreal Forum (16,074; 200' × 85'). Training camp: Montreal.

SCOUTING REPORT

OFFENSE: The once-proud fleet attack of the Canadiens has slowed. It certainly has not downshifted to a crawl, but it should be made clear that the Habs are not nearly as explosive and dominant as they once were. Still, their 360 goals were fourth-best in the league last season—a total Montreal may be hard-pressed to meet this time. Guy Lafleur is old and looking older every day; his goal total plunged to 27. The fact of the matter is, the best members of the old veteran crew are slipping.

Steve Shutt was benched at times last season. Doug Jarvis can't do it like he used to do it. Bob Gainey isn't as effective as he once was. He even failed to win the Selke Trophy as best defensive forward for the first time since the award was established four years ago.

Players once thought to be the next generation of stars have faded. Doug Risebrough was often mentioned in trades. Doug Wickenheiser, a former No. 1 draft pick, hasn't been given much of a chance to play. The Canadiens may be forced to give it to him this season. Coming off a stunning upset in the first round of the playoffs last season, Montreal might be in for several changes. The key player is Keith Acton, one of the best young centers around and the team's leading scorer with 88 points. The Canadiens hope more help will come from first-round draft pick Alain Heroux. At least, the Canadiens still have size and muscle with Mario Tremblay and Chris Nilan, who is best remembered for being suspended for throwing a puck at Pittsburgh's Paul Baxter.

DEFENSE: The question before the court is, will any team other than the Canadiens produce the best goals-against average? With a trio of rock-solid defensemen such as Rod Langway, Brian Engblom and Larry Robinson, the answer is no. What it took to end the team's stranglehold on the Vezina Trophy was a change in the definition of the award. The Vezina now goes to the goaltender judged to be the most valuable. The award for best goals-against average is now named the Williams Jennings Trophy. Last season it was shared by Denis Herron and rookie Rick Wamsley.

Larry Robinson is still one of NHL's top defensemen.

It was Herron who had the lowest average in the league (2.64) but Wamsley who played in the most games of any Montreal goalie (38). If there are those who believe Wamsley won't have similar success this season, rest assured the Canadiens are prepared. They also have Richard Sevigny, who was the rookie sensation two years ago before being left out last season. Goaltending won't be a problem for Montreal.

There are few problems anywhere on the blue line. The Canadiens allowed just 223 goals, fewest in the league. Besides their Big Three on defense, they have Gaston Gingras, the owner of a booming shot, and Robert Picard, still terribly inconsistent but nevertheless hiding untapped potential.

OUTLOOK: The Canadiens have been putting too much pressure on their defense and until now the defense has survived in masterful fashion. It will continue to survive, but not as masterfully. Montreal's inability to be as explosive as it used to be will leave the goalies fighting more shots. If any one of the Big Three—Robinson, Engblom or Langway—slumps, the Canadiens might be in for trouble.

CANADIEN ROSTER

No.	Player	Pos.	Hgt.	Wgt.	Born	1981-82	G	A	Pts.	PIM
12	Keith Acton	C	5-8	167	4-15-58/Peterborough, Ont.	Montreal	36	52	88	88
	Jeff Brubaker	LW	6-2	210	2-24-58/Hagerstown, Md.	Montreal	0	1	1	32
						Nova Scotia	28	12	40	258
	Guy Carbonneau	C	5-10	165	3-18-60/Sept. Isles, Que.	Nova Scotia	27	67	94	126
	Dan Daoust	C	5-10	153	2-29-60/Kirkland Lake, Ont.	Nova Scotia	25	39	64	77
3	Brian Engblom	D	6-2	200	1-27-57/Winnipeg, Man.	Montreal	4	29	33	76
23	Bob Gainey	LW	6-1	195	12-13-53/Peterborough, Ont.	Montreal	21	24	45	24
2	Gaston Gingras	D	6-0	191	2-13-59/North Bay, Ont.	Montreal	6	18	24	28
15	Rejean Houle	RW	5-11	165	10-25-49/Rouyn, Que.	Montreal	11	32	43	34
20	Mark Hunter	RW	6-2	200	11-12-62/Petrolia, Ont.	Montreal	18	11	29	143
	Yvan Joly	RW	5-8½	165	2-6-59/Hawksburg, Ont.	Nova Scotia	20	28	48	75
21	Doug Jarvis	C	5-9	172	3-24-55/Brantford, Ont.	Montreal	20	28	48	20
34	Bill Kitchen	D	6-11	195	7-16-60/Schoneberg, Ont.	Nova Scotia	3	17	20	137
						Montreal	0	0	0	7
10	Guy Lafleur	RW	6-0	185	9-20-50/Thursox, Que.	Montreal	27	57	84	24
17	Rod Langway	D	6-3	210	5-3-57/Maag, Taiwan	Montreal	5	34	39	116
26	Craig Laughlin	RW	5-11	198	9-19-57/Toronto, Ont.	Montreal	12	11	23	33
						Nova Scotia	14	15	29	16
6	Pierre Mondou	RW-C	5-10	175	11-27-55/Sorel, Que.	Montreal	35	33	68	57
31	Mark Napier	RW	5-10	185	1-28-57/Toronto, Ont.	Montreal	40	41	81	14
30	Chris Nilan	RW	6-0	200	2-9-58/Boston, Mass.	Montreal	7	4	11	204
24	Robert Picard	D	6-2	211	5-25-57/Montreal, Que.	Montreal	2	26	28	106
8	Doug Risebrough	RW	5-11	180	1-1-54/Kitchener, Ont.	Montreal	15	18	33	116
19	Larry Robinson	D	6-3	215	6-2-51/Marvelville, Ont.	Montreal	12	47	59	41
22	Steve Shutt	LW	5-11	180	7-1-52/Toronto, Ont.	Montreal	31	24	55	40
14	Mario Tremblay	RW	6-0	185	9-2-56/Montreal, Que.	Montreal	33	40	73	66
25	Doug Wickenheiser	C	6-1	199	3-30-61/Regina, Sask.	Montreal	12	23	35	43

No.	Player	Pos.	Hgt.	Wgt.	Born	1981-82	GP	GA	SO	Avg.
	Mark Holden	G	5-10	165	6-12-57/Weymouth, Mass.	Nova Scotia	44	142	0	3.36
						Montreal	1	0	0	0.00
32	Denis Herron	G	5-10	155	6-18-52/Chambly, Que.	Montreal	27	68	3	2.64
33	Rich Sevigny	G	5-8	172	4-11-57/Montreal, Que.	Montreal	19	53	0	3.10
1	Rick Wamsley	G	5-11	195	5-25-59/Simcoe, Ont.	Montreal	38	101	2	2.75

CANADIEN PROFILES

MARK NAPIER 25 5-10 185   **Forward**

Hits the Mark . . . Led team in goals . . . Has lightning-quick shot
and skates like the wind . . . Another unhappy Hab . . . Has threatened to become free agent . . . A No. 1 draft who spent three
seasons in WHA . . . Was only 18 when he made pro debut with
Toronto Toros . . . Was WHA Rookie of the Year in 1976 . . . Born
Jan. 28, 1957, in Toronto . . . A lefthanded shooter who plays right
wing . . . Has also played center . . . Led club in important-goals
category with 10 . . . Rather gentle . . . Had only 14 penalty minutes . . . Could be on verge of superstardom . . . Favorite of crowd
for his eye-pleasing end-to-end rushes.

Year	Club	GP	G	A	Pts.
1975-76	Toronto (WHA)	78	43	50	93
1976-77	Birmingham (WHA) ...	80	60	36	96
1977-78	Birmingham (WHA) ...	79	33	32	65
1978-79	Montreal	54	11	20	31
1979-80	Montreal	76	16	33	49
1980-81	Montreal	79	35	36	71
1981-82	Montreal	80	40	41	81
	Totals	526	238	248	486

BOB GAINEY 28 6-2 195   **Forward**

Mr. Defense . . . Has won Frank Selke trophy as outstanding defensive forward four times . . . Truth is, it was his play that inspired
trophy to begin with . . . A hard-nosed and clean bodychecker who
wraps opponents in a tangle of arms and legs . . . Irony is, he
missed check that led to winning Quebec goal that ousted Canadiens from playoffs in first round last season . . . Born Dec. 13,
1953, in Peterborough, Ont. . . . Was playoff MVP when Montreal
won 1979 Stanley Cup . . . Well-liked and articulate . . . Has knack
for getting big score . . . Led Canadiens with three shorthanded
goals . . . Will go down as greatest defensive forward of all time.

Year	Club	GP	G	A	Pts.
1973-74	Montreal	66	3	7	10
1974-75	Montreal	80	17	20	37
1975-76	Montreal	78	15	13	28
1976-77	Montreal	80	14	19	33
1977-78	Montreal	66	15	16	31
1978-79	Montreal	79	20	18	38
1979-80	Montreal	64	14	19	33
1980-81	Montreal	78	23	24	47
1981-82	Montreal	79	21	24	45
	Totals	670	142	160	302

GUY LAFLEUR 31 6-0 185   Forward

Still called the Flower... Wilting now... No longer dominates
the game like he once did... Said to be on trading block... Once
an institution... Was second player to Phil Esposito to score at
least 50 goals five straight seasons... Retains crackling shot and
breakneck speed... Has been hampered by injuries last two seasons... Born Sept. 30, 1951, in Thurso, Que.... Was involved
in auto accident that got headlines across Canada in March,
1980... Crashed into metal sign which cut his ear, requiring plas-
tic surgery... Had disappointing finale against Soviets in 1981
Canada Cup... Still has charm and grace and charisma... Will
go down as one of best right wings in history.

Year	Club	GP	G	A	Pts.
1971-72	Montreal	73	29	35	64
1972-73	Montreal	69	28	27	55
1973-74	Montreal	73	21	35	56
1974-75	Montreal	70	53	66	119
1975-76	Montreal	80	56	69	125
1976-77	Montreal	80	56	80	136
1977-78	Montreal	78	60	72	132
1978-79	Montreal	80	52	77	129
1979-80	Montreal	74	50	75	125
1980-81	Montreal	51	27	43	70
1981-82	Montreal	66	27	57	84
	Totals	794	459	636	1095

KEITH ACTON 24 5-8 167   Forward

The Habs' center of attention... He ought to spell it Action
... Sprouted into club's leading scorer... Small, but speedy and
surprisingly tough... Led Canadiens with 10 power-play
goals... Also led in effort and attitude... Tied for club lead with
five game-winners... Beat out No. 1 draft pick Doug Wickenheiser for spot on team two years ago... Born April 15, 1958,
in Peterborough, Ont.... Raised eyebrows with 45-goal season
for Nova Scotia minor-league team... A sixth-round pick who
made it big... Exciting bodychecker... Persistent... Never
tires... Listed first alphabetically in NHL Guide.

Year	Club	GP	G	A	Pts.
1979-80	Montreal	2	0	1	1
1980-81	Montreal	61	15	24	39
1981-82	Montreal	78	36	52	88
	Totals	141	51	77	128

ROD LANGWAY 25 6-3 210   Defenseman

Hot Rod . . . Emerging as one of league's best blueliners . . . A crisp checker who doesn't care to score . . . Quietly effective . . . Gained notice with exceptional play for Team USA in 1981 Canada Cup . . . Idled parts of last season with knee injury . . . Was thrilled to meet President Reagan on White House trip during all-star break . . . Idolized Phil Esposito as youngster growing up in Massachusetts, then antagonized Esposito with hard checks in celebrated feud in 1979 Stanley Cup finals against Rangers . . . Born May 3, 1957, in Maag, Taiwan . . . He's an American whose parents lived in Far East briefly before settling outside Boston . . . Quotable, with very engaging personality.

Year	Club	GP	G	A	Pts.
1977-78	Birmingham (WHA) ...	52	3	18	21
1978-79	Montreal	45	3	4	7
1979-80	Montreal	77	7	29	36
1980-81	Montreal	80	11	34	45
1981-82	Montreal	66	5	34	39
	Totals	320	29	119	148

BRIAN ENGBLOM 27 6-2 200   Defenseman

Probably Canadiens' best defenseman the last two seasons . . . Strong checker who gives hits and takes them . . . And handles puck well . . . Was among NHL's plus-minus leader at an eye-opening plus 78 . . . A coming star and one of most coveted defensemen in league . . . Stronger than he looks . . . Doesn't score goals and doesn't want to . . . Born Jan. 27, 1955, in Winnipeg . . . Attended University of Wisconsin, where he played for Team USA coach Bob Johnson . . . Was rare second-round draft out of college . . . Went to Nova Scotia, where he was named AHL's best defensive defenseman . . . Couldn't be more consistent if he tried.

Year	Club	GP	G	A	Pts.
1977-78	Montreal	28	1	2	3
1978-79	Montreal	62	3	11	14
1979-80	Montreal	70	3	20	23
1980-81	Montreal	80	3	25	28
1981-82	Montreal	76	4	29	33
	Totals	316	14	87	101

RICK WAMSLEY 23 5-11 195   Goaltender

Literally came out of nowhere to pry No. 1 goalie job loose from veteran Denis Herron and backup Richard Sevigny...His 2.75 goals-against average was second-best behind only Herron, but he played in 11 more games...Also, 23-7-7 record was among league's best...Turned in two shutouts...Knock on him is he plays behind best defense around and rarely dominates a game...Born May 25, 1959, in Simcoe, Ont....Had rare distinction of playing for three different junior teams, although he was OHA's leading goalie for Brantford...Was in net for Dale Hunter's goal at 22 seconds of overtime which knocked Montreal out of playoffs.

Year	Club	GP	G	A	Pts.
1980-81	Montreal	5	8	1	1.90
1981-82	Montreal	38	101	2	2.75
	Totals	43	109	3	2.66

LARRY ROBINSON 31 6-3 215   Defenseman

Mr. Robinson...Strong; tough and mean if he has to be...A perfect gentleman off the ice...Past winner of Norris Trophy as best defenseman and several times an all-star...Past his prime but remains one of best around...Looks lean and gangly, but is very muscular...Anchored defense for teams that won four straight Stanley Cups in 1970s...Born June 2, 1951, in Winchester, Ont....A chicken farmer in the offseason...A class individual...Still very much a team leader...Will talk about sport, politics or life...Rattles opponents with checks...Rattles forwards with enterprising defense.

Year	Club	GP	G	A	Pts.
1972-73	Montreal	36	2	4	6
1973-74	Montreal	78	6	20	26
1974-75	Montreal	80	14	47	61
1975-76	Montreal	80	10	30	40
1976-77	Montreal	77	19	66	85
1977-78	Montreal	80	13	52	65
1978-79	Montreal	67	16	45	61
1979-80	Montreal	72	14	61	75
1980-81	Montreal	65	12	38	50
1981-82	Montreal	71	12	47	59
	Totals	706	118	410	528

STEVE SHUTT 30 5-11 180 Forward

Production halved by injuries and spotty play...Even went through embarrassing benching in midseason...Yet he has been one of premier goal-scorers in league for long time...His 60 led NHL in 1976–77...Is swift and has quick shot...Handsome and debonaire...Often seen at Montreal late-night spots...Very off-beat guy who enjoys the good life...Once claimed he wanted to ride down Ste. Catherine's Street in his Bentley—naked...Born July 1, 1952, in Toronto...Loves rock music...Turned down lucrative offer to play in WHA and signed with Canadiens; he hasn't regretted it...Brother Byron plays in International League.

Year	Club	GP	G	A	Pts.
1972-73	Montreal	50	8	8	16
1973-74	Montreal	70	15	20	35
1974-75	Montreal	77	30	35	65
1975-76	Montreal	80	45	34	79
1976-77	Montreal	80	60	45	105
1977-78	Montreal	80	49	37	86
1978-79	Montreal	72	37	40	77
1979-80	Montreal	77	47	42	89
1980-81	Montreal	77	35	38	73
1981-82	Montreal	57	31	24	55
	Totals	720	357	323	680

MARIO TREMBLAY 26 6-0 185 Forward

Tough, gutsy right wing who has harder time keeping his temper than he does scoring goals...Smallest thing will set him off...Not very popular among opponents...Likes to work along boards picking up loose pucks...Underestimated as a shooter...Broke into lineup at only 19 years old and hasn't stopped hustling since...Born Sept. 2, 1956, in Alma, Que...Has uncanny way of scoring key goals...Also can throw big punch...Won't back down from anyone...Should learn to control temper...Probably won't...The epitome of the unsung hero...A real firecracker with short fuse.

Year	Club	GP	G	A	Pts.
1974-75	Montreal	63	21	18	39
1975-76	Montreal	71	11	16	27
1976-77	Montreal	74	18	28	46
1977-78	Montreal	56	10	14	24
1978-79	Montreal	76	30	29	59
1979-80	Montreal	77	16	26	42
1980-81	Montreal	77	25	38	63
1981-82	Montreal	80	33	40	73
	Totals	574	164	209	373

Rick Wamsley lost only seven times last season.

COACH BOB BERRY: Strict disciplinarian who roped in Canadiens from first day on job . . . Didn't permit smoking in dressing room and that included even Guy Lafleur . . . Has no-nonsense approach which can grate on veterans . . . Yet is sensible and valued as a good strategian . . . Got marginally-talented Los Angeles Kings a fourth-place finish in regular season two years ago . . . First-round upset by Rangers in 1981 got him into trouble with owner Dr. Jerry Buss . . . Wanted to renegotiate contract and accepted Montreal offer when Buss refused . . . Born Nov. 29, 1943, in Montreal . . . Scored 159 goals in seven years as Kings' left wing . . . Started career with Canadiens . . . Outstanding college athlete at George Williams University who had minor-league offer from Houston Astros and scholarship offer for football from University of Kentucky.

GREATEST CENTER

Some players set their sights on records, others set those records and still others set the standard by which the record-setters are measured. On the team which has set the standard for the NHL with 22 Stanley Cups, Jean Beliveau set the standard by which other centers will be measured for years to come.

There were many great contemporaries who were the heart of their clubs. But to those who knew him and the Canadiens, Beliveau was the soul of the great Montreal teams. He was the Hart Trophy winner as MVP twice and it is another measure of his fame and durability that the award came eight years apart, in 1956 and 1964. He won the scoring championship in 1956, won the Conn Smythe Trophy as playoff MVP in 1965 and was a first- or second-team all-star 11 times in 18 seasons.

He was nicknamed Le Gros Bill (Big Bill) and he certainly had a knack for making the big play. He was able to do it despite an assortment of injuries, including once having his sight imperiled by being struck in the eye with a stick. He also did it with flair and grace. Time after time, Beliveau would shrink from the spotlight so a teammate could share the credit. He was class and charisma and dignity.

He still is in a public-relations position for the Canadiens. He completed his career with 507 goals, eighth on the all-time list, and 1,219 points. But that doesn't begin to tell the story of Beliveau's contributions. The legends of his fire and determination and his quiet grace do that.

ALL-TIME CANADIEN LEADERS

GOALS: Steve Shutt, 60, 1976-77
 Guy Lafleur, 60, 1977-78
ASSISTS: Pete Mahovlich, 82, 1974-75
POINTS: Guy Lafleur, 136, 1976-77
SHUTOUTS: George Hainsworth, 22, 1928-29

NEW JERSEY DEVILS

TEAM DIRECTORY: Owner: John McMullen; GM-Coach: Bill MacMillan; VP Operations: Max McNab; Dir. Player Personnel: Bert Marshall; Dir. Pub. Rel.: Kevin O'Brien. Home ice: Byrne Meadowlands Arena (19,000; 200' x 85'). Colors: White, red and green.

SCOUTING REPORT

OFFENSE: Puny? Impotent? Weak? Not strong enough? Try non-existent!

As the Colorado Rockies, the team scored 241 goals. At least, they outscored Wayne Gretzky. The club's leading sniper, Don Lever, scored 30 goals. Some good efforts defensively were wasted because the team couldn't beg, borrow or steal a goal or two.

The team's problem is that it is three decades too late. The scoring stats resemble those of a club in the 1940s: a 30-goal shooter and a few with 20.

Lever (30 goals, 69 points) and Bob MacMillan (22 goals, 61 points), acquired in a trade with Calgary for the club's one bona fide sniper, Lanny McDonald, led the Rockies. Steve Tambellini (29, 59) and Brent Ashton (24 goals) are solid NHL players.

The remainder of the forward cast is ordinary—Aaron Broten, Dwight Foster, Bob Miller and Stan Weir. Two forwards who had strong efforts in 1980-81 but slumped badly last season need to make comebacks if the team is to have any hope. Center Merlin Malinowski sagged to 13 goals and 41 points after 25 goals and 62 points in 1980-81; young winger Paul Gagne slipped to 10 goals in 59 games after scoring 25 goals in 61 games the year before.

The team can only hope that its first-round draft pick, center Rocky Trottier, really is a chip off the old block that produced brother Bryan.

DEFENSE: The club's best backliner, Rob Ramage, was granted his wish to be traded and he's now a St. Louis Blue. That means the defense will be journeymen and kids.

There are two youngsters of promise. Joe Cirella spent most of 1981-82 with the NHL club before returning to junior hockey and the club drafted promising Ken Daneyko.

The team's best rearguard could be Tapio Levo, 26, who showed plenty of ability in his rookie season out of Finland. That term was reduced to 34 games by a broken wrist.

Goalie Glenn Resch looks to better things in New Jersey.

Veterans Bob Lorimer, Joel Quenneville and Mike Kitchen round out an undistinguished cast.

The best Rockie in a rocky season was goalie Chico Resch, who toiled valiantly with a minimum of aid. His 4.03 average in 61 games doesn't sound that impressive. If he hadn't played well, it would have been 8.03.

OUTLOOK: Early indications are that the team will attract large crowds to the new Brendan Byrne Arena in the Meadowlands. The poor lads, accustomed to performing in front of 6,000 or so

DEVIL ROSTER

No.	Player	Pos.	Hgt.	Wgt.	Born	1981-82	G	A	Pts.	PIM
28	Bob Attwell	RW	6-1	190	12-26-59/Spokane, Wash.	Fort Worth	31	36	67	66
	Brent Ashton	LW	6-1	209	5-18-60/Saskatoon, Sask.	Colorado	24	36	60	26
	Aaron Broten	C	5-10	168	11-14-60/Roseau, Minn.	Colorado	15	24	39	6
						Fort Worth	15	21	36	11
	Dave Cameron	C	6-0	185	7-29-58/Charlottetown, PEI	Colorado	11	12	23	103
						Fort Worth	0	0	0	0
	Joe Cirella	D	6-2	190	5-9-63/Hamilton, Ont.	Colorado	7	12	19	52
	Bob Crawford	LW	5-8	155	5-27-60/New York, N.Y.	Colorado	23	31	54	45
	Jim Dobson	RW	6-1	185	2-29-60/Winnipeg, Man.	Minn-Colo.	0	0	0	6
						Nash-FtWor.	34	25	59	94
	Dwight Foster	RW-C	5-11	195	4-2-57/Toronto, Ont.	Colorado	12	19	31	41
17	Paul Gagne	LW	5-10	178	2-6-62/Iroquois Falls, Ont.	Colorado	10	12	22	17
	Peter Gustavsson	LW	6-1	188	3-30-58/Bollebgd, Swe.	Fort Worth	8	11	19	4
						Colorado	0	0	0	0
2	Jack Hughes	D	6-1	205	7-20-57/Somerville, Mass.	Colorado	0	0	0	13
						Fort Worth	7	25	32	158
	Dave Kasper	C	5-10	154	2-12-64/Montreal, Que.	Sherbrooke	20	24	44	92
	Christer Kellgren	RW	6-0	173	8-15-58/Gothenburg, Swe.	Colorado	0	0	0	0
						Fort Worth	9	10	19	6
	Veli-Pekka Ketola	C	6-3	220	3-28-48/Pori, Fin.	Colorado	9	5	14	4
26	Mike Kitchen	D	5-10	185	2-1-56/Newmarket, Ont.	Colorado	1	8	9	60
						Fort Worth	1	5	6	16
	Bob Lorimer	D	6-1	200	8-25-53/Toronto, Ont.	Colorado	5	15	20	68
	Jeff Larmer	RW	5-11	180	— / —	Kitchener	51	44	95	95
	Don Lever	LW	5-11	185	11-14-52/S. Porcupine, Ont.	Cal-Colo.	30	39	69	26
	Tapio Levo	D	6-2	200	9-24-55/Pori, Fin.	Colorado	9	13	22	14
16	Merlin Malinowski	C	6-0	190	9-29-58/N. Battleford, Sask.	Colorado	13	28	41	32
	Graeme Nicolson	D	6-0	188	1-13-58/North Bay, Ont.					
	Bob MacMillan	C-LW	5-11	185	12-3-52/Charlottetown, PEI	Calg-Colo.	22	39	61	41
	Kevin Maxwell	C	5-9	165	3-30-60/Edmonton, Alta.	Nashville	4	2	6	6
						Minn-Colo.	6	9	15	52
	Bob Miller	RW-C	5-11	185	9-28-56/Medford, Mass.	Colorado	11	20	31	27
						Fort Worth	9	8	17	17
7	Randy Pierce	RW	5-11	187	11-23-57/Arnprior, Ont.	Colorado	0	0	0	4
						Fort Worth	6	6	12	19
	Jukka Porvari	LW	5-11	175	1-19-54/Tampere, Fin.	Colorado	2	6	8	0
	Joel Quenneville	D	6-0	187	9-15-58/Windsor, Ont.	Colorado	5	10	15	55
	Steve Tambellini	C	5-11	184	5-14-58/Trail, B.C.	Colorado	29	30	59	
	Rocky Trottier	C	5-11	185	4-11-64/Climax, Sask.	Billings	13	21	34	36
29	Yvon Vautour	RW	6-0	200	9-10-56/St. John's, N.S.	Colorado	1	2	3	18
	Pat Verbeek	C	5-8	176	5-24-64/Sarnia, Ont.	Sudbury	37	51	88	180
	Joe Ward	C	6-0	178	2-11-61/Sarnia, Ont.	Fort Worth	6	15	21	12
	Stan Weir	C	6-1	180	3-17-52/Ponoka, Alta.	Edmon-Colo.	5	16	21	9
	John Wensink	LW	6-0	200	4-1-53/Cornwall, Ont.	Colorado	5	3	8	152

							GP	GA	SO	Avg.
	Steve Janaszak	G	5-8	160	1-7-57/St. Paul, Minn.	Colorado	2	13	0	7.80
							Fort Worth	37	152	2	4.65
	Rick Laferriere	G	5-9	165	1-3-61/Hawksbury, Ont.	Colorado	1	1	0	3.00
							Fort Worth	37	189	1	5.26
1	Glenn Resch	G	5-9	165	4-17-48/Regina, Sask.	Colorado	61	230	0	4.03

in Denver, could have stage fright with all those folks watching them.

Bill MacMillan, who admits to making mistakes in his first season as GM, will now wear the coaching hat, too. Marshall Johnston, last year's coach, will assist.

The team has come down from the hills to sea level but there's still a big mountain for it to climb.

DEVIL PROFILES

DON LEVER 30 5-11 185   Forward
Diligent veteran who plays strongly both ways... Traded to Rockies in 1981-82 with Bob MacMillan by Calgary for Lanny McDonald... Had 30 goals and 69 points to lead team in scoring ... Has 256 goals in ten NHL seasons... Plays all three forward positions and is a good penalty-killer... Born Nov. 14, 1952, in South Porcupine, Ont.... Was Most Valuable Player in Ontario Major Junior hockey with Niagara Falls Flyers... Vancouver's first-round draft pick in 1972... Spent 7½ seasons with Canucks ... Played in 437 consecutive games in one stretch... Traded to Flames in 1980 with Brad Smith for Ivan Boldirev and Darcy Rota.

Year	Club	GP	G	A	Pts.
1972-73	Vancouver	78	12	26	38
1973-74	Vancouver	78	23	25	48
1974-75	Vancouver	80	38	30	68
1975-76	Vancouver	80	25	40	65
1976-77	Vancouver	80	27	30	57
1977-78	Vancouver	75	17	32	49
1978-79	Vancouver	71	23	21	44
1979-80	Vanc.-Atl.	79	35	33	68
1980-81	Calgary	62	26	31	57
1981-82	Calg.-Colo.	82	30	39	69
	Totals	765	256	307	563

BOB MacMILLAN 29 5-11 185   Forward
Versatile player with good skill in all areas of the game... Younger brother of team's GM Bill MacMillan... Joined Rockies with Don Lever from Calgary in 1982 deal for Lanny McDonald... Had 22 goals, 61 points... Also logged time the Minnesota in WHA, Rangers, St. Louis, Atlanta... Best season was 1978-79 with Atlanta when he had 108 points and won Lady Byng Trophy as

most gentlemanly player . . . He feels that season was a fluke . . . "I'm not a consistent 100-point player," he says . . . Excellent skater . . . Gregarious guy who's a good interview.

Year	Club	GP	G	A	Pts.
1972-73	Minnesota (WHA)	75	13	27	40
1973-74	Minnesota (WHA)	78	14	34	48
1974-75	New York R.	22	1	2	3
1975-76	St. Louis	80	20	32	52
1976-77	St. Louis	80	19	39	58
1977-78	St. L.-Atl	80	38	33	71
1978-79	Atlanta	79	37	71	108
1979-80	Atlanta	77	22	39	61
1980-81	Calgary	77	28	35	63
1981-82	Calg.-Col.	80	22	39	61
	Totals	728	214	351	565

BRENT ASHTON 22 6-1 209   Forward

Joined the Rockies in 1981 in complicated "Czech" deal . . . Scored 24 goals, 60 points and was one of club's most consistent performers . . . Came to team from Vancouver as compensation for Canucks' signing of Jiri Bubla, who had been drafted from Czech nationals by Rockies . . . Versatile forward who can play all three positions . . . Born May 18, 1960, in Saskatoon, Sask. . . . Big scorer in junior hockey with Saskatoon Blades . . . Second-round draft pick in 1979 . . . A competitive water skier in his teens . . . Fine all-around athlete who carries a seven handicap in golf.

Year	Club	GP	G	A	Pts.
1979-80	Vancouver	47	5	14	19
1980-81	Vancouver	77	18	11	29
1981-82	Colorado	80	24	36	60
	Totals	204	47	61	108

STEVE TAMBELLINI 24 6-0 190   Forward

Slick, smart center, solid scorer, fine playmaker . . . Had 29 goals, 59 points in first full season as Rockie . . . Joined team from Islanders with Chico Resch late in 1980-81 season in exchange for Mike McEwen . . . Born May 14, 1958, in Trail, B.C. . . . His father, Addie Tambellini, played for Trail Smoke Eaters, the last Canadian team to win the world tournament in 1961 . . . Was junior star with Lethbridge Broncos (115 points in 1977-78) . . . Islanders' first-round draft choice in 1978 . . . Has the potential to be a front-line center.

Year	Club	GP	G	A	Pts.
1978-79	New York I.	1	0	0	0
1979-80	New York I.	45	5	8	13
1980-81	N.Y.I.-Col.	74	25	29	54
1981-82	Colorado	79	29	30	59
	Totals	199	59	67	126

GLENN RESCH 34 5-9 165   Goaltender

Had an exceptional 1981-82 season despite team's poor record . . . Played in 62 games, most with a heavy load of shots, and built a 4.03 average . . . Won Bill Masterton Trophy for sportsmanship, perseverance and dedication . . . Quick, agile, excellent technically . . . Was a mainstay of Islanders through the 1970s . . . Traded to Rockies late in 1980-81 season with Steve Tambellini for Mike McEwen . . . Born July 10, 1948, in Moose Jaw, Sask. . . . Attended University of Minnesota-Duluth . . . His 2.83 career average is among best of active goalies . . . Outgoing and gregarious, among most popular players in game.

Year	Club	GP	GA	SO	Avg.
1973-74	New York I.	2	6	0	3.00
1974-75	New York I.	25	59	3	2.47
1975-76	New York I.	44	88	7	2.07
1976-77	New York I.	46	103	4	2.28
1977-78	New York I.	45	112	3	2.55
1978-79	New York I.	43	106	2	2.50
1979-80	New York I.	45	132	3	3.04
1980-81	N.Y.I.-Col.	40	121	3	3.20
1981-82	Colorado	61	230	0	4.03
	Totals	351	957	25	2.83

MERLIN MALINOWSKI 24 6-0 190   Forward

Talented player who sagged in 1981-82 after strong 25 goals, 62 points previous term . . . Did finish schedule well but totals of 13 goals and 41 points were a big disappointment . . . Smart, smooth skater and puckhandler . . . Fine stickhandler . . . Born Sept. 25, 1958, in North Battleford, Sask. . . . Played junior hockey in Medecine Hat, Alta. . . . Second-round draft choice in 1978 . . . Divided first two pro seasons between Rockies and minors . . . Big season in 1979-80 with Fort Worth in Central League (76 points) and he led all playoff scorers.

Year	Club		GP	G	A	Pts.
1978-79	Colorado	....	54	6	17	23
1979-80	Colorado	....	10	2	4	6
1980-81	Colorado	....	69	25	37	62
1981-82	Colorado	....	69	13	28	41
	Totals	....	202	46	86	132

DWIGHT FOSTER 25 5-11 195   Forward

One of the NHL's big flops in 1981-82 . . . Signed as a free agent by Rockies from Boston . . . Compensation was two draft picks, including first overall selection in 1982 . . . Worked hard but had only 12 goals, 31 points . . . Still young enough and owns the talent to bounce back . . . Tough, good skater, solid defensively . . . Born Apr. 2, 1957, in Toronto . . . Junior star with Kitchener Rangers . . . First-round draft choice in 1977 . . . Hampered by knee injury in first two pro seasons . . . Had good 1980-81 season with Bruins when he scored 24 goals.

Year	Club		GP	G	A	Pts.
1977-78	Boston	....	14	2	1	3
1978-79	Boston	....	44	11	13	24
1979-80	Boston	....	57	10	28	38
1980-81	Boston	....	77	24	28	52
1981-82	Colorado	....	70	12	19	31
	Totals	....	262	59	89	148

BOB LORIMER 29 6-1 200   Defenseman

One of the NHL premier "defensive" defensemen . . . Not a high scorer but efficient in own zone at moving the puck and clearing the front of the net . . . Joined Rockies from Islanders, where he was a regular on two Stanley Cup winners . . . Traded with Dave Cameron for future first-round draft pick . . . Born Aug. 25, 1953, in Toronto . . . Postponed pro career to attend Michigan Tech, where he played college hockey and earned degree in business administration . . . Spent two seasons in minors before becoming Islander regular in 1978-79.

Year	Club	GP	G	A	Pts.
1976-77	New York I.	1	0	1	1
1977-78	New York I.	5	1	0	1
1978-79	New York I.	67	3	18	21
1979-80	New York I.	74	3	16	19
1980-81	New York I.	73	1	12	13
1981-82	Colorado	79	5	15	20
	Totals	299	13	62	75

TAPIO LEVO 26 6-2 200   Defenseman

Started rookie NHL season strongly, then missed 50 games because of a broken wrist . . . Big, strong backliner who moves the puck well and has devastating shot from the point . . . Born Sept. 24, 1956, in Pori, Finland . . . Was major star in Finland . . . Played in the world championship tournament four times . . . Was captain of Finnish team in the 1980 Olympics at Lake Placid . . . All-star in Finnish Elite league with Pori Assat club . . . Several NHL teams made offers to him . . . "He can be a fine NHL defenseman," said team GM Bill MacMillan.

Year	Club	GP	G	A	Pts.
1981-82	Colorado	34	9	13	22

PAUL GAGNE 20 5-10 180   Forward

Promising youngster who slipped to 10 goals, 22 points in sophomore season in which he played 59 games because of injuries. . . . Youngest player in the NHL at 18 in 1980-81 when he scored 25 goals in 61 games . . . Strong skater with good scoring touch . . . Second in shooting percentage behind Charlie Simmer as a rookie with 25 goals on 99 shots . . . Born Feb. 6, 1962, in Iroquois Falls, Ont . . . Junior all-star with Windsor Spitfires with

48 goals, 101 points in 1979-80 . . . First-round draft choice in 1980.

Year	Club	GP	G	A	Pts.
1980-81	Colorado	61	25	17	42
1981-82	Colorado	59	10	12	22
	Totals	120	35	29	64

COACH BILL MacMILLAN: Coach two seasons ago, general manager last year, now he steps into both shoes at once . . . One of the keenest young minds in the game . . . Was worried that his job might be terminated when team changed ownership in offseason, but new boss John McMullen named him coach-GM because "you have to maintain a sense of continuity" . . . Skated for seven years in NHL and played integral part in the building of the New York Islanders . . . Played four years with Islanders and eventually served as assistant coach to Al Arbour in 1979-80, when Isles captured first Stanley Cup . . . Has minor-league coaching experience, too, and was named Coach of the Year in the Central Hockey League in his first year behind the bench (1978-79) . . . Born March 7, 1943, in Charlottetown, Prince Edward Island . . . Younger brother Bob is star with Calgary Flames.

GREATEST CENTER

Because the team has had a rather sad history in three different locations—Kansas City as the Scouts, Denver as the Colorado Rockies and now New Jersey—few players of great distinction have worn its various sweaters.

Thus, the club's best center is a man who played only 170 games over three seasons, one in Kansas City and almost two in Denver, Paul Gardner.

The son of former NHL great Cal Gardner, Paul was a first-round draft choice of the Scouts in 1975. In his 170 games with the club, Gardner scored 83 goals and had 77 assists for 160 points.

Not an exceptional skater, Gardner has the scoring touch around the net, the ability to shoot or deflect pucks into small openings with deadly accuracy.

He was traded to the Toronto Maple Leafs and on to the Pittsburgh Penguins, where he has continued to be a fine goal-scorer.

ALL-TIME DEVIL LEADERS

GOALS: Wilf Paiement, 41, 1976-77
ASSISTS: Wilf Paiement, 56, 1977-78
POINTS: Wilf Paiement, 87, 1977-78
SHUTOUTS: Doug Favell, 1, 1977-78
Bill Oleschuk, 1, 1978-79
Bill McKenzie, 1, 1979-80

Paul Gagne hopes to regain 25-goal form of 1980-81.

NEW YORK ISLANDERS

TEAM DIRECTORY: Chairman of the Board: John Pickett; Pres.-GM: William A. Torrey; Dir. Pub. Rel.: Les Wagner; Coach: Al Arbour. Home ice: Nassau Coliseum (15,271; 200' × 85'). Colors: White, blue and orange. Training camp: Cantiague Park, N.Y.

SCOUTING REPORT

OFFENSE: The defending Stanley Cup champions have 10 capable goal-scorers among their forwards, led, of course, by Mike Bossy. Other dangerous scorers are Bryan Trottier, a marvelous all-around center; John Tonelli, Clark Gillies, Bob Bourne, brothers Duane and Brent Sutter, Bob Nystrom, Anders Kallur, Butch Goring and Wayne Merrick.

"They're loaded with really good scorers," says Ranger veteran Carol Vadnais. "Solid at center, solid at wings, solid every place up front."

The Islanders ranked second in offense in the NHL last season with a team-record 385 goals and for the third consecutive season had the best power play in the league. As might be expected, they were the most accurate shooting team in hockey, scoring on a remarkably high 15.6 per cent of their shots. Promising new forwards Greg Gilbert and Dave Simpson could win jobs this season.

DEFENSE: Coach Al Arbour always has stressed team defense and positional play without the puck. The Islanders, seldom caught out of position without the puck, ranked second in the league in defense last season. The defense corps, led by Denis Potvin, a dangerous offensive threat, is deep in talent with Michael McEwen, Stefan Persson, Tomas Jonsson, Ken Morrow, Dave Langevin and Gord Lane. Rookie Paul Boutilier may get a shot at a job.

Few mistakes are made inside the Islanders' defensive zone and giveaways are rare. The penalty killing, fourth-best in the NHL in 1981-82, is outstanding and, with an explosive power play, gives the Islanders the best speciality teams in the league.

Bill Smith has proved to be one of the best goaltenders under playoff pressure in helping the Islanders win three consecutive Stanley Cups. He is backed up by Roland Melanson, a bright young prospect. Kelly Hrudey, up from the minor leagues, could become Smith's backup goalie this season.

OUTLOOK: Three straight Stanley Cups. Can the Islanders make it four straight in 1983 and then challenge Montreal's record five consecutive Stanley Cups won from 1956 through 1960?

"I definitely think they can," says Jean Beliveau, who played with 10 Stanley Cup champion Canadiens' teams. "The Islanders are very similar to the Montreal teams I was with for five straight Cups. Like us, they have no major weakness. They are very strong in goal, have a great defense and so many forwards who score goals and check very well. When we won the five Cups, we had very good power-play units and penalty-killers. The Islanders have great penalty-killing and a great power play, too."

It's not only the players who have made the Islanders so suc-

Large Clark Gillies had career-high 38 goals last season.

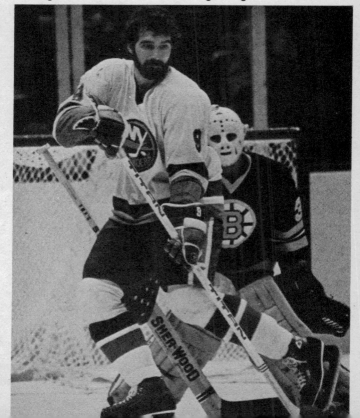

ISLANDER ROSTER

No.	Player	Pos.	Hgt.	Wgt.	Born	1981-82	G	A	Pts.	PIM
	Bruce Affleck	D	6-0	205	5-5-54/Salmon Arm, B.C.	Indianapolis	5	17	22	4
22	Mike Bossy	RW	6-0	185	1-22-57/Montreal, Que.	Islanders	64	83	147	22
14	Bob Bourne	C-LW	6-2	203	6-21-54/Kindersley, Sask.	Islanders	27	26	53	77
25	Bill Carroll	RW	5-10	191	1-19-59/Toronto, Ont.	Islanders	9	20	29	32
	Kelly Davis	D	6-0	198	9-23-58/Grand Prairie, Alta.	Indianapolis	2	12	24	100
17	Greg Gilbert	LW	6-1	194	1-22-62/Mississauga, Ont.	Islanders	1	0	1	0
						Toronto (OHL)	41	67	108	119
9	Clark Gillies	LW	6-3	218	4-4-54/Moose Jaw, Sask.	Islanders	38	39	77	75
91	Butch Goring	C	5-9	165	10-22-49/St. Boniface, Man.	Islanders	15	17	32	10
	Mats Hallin	LW	6-2	202	3-19-58/Eskilstona, Swe.	Indianapolis	25	32	57	113
	Neil Hawryliw	C	5-11	191	11-19-55/Fielding, Sask.	Islanders	0	0	0	0
						Indianapolis	20	14	34	89
	Mike Hordy	D	5-10	180	10-10-56/Thunder Bay, Ont.	Indianapolis	17	49	66	86
	Randy Johnston	D	5-11	184	6-2-58/Brampton, Ont.	Indianapolis	7	34	41	71
3	Tomas Jonsson	D	5-10	176	4-12-60/Falun, Swe.	Islanders	9	25	34	51
28	Anders Kallur	RW-C	5-10	175	7-6-52/Ludvika, Swe.	Islanders	18	22	40	18
24	Gordie Lane	D	6-1	180	3-31-53/Brandon, Man.	Islanders	0	13	13	98
26	Dave Langevin	D	6-2	215	5-15-54/St. Paul, Minn.	Islanders	1	20	21	82
	Red Laurence	C	5-9	173	6-27-57/Galt, Ont.	Indianapolis	43	55	98	43
	Tim Lockridge	D	6-0	204	1-18-59/Barrie, Ont.	Indianapolis	2	12	14	146
29	Hector Marini	RW	6-1	204	1-27-57/Timmins, Ont.	Islanders	4	9	13	53
2	Mike McEwen	D	6-1	185	8-10-58/Hornepayne, Ont.	Islanders	10	39	49	50
	Garth McGuigan	C	6-0	191	2-16-56/Charlottetown, PEI	Indianapolis	24	51	75	112
11	Wayne Merrick	C	6-1	190	4-23-52/Sarnia, Ont.	Islanders	12	27	39	20
6	Ken Morrow	D	6-4	210	10-17-56/Davison, Mich.	Islanders	1	18	19	56
23	Bob Nystrom	RW	6-1	200	10-10-52/Stockholm, Swe.	Islanders	22	25	47	103
7	Stefan Persson	D	6-1	187	12-22-54/Umea, Swe.	Islanders	6	37	43	99
5	Denis Potvin	D	6-0	205	10-29-53/Ottawa, Ont.	Islanders	24	37	61	83
	Dave Simpson	C	6-0	187	3-3-62/London, Ont.	Indianapolis	0	1	1	0
						London	67	88	155	
	Charlie Skjodt	C	6-0	187	6-10-56/North Bay, Ont.	Indianapolis	40	55	95	58
21	Brent Sutter	C	5-11	175	6-10-62/Viking, Alta.	Islanders	21	22	43	114
						Lethbridge	46	34	80	162
12	Duane Sutter	RW	6-1	181	3-6-60/Viking, Alta.	Islanders	18	35	53	100
27	John Tonelli	LW	6-1	195	3-23-57/Hamilton, Ont.	Islanders	35	58	93	57
19	Bryan Trottier	C	5-10	205	7-17-56/Val Marie, Sask.	Islanders	50	79	129	88
	Monte Trottier	C	5-10	170	8-25-61/Val Marie, Sask.	Indianapolis	10	15	25	142

							GP	GA	SO	Avg.
	Rob Holland	G	6-1	182	9-10-57/Montreal, Que.	Indianapolis	30	95	0	3.41
	Kelly Hrudey	G	5-10	182	1-13-61/Edmonton, Alta.	Indianapolis	51	149	1	2.95
1	Roland Melanson	G	5-10	178	6-28-60/Moncton, N.B.	Islanders	36	114	0	3.23
31	Billy Smith	G	5-10	185	12-12-50/Perth, Ont.	Islanders	46	133	0	2.97

cessful. "The Islanders have such a great organization, like we had in Montreal," said Beliveau. The Islanders needed only four seasons to become a league power after joining the NHL as an expansion team in 1972-73 and experiencing two dismal seasons. In 10 years in the NHL they have done three times what the rival Rangers have not done once in 42 years: win the Stanley Cup. Outstanding talent selection and wise drafting by General Manager Bill Torrey and former assistant general manager Jim Devellano have made the Islanders what they are today—the best team in hockey. They should remain the best.

ISLANDER PROFILES

MIKE BOSSY 25 6-0 185   Forward

Hockey's most dynamic pure shooter and goal-scorer... A threat to score from almost any position in the offensive zone... Blessed with remarkably quick, accurate shot and can pin-point where he wants it to go... Dangerous wrist or slap shot from either left or right angles, often shoots directly upon receiving pass... Needs no time to set up puck for shot... Winner of Conn Smythe Trophy as playoff MVP in Islanders' third consecutive Stanley Cup victory... Has uncanny natural instinct for being in perfect scoring position... Has scored an incredible 305 goals and 575 points in only 317 games in five seasons in NHL... Born Jan. 22, 1957, in Montreal... Fourteen teams which overlooked him in 1977 amateur draft were badly embarrassed... Has 113 power-play goals, 42 game-winning goals in career... A hockey star since childhood who once scored 21 goals in a game in youth hockey.

Year	Club	GP	G	A	Pts.
1977-78	New York I.	73	53	38	91
1978-79	New York I	80	69	57	126
1979-80	New York I.	75	51	41	92
1980-81	New York I.	79	68	51	119
1981-82	New York I.	80	64	83	147
	Totals	387	305	270	575

BRYAN TROTTIER 26 5-10 205   Forward

"Best all-around player in hockey," says Rangers' coach Herb Brooks... "He does everything well," says former star Phil Esposito... Has 760 points in 540 games in seven-year NHL career... Strong, durable, relentless checker... Reached 50-goal plateau last season and set playoff assist record . . . So strong his bodychecks can leave opponents dizzy from the impact . . . Tireless worker who excels as forechecker, backchecker and penalty killer . . . Born July 17, 1956, in Val Marie, Sask. . . . Scored on 23 per cent of his shots . . . May be best center in NHL at winning faceoffs . . . Destroyed Rangers' centers on faceoffs in last two playoffs with 85-44 record in 1981, 142-52 record last year . . . Shared team lead of 10 winning goals with Mike Bossy last season . . . His plus-70 rating was third in NHL behind Edmonton's Wayne Gretzky (plus-81) and Montreal's Brian Engblom (plus-78) . . . Has scored 92 power-play goals, 46 winning goals in career.

Year	Club	GP	G	A	Pts.
1975-76	New York I.	80	32	63	95
1976-77	New York I.	76	30	42	72
1977-78	New York I.	77	46	77	123
1978-79	New York I.	76	47	87	134
1979-80	New York I.	78	42	62	104
1980-81	New York I.	73	31	72	103
1981-82	New York I.	80	64	83	147
	Totals	540	292	486	778

CLARK GILLIES 28 6-3 218   Forward

Nicknamed "Jethro" because of his resemblance to the actor in the Beverly Hillbillies TV show . . . Can intimidate opponents with his fierce stare . . . Doesn't look for trouble but he's not the sort other players want to anger and fight . . . Rangers' Ed Hospodar unwisely started a fight with Islanders' giant-sized left wing last season . . . He ended up in a pool of blood on the ice with a broken jaw from one Gillies punch . . . Born April 7, 1954, in Moose Jaw, Sask. . . . Friendly, well-spoken man off the ice . . . Always mild-mannered and polite . . . Not a cheap-shot artist on ice . . . Played minor-league baseball for one year for Houston Astros . . . Took batting practice at Shea Stadium two years ago before charity softball game and impressed Mets' players and coaches with his ability to hit.

Year	Club	GP	G	A	Pts.
1974-75	New York I.	80	25	22	47
1975-76	New York I.	80	34	27	61
1976-77	New York I.	70	33	22	55
1977-78	New York I.	80	35	50	85
1978-79	New York I.	75	35	56	91
1979-80	New York I.	73	19	35	54
1980-81	New York I.	80	33	45	78
1981-82	New York I.	79	38	39	77
	Totals	617	252	296	548

JOHN TONELLI 25 6-1 195   **Forward**

Symbolizes hard-working, team-play concept which has helped Islanders dominate NHL... Hero of tense first-round playoff victory over Pittsburgh... Scored tying goal with 2:21 to play in third period and added sudden-death overtime goal after 6:19 in clinching fifth game to avert playoff elimination... Strong, sturdy left wing with tremendous endurance and stamina... Persistent checker who keeps pressure on opponents... Nothing fancy about his style of play... Born March 23, 1957, in Hamilton, Ont.... Developed into high-scoring threat with 93 points last season, many of his 58 assists the result of vigorous work in corners or behind the net.

Year	Club	GP	G	A	Pts.
1975-76	Houston (WHA)	79	17	14	31
1976-77	Houston (WHA)	80	24	31	55
1977-78	Houston (WHA)	65	23	41	64
1978-79	New York I.	73	17	39	56
1979-80	New York I.	77	14	30	44
1980-81	New York I.	70	20	32	52
1981-82	New York I.	80	35	58	93
	Totals	524	150	245	395

DENIS POTVIN 29 6-0 205   **Defenseman**

A defenseman with Bobby Orr's rare ability to control the game and the tempo of play... At his best directing Islanders' strong power play... Seldom misses the net with his fast, low slap shot from blue line... Skilled puckhandler and passer... Islanders' captain... Always seems to play his best in important games... Born Oct. 29, 1953, in Ottawa, Ont.... Ten-year veteran who became eligible for free agency in June... Islanders could not function as effectively without his presence on ice... Experienced occasional slumps and defensive lapses last season but was a dominant force in playoffs... Intelligent, sophisticated man.

Year	Club	GP	G	A	Pts.
1973-74	New York I.	77	17	37	54
1974-75	New York I.	79	21	55	76
1975-76	New York I.	78	31	67	98
1976-77	New York I.	80	25	55	80
1977-78	New York I.	80	30	64	94
1978-79	New York I.	73	31	70	101
1979-80	New York I.	31	8	33	41
1980-81	New York I.	74	20	56	76
1981-82	New York I.	60	24	37	61
	Totals	632	207	474	681

BOB NYSTROM 30 6-1 200 Forward

Has become a master of scoring dramatic sudden-death overtime playoff goals...His overtime goal in 1980 gave Islanders their first Stanley Cup championship in win over Flyers...Works effectively at right wing on line with John Tonelli and Wayne Merrick...A player whose statistics don't give a true indication of his value to team...Dedicated team player, hard-worker, checker and defensive player...Born Oct. 10, 1952, in Stockholm, Sweden, but raised in Kamloops, B.C....Ten-year veteran who has scored 207 career goals...Ideal team player who does his job without complaining...A rugged player...Has played more games than any player in Islanders' history.

Year	Club	GP	G	A	Pts.
1972-73	New York I.	11	1	1	2
1973-74	New York I.	77	21	20	41
1974-75	New York I.	76	27	28	55
1975-76	New York I.	80	23	25	48
1976-77	New York I.	80	29	27	56
1977-78	New York I.	80	30	29	59
1978-79	New York I	78	19	20	39
1979-80	New York I.	67	21	18	39
1980-81	New York I.	79	14	30	44
1981-82	New York I.	74	22	25	47
	Totals	702	207	223	430

MICHAEL McEWEN 26 6-1 185 Defenseman

Rangers and Colorado Rockies made mistakes by trading him...Islanders' GM Bill Torrey made a wise move acquiring him in 1981 trade...Has lightning-fast shot from blue line and skating moves to match...Starred in 1976-77 as Ranger rookie and became a 20-goal scoring defenseman two seasons later...Born Aug. 10, 1956, in Hornepayne, Ont....Sent to Colorado in 1979 as part of Rangers' trade for Barry Beck...Offense-minded defenseman who is improving his play in the defensive zone under coaching of Al Arbour...Introverted young athlete...Prefers to be known as Michael instead of Mike.

Year	Club	GP	G	A	Pts.
1976-77	New York R.	80	14	29	43
1977-78	New York R.	57	5	13	18
1978-79	New York I.	80	20	38	58
1979-80	N.Y.R.-Col.	76	12	47	59
1980-81	Col.-N.Y.I.	78	11	38	49
1981-82	New York I.	73	10	39	49
	Totals	447	72	204	276

BOB BOURNE 28 6-2 203   Forward

One of hockey's swiftest, most graceful skaters . . . Always a threat to penetrate behind opposing defensemen with his quick, clever moves . . . Used either at center or left wing . . . Excels in defensive part of game as checker and penalty killer . . . A versatile player . . . Adept at scoring shorthanded goals . . . Born June 21, 1954, in Kindersley, Sask. . . . Receives and delivers passes well while in full stride . . . Has been a 30-goal scorer three times . . . Uses his speed effectively to create two-on-one rushes and breakaways . . . Islanders acquired him in 1974 from Kansas City Scouts . . . Played minor-league baseball in Houston Astros' farm system.

Year	Club	GP	G	A	Pts.
1974-75	New York I.	77	16	23	39
1975-76	New York I.	14	2	3	5
1976-77	New York I.	75	16	19	35
1977-78	New York I.	80	30	33	63
1978-79	New York I.	80	30	31	61
1979-80	New York I.	73	15	25	40
1980-81	New York I.	78	35	41	76
1981-82	New York I.	76	27	26	53
	Totals	553	171	201	372

DAVE LANGEVIN 28 6-2 215   Defenseman

Scored winning goal with 60-foot slap in Islanders' playoff clinching 5-3 conquest of Rangers . . . Not noted for his goal-scoring, however, notching only one regular-season goal last season, only five in three NHL seasons . . . Underrated defensive defenseman specializing in clearing puck from his zone, blocking shots and bodychecking opposing forwards out of play . . . Had impressive plus-34 rating last season and was plus-40 in 1980–81 . . . Born May 15, 1954, in St. Paul, Minn. . . . Played college hockey at University of Minnesota in Duluth . . . Played three years with Edmonton in WHA before joining Islanders . . . Nicknamed "Bam Bam" for his robust bodychecks.

Year	Club	GP	G	A	Pts.
1976-77	Edmonton (WHA)	77	7	16	23
1977-78	Edmonton (WHA)	62	6	22	28
1978-79	Edmonton (WHA)	77	6	21	27
1979-80	New York I.	76	3	13	16
1980-81	New York I.	75	1	16	17
1981-82	New York I.	73	1	20	21
	Totals	440	24	108	132

BILL SMITH 31 5-10 185 — Goaltender

Smitty... Has finally gained the recognition he deserves as one of the best playoff goalies in recent hockey history... Has a remarkable career record of 59-21 in playoffs and was outstanding in last season's march to the Stanley Cup... Made a seemingly impossible save on point-blank shot by Rangers' Reijo Ruotsalainen to stave off Ranger comeback in Islanders' clinching sixth-game win... Started NHL career in 1971 with Los Angeles ... Became only goalie in NHL history to score a goal Nov. 28, 1979, against Colorado... Born Dec. 12, 1950, in Perth, Ont.... Tough, feisty goalie who allows no one to roam too close to his goal crease... Hockey's most aggressive netminder, with 316 career penalty minutes in 424 games... Led NHL with 32-9-4 mark last season... Has 192-135-79 career goaltending record.

Year	Club	GP	GA	SO	Avg.
1971-72	Los Angeles	5	23	0	4.60
1972-73	New York I.	37	147	0	4.16
1973-74	New York I.	46	134	0	3.07
1974-75	New York I.	58	156	3	2.78
1975-76	New York I.	39	98	3	2.61
1976-77	New York I.	36	87	2	2.50
1977-78	New York I.	38	95	2	2.65
1978-79	New York I.	40	108	1	2.87
1979-80	New York I	38	104	2	2.95
1980-81	New York I.	41	129	2	3.20
1981-82	New York I.	46	133	0	2.97
	Totals	424	1214	15	2.99

COACH AL ARBOUR: Nicknamed "Radar" because he's one of the few players in hockey history to have worn glasses while playing... Spent 12 years as a defensive defenseman in NHL with Detroit, St. Louis, Chicago and Toronto... In 28 years in hockey as a player and coach, he's missed being in the playoffs only once... Calm, stoic man who always appears unruffled behind the bench... Players know better... He can explode in anger when Islanders aren't playing well... Born Nov. 1, 1932, in Sudbury, Ont.... Made NHL coaching debut with St. Louis in 1970... Became Islanders' coach in 1973–74... Strong advocate of disciplined positional play and team defense... Has career coaching record of 381-202-135 in nine seasons as Islanders' coach and playoff coaching record of 78-39 . . . His overall NHL regular-season coaching record of 432-242-160 is among the best in the league . . . Friendly, scholarly-looking man respected by players and coaching peers.

GREATEST CENTER

Phil Esposito, the highest-scoring center in hockey history, was talking about Bryan Trottier, the three-time Stanley Cup champion Islanders' all-around center.

"Trottier does everything Wayne Gretzky does and does a lot more things, too," said Esposito. "The guy's a great center. He's the most complete center in the league. He's better than I was."

Esposito may get a slight argument there. He scored 717 goals in his brilliant career, 76 in one season. Gretzky scored a record 92 goals last season.

"I'm certainly not knocking Gretzky; he's phenomenal," said Esposito. "He's got the edge in goals on Trottier. But nothing bothers Trottier."

The Islanders' gifted center achieved a personal high with 50 goals last season and probably could score more except that he's cast in a playmaking role. He forechecks and backchecks vigorously. He's an outstanding penalty killer. He's exceptionally skilled on power plays. He may be the best in the league at winning faceoffs. And he scores, too (760 points in seven seasons).

But his strongest point may be his bodychecking. He is one of the hardest-hitting, most aggressive forwards of high-quality skill in the game. A perfect example of the impact and power of a Trottier bodycheck was in the second game of the playoff final last season. He checked Vancouver's Gerry Minor so hard that it knocked out a pane of protective glass at Nassau Coliseum and sent Minor flying over the boards.

"And he didn't really hit the guy that hard," joked Islanders' coach Al Arbour.

ALL-TIME ISLANDER LEADERS

GOALS: Mike Bossy, 69, 1978-79
ASSISTS: Bryan Trottier, 87, 1978-79
POINTS: Mike Bossy, 147, 1981-82
SHUTOUTS: Glenn Resch, 7, 1975-76

NEW YORK RANGERS

TEAM DIRECTORY: Pres.: John H. Krumpe; VP-GM: Craig Patrick; Bus. Mgr.-Dir. Pub. Rel.: John Halligan; Coach: Herb Brooks. Home ice: Madison Square Garden (17,500; 200′ × 85′). Colors: Blue, red and white. Training camp: Rye, N.Y.

SCOUTING REPORT

OFFENSE: "We have to upgrade our offense, be more of a goal-scoring threat," says Herb Brooks, who in his first season as coach gave the Rangers a sense of purpose and order and brought respect back to a troubled organization. "But, in trying to be more of an offensive team, we don't want to sacrifice the defensive aspect of our game," says Brooks.

It took time for the Rangers to adapt to Brooks' innovative, European-style of attack, which he calls "motion offense"—players with or without the puck constantly moving, bobbing, weaving, circling, dropping back in center ice to regroup, criss-crossing to confuse opponents accustomed to the standard straight-ahead, up-and-down game. The problem with Brooks' system is that it takes almost perfection to execute properly. One false move and the Rangers are caught out of position without the puck. They often were victims of their own system, failing to make the transition from offense to defense.

Mike Rogers, Ron Duguay, rookie Mark Pavelich and hard-working Eddie Johnstone provide most of the offense among the forwards. Except for Don Maloney, left wing is a problem position. There is also a need for a center who can consistently win faceoffs. Brooks constantly juggled lines last season, using more than 100 different combinations. He must find compatable lines that can play and stay together this season.

The Ranger power play was a joke for most of last season.

DEFENSE: The Rangers' finished eighth in team defense in the NHL, an improvement over recent seasons. But they still were guilty of excessive giveaways, more than 100 of which led to opponents' goals. The penalty-killing was outstanding at times, dreadful at others. Barry Beck is the dominant force among the corps of defensemen, which received generally good performances from Dave Maloney, Tom Laidlaw, veteran Carol Vadnais and Finnish rookie Reijo Ruotsalainen, an offensive defenseman with defensive shortcomings. Rookie Andre Dore had a fine season. Ron Greschner, plagued by injuries, may move to forward this season if his recurring back ailment finally heals.

Rookie goaltender Steve Weeks, described by Brooks as "our goalie of the future," had an outstanding first half of the season. Journeyman Eddie Mio came through splendidly in the second half. Injury-prone John Davidson and Steve Baker, both of whom sat out most of last season with injuries, will create job competition in training camp this season.

Trade for Mike Rogers proved cause for Ranger joy.

RANGER ROSTER

No.	Player	Pos.	Hgt.	Wgt.	Born	1981-82	G	A	Pts.	PIM
14	Mike Allison	C	6-0	202	3-28-61/Ft. Francis, Ont.	Rangers	7	15	22	74
						Springfield	0	0	0	0
21	Mike Backman	RW	5-10	175	1-2-53/Halifax, N.S.	Rangers	0	2	2	4
						Springfield	24	27	51	147
3	Barry Beck	D	6-3	215	6-3-57/Vancouver, B.C.	Rangers	9	29	38	111
6	Tim Bothwell	D	6-3	190	5-6-55/Vancouver, B.C.	Rangers	0	3	3	10
						Springfield	0	4	4	7
	Gary Burns	C	6-1	190	1-15-55/Cambridge, Mass.	Springfield	27	39	66	73
20	Cam Connor	LW	6-2	200	8-1-54/Winnipeg, Man.	Springfield	17	34	51	195
	Gary DeGrio	LW/RW	5-11	180	2-16-60/Duluth, Minn.	Minnesota-Dul.	18	17	35	18
33	Andre Dore	D	6-2	200	2-11-58/Montreal, Que.	Rangers	4	16	20	64
						Springfield	3	8	11	20
10	Ron Duguay	C-RW	6-2	210	7-6-57/Sudbury, Ont.	Rangers	40	36	76	82
22	Nick Fotiu	LW	6-2	200	5-25-52/Staten Isl., N.Y.	Rangers	8	10	18	151
38	Robbie Ftorek	C	5-8	160	1-2-52/Needham, Mass.	Que.-Rangers	9	33	42	28
4	Ron Greschner	D	6-2	185	12-33-54/Goodsoil, Sask.	Rangers	5	11	16	16
15	Anders Hedberg	RW	5-11	176	2-25-51/Ornskoldsvik, Swe.	Rangers	0	1	1	0
23	Ed Hospodar	D-RW	6-2	205	2-5-59/Bowling Green, Ohio	Rangers	3	8	11	152
	John Hughes	D	5-11	180	3-18-54/Charlottestown, PEI	Springfield	1	33	34	169
17	Eddie Johnstone	RW	5-9	175	3-2-54/Brandon, Man.	Rangers	30	28	58	57
	Chris Kontos	C	6-1	196	12-10-63/Toronto, Ont.	Toronto(OHL)-Sud.	42	62	104	86
2	Tom Laidlaw	D	6-2	215	4-15-58/Brampton, Ont.	Rangers	3	18	21	104
	Claude Larose	LW	5-10	175	5-17-55/St. John, Que.	Springfield	30	36	66	12
28	Mikko Leinonen	C	6-0	175	7-15-55/Tampere, Fin.	Springfield	4	2	6	2
						Rangers	11	19	30	18
	Jim Malone	C	6-1	180	2-20-62/Chatham, N.B.	Toronto (OHL)	24	28	52	127
26	Dave Maloney	D	6-1	195	7-31-56/Kitchener, Ont.	Rangers	13	36	49	105
12	Don Maloney	LW	6-1	190	9-5-58/Kitchener, Ont.	Rangers	22	36	58	73
9	Rob McClanahan	RW	5-10	180	1-9-58/St. Paul, Minn.	Bing-Spring	15	23	38	21
						Hart-Rangers	5	12	17	21
	Mark Morrison	C	5-9	155	3-11-63/Delta, B.C.	Victoria	48	66	114	83
11	Ulf Nilsson	C	5-11	176	5-11-50/Laksand, Swe.	Springfield	0	0	0	0
40	Mark Pavelich	C	5-7	165	2-28-58/Eveleth, Minn.	Rangers	33	43	76	67
27	Mike Rogers	C	5-8	175	10-24-54/Calgary, Alta.	Rangers	38	65	103	43
29	Reijo Ruotsalainen	D	5-7	170	4-1-60/Kaakkuri, Fin.	Rangers	18	38	56	27
16	Dave Silk	RW	5-11	190	1-1-58/Scituate, Mass.	Rangers	15	20	35	39
5	Carol Vadnais	D	6-1	190	9-25-45/Montreal, Que.	Rangers	5	6	11	45
8	Steve Vickers	LW	6-0	180	4-21-51/Toronto, Ont.	Rangers	9	11	20	13
						Springfield	4	6	10	14
25	Peter Wallin	C	5-10	175	4-30-57/Stockholm, Swe.	Rangers	2	9	11	12
						Springfield	4	10	14	8
	Bart Wilson	D	6-1	196	8-8-61/Kingston, Ont.	Springfield	12	26	38	170
19	Tom Younghans	RW	5-11	175	1-22-53/St. Paul, Minn.	Minn-Rang	4	5	9	17
						Springfield	4	0	4	16

No.	Player	Pos.	Hgt.	Wgt.	Born	1981-82	GP	GA	SO	Avg.
35	Steve Baker	G	6-3	200	5-6-57/Braintree, Mass.	Rangers	6	33	0	6.04
						Springfield	11	42	0	5.01
30	John Davidson	G	6-3	205	2-27-53/Ottawa, Ont.	Rangers	1	1	0	1.00
						Springfield	8	24	0	3.30
41	Ed Mio	G	5-10	180	1-31-54/Windsor, Ont.	Wichita	11	46	0	4.20
						Rangers	25	89	0	3.56
	Rick Strack	G	6-0	170	11-30-58/Lake Placid, N.Y.	Springfield	49	168	0	3.70
	John Vanbiesbrouck	G	5-7	165	9-4-63/Detroit, Mich.	Rangers	1	1	0	1.00
						Slt. St. Marie	31	102	0	3.62
31	Steve Weeks	G	5-10	175	6-30-58/Scarborough, Ont.	Rangers	49	179	1	3.77

OUTLOOK: Despite a poor start and the Rangers' usual injury jinx (they led the league with 539 games missed through player injuries and ailments), Brooks gave the teams' frustrated fans new hope. The Rangers still haven't won the Stanley Cup since 1940 but at least they were interesting and competitive last season.

"We should be better this season . . . if we avoid injuries," said Brooks. Last season he was without such important forwards as Anders Hedberg and Ulf Nilsson for virtually the entire season. Oddly, the Rangers played better on the road than at home. The team has speed among its forwards but lacks size. Brooks believes last season's second-place Patrick Division finish, highest position in the standings in seven years, is an indication of better days ahead. He views Finnish center Mikko Leinonen, who scored a record six assists in one playoff game, as a player who could become a dominant offensive force this season.

The team, though, appears to have too many holes to seriously threaten the Islanders' reign.

RANGER PROFILES

MIKE ROGERS 28 5-8 175   Forward

If Rogers were a car, Ranger GM Craig Patrick could be charged with grand theft auto . . . Lowly Hartford Whalers foolishly traded him to Rangers despite back-to-back 105-point seasons . . . Gave revitalized Rangers dominant high-scoring center they lacked . . . Scored points in 65 of 80 games . . . Became only third player in Ranger history to score 100 or more points in one season, leading team with 38 goals, team-record 65 assists, 103 points . . . Set Ranger record with 16-game scoring streak . . . Born Oct. 24, 1954, in Calgary . . . Slick, quick, hard to check . . . Outstanding at winning faceoffs . . . Had not missed a game in five years until ankle injury felled him in last year's playoffs . . . Starred for five years in WHA.

Year	Club	GP	G	A	Pts.
1974-75	Edmonton (WHA)	78	35	48	83
1975-76	Edm.-N.E. (WHA)	80	30	29	59
1976-77	New England (WHA) .	78	25	57	82
1977-78	New England (WHA) .	80	28	43	71
1978-79	New England (WHA) .	80	27	45	72
1979-80	Hartford	80	44	61	105
1980-81	Hartford	80	40	65	105
1981-82	New York R.	80	38	65	103
	Totals	636	267	413	680

RON DUGUAY 25 6-2 210   **Forward**

Doogie or Doogs... Name mentioned almost as much in gossip
columns as it is in sports pages for his highly-publicized social
life and involvement with celebrities... Enjoys living a fast life
on and off the ice... High-energy skater and checker... Convinced
many of his skeptics that he's a quality player with 40-goal season
in 1981–82... Plays right wing or center... Has tremendous
breakaway speed... Born July 6, 1957, in Sudbury, Ont.... Excels
as penalty killer... Has impressive plus-18 rating last season but
still has occasional defensive lapses... Does modeling in offseason... Groupies of all ages adore him... Hardcore Ranger
fans either love him or hate him.

Year	Club	GP	G	A	Pts.
1977-78	New York R.	71	20	20	40
1978-79	New York R.	79	27	36	63
1979-80	New York R.	73	28	22	50
1980-81	New York R.	50	17	21	38
1981-82	New York R.	72	40	36	76
	Totals	345	132	135	267

MARK PAVELICH 24 5-7 165   **Forward**

Leads Rangers in nicknames: Pav... Pac Man... Fishin' Magician... Mark The Shark... Proved scouts from other teams who
claimed he was too small to play in NHL were wrong... Overlooked
in draft and signed as a free agent... Had outstanding rookie
season, setting Ranger rookie records with 33 goals, 43 assists,
76 points, 12 power-play goals... "Pav is the ultimate rink rat,"
says coach Herb Brooks, who often has to run Pavelich off the
ice after practice has ended... Starred for Brooks' gold-medal
1980 U.S. Olympic team... Born Feb. 28, 1958, in Eveleth,
Minn.... Led Rangers with plus-21 rating and was important in
teammate Ron Duguay scoring 40 goals... Quiet almost to the
point of shyness... Loves fishing and the outdoors... Carries
fishing rod along on road trips... "If I could earn a living just
fishing, that's what I'd do with the rest of my life," he says.

Year	Club	GP	G	A	Pts.
1981-82	New York R.	79	33	43	76

EDDIE JOHNSTONE 28 5-9 175 Forward

Known to teammates as E.J. or Ciggy...Few players work harder...Had his second straight 30-goal season...Capable of playing all three forward positions...Outstanding penalty killer...Lack of size doesn't prevent him from playing a tough, grinding style of game...Needs six goals to reach 100 for his NHL career...Born March 2, 1954, in Brandon, Man....."You don't get anywhere without working hard all the time" is his favorite expression...A notorious streak scorer who usually plays his best in the second half of the season...Excelled on line with Robbie Ftorek and Don Maloney...Outstanding all-around athlete in high school who had a chance to be a pro baseball catcher.

Year	Club	GP	G	A	Pts.
1974-75	Michigan (WHA)	23	4	4	8
1975-76	New York R.	10	2	1	3
1977-78	New York R.	53	13	13	26
1978-79	New York R.	30	5	3	8
1979-80	New York R.	78	14	21	35
1980-81	New York R.	80	30	38	68
1981-82	New York R.	68	30	28	58
	Totals	342	98	108	206

DON MALONEY 24 6-1 190 Forward

Injured right knee forced him to miss 26 games last season... Rangers started their move to reach second place when he returned to the lineup...Outstanding team player and vigorous worker, especially in corners and along the side boards...Doesn't always get the recognition he deserves...Injuries have set him back in each of the last two seasons...Born Sept. 5, 1958, in Lindsay, Ont....Noted for his ability to dig the puck free from scrambles in the corners and to score from in front of the net on rebounds and tip-ins...Younger brother of Ranger defenseman Dave Maloney.

Year	Club	GP	G	A	Pts.
1978-79	New York R.	28	9	17	26
1979-80	New York R.	79	25	48	73
1980-81	New York R.	61	29	23	52
1981-82	New York R.	54	22	36	58
	Totals	222	85	124	209

BARRY BECK 25 6-3 215   **Defenseman**

Bubba... Perhaps the most dominating defenseman in the defensive end of the ice in the league because of his size, strength and ability to neutralize rival forwards with jarring bodychecks ... Capable of rushing with the puck and being a dynamic offensive threat but played more of a defensive role last season... Seldom makes a bad play... Feared so much as a fighter that few opposing players challenge him... Born June 3, 1957, in Vancouver... Has developed into a forceful, respected team leader as Rangers' captain... Works with underprivileged children in New York area.

Year	Club	GP	G	A	Pts.
1977-78	Colorado	75	22	38	60
1978-79	Colorado	63	14	28	42
1979-80	Col.-N.Y.R.	71	15	50	65
1980-81	New York R.	75	11	23	34
1981-82	New York R.	60	9	29	38
	Totals	344	71	168	239

DAVE MALONEY 26 6-1 195   **Defenseman**

Made his Ranger debut at 18 after being drafted as a 17-year-old in 1974... Enjoyed his best all-around season in 1981–82 with 13 goals, 49 points... "I'm a big fan of Dave Maloney," says Herb Brooks... Served briefly as Ranger captain... Was freed from role as defensive defenseman last season and responded with several spectacular scoring rushes... Steady behind the blue line and a clever breakout passer who fit perfectly into Brooks' "motion" system of play... Led Rangers in game-winning goals... Born July 31, 1956, in Kitchener, Ont.... Career hampered by injuries in early years with Rangers... Has matured and reduced tendency to be charged with excessive penalties... Plays well on defense when paired with veteran Carol Vadnais... Works for brokerage house on Wall Street in offseason.

Year	Club	GP	G	A	Pts.
1974-75	New York R.	4	0	2	2
1975-76	New York R.	21	1	3	4
1976-77	New York R.	66	3	18	21
1977-78	New York R.	56	2	19	21
1978-79	New York R.	76	11	17	28
1979-80	New York R.	77	12	25	37
1980-81	New York R.	79	11	36	47
1981-82	New York R.	64	13	36	49
	Totals	443	53	156	209

REIJO RUOTSALAINEN 22 5-7 170   Defenseman

Rexi . . . Small, blond defenseman from Finland has terrific skating speed and elusive moves . . . Also has one of the quickest and hardest shots in the league but often fails to put his shots on net . . . Had difficulty adapting to North American style of play in first half of last season but finally adjusted during second half . . . "Rexi may be the best pure skater in the league," said coach Herb Brooks . . . Born April 1, 1960, in Oulu, Finland . . . Led Rangers with 247 shots on goal and set team scoring records for goals, assists and points by a rookie defenseman . . . Doesn't speak much English . . . Teamed with big Barry Beck to give Rangers a Mutt and Jeff defense tandem.

Year	Club	GP	G	A	Pts.
1981-82	New York R.	78	18	38	56

STEVE WEEKS 24 5-10 165   Goaltender

Played a vital role in his rookie season . . . Rangers were left without an experienced goaltender when John Davidson and Steve Baker were lost for the season with injuries in October . . . Took over as No. 1 goalie and carried the team on his back for most of the season with outstanding play in goal . . . Finished season with 23-16-9 record in 49 games . . . Set Ranger record with 15-game unbeaten streak (10-0-5) . . . Born June 30, 1958, in Scarborough, Ont. . . . Nicknamed "Weeksie" . . . Studied forestry at Northern Michigan University and was a teammate of Ranger defenseman Tom Laidlaw . . . Seldom beaten on breakaways . . . "He's our goalie of the future," says Herb Brooks.

Year	Club	GP	GA	SO	Avg.
1980-81	New York R.	1	2	0	2.00
1981-82	New York R.	49	179	1	3.77
	Totals	50	181	1	3.73

EDDIE MIO 28 5-10 180   **Goaltender**

Acquired Dec. 11 from Edmonton's Wichita minor-league team in another smart move by GM Craig Patrick... Rangers needed an experienced goalie to share workload with Steve Weeks... Mio came through perfectly... Became a crowd favorite in Madison Square Garden with his darting, diving, spectacular style of play... Lost only six of 25 games... Born Jan. 31, 1954, in Windsor, Ont.... Starred in Rangers' playoff conquest of Flyers and in losing playoff effort against Stanley Cup champion Islanders... Proved last season he belongs in NHL, not in minor leagues.

Year	Club	GP	GA	SO	Avg.
1977-78	Indianapolis (WHA) ...	17	64	0	4.27
1978-79	Ind.-Edm. (WHA)	27	84	2	3.85
1979-80	Edmonton	34	120	1	4.21
1980-81	Edmonton	43	155	0	3.89
1981-82	New York R.	25	89	0	3.56
	Totals	146	512	3	3.93

COACH HERB BROOKS: May have set an NHL coaching record in his rookie season for diagramming X's and O's and dreaming up new plays on paper table napkins in hotels and restaurants across the country... The thinking man's coach... An innovator whose self-designated "motion" system of play helped turn the troubled Rangers into a respected team after a dreadful start... Skeptics believed he would have trouble coaching in NHL with no experience and a coaching philosophy new to professional hockey... Intense, dedicated American-born coach proved them wrong... Quickly gained the respect of his players and coaching peers for his coaching techniques... Has given the enigmatic Rangers a sense of purpose and order after years of turmoil and coaching changes... Born Aug. 5, 1937, in St. Paul, Minn.... Military-minded man who believes in dedication, discipline and hard work but is fair and understanding with his players... An outstanding motivator of athletes... Would make an ideal Marine Corps officer... Brilliant college coach at University of Minnesota... Became a national hero by coaching 1980 U.S. Olympic team to stunning upset of Russians and gold-medal victory at Lake Placid... Appreciated and respected for his honest dealing with the press.

GREATEST CENTER

When Madison Square Garden public address announcer Carl Martin introduced Jean Ratelle to the crowd in pre-game ceremonies before the Phil Esposito Foundation Masters of Hockey benefit game last season, the fans responded with a long and affectionate standing ovation.

It was not surprising. For 16 seasons from 1961 to 1975, Ratelle established himself as one of the best centers in NHL history for the Rangers.

"Jean Ratelle was a good example of the perfect center," said former Montreal Canadiens' star center Jean Beliveau. "He was a great passer and playmaker, very unselfish, a good team player."

Known best as Ratty, the tall, graceful, smooth-skating center is best remembered for the smooth passes he made to linemates Rod Gilbert and Vic Hadfield. His passes had a featherly touch and seldom missed their mark. He set a Ranger record in 1971-72 by scoring 109 points in his first 63 games.

He was leading the NHL in scoring when he was accidentally struck by a shot by teammate Dale Rolfe. He broke an ankle and didn't play for the remainder of the season.

"I've always felt we might have won the Cup that year if Ratty hadn't been hurt," said Gilbert.

An outstanding defensive player who excelled at winning faceoffs, Ratelle was involved in the big trade of 1975 in which he and Brad Park were sent to Boston for Phil Esposito and Carol Vadnais. Ranger fans criticized the trade. Ranger management believed Ratelle's career would soon be over. They were wrong.

Ratelle became a 100-point scorer for the second time and starred for five seasons with the Bruins. He retired to become a Bruins' assistant coach following the 1980-81 season. In 21 NHL seasons, he scored 491 goals and 1,267 points in 1,281 games.

ALL-TIME RANGER LEADERS

GOALS: Vic Hadfield, 50, 1971-72
ASSISTS: Mike Rogers, 65, 1981-82
POINTS: Jean Ratelle, 109, 1971-72
SHUTOUTS: John Roach, 13, 1928-29

PHILADELPHIA FLYERS

TEAM DIRECTORY: Chairman of Exec. Comm.: Edward Snider; Chairman of Board: Joseph Scott; Pres.: Bob Butera; Dir. Player Personnel: Marcel Pelletier; Dir. Press Rel.: Joe Kadlec; Coach: Bob McCammon. Home ice: The Spectrum (17,077; 200' × 85'). Colors: Orange and white. Training camp: Portland, Me., and Philadelphia.

SCOUTING REPORT

OFFENSE: The Flyers, a defense-oriented team, have acquired more of an offensive image. They ranked eighth in offense last season and still rely heavily upon their vigorous forechecking to creat scoring chances. Bobby Clarke has entered the sunset side of his brilliant career but still is a gifted playmaking artist. Bill Barber, always reliable, is regarded by most opposing players as the best all-around left wing in the league. Ron Flockhart had an outstanding rookie season and Brian Propp proved he's a quality goal-scorer.

Ray Allison and Tim Kerr are impressive new faces among the forwards and, of course, there's rugged Paul Holmgren to plant himself in front of opposing goalies to screen and deflect shots. Acquiring veteran Darryl Sittler from Toronto was another offensive plus. Although feisty Ken Linseman led the Flyers with 92 points, management and many fans don't believe he had a good season.

DEFENSE: Defensively, the Flyers have slipped badly from their Stanley Cup championship seasons of the mid-1970s. They allowed a team-record 313 goals last season and their penalty-killing ranked 17th in the league, the worst in team history. Once one of the best penalty-killing teams in the NHL, the penalty-prone Flyers allowed a whopping 102 power-play goals last season, a league record.

The backchecking from forwards was generally subpar last season. But the biggest problem was the lack of defense by defensemen in their own zone. Behn Wilson was inconsistent, lost his composure and committed too many damaging penalties. Bob Dailey played in only 12 games and an injury has jeopardized his career. Jimmy Watson, once one of the Flyers' most effective two-way defensemen, didn't seem the same following back surgery. The acuisition of Brad Marsh, a good shot-blocker, helped. Opponents generally found it easy to take advantage of the Flyers' immobile corps of defensemen.

Ron Flockhart scored 33 times in his rookie season.

"They looked pretty bad behind the blue line," said Fred Shero, a former Flyers' coach.

Goaltending is a problem, too. It hasn't been the same since an eye injury forced Bernie Parent to retire. Grumpy Pete Peeters was inconsistent last season and was traded to Minnesota. Rick St. Croix was also inconsistent, so Pelle Lindbergh, whom Flyers' management rates highly, may emerge as No. 1 goalie this season.

OUTLOOK: My, how the mighty have fallen! The once-proud Flyers' record last season was their poorest since 1972-73. For the first time in nine years, they failed to finish first or second in their division.

"We just couldn't find any kind of consistency," said Keith Allen, Philadelphia's respected general manager. "We have to stop hurting ourselves by taking so many bad penalties," said personnel director Marcel Pelletier.

The situation became so bad that management fired Pat Quinn as coach late in the season, giving the job to Bob McCammon.

FLYER ROSTER

No.	Player	Pos.	Hgt.	Wgt.	Born	1981-82	G	A	Pts.	PIM
	Greg Adams	LW	6-2	188	5-31-60/Fuller Lake, B.C.	Maine	16	22	38	251
						Philadelphia	4	15	19	105
	Ray Allison	RW	5-9	178	3-4-59/Cranbrook, B.C.	Philadelphia	17	37	54	104
						Maine	15	13	28	75
6	Fred Arthur	D	6-3	204	3-9-61/Toronto, Ont.	Philadelphia	1	7	8	47
7	Bill Barber	LW	6-0	190	7-11-52/Callander, Ont.	Philadelphia	45	44	89	85
	Reid Bailey	D	6-2	198	5-28-56/Toronto, Ont.	Philadelphia	0	0	0	23
						Maine	4	26	30	53
5	Frank Bathe	D	6-1	190	9-27-54/Oshawa, Ont.	Philadelphia	1	3	4	68
	Mark Botell	D	6-4	212	8-27-61/Scarborough, Ont.	Philadelphia	4	10	14	31
						Maine	3	15	18	41
28	Mike Busniuk	D	6-3	200	12-13-51/Thunder Bay, Ont.	Maine	12	27	39	202
	Lindsay Carson	C	6-2	182	11-21-60/Oxbow, Sask.	Maine	20	32	52	92
						Philadelphia	0	1	1	32
16	Bobby Clarke	C	5-10	185	8-13-49/Flin Flon, Man.	Philadelphia	17	46	63	154
35	Glen Cochrane	D	6-2	200	1-29-58/Cranbrook, B.C.	Philadelphia	6	12	18	329
2	Bob Dailey	D	6-5	220	5-3-53/Kingston, Ont.	Philadelphia	1	5	6	22
	Pete Dineen	D	5-11	181	6-16-60/Kingston, Ont.	Maine	8	12	20	156
	Paul Evans	C	5-9	180	5-2-54/Toronto, Ont.	Maine	33	57	90	42
11	Ron Flockhart	C	5-11	175	10-10-60/Smithers, B.C.	Philadelphia	33	39	72	44
22	Tom Gorence	C-RW	6-0	185	3-11-57/St. Paul, Minn.	Philadelphia	5	8	13	8
15	Al Hill	LW	6-0	170	4-22-55/Nanaimo, B.C.	Philadelphia	6	13	19	58
24	Bob Hoffmeyer	D	6-0	182	7-7-55/Dodsland, Sask.	Philadelphia	7	20	27	142
						Maine	6	8	14	57
17	Paul Holmgren	LW	6-3	210	12-2-55/St. Paul, Minn.	Philadelphia	9	22	31	183
12	Tim Kerr	C	6-3	215	1-5-60/Windsor, Ont.	Philadelphia	21	30	51	138
14	Ken Linseman	C	5-11	175	8-11-58/Kingston, Ont.	Philadelphia	24	68	92	275
8	Brad Marsh	D	6-2	215	3-31-58/London, Ont.	Cal.-Phil.	2	23	25	116
	Brad McCrimmon	D	5-10	186	3-29-59/Dodsland, Sask.	Boston	1	8	9	83
	Dave Michayluk	RW	5-11	182	5-18-62/Wakaw, Sask.	Regina	62	111	173	128
21	Gary Morrison	LW	6-2	200	11-8-55/Detroit, Mich.	Maine	13	10	23	52
						Philadelphia	0	0	0	2
26	Brian Propp	LW	5-9	185	2-15-59/Neudorf, Sask.	Philadelphia	44	47	91	117
23	Ilkka Sinisalo	LW	6-1	190	7-10-58/Valeakoski, Fin.	Philadelphia	15	22	37	22
	Steve Smith	D	5-9	202	4-4-63/Trenton, Ont.	Philadelphia	0	1	1	0
9	Darryl Sittler	C	6-0	190	9-18-50/Kitchener, Ont.	Tor.-Phila.	32	38	70	74
	Ron Sutter	C	5-11	165	12-2-63/Viking, Alta.	Lethbridge	38	54	92	207
	Barry Tabodondung	LW	5-8	207	3-4-61/Parry Sound, Ont.	Maine	11	15	26	166
	Mark Taylor	C	5-11	185	6-1-58/Vancouver, B.C.	Maine	32	48	80	42
20	Jim Watson	D	6-0	190	8-19-52/Smithers, B.C.	Philadelphia	3	9	12	99
	Gordie Williams	RW	5-11	175	4-10-60/Saskatoon, Sask.	Maine	31	25	56	35
						Philadelphia	0	0	0	2
3	Behn Wilson	D	6-3	215	12-19-58/Kingston, Ont.	Philadelphia	13	23	36	135

No.	Player	Pos.	Hgt.	Wgt.	Born	1981-82	GP	GA	SO	Avg.
	Bob Froese	G	5-11	178	6-30-58/St. Catherine's, Ont.	Maine	33	104	2	3.28
31	Pelle Lindbergh	G	5-9	160	3-24-59/Stockholm, Swe.	Philadelphia	8	35	0	4.38
						Maine	25	83	0	3.31
30	Rick St. Croix	G	5-10	160	1-3-55/Kenora, Ont.	Philadelphia	29	112	0	3.89

"We need to show greater discipline as a team," said McCammon. "We have to get back to the old Flyers' style of good defensive play." It still may not be enough to catch the Islanders.

FLYER PROFILES

BOBBY CLARKE 33 5-10 185   **Forward**
Now into the sunset side of a brilliant career but still regarded by rivals as one of the best team players in the game . . . Never stops working in all three zones . . . An unselfish athlete from the old school . . . Fierce competitor who hates to lose . . . Outstanding team leader who has served as Flyers' captain and playing assistant coach . . . Plays the game the way Gordie Howe and Maurice (Rocket) Richard did: not shy about giving an opponent a jab with his elbow or stick . . . Born Aug. 13, 1949, in Flin Flon, Man. . . . Outstanding all-around center who excels at winning faceoffs, forechecking, backchecking, killing penalties and setting up plays with crisp power-play passes . . . Has won Hart Trophy as NHL MVP three times . . . Thirteen-season Flyers' veteran who seems destined to become coach or general manager when playing career is over . . . Overcame diabetes to achieve fame in hockey.

Year	Club	GP	G	A	Pts.
1969-70	Philadelphia	76	15	31	46
1970-71	Philadelphia	77	27	36	63
1971-72	Philadelphia	78	35	46	81
1972-73	Philadelphia	78	37	67	104
1973-74	Philadelphia	77	35	52	87
1974-75	Philadelphia	80	27	89	116
1975-76	Philadelphia	76	30	89	119
1976-77	Philadelphia	80	27	63	90
1977-78	Philadelphia	71	21	68	89
1978-79	Philadelphia	80	16	57	73
1979-80	Philadelphia	76	12	57	69
1980-81	Philadelphia	80	19	46	65
1981-82	Philadelphia	62	17	37	54
	Totals	991	318	738	1056

BILL BARBER 30 6-0 190   **Forward**
Pound for pound, generally regarded as hockey's best all-around left wing . . . Does everything well . . . Durable and consistent . . . Seldom plays a bad game or makes mistakes . . . Flyers' captain . . . Has averaged 37 goals in 10 years with Flyers

... Outstanding cornerman and defensive player ... Can also play center ... Born July 11, 1952, in Callander, Ont. ... Has scored 30 or more goals in nine of 10 NHL seasons ... Seldom becomes unruffled, always plays with poise ... Outstanding power-play pointman with deadly slap and wrist shots ... Good burst of speed when on the move ... Has 96 career power-play goals ... Finished third in NHL with 350 shots last season behind Wayne Gretzky (369) and Marcel Dionne (351).

Year	Club	GP	G	A	Pts.
1972-73	Philadelphia	69	30	34	64
1973-74	Philadelphia	75	34	35	69
1974-75	Philadelphia	79	34	37	71
1975-76	Philadelphia	80	50	62	112
1976-77	Philadelphia	73	20	35	55
1977-78	Philadelphia	80	41	31	72
1978-79	Philadelphia	79	34	46	80
1979-80	Philadelphia	79	40	32	72
1980-81	Philadelphia	80	43	42	85
1981-82	Philadelphia	80	45	44	89
	Totals	774	371	398	769

BRIAN PROPP 23 5-9 185   Forward

Quiet, self-effacing left wing with ability to block out pressure and distractions of fans with remarkable self-discipline ... Has missed only one game in three seasons with Flyers ... Had his best season in 1981–82 with 44-goal, 91-point effort ... Cast in the mold of most Flyers with a competitive, aggressive personality on ice ... Born Feb. 15, 1959, in Lanigan, Sask. ... Breaks free from checks and into open ice for passes and shots as well as any forward in NHL ... Flyers' No. 1 draft pick in 1979 after scoring 94 goals and 194 points in junior hockey for Brandon Wheat Kings.

Year	Club	GP	G	A	Pts.
1979-80	Philadelphia	80	34	41	75
1980-81	Philadelphia	79	26	40	66
1981-82	Philadelphia	80	44	47	91
	Totals	239	104	128	232

KEN LINSEMAN 24 5-11 175   Forward

Nicknamed "The Rat" by some of his Flyers' teammates ... Many opponents have even less flattering names for him because of his feisty, pestiferous tactics and verbal harrassment during games ...Has the speed to dodge checkers and gets from point A to point B more swiftly than most players...Playmaking center with good short-passing ability who led Flyers in scoring last season...Born Aug. 11, 1958, in Kingston, Ont....Wiry, sharp-faced guy...Flyers drafted him in 1978 from WHA, using draft pick held by Rangers but forfeited by signing Fred Shero as coach while still legally under contract to Flyers.

Year	Club	GP	G	A	Pts.
1977-78	Birmingham (WHA) ...	71	38	38	76
1978-79	Philadelphia	30	5	20	25
1979-80	Philadelphia	80	22	57	79
1980-81	Philadelphia	51	17	30	47
1981-82	Philadelphia	79	24	68	92
	Totals	311	106	213	319

DARRYL SITTLER 32 6-0 190   Forward

Acquired midway through last season from Toronto...Veteran of 12 outstanding seasons with Maple Leafs who tired of playing for a dreadful team and demanded to be traded...Victim of constant criticism by Maple Leafs' outspoken owner Harold Ballard, despite valuable contributions he made to Maple Leafs and popularity among Toronto fans...One of hockey's best centers and most respected veterans...A welcome addition to Flyers...Born Sept. 18, 1950, in Kitchener, Ont....Holds most Toronto scoring records...Needs only 52 points to reach 1,000 for his career...Has two 100-point seasons to his credit...After slow start with Flyers, finished last season with 14 goals, 32 points in 35 games with Philadelphia.

Year	Club	GP	G	A	Pts.
1970-71	Toronto	49	10	8	18
1971-72	Toronto	74	15	17	32
1972-73	Toronto	78	29	48	77
1973-74	Toronto	78	38	46	84
1974-75	Toronto	72	36	44	80
1975-76	Toronto	79	41	59	100
1976-77	Toronto	73	38	52	90
1977-78	Toronto	80	45	72	117
1978-79	Toronto	70	36	51	87
1979-80	Toronto	73	40	57	97
1980-81	Toronto	80	43	53	96
1981-82	Tor.-Phil.	73	32	38	70
	Totals	879	403	545	948

RON FLOCKHART 22 5-11 175   Forward

Represents another of GM Keith Allen's smart decisions
... Overlooked in draft but signed by Flyers as free agent... Slow
developer who needed a season with Flyers' farm team in Maine
to fully adjust to the pro game ... Had an outstanding rookie season
with 33 goals, 72 points... More of a finesse player than some
of his overly physical teammates ... Developing into a steady two-
way center with ability to win faceoffs... Born Oct. 10, 1960,
in Smithers, B.C.... Younger brother of Rob Flockhart, who has
played for Minnesota and Vancouver.

Year	Club	GP	G	A	Pts.
1980-81	Philadelphia	14	3	7	10
1981-82	Philadelphia	72	33	39	72
	Totals	86	36	46	82

PAUL HOLMGREN 26 6-3 210   Forward

American-born right wing who played college hockey under
Ranger coach Herb Brooks at University of Minnesota ... A guard
and linebacker in high-school football with the size to make a
good tight end in pro football ... Opponents often complain that
he throws "blocks" and "tackles" on ice more suited for the gridiron
than a hockey rink ... One of the league's strongest men and most
feared fighters ... Awesome bodychecker and cornerman ... Showed
he has scoring skill with 30-goal season and 10 goals in 18 playoff
games in 1979-80 but limited to nine goals in 41 games during
injury-marred 1981–82 season ... Born Dec. 2, 1955, in St. Paul,
Minn.... Has 1,317 penalty minutes in only seven seasons with
Flyers ... Must learn to show more restraint and stop taking bad
penalties ... Was once suspended for shoving referee Andy Van
Hellemond.

Year	Club	GP	G	A	Pts.
1975-76	Minn. (WHA)-Phil.	52	14	16	30
1976-77	Philadelphia	59	14	12	26
1977-78	Philadelphia	62	16	18	34
1978-79	Philadelphia	57	19	10	29
1979-80	Philadelphia	74	30	35	65
1980-81	Philadelphia	77	22	37	59
1981-82	Philadelphia	41	9	22	31
	Totals	422	124	150	274

BEHN WILSON 23 6-3 215   Defenseman

Bright, introspective red-haired defenseman with fiery temper which often works against him...Widely criticized for hitting Rangers' Reijo Ruotsalainen in the face with the blade of his stick last season, an act which led to a suspension...Has the size and ability to become one of the league's most dominant defensemen but has yet to reach full potential...Must learn to control temper and play a more team-oriented game...Born Dec. 19, 1958, in Toronto...Excellent skater, shooter, puck-carrier and bodychecker...Tough man to beat in a fight...Studies economics in off-season at University of Toronto...Interested in dramatic acting...Not overly popular with fans and some rival players.

Year	Club	GP	G	A	Pts.
1978-79	Philadelphia	80	13	36	49
1979-80	Philadelphia	61	9	25	34
1980-81	Philadelphia	77	16	47	63
1981-82	Philadelphia	59	13	23	36
	Totals	277	51	131	182

JIMMY WATSON 30 6-0 190   Defenseman

Made comeback last season following back surgery which threatened to end his playing career...No longer able to play with as much mobility as before..."Jimmy showed a lot of courage last season after his operation and should be more effective this season," says Flyers' personnel director Marcel Pelletier...Starred with Flyers' Stanley Cup champion teams in 1974 and 1975...Friendly, cheerful athlete well-liked by teammates and the press for his enthusiasm and determination...Born Aug. 19, 1952, in Smithers, B.C....An outstanding rusher and two-way defenseman before undergoing surgery...Brother of former Flyers' defenseman Joe Watson, who now scouts for Flyers.

Year	Club	GP	G	A	Pts.
1972-73	Philadelphia	4	0	1	1
1973-74	Philadelphia	78	2	18	20
1974-75	Philadelphia	68	7	18	25
1975-76	Philadelphia	79	2	34	36
1976-77	Philadelphia	71	3	23	26
1977-78	Philadelphia	71	5	12	17
1978-79	Philadelphia	77	9	13	22
1979-80	Philadelphia	71	5	18	23
1980-81	Philadelphia	18	2	2	4
1981-82	Philadelphia	76	3	9	12
	Totals	613	38	148	186

PELLE LINDBERGH 23 5-9 160   Goaltender

Flyers finally will find out this season how good he is . . . Expected
to take over as No. 1 goalie for Pete Peeters, traded to Bruins in
June . . . Must beat out Rick St. Croix for No. 1 goaltending
job . . . Rated as potential star by many NHL scouts . . . Ranked as
one of Europe's best goalies while playing for Swedish National
Team and in 1980 Olympics . . . Flyers drafted him in
1979 . . . Smashing success in first pro season with Flyers' Maine
American League farm team in 1980-81 with 3.26 average, winning awards as AHL MVP, Rookie of Year and all-star
honors . . . Born May 24, 1959, in Stockholm, Sweden . . . Made
NHL debut last season and was shaky with 4.38 average in eight
games . . . Has outstanding shot anticipation, plays stand-up style
but has tendency of European goalies to stay back too far in
crease . . . "He can become a star," says former all-star goalie
Bernie Parent, who'll work with Lindbergh this season as Flyers'
new assistant coach.

Year	Club	GP	GA	SO	Avg.
1981-82	Philadelphia	8	35	0	4.38

COACH BOB McCAMMON: Neil Simon must have had him
in mind when he wrote the script for the play
and movie, "Chapter Two" . . . On his second
tour of duty coaching Flyers . . . Succeeded
Fred Shero as coach in 1978–79 but was de-
moted to Flyers' Maine farm team after only
50 games, despite a winning record (22-17-
11) . . . Flyers gave him a second chance as
coach last season when, with only eight games
remaining in regular season, they dismissed Pat Quinn as coach
and promoted McCammon again from minor leagues . . . Rallied
slumping Flyers to 4-2-2 record . . . Also given title of assistant
general manager . . . Born April 14, 1941, in Kenora, Ont. . . . Has
outstanding record as coach in International and American
Leagues, winning four championships in nine years . . . Spent 13
years as minor-league defenseman, mostly in International
League . . . Vocal, enthusiastic coach behind bench . . . Has developed
many of Flyers' younger players with Maine minor-league team.

Rick St. Croix will vie with Pelle Lindbergh for net spot.

GREATEST CENTER

Few players in hockey history have overcome greater adversity to reach stardom than Bobby Clarke, the Flyers' inspirational leader and perhaps the hardest working player in the last decade.

"Bobby Clarke is the sort of player who would do well in any era of the game, today or in the old days," said Gordie Howe, highest-scoring player in the history of the game. "He's a natural-born leader."

For 13 seasons, the slender, blond center known to teammates as "Clarkie" has been an unrelenting checker and playmaker for the Flyers, showing the hustle and determination and fierce pride in winning that Pete Rose has shown in baseball.

He almost didn't get the chance, despite a brilliant junior career with the Flin Flon Bombers. Clarke has been a diabetic since boyhood. Doctors suggested that it would be difficult for him to expect to successfully make a career in professional sports, especially one so physically demanding as hockey. Most scouts didn't believe he would have enough stamina to last in the NHL, so he was not chosen by an NHL team until the second round of the 1969 amateur draft.

His diabetic condition has never been a problem during a brilliant career in which he has won acclaim as one of the best all-around centers the modern game has known. He has served as Flyers' team captain and assistant coach, has scored more than 1,000 points in his career, and has helped the Flyers win two Stanley Cups. He's 33 now and his scoring production has slipped but he still plays hard and aggressively.

ALL-TIME FLYER LEADERS

GOALS: Reggie Leach, 61, 1975-76
ASSISTS: Bobby Clarke, 89, 1974-75, 1975-76
POINTS: Bobby Clarke, 119, 1975-76
SHUTOUTS: Bernie Parent, 12, 1973-74, 1974-75

PITTSBURGH PENGUINS

TEAM DIRECTORY: Owner: Edward DeBartolo; GM: Baz Bastien; Dir. Player Personnel: Ken Schinkel; Dir. Media Relations: Terry Schiffhauer; Coach: Ed Johnston. Home ice: Civic Arena (16,033; 200' × 85'). Training camp: Pittsburgh and Erie, Pa.

SCOUTING REPORT

OFFENSE: The Penguins have an awesome power play, scoring an NHL-record 99 goals with manpower advantages last season. Trouble is, they don't score as consistently in even-strength situations and that mystifies coach Ed Johnston. "We're capable of scoring more goals than we do," he says.

One problem is that Penguins' forwards don't always apply sufficient forechecking pressure against opponents to force giveaways and create scoring chances. Penguins' forwards aren't noted, either, for their backchecking or overall team defense as a group and often are beaten in puck control and offensive rushes.

Rick Kehoe, Mike Bullard and Paul Gardner are dangerous scoring threats among the forwards, producing 106 goals, 48 on

Michel Dion almost stunned the Islanders in the playoffs.

power plays, last season. But then the goal-scoring drops off drastically. Pat Boutette is an energetic force in front of the net and in the corners and George Ferguson has a reputation for scoring important goals.

The Penguins need more goal-scoring from players such as Greg Malone, Rick MacLeish and Rod Schutt. They ranked a poor 15th in offense last season and must improve to be more successful this season.

DEFENSE: Randy Carlyle, a former Norris Trophy winner as the league's outstanding defenseman, is a catalyst, as vital to the Penguins as Denis Potvin is to the Islanders. He's an excellent rusher and playmaker and one of the best as a power-play pointman but his occasional defensive lapses hurt the team. Paul Baxter and Pat Price accumulated 729 penalty minutes between them but are developing into competent defensemen.

The Penguins don't have much depth on defense behind the hard-hitting Baxter and Price. They must upgrade positional play in their defensive zone, as well as reducing giveaways caused by careless puck-clearing and vulnerability to enemy forechecking. The penalty-killing was shabby last season: 92 power-play goals against in 398 shorthanded situations, the most in the league. Obviously, Pittsburgh's aggressive style of play sometimes works to its disadvantage.

Goaltender Michel Dion was brilliant last season, the master of making seemingly impossible, spectacular saves. He played in 62 games and was in net for 25 of the team's 31 wins. If he gets better support in 1982-83, the Penguins could rise in the standings.

OUTLOOK: Defenseman Mario Faubert missed most of last season with a broken leg and his return should help the team. The Penguins made some progress last season but not as much as expected. They finished second in penalty minutes in the NHL and must eliminate taking needless penalties. The team is well-coached but continues to struggle on the road. They finished 12th in the league in 1981-82 and in 14 years in the NHL have had only four winning records. They should make it five this year if their offense picks up.

PENGUIN PROFILES

RICK KEHOE 31 5-11 180   Forward
Second-highest scorer in Penguins' history with 524 points, trailing leader Jean Pronovost by only 79 points...Goal-scoring

PENGUIN ROSTER

No.	Player	Pos.	Hgt.	Wgt.	Born	1981-82	G	A	Pts.	PIM
4	Paul Baxter	D	5-11	205	10-28-55/Winnipeg, Man.	Pittsburgh	9	34	43	407
	John Bednarski	D	5-10	185	7-4-52/Thunder Bay, Ont.	Erie	9	30	39	61
15	Pat Boutette	RW	5-8	180	3-1-52/Windsor, Ont.	Pittsburgh	23	51	74	230
22	Mike Bullard	C	5-10	185	3-10-61/Ottawa, Ont.	Pittsburgh	37	27	64	91
25	Randy Carlyle	D	5-10	200	4-19-56/Sudbury, Ont.	Pittsburgh	11	64	75	131
16	Marc Chorney	D	6-0	200	11-8-59/Edmonton, Alta.	Pittsburgh	1	6	7	63
						Erie	1	3	4	4
5	Mario Faubert	D	6-1	175	12-2-54/Valleyfield, Que.	Pittsburgh	4	8	12	14
	Tony Feltrin	D	6-1	195	12-6-61/Nanaimo, B.C.	Pittsburgh	0	0	0	4
						Erie	4	13	17	115
11	George Ferguson	C	6-0	190	8-22-52/Trenton, Ont.	Pittsburgh	22	31	53	45
20	Paul Gardner	C	6-0	195	3-5-56/Toronto, Ont.	Pittsburgh	36	33	69	28
	Rob Garner	RW	5-11	180	8-17-58/Weston, Ont.	Erie	25	27	52	62
26	Steve Gatzos	RW	5-11	182	6-22-61/Toronto, Ont.	Pittsburgh	6	8	14	14
						Erie	18	19	37	67
	Jim Hamilton	RW	6-0	180	1-18-57/Barrie, Ont.	Pittsburgh	5	3	8	2
						Erie	27	17	44	51
6	Greg Hotham	D	5-11	185	3-9-56/London, Ont.	Tor.-Pitts.	4	6	10	16
						Cincinnati	10	33	43	94
17	Rick Kehoe	RW	5-11	180	7-15-51/Windsor, Ont.	Pittsburgh	33	52	85	8
10	Peter Lee	RW	5-10	174	1-2-56/Ellesbro, Eng.	Pittsburgh	18	16	34	98
7	Rick MacLeish	C-LW	5-11	185	1-3-50/Cunningham, Ont.	Hart.-Pitt.	19	28	47	44
12	Greg Malone	C	6-0	190	3-8-56/Fredericton, N.B.	Pittsburgh	15	24	39	125
2	Pat Price	D	6-2	205	3-24-55/Nelson, B.C.	Pittsburgh	7	31	38	322
23	Gary Rissling	LW	5-9	169	8-18-56/Saskatoon, Sask.	Erie	7	15	22	185
						Pittsburgh	0	0	0	55
34	Andre St. Laurent	C	5-10	168	2-16-53/Rouyn, Que.	LA-Pitt.	10	9	19	32
						New Haven	7	9	16	58
27	Rod Schutt	LW	5-9	185	10-13-56/Bancroft, Ont.	Pittsburgh	8	12	20	42
						Erie	12	15	27	40
	Doug Sheddon	C	6-0	184	4-26-61/Wallaceburg, Ont.	Pittsburgh	10	15	25	12
						Erie	4	6	10	14
28	Bobby Simpson	LW	6-0	190	11-17-56/Caughnawaga, Que.	Pittsburgh	9	9	18	4
						Erie	25	23	48	45
3	Ron Stackhouse	D	6-3	185	8-26-49/Haliburton, Ont.	Pittsburgh	2	19	21	102
	Rick Sutter	RW	5-11	170	12-2-63/Viking, Alta.	Lethbridge	38	31	69	263
16	Bennett Wolf	D	6-3	205	10-23-59/Kitchener, Ont.	Pittsburgh	0	0	0	2
						Erie	0	4	4	148

No.	Player	Pos.	Hgt.	Wgt.	Born	1981-82	GP	GA	SO	Avg.
29	Michel Dion	G	5-10	185	2-11-54/Granby, Que.	Pittsburgh	62	226	0	3.79
30	Gary Edwards	G	5-10	165	10-5-47/Toronto, Ont.	St. L.-Pitt.	16	67	1	4.21
	Gord Laxton	G	5-10	175	3-16-55/Montreal, Que.	Erie	31	172	0	6.17
	Nick Ricci	G	5-10	160	6-3-59/Niagara Falls, Ont.	Pittsburgh	3	14	0	5.25
						Erie	40	175	0	4.66

dropped from team-record 55 goals in 1980–81 to 33 last season but achieved career high of 52 assists and again led Penguins in scoring within 85 points . . . One of the best in the league at scoring power-play goals . . . Quick-moving right wing with scoring ability from close to net or on long-range shots from slot, blue line or faceoff circles . . . Born July 15, 1951, in Windsor, Ont. . . . Started NHL career in 1971–72 with Maple Leafs, who made a major mistake by trading him to Pittsburgh . . . Scored in overtime to beat Islanders in playoff game last season . . . Member of elite 300-goal club with 324 career goals.

Year	Club	GP	G	A	Pts.
1971-72	Toronto	38	8	8	16
1972-73	Toronto	77	33	42	75
1973-74	Toronto	69	18	22	40
1974-75	Pittsburgh	76	32	31	63
1975-76	Pittsburgh	71	29	47	76
1976-77	Pittsburgh	80	30	27	57
1977-78	Pittsburgh	70	29	21	50
1978-79	Pittsburgh	57	27	18	45
1979-80	Pittsburgh	79	30	30	60
1980-81	Pittsburgh	80	55	33	88
1981-82	Pittsburgh	71	33	52	85
	Totals	768	324	331	655

RANDY CARLYLE 26 6-10 200   Defenseman

Another player Maple Leafs regret trading to Pittsburgh . . . Outstanding rushing, scoring, playmaking defenseman who was named to all-star team and won Norris Trophy as hockey's leading defenseman in 1980–81 . . . Blue-line leader of Pittsburgh's dangerous power play . . . Holds virtually every major scoring record for Penguin defensemen and has assisted on 131 goals in last two seasons . . . "Offensively, he's as good as any defenseman there is in the game," says the Rangers' Barry Beck . . . Born April 19, 1956, in Sudbury, Ont. . . . Rugged player who plays a physical game . . . Gifted passer when leading rushes through center ice . . . Some rivals question his skills under forechecking pressure in defensive zone . . . Crowd favorite among critical Pittsburgh fans.

Year	Club	GP	G	A	Pts.
1976-77	Toronto	45	0	5	5
1977-78	Toronto	49	2	11	13
1978-79	Pittsburgh	70	13	34	47
1979-80	Pittsburgh	67	8	28	36
1980-81	Pittsburgh	76	16	67	83
1981-82	Pittsburgh	73	11	64	75
	Totals	380	50	209	259

PAUL GARDNER 26 6-0 195   **Forward**

Victim of sneak attack by Winnipeg's Jimmy (The Ox) Mann . . . Suffered broken jaw and missed 21 games from incident in which Mann was suspended and charged with assault . . . "It was sickening to watch what Mann did to him and losing Gardner for so long hurt our club," says Penguins' coach Ed Johnston . . . Still scored 36 goals and 69 points in 59 games and led league with 21 power-play goals . . . Another of several former Maple Leafs who have helped Penguins become a force within NHL . . . Born March 5, 1956, in Fort Erie, Ont. . . . Elusive, smooth-skating center with natural goal-scoring instincts . . . Extremely accurate shooter who scored on 22.9 per cent of his shots last season . . . Son of former NHL star Cal Gardner.

Year	Club	GP	G	A	Pts.
1976-77	Colorado	60	30	29	59
1977-78	Colorado	46	30	22	52
1978-79	Colo.-Tor.	65	30	28	58
1979-80	Toronto	45	11	13	24
1980-81	Pittsburgh	62	34	40	74
1981-82	Pittsburgh	59	36	33	69
	Totals	337	171	165	336

PAT BOUTETTE 30 5-8 180   **Forward**

Rivals complain about the feisty, tough left wing because of his aggressive style of play and willingness to hit and be hit in corners and along boards . . . Penguins acquired him from Hartford as compensation for signing of free-agent goalie Greg Millen in 1981 . . . Nicknamed "Bash" . . . Played college hockey at University of Minnesota of Duluth . . . Born March 1, 1952, in Windsor, Ont. . . . Another former Maple Leaf on Penguins' roster . . . At his best in the rough-going in front of the net . . . Always willing to fight . . . Led Penguins' forwards with 230 penalty minutes last season and has spent 985 minutes in penalty box in eight-year NHL career.

Year	Club	GP	G	A	Pts.
1975-76	Toronto	77	10	22	32
1976-77	Toronto	80	18	18	36
1977-78	Toronto	80	17	19	36
1978-79	Toronto	80	14	19	33
1979-80	Tor.-Hart.	79	13	35	48
1980-81	Hartford	80	28	52	80
1981-82	Pittsburgh	80	23	51	74
	Totals	556	123	216	339

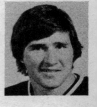

MIKE BULLARD 21 5-10 185   Forward

General Manager Baz Bastien made a smart choice when Penguins selected young, all-around center in first round of 1980 draft...Made a good showing in 1980–81 playoffs and followed that up with 37-goal rookie season...The fifth most accurate shooter in NHL in 1981–82, scoring on 24.8 per cent of his shots...Scored 156 goals, 356 points in 174 games in brilliant three-year career with Brantford in Ontario Junior Hockey Association...Finished first NHL season with minus-1 rating, outstanding in that Penguins surrendered 27 more goals than they scored...Born March 10, 1961, in Ottawa, Ont....Led Pittsburgh with five game-winning goals...Difficult for opponents to check and doesn't back away from physical aspect of play.

Year	Club	GP	G	A	Pts.
1980-81	Pittsburgh	15	1	2	3
1981-82	Pittsburgh	75	37	27	64
	Totals	90	38	29	67

PAUL BAXTER 26 5-11 205   Defenseman

Led NHL with 407 penalty minutes last season...An antagonizing player opponents often accuse of stirring up trouble verbally and with his rough style of play...Caused Rangers' Barry Beck to lose his cool and leave his bench to fight, resulting in suspension that angered Rangers...Challenged Rangers' tough Nick Fotiu and more than held his own in short but furious scrap...A much better defenseman than some people give him credit for being...Born Oct. 25, 1956, in Winnipeg...Originally drafted by Penguins in 1975 but played four years for Quebec in WHA before joining Penguins as a free agent in 1980–81 season...Has 1,742 penalty minutes in eight seasons of pro hockey.

Year	Club	GP	G	A	Pts.
1974-75	Cleveland (WHA)	5	0	0	0
1975-76	Cleveland (WHA)	67	3	7	10
1976-77	Quebec (WHA)	66	6	17	23
1977-78	Quebec (WHA)	76	6	29	35
1978-79	Quebec (WHA)	76	10	36	46
1979-80	Quebec	61	7	13	20
1980-81	Pittsburgh	51	5	14	19
1981-82	Pittsburgh	76	9	34	43
	Totals	478	46	150	196

PAT PRICE 27 6-2 205   Defenseman

Joins Baxter of the other half of the Penguins' "mean-team" defense... Served 322 minutes in penalties last year... "Pat made big improvements in his overall play last season," says Pittsburgh assistant coach Mike Corrigan, a former NHL forward... "I finally feel I've got my game together and am with a team that appreciates what I can do," says Price, who played with Islanders and Edmonton, in WHA and minor leagues before fully establishing himself last season... Born March 24, 1955, in Nelson, B.C.... A former No. 1 draft choice of Stanley Cup champion Islanders... Plays a defensive style of game and enjoys bodychecking but has scoring ability, too.

Year	Club	GP	G	A	Pts.
1974-75	Vancouver (WHA)	68	5	29	34
1975-76	New York I.	4	0	2	2
1976-77	New York I.	71	3	22	25
1977-78	New York I.	52	2	10	12
1978-79	New York I.	55	3	11	14
1979-80	Edmonton	75	11	21	32
1980-81	Edm.-Pitt.	63	8	34	42
1981-82	Pittsburgh	77	7	31	38
	Totals	465	39	160	199

GREG MALONE 26 6-0 190   Forward

Penguins still waiting for potentially high-quality center to regain form he snowed in 1978−79 as 35-goal scorer... Had modest 15-goal season in 1981−82 in comeback from a serious knee injury... More of a playmaking center than a goal-scorer and holds Penguins' record of six assists in one game... Was Penguins' second-round draft choice in 1976... Born March 8, 1956, in Chatham, N.B.... Mentioned in trade rumors in past but Penguins still have faith in his ability to reach full potential... Has good scoring touch close to net and has ability to win faceoffs... Older brother of Jim Malone, Rangers' first draft choice in 1980... Rangers have expressed interest in acquiring him in trade.

Year	Club	GP	G	A	Pts.
1976-77	Pittsburgh	66	18	19	37
1977-78	Pittsburgh	78	18	43	61
1978-79	Pittsburgh	80	35	30	65
1979-80	Pittsburgh	51	19	32	51
1980-81	Pittsburgh	62	21	29	50
1981-82	Pittsburgh	78	15	24	39
	Totals	415	126	177	303

RICK MacLEISH 32 5-11 185   Forward

Twelve-year NHL veteran who starred during 11 seasons with Flyers . . . A 50-goal, 100-point scorer with Philadelphia in 1972–73 and member of Flyers' Stanley Cup championship teams in 1974 and 1975 . . . Traded by Flyers to Hartford after 1980–81 season and traded again to Pittsburgh midway through last season . . . Has scored 339 career goals . . . Didn't adjust well to trading and scored only 19 times last season, his poorest production in NHL career . . . Penguins confident he'll regain his form this season . . . Born Jan. 3, 1950, in Lindsay, Ont. . . . A natural skater with great speed and blazing wrist and slap shots . . . Low-key chap who takes everything in stride . . . Equally at home at center or left wing.

Year	Club	GP	G	A	Pts.
1970-71	Philadelphia	26	2	4	6
1971-72	Philadelphia	17	1	2	3
1972-73	Philadelphia	78	50	50	100
1973-74	Philadelphia	78	32	45	77
1974-75	Philadelphia	80	38	41	79
1975-76	Philadelphia	51	22	23	45
1976-77	Philadelphia	79	49	48	97
1977-78	Philadelphia	76	31	39	70
1978-79	Philadelphia	71	26	32	58
1979-80	Philadelphia	78	31	35	66
1980-81	Philadelphia	78	38	36	74
1981-82	Hart.-Pitt.	74	19	28	47
	Totals	786	339	383	722

MICHEL DION 28 5-10 185   Goaltender

Soared to prominence last season with spectacular play for team not always noted for its defensive work . . . Was brilliant in playoff loss to champion Islanders, making a profusion of seemingly impossible saves . . . "Dion was simply unbelievable," said coach Ed Johnston, a former prominent NHL goalie . . . Was chosen to play in 1982 All-Star Game . . . Ironman goalie who played in 62 games and accounted for 25 of Pittsburgh's 31 wins . . . Lightning-fast reflexes enable him to make spectacular saves in goal-mouth scrambles and on second and third rebounds following initial shot . . . "Dion's unreal on breakaways," said Rangers' Ron Duguay after Dion robbed him of goals on three breakaways in game last season . . . Born Feb. 11, 1954, in Granby, Quebec . . . Penguins made smart move signing him as free agent when Greg Millen signed with Hartford as free agent . . . Former star in WHA.

Year	Club	GP	GA	SO	Avg.
1974-75	Indianapolis (WHA) ...	1	4	0	4.00
1975-76	Indianapolis (WHA) ...	31	85	0	2.74
1976-77	Indianapolis (WHA) ...	42	128	1	3.36
1977-78	Cincinnati (WHA)	45	140	4	3.57
1978-79	Cincinnati (WHA)	30	93	0	3.32
1979-80	Quebec	50	171	2	3.70
1980-81	Que.-Winn.	26	122	0	5.07
1981-82	Pittsburgh	62	226	0	3.79
	Totals	287	969	7	3.62

COACH ED JOHNSTON: "E.J." ... Good guy who is well-liked and respected by all who have known him in long NHL career ... Spent 16 years in NHL as goaltender with Boston, Toronto, St. Louis and Chicago ... Last NHL goalie to play in every game, appearing in all 70 games for 1963-64 Bruins ... Member of Bruins' Stanley Cup championship teams of 1970 and 1972 ... Win or lose, always easygoing, approachable and helpful in post-game press interviews after game, as a goalie and as a coach ... Easy-going manner hides fact that he's intense and high-strung during games ... Born Nov. 24, 1935, in Montreal ... Fair but firm coach players enjoy working for ... Did outstanding job as Chicago coach in 1979-80 but was victimized by management politics ... Named Penguins' coach July 15, 1980 ... Gaining reputation among fellow coaches as smart tactician and motivator of palyers ... With 95-100-45 record in three years as NHL coach, needs five wins to reach 100 for career.

GREATEST CENTER

Syl Apps Jr. never gained the acclaim of his famous father, Hockey Hall of Fame member Syl Apps Sr., who started with the Toronto Maple Leafs from 1936 to 1948. But when Penguins' fans relive the past, they recall the younger Apps as the team's most effective center since the city gained an NHL franchise in 1967.

Apps spent eight seasons with the Penguins from 1970 to 1978, establishing himself as a gifted playmaking center who played hard but clean hockey. He set up his wings for shots with accurate passes better than any center the Penguins have had.

His most memorable game was March 24, 1971, when he tied the NHL record with four assists in one period, the third period of an 8-2 conquest of Detroit. He set a Penguins' record of six points in one game Dec. 13, 1972, scoring three goals and assisting on three others against the Islanders.

A slender, dark-haired athlete who played hockey at Princeton University, Apps' best years with the Penguins were the seasons from 1972-73 through 1975-76, when he set a team record with 67 assists.

Apps was acquired by Pittsburgh Jan. 26, 1971, in a trade with the Rangers for Glen Sather. The Penguins traded him to Los Angeles as part of a 1977 trade for Dave Schultz. He retired after the 1979-80 season. He is the third-highest career scorer in Penguins' history and his 349 career assists are a Pittsburgh record. He scored 151 goals and 500 points in 495 games as a Penguin.

ALL-TIME PENGUIN LEADERS

GOALS: Rick Kehoe, 55, 1980-81
ASSISTS: Syl Apps, 67, 1975-76
          Randy Carlyle, 67, 1980-81
POINTS: Pierre Larouche, 111, 1975-76
SHUTOUTS: Les Binkley, 6, 1967-68

QUEBEC NORDIQUES

TEAM DIRECTORY: Pres.: Marcel Aubut; GM: Maurice Filion; Asst. GM: Martin Madden; Dir. Player Per.: Gilles Leger; Dir. Pub. Rel.: Marius Fortier; Coach: Michel Bergeron. Home ice: Quebec Coliseum (15,153; 200′ × 85′). Colors: Blue, white and red. Training camp: Quebec City, Que.

SCOUTING REPORT

OFFENSE: The Nordiques play games that end up like the scores of lacrosse contests. They win 9-2 or they lose 8-6 and all the time they are terribly inconsistent, however exciting. They could be ready to change. While enjoying their stunning drive to the

Nordique Czech-mates: The flying Stastny brothers.

Stanley Cup semifinals, the Nordiques learned that defense is a part of the game, too. That could make them dangerous. Their offense already stacks up as a fearsome collection of snipers.

Peter Stastny, merely one of the best centers in the world, had an eye-opening 139 points last season. He was one of five 30-goal scorers and, simply, a rage at times. But he doesn't do it alone and that makes the Nordiques a lightning-quick and well-balanced team. There are his brothers Anton and Marian, Real Cloutier and Michel Goulet, who might be one of the most underrated wings in the game.

The addition of Wilf Paiement's size didn't hurt the Nordiques and if Dale Hunter ever learns to use his stick for something besides an axe, he could be a help, too. So deep are the Nordiques with the likes of Marc Tardif that Jacques Richard, a 50-goal scorer the year before, couldn't crack the lineup much of the time last season. That's what 356 goals, the fourth highest total in the NHL, can do.

Where the Nordiques' attack is tender is their ability to wear down opponents. Many of the forwards are lean and frail. Although some players try to be aggressive, there aren't enough of them. Usually, players such as a Hunter just get the Nordiques in trouble with penalties that keep Quebec off its own power-play, which happens to be among the league's best.

DEFENSE: Okay, 345 goals against does not look good, but Quebec's defense really shouldn't be as bad as it looks. Dave Pichette handles the puck well and Mario Marois is exceedingly tough and absolutely fearless. Old hand Andre Dupont isn't quite the player he used to be, but he adds size and physical play.

Still, the Nordiques need help. Their positional play leaves a lot to be desired and there really isn't one scoring threat from the blueline corps. Wally Weir is strong and a good checker, but the Nordiques are going to have to find consistency from players such as Jean Hamel, Gaston Therrien or Normand Rochefort, who was a surprise in the playoffs. Maybe Michel Petit, the team's first-round draft choice, will help. If that can be accomplished, Quebec's potential could be limitless. The defense has to learn to stand up to pressure, rather than wilt under it. There are times when their poise melts like an ice cream cone in August.

Goaltender Dan Bouchard shoulders the blame for the holes in the defense and sometimes he doesn't even do that. Bouchard played well in the early playoff rounds, not so well in the later rounds and therein is the story of his career. Backup John Garrett is bright, witty and quotable and the Nordiques might be depending on him more this season.

NORDIQUE ROSTER

No.	Player	Pos.	Hgt.	Wgt.	Born	1981-82	G	A	Pts.	PIM
14	Pierre Aubry	C	5-10	195	4-15-60/Cape de la Madeline, Que.	Quebec	10	13	23	27
						Fredericton	6	5	11	10
9	Real Cloutier	RW	5-10	185	7-30-56/St. Emile, Que.	Quebec	37	60	97	34
19	Alain Cote	LW	5-10	203	5-3-47/Matone, Que.	Quebec	15	16	31	82
15	Richard David	LW	6-2	205	4-8-58/N.D. dela Salette, Que.	Quebec	1	1	2	4
						Fredericton	51	32	83	18
28	Andre Dupont	D	6-0	205	7-27-49/Three Rivers, Que.	Quebec	4	12	16	100
	Jere Gillis	LW	6-1	190	1-18-57/Bend, Que.	Rang-Que.	5	10	15	16
						Fredericton	2	17	19	10
16	Michel Goulet	LW	6-1	195	4-21-60/Perihonqua, Que.	Quebec	42	42	84	48
4	Jean Hamel	D	5-11	182	6-6-52/Asbestos, Que.	Quebec	1	6	7	32
						Fredericton	2	4	6	19
17	Pat Hickey	LW	5-10	170	3-8-55/Toronto, Ont.	Rang.-Que.	15	15	30	36
33	Dale Hoganson	D	5-10	180	7-8-49/N. Battleford, Sask.	Quebec	0	6	6	16
						Fredericton	2	4	6	18
32	Dale Hunter	C	5-9	187	7-31-60/Oil Springs, Ont.	Quebec	22	50	72	272
	Terry Johnson	D	6-3	210	11-28-58/Calgary, Alta.	Fredericton	0	6	6	135
						Quebec	0	1	1	5
25	Pierre Lacroix	D	5-11	185	4-11-59/Quebec City, Que.	Quebec	4	23	27	74
22	Mario Marois	D	5-11	170	12-15-57/Lovette, Que.	Quebec	11	32	43	161
11	Basil McRae	LW	6-2	199	1-5-61/Beaverton, Ont.	Quebec	4	3	7	69
						Fredericton	11	15	26	175
	Randy Moller	D	6-2	205	8-23-63/Calgary, Alta.	Quebec	0	0	0	0
27	Wilf Paiement	RW	6-1	205	10-16-55/Earlton, Ont.	Tor.-Quebec	25	46	71	221
29	Dave Pichette	D	6-3	192	2-4-60/Grand Falls, N.S.	Quebec	7	30	37	152
23	Jacques Richard	LW	5-11	175	10-7-52/Quebec City, Que.	Quebec	26	41	77	77
5	Normand Rochefort	D	6-1	200	1-28-61/Trois Riveres, Que.	Quebec	4	14	18	115
20	Anton Stastny	LW	5-9	175	8-5-59/Bratislava, Czech.	Quebec	26	46	72	16
18	Marian Stastny	RW	5-10	193	1-8-53/Bratislava, Czech.	Quebec	35	54	89	27
26	Peter Stastny	C	5-10	190	9-18-56/Bratislava, Czech.	Quebec	46	93	139	91
	Christian Tanguay	C	5-10	190	8-4-62/Beauport, Que.	Quebec	0	0	0	0
						Trois Riveres	52	55	107	27
8	Marc Tardif	LW	6-1	180	6-12-49/Granby, Que.	Quebec	39	31	70	55
10	Gaston Therrien	D	5-10	196	5-27-60/Montreal, Que.	Fredericton	11	42	53	75
						Quebec	0	7	7	6
	Tim Tookey	C	5-11	185	8-29-60/Edmonton, Alta.	Washington	8	8	16	35
						Hershey-Fred.	10	19	29	26
2	Wally Weir	D	6-2	195	6-3-54/Verdun, Que.	Quebec	3	5	8	173

No.	Player	Pos.	Hgt.	Wgt.	Born		GP	GA	SO	Avg.
35	Dan Bouchard	G	6-0	185	12-12-50/Val D'Or, Que.	Quebec	60	230	1	3.86
1	John Garrett	G	5-8	175	6-17-51/Toronto, Ont.	Quebec-Hart.	28	125	0	4.75
	Clint Malarchuk	G	5-10	165	5-1-61/Edmonton, Alta.	Quebec	2	14	0	7.00
						Fredericton	51	253	0	5.12

OUTLOOK: The Nordiques are a team going somewhere, but how quickly they arrive at that destination is a matter for coach Michel Bergeron to study. The way the team can pour shots at opponents often relieves pressure from a questionable defense. But even a questionable defense has to have answers once in a while. If the Nordiques reply in the right fashion, another berth in the semifinals is certainly not out of the question. But if the Nordiques insist on relying on their mecurial offense, the season, like Bergeron's temper, will be short.

NORDIQUE PROFILES

PETER STASTNY 26 5-10 190   **Forward**
Peter the Great...Extraordinary playmaker who is certified as one of top centers in the world...Was league's third-leading scorer behind only Wayne Gretzky and Mike Bossy...Set club records with 93 assists and 139 points...Also led team with 16 power-play goals...Made headlines with brother Anton after defection from Czechoslovakia before 1980–81 season...Born Sept. 18, 1956, in Bratislava, Czechoslovakia...Was Calder Trophy winner after setting rookie record with 109 points...The middle-aged of the three Stasny brothers, but the one teammates call "The Boss"...Doesn't mind playing hard-nosed North American style...Had eight-point game against Washington, Feb. 22, 1981.

Year	Club	GP	G	A	Pts.
1980-81	Quebec	79	39	70	109
1981-82	Quebec	80	46	93	139
	Totals	159	85	163	248

ANTON STASTNY 23 5-9 175   **Forward**
Baby brother...Always smiling...Big practical joker...Plays Costello to Peter's Abbott...Along with Peter, set NHL record for most points (16) in one game by two brothers...Quick and has lightning shot...Former member of Czechoslovakian National Team...Terrific one-on-one...Even terrific one-on-two...Born Aug. 5, 1959, in Bratislava, Czechoslovakia...Already one of the best left wings around...Looks more like

Marian than Peter . . . Once pretended to be reporter, standing with newspapermen who were interviewing Peter . . . Takes pass on his backhand as well as anyone . . . Best acceleration of all three brothers . . . Is deadly accurate . . . Will only get better . . . Extremely popular with teammates and fans.

Year	Club	GP	G	A	Pts.
1980-81	Quebec	80	39	46	85
1981-82	Quebec	68	26	46	72
	Totals	148	65	92	157

MARIAN STASTNY 29 5-10 193   Forward

Three's a charm . . . Joined Peter and Anton on a line after defecting from Czechoslovakia . . . Helped arranged his brothers' defections but remained home with family . . . Punished by being kicked off National Team . . . Publicly denounced brothers in ruse to win confidence of government officials . . . Made home improvements, luring officials into thinking he wouldn't defect . . . Vacationed in other East Bloc countries, then skipped with wife and three children to Austria and on to Canada . . . Born Jan. 8, 1953, in Bratislava, Czechoslovakia . . . Played right wing for Peter and Anton much of the season . . . Played well in first-round upset of Montreal . . . Had 13 power-play goals during season . . . Oldest of the three Stastnys . . . Owns bar outside Quebec named Dix-Huit . . . That's French for 18, his number.

Year	Club	GP	G	A	Pts.
1981-82	Quebec	74	35	54	89

MICHEL GOULET 22 6-1 195   Forward

Michel, my belle . . . Exciting left wing who knows how to put puck in the net . . . Players say he could shoot a gold ball through a doughnut . . . Exceptional skater who is a dangerous penalty killer . . . Tied for league lead with six shorthanded goals . . . Added two more shorthanded goals in playoffs . . . Led team with five game-tying goals and plus-minus figure of plus-36...Third in scoring and first in thrill-a-minute skating...Especially important to power-play unit...Born April 21, 1960, in Peribonqua, Que....Debuted as 18-year-old in WHA with Birmingham Bulls...Was first player to sign a contract that was written in French...Tailor-made for Nordiques' weaving, curling offense...Dangerous with the puck and without it...Stronger than he looks...Good instinct and superior anticipation.

Year	Club	GP	G	A	Pts.
1978-79	Birmingham (WHA) ...	78	28	30	58
1979-80	Quebec	77	22	32	54
1980-81	Quebec	76	32	39	71
1981-82	Quebec	80	42	42	84
	Totals	311	124	143	267

DANIEL BOUCHARD 31 6-0 185   Goaltender

Dandy Dan...Experienced goalie who has found home with Nordiques...Rapped throughout career for nonchalance...Had only three career playoff wins entering last season...Equalled that in one series when Nordiques upset Montreal in first round...Has got religion...Began career with Atlanta...Hot temper and moodiness made him unpopular with teammates as he was quick to blame others for losses...Born Dec. 12, 1950, in Val D'Or, Que....Traded by Calgary midway through '80–81 season...Lost only five of 29 games the rest of way for Nordiques...Played in 60 games last season...Finished second in league with 27 wins...Still terribly inconsistent...Moves like Tony Esposito one game and Tony Orlando the next...Has two favorite words for reporters: "No comment."

Year	Club	GP	GA	SO	Avg.
1972-73	Atlanta	34	100	2	3.09
1973-74	Atlanta	46	123	5	2.77
1974-75	Atlanta	40	111	3	2.77
1975-76	Atlanta	47	113	2	2.54
1976-77	Atlanta	42	139	1	3.51
1977-78	Atlanta	58	153	2	2.75
1978-79	Atlanta	64	201	3	3.33
1979-80	Atlanta	53	163	2	3.18
1980-81	Calg.-Que.	43	143	2	3.43
1981-82	Quebec	60	230	1	3.86
	Totals	487	1476	23	3.14

ANDRE DUPONT 33 6-0 205   Defenseman

Still "The Moose"...Large arms, large shoulders, large head...Tough, aggressive and mean when he wants to be...Had added needed strength to porous defense...Made name for himself on Flyer teams that won two straight Stanley Cups...Ranks fourth in career penalty minutes...Had a mere 100 last season, lowest total in years...Named team captain in 1981 because of leadership qualities...Toiled in minors and let go by Rangers...Played in St. Louis but developed under Fred Shero in Philadelphia...Born July 27, 1949, in Trois Rivieres, Que....Doesn't score much, but that's not his game anyway...Getting older and not as crushing a checker as he used to be...Gets by on experience and persistence...Just a good guy to have around.

Year	Club	GP	G	A	Pts.
1970-71	New York R.	7	1	2	3
1971-72	St. Louis	60	3	10	13
1972-73	St.L.-Phil.	71	4	26	30
1973-74	Philadelphia	75	3	20	23
1974-75	Philadelphia	80	11	21	32
1975-76	Philadelphia	75	9	27	36
1976-77	Philadelphia	69	10	19	29
1977-78	Philadelphia	69	2	12	14
1978-79	Philadelphia	77	3	9	12
1979-80	Philadelphia	58	1	7	8
1980-81	Quebec	63	5	8	13
1981-82	Quebec	60	4	12	16
	Totals	764	56	173	229

JACQUES RICHARD 30 5-11 175   Forward

Was comedown player of the year after being comeback player of the year...Missed 21 games due to injury and poor play...Used to be known as King Richard...Hardly played in playoffs and was bitter about it...The fall came just a year after the rise...Was team's leading scorer in his first full season after being obtained from Buffalo...That ended intriguing odyssey...Was second player (behind Billy Harris) selected in 1972 amateur draft...Failed with Atlanta and toiled in minors before being promoted by Buffalo...Wound up in Quebec and was quickly turned on by hometown fans...Born Oct. 7, 1952, in Quebec City, not far from Le Colisee...Was junior teammate of Guy Lafleur...Sensitive guy who is deadly around net...Was as confused last season as he was confident the year before...Good in clutch . . . Needs to be handled with kid gloves . . . An avid golfer in the offseason.

Year	Club	GP	G	A	Pts.
1972-73	Atlanta	74	13	18	31
1973-74	Atlanta	78	27	16	43
1974-75	Atlanta	63	17	12	29
1975-76	Buffalo	73	12	23	35
1976-77	Buffalo	21	2	0	2
1978-79	Buffalo	61	10	15	25
1979-80	Quebec	14	3	12	15
1980-81	Quebec	78	52	51	103
1981-82	Quebec	59	15	26	41
	Totals	521	151	173	324

REAL CLOUTIER 26 5-10 185   Forward

He's for Real . . . Outstanding offensive player who is prone to streakiness . . . Has thunderous shot . . . Was second on club in assists and points . . . Holdover from Quebec team that won 1976–77 Avco Cup . . . Turned pro at age 18 . . . Was youngest player ever to score 60 goals in a professional league . . . Scored a hat trick in first NHL game . . . Can be tempermental . . . Born July 30, 1956, in St. Emile, Que. . . . Injury-prone . . . Will never live down breaking ankle in charity softball game that caused him to miss three months of '80–81 season . . . Sometimes complains he doesn't get puck enough . . . Nicknamed "Buddy" . . . Named to 1980 all-star team . . . Still searching for consistency that would make him superstar.

Year	Club	GP	G	A	Pts.
1974-75	Quebec (WHA)	63	26	27	53
1975-76	Quebec (WHA)	80	60	54	114
1976-77	Quebec (WHA)	76	66	75	141
1977-78	Quebec (WHA)	73	56	73	129
1978-79	Quebec (WHA)	77	75	54	129
1979-80	Quebec	67	42	46	88
1980-81	Quebec	34	15	16	31
1981-82	Quebec	67	37	60	97
	Totals	537	377	405	782

WILF PAIEMENT 27 6-1 205   Forward

Wilfie . . . Acquired at trading deadline in deal that sent Miroslav Frycer to Toronto . . . Delighted to be in Quebec City and showed it . . . Added spark and spunk to small lineup . . . Not afraid to be physical . . . A hard and persistent checker . . . Strong, fast and useful in every situation . . . Fans particularly like his tireless chasing of the puck . . . Thought to be a head-case but wasn't a problem with Nordiques . . . Born Oct. 16, 1955, in Earlton, Ont. . . . Youngest of 16 children . . . Spent summers farming and lumberjacking . . . Drafted at 17 by Kansas City Scouts and shipped by Colorado to Toronto in bombshell trade for Lanny MacDonald . . . Scored 13 points in his first eight games for Quebec . . . Rugged right wing who also knows how to score . . . May be best deal Nordiques ever made . . . Good on the ice or on the bench . . . Likes to cheerlead.

Year	Club	GP	G	A	Pts.
1974-75	Kansas City	78	26	13	39
1975-76	Kansas City	57	21	22	43
1976-77	Colorado	78	41	40	81
1977-78	Cororado	80	31	56	87
1978-79	Colorado	65	24	36	60
1979-80	Col.-Tor.	75	30	44	74
1980-81	Toronto	77	40	57	97
1981-82	Tor.-Que.	77	25	46	71
	Totals	587	238	314	552

DALE HUNTER 22 5-9 187   Forward

Player you hate to play against . . . Player you love to have on your team . . . Chippy, dirty and smart-alecky . . . Likes to frustrate opponents . . . Thinks elbow is part of his equipment so he uses it . . . Nevertheless, is smart and valuable . . . A real comer . . . Already has two overtime goals to his credit . . . Scored biggest goal in history of the franchise when he beat Rick Wamsley in overtime to give Nordiques first-round playoff victory over Montreal . . . That also gave him victory over brother Mark, who plays for Canadiens . . . Was in penalty box when Mark scored goal to beat Nordiques in fourth game of series . . . Brother Dave plays for Edmonton . . . Born July 31, 1960, in Oil Springs, Ont. . . . Does good imitation of Ken Linseman . . . Always plays against best centers . . . Has been Quebec's most penalized player the last two seasons with total of 498 minutes . . . Small, but don't let that fool you . . . Will occasionally use his stick even to score goals.

Year	Club	GP	G	A	Pts.
1980-81	Quebec	80	19	44	63
1981-82	Quebec	80	22	50	72
	Totals	160	41	94	135

COACH MICHEL BERGERON: Quietly intelligent but colorful
coach whose stock is very high. . . . Has molded

team into Stanley Cup semifinalist after year
of misdirection . . . Quotable and very descrip-
tive . . . Once described Nordiques as "cute little
baby" and rival Canadiens like "little boy who
throws rock through window" . . . Enjoys con-
versation . . . But a real battler behind the
bench . . . Called "the Tiger of Quebec" for his
yelling and screaming . . . "One of the most underrated coaches in
league," according to Islander GM Bill Torrey . . . Has developed
one of league's best power plays . . . Very good at knowing how
to use best player in crucial situations . . . Never played in NHL
or WHA . . . Was extremely successful junior coach in Trois
Rivieres . . . Lifetime Quebecker . . . Born June 12, 1946, in
Montreal . . . Coached and played youth hockey . . . Astute and
witty . . . Took over with team in turmoil and led it to .500 record
under him . . . Transmits confidence to team . . . Says most successful way to build a franchise is not to fire the coach . . .
Well-liked by players and fans.

GREATEST CENTER

There once was a team called the Quebec Nordiques which
once played in a league called the World Hockey Association. It
was a team largely made up of French Canadians in order to appeal
to the overwhelming French-speaking population in the city. The
hero of this French team in a French city in a French province
was born and raised in Needham, Massachusetts. His name was
Robbie Ftorek.

Probably no one did more for the identity of the Nordiques
than the American-born Ftorek. So grateful were the Nordiques,
in fact, that when Ftorek requested a trade to the New York
Rangers last season because of the heavy Canadian taxes, the
Nordiques accomodated him without bitterness and with well
wishes. Not only was Ftorek the captain of the Nordiques, he was
their leader on and off the ice. He learned French. He delighted
in the culture of the Quebecois. And he made all the right plays.

Ftorek's stay in Quebec was too brief, just two years, but he
confirmed his reputation that was earned in other stops along the
WHA trail. Ftorek scored 117 points in Phoenix and 59 goals in
Cincinnati and although injuries kept him sidelined much of his
time in Quebec, he was popular among fans, even worshipped by
them. Not bad for a kid who grew up outside Boston and made

his name early in high school. Those who remember Ftorek from those days remember a high school tournament in which an opponent vowed his team would hold Ftorek to less than three goals. Well, Ftorek scored four goals. And then the second period began. He finished with six, or so the story goes.

It should be mentioned that Ftorek's productive season in Phoenix still ranks as the most points ever scored by an American in a professional league. Ftorek is 5-8, but his size isn't what is important. His heart is. Robbie Ftorek has a very big heart.

ALL-TIME NORDIQUE LEADERS

GOALS: Real Cloutier, 75, 1978-79
ASSISTS: Peter Stastny, 93, 1981-82
POINTS: Marc Tardif, 154, 1977-78
SHUTOUTS: Richard Brodeur, 3, 1978-79
                 Jim Corsi, 3, 1978-79

Michel Goulet tied for NHL lead with six shorthanded goals.

ST. LOUIS BLUES

TEAM DIRECTORY: Chairman: William Stiritz; Pres.-GM-Coach: Emile Francis; Dir. Pub. Rel.: Susie Mathieu. Home ice: St. Louis Checkerdome (17,967; 200' x 85'). Colors: White, blue and gold. Training camp: Regina, Saskatchewan.

SCOUTING REPORT

OFFENSE: Although the Blues' attack skidded by 37 goals from the 1980-81 production, the parts are all there for a solid, productive offense. The sag can be attributed to the shoulder injury of winger Wayne Babych, who went from 52 goals in 1980-81 to 19 in 51 games last season.

The Blues can send out two superior forward lines. Bernie Federko (30 goals, 92 points), Brian Sutter (39 goals) and Joe Mullen (25, 59 in 45 games) totalled 50 points in 10 playoff games and have all the ingredients of a splendid line. Mullen learned his trade in 2½ minor league seasons and is quick, strong and deadly around the net.

Blake Dunlop (78 points), Jorgen Pettersson (38 goals) and Babych form a solid, skilled second line.

When Emile Francis took over as coach late in the schedule, he moved big, swift, tough winger Perry Turnbull (33 goals) to center, flanked by bellicose youngsters Perry Anderson and Mark Reeds, on a splendid wrecking-crew line.

The addition of defenseman Rob Ramage gives the Blues a factor the club has lacked: a strong rusher on the blueline. Jack Brownschidle moves the puck well, too, and young Rik Wilson and Jim Pavese show promise in that area.

DEFENSE: The Blues' defensive mark slipped by 68 goals last season and tightening down the hatches is Francis' main target. Only the Colorado Rockies surrendered as many goals as the Blues did on the road—214 in 40 games—and Francis will demand much more solid work on foreign turf.

Goalie Mike Liut, the sensation of 1980-81 with a 3.34 average in 61 games, had a 4.06 average in 64 matches last season. Many Blue watchers claim he played just as well but lacked the tight support in front of him. Liut and Glen Hanlon, acquired from Vancouver, give the Blues a strong one-two parlay.

Disheartened by the whole Rockie scene, Ramage, 23, should blossom towards all-star territory with the Blues. He's big, strong and talented.

Joey Mullen tallied 25 goals in only 45 games with Blues.

Brownschidle, Ed Kea and Rick LaPointe are competent big leaguers and if veteran Guy Lapointe, a late-season addition, can stay healthy and enthusiastic, he'll be a big boost.

Wilson and Pavese are promising kids with abundant talent. Scott Campbell, an 1981 acquisition from the Winnipeg Jets, will help immeasurably if has recovered from a severe asthmatic condition that limited his duty to three games in 1981-82. There's optimism that he'll be able to play.

BLUE ROSTER

No.	Player	Pos.	Hgt.	Wgt.	Born	1981-82	G	A	Pts.	PIM
12	Perry Anderson	LW	6-0	194	10-14-61/Barrie, Ont.	St. Louis	1	2	3	0
						Salt Lake	32	32	64	117
10	Wayne Babych	RW	5-11	191	6-6-58/Edmonton, Alta.	St. Louis	19	25	44	51
25	Bill Baker	D	6-1	195	11-29-56/Grand Rapids, Minn.	Col.-St. L.	3	8	11	67
						Fort Worth	0	2	2	20
16	Jack Brownschidle	D	6-2	195	10-2-55/Buffalo, N.Y.	St. Louis	5	33	38	26
14	Blair Chapman	RW	6-0	184	6-13-56/Lloydminster, Sask.	St. Louis	6	11	17	8
						Salt Lake	1	0	1	0
27	Bobby Crawford	RW	5-11	177	4-6-59/Belleville, Ont.	St. Louis	0	1	1	0
						Salt Lake	54	45	99	43
26	Mike Crombeen	RW	5-11	192	7-16-57/Sarnia, Ont.	St. Louis	19	8	27	32
19	Blake Dunlop	C	5-11	175	4-4-53/Hamilton, Ont.	St. Louis	25	53	78	32
24	Bernie Federko	C	6-0	190	5-12-56/Foam Lake, Sask.	St. Louis	30	62	92	70
	Richie Hansen	C	5-10	175	10-30-55/New York, N.Y.	St. Louis	0	2	2	0
						Salt Lake	29	81	110	52
	Steve Harrison	D	5-11	190	4-25-58/Scarborough, Ont.	Salt Lake	12	46	58	63
2	Gerry Hart	D	5-9	180	1-1-48/Flin Flon, Sask.	St. Louis	0	1	1	100
17	Ed Kea	D	6-3	190	1-19-48/Collingwood, Ont.	St. Louis	2	14	16	62
28	Ralph Klassen	C	5-11	175	9-15-55/Muenster, Sask.	St. Louis	3	7	10	6
	Neil Labatte	D	6-2	175	4-24-57/Toronto, Ont.	St. Louis	0	0	0	6
						Salt Lake	7	24	31	86
5	Guy Lapointe	D	6-0	186	3-18-48/Montreal, Que.	Mont.-St. L.	1	25	26	76
18	Rick LaPointe	D	6-2	200	8-2-55/Victoria, B.C.	St. Louis	2	20	22	127
	Alain Lemieux	C	6-0	185	5-29-61/Montreal, Que.	St. Louis	0	1	1	0
						Salt Lake	41	42	83	61
	John Markell	LW	5-10	180	3-10-56/Cornwall, Ont.	Salt Lake	19	53	72	33
7	Joe Mullen	RW	5-9	180	2-26-57/New York, N.Y.	Salt Lake	21	27	48	12
						St. Louis	25	34	59	4
	Doug Palazzari	C	5-5	170	11-3-52/Everleth, Minn.	Salt Lake	34	41	75	44
6	Larry Patey	C	6-1	180	2-17-53/Toronto, Ont.	St. Louis	14	12	26	97
	Jim Pavese	D	6-2	204	6-8-62/New York, N.Y.	St. Louis	2	9	11	67
22	Jorgen Pettersson	LW	6-2	185	7-11-56/Gothenberg, Swe.	St. Louis	38	31	69	28
	Rob Ramage	D	6-2	196	1-11-59/Byron, Ont.	Colorado	13	29	42	201
33	Mark Reeds	RW	5-10	188	1-24-60/Burlington, Ont.	St. Louis	1	3	4	0
						Salt Lake	22	24	46	55
20	Bill Stewart	D	6-2	190	10-6-57/Toronto, Ont.	St. Louis	0	5	5	25
						Salt Lake	2	12	14	93
11	Brian Sutter	LW	5-11	180	10-7-56/Viking, Alta.	St. Louis	39	36	75	239
	John Taft	D	6-2	185	3-8-54/Minneapolis, Minn.	St. Louis	6	16	22	46
9	Perry Turnbull	LW	6-2	200	3-9-59/Bentley, Alta.	St. Louis	33	26	59	161
	Alain Vigneault	D	6-0	194	5-14-61/ —	St. Louis	1	2	3	43
						Salt Lake	2	10	12	266
34	Rik Wilson	D	6-0	180	6-17-62/Long Beach, Calif.	St. Louis	3	18	21	24
21	Mike Zuke	C	6-0	180	4-16-54/Sault Ste. Marie, Ont.	St. Louis	13	40	53	41

No.	Player	Pos.	Hgt.	Wgt.	Born	1981-82	GP	GA	SO	Avg.
31	Glen Hanlon	G	6-0	171	2-20-57/Brandon, Man.	Van.-St. L.	30	114	1	4.05
1	Mike Liut	G	6-2	180	1-7-56/Weston, Alta.	St. Louis	64	250	2	4.06
	Rick Heinz	G	5-10	165	5-30-55/Essex, Ont.	St. L-Van.	12	44	1	4.34
						Salt Lake	19	71	0	3.65
	Paul Skidmore	G	6-0	175	7-22-56/Smithtown, N.Y.	St. Louis	2	6	0	3.00
						Salt Lake	50	192	3	3.85

Undoubtedly, Francis will inspire the Blues' forwards to check much more thoroughly than they did last season.

OUTLOOK: The pieces are all there for the Blues to be among the best four or five clubs in the NHL. The team moved away from the strong, two-way hockey that characterized their excellent 1980-81 campaign but Francis, a firm believer in fundamental hockey, will encourage them to play that way.

BLUE PROFILES

WAYNE BABYCH 24 5-11 191   **Forward**
Arrived as major star with 54 goals in 1980-81 season... Injuries limited action to 51 games last term when he had 19 goals, 44 points... Big, strong, excellent skater, awesome shot, combative nature... Born June 6, 1958, in Edmonton... Junior star with Portland Winterhawks... Blues' first-round draft pick in 1978... Had 26 and 27 goals in first two NHL seasons... He and brother Dave of Winnipeg Jets married twin sisters during offseason... Good enough baseball player to be offered pro contract by Montreal Expos.

Year	Club	GP	G	A	Pts.
1978-79	St. Louis	67	27	36	63
1979-80	St. Louis	59	26	35	61
1980-81	St. Louis	78	54	42	96
1981-82	St. Louis	51	19	25	44
	Totals	255	126	138	264

JACK BROWNSCHIDLE 27 6-2 195   **Defenseman**
Has steadily developed into solid NHL defenseman... Enters sixth season with Blues, parts of two spent in minors... Good puck-handler and skater, strong on power play... Has upgraded defensive play noticeably in past two seasons... Born Oct. 2, 1955, in Buffalo... Played college hockey at Notre Dame... Blues' fifth-round choice, 99th player picked, in 1977 entry draft... Divided first two pro seasons between Blues and Salt Lake of

CHL . . . Earned 26 penalty minutes in 1981-82, highest total of career.

Year	Club	GP	G	A	Pts.
1977-78	St. Louis	40	2	15	17
1978-79	St. Louis	64	10	24	34
1979-80	St. Louis	77	12	32	44
1980-81	St. Louis	71	5	23	28
1981-82	St. Louis	80	5	33	38
	Totals	332	34	127	161

BLAKE DUNLOP 29 5-11 175 Forward

A late bloomer . . . Had mediocre success in whirls with Minnesota and Philadelphia, logging much time in minors . . . Traded to Blues with Rick LaPointe by Flyers in 1979 for goalie Phil Myre . . . Had 45 points in first Blues' season, then exploded . . . Counted 87 points in 1980-81 and won Masterton Trophy for dedication and perseverance . . . Last season, he had 78 points . . . Born in Hamilton, Ont., on Apr. 18, 1953 . . . Standout junior with Ottawa 67s . . . North Stars' second-round pick in 1973 draft . . . Not especially fast but very smart with puck . . . Was a top junior tennis player.

Year	Club	GP	G	A	Pts.
1973-74	Minnesota	12	0	0	0
1974-75	Minnesota	52	9	18	27
1975-76	Minnesota	33	9	11	20
1976-77	Minnesota	3	0	1	1
1977-78	Philadelphia	3	0	1	1
1978-79	Philadelphia	66	20	28	48
1979-80	St. Louis	72	18	27	45
1980-81	St. Louis	80	20	67	87
1981-82	St. Louis	77	25	53	78
	Totals	398	101	206	307

BERNIE FEDERKO 26 6-0 190 Forward

In front ranks of NHL's centers . . . Smooth, slick, smart, one of the best passers in league . . . Has produced 95, 94, 104 and 92 points in last four seasons to demonstrate consistency . . . Tough competitor, aggressive forechecker . . . Born May 12, 1956, in Foam Lake, Sask. . . . Played junior hockey with Saskatoon Blades . . . First-round draft pick in 1976 . . . Top rookie in CHL in 1976-77 although he was promoted to Blues late in season . . . Had

18 points in 10 playoff games last spring...Key man for team, a premier player at the peak of his career.

Year	Club	GP	G	A	Pts.
1976-77	St. Louis	31	14	9	23
1977-78	St. Louis	72	17	24	41
1978-79	St. Louis	74	31	64	95
1979-80	St. Louis	79	38	56	94
1980-81	St. Louis	78	31	73	104
1981-82	St. Louis	74	30	62	92
	Totals	408	161	288	449

RICK LaPOINTE 27 6-2 200   **Defenseman**

Anchor of the Blues' blueline...More efficient than spectacular...Strong defensively, uses size and strength to control corners and front of net...Moves the puck well...Joined team with Blake Dunlop from Philadelphia for goalie Phil Myre in trade that was important in Blues' rebirth...Born Aug. 2, 1955, in Victoria, B.C....Top junior with Victoria Cougars...Detroit's first-round draft pick in 1975...Spent two seasons with Red Wings, then was traded to Flyers.

Year	Club	GP	G	A	Pts.
1975-76	Detroit	80	10	23	33
1976-77	Det.-Phil.	71	3	19	22
1977-78	Philadelphia	47	4	16	20
1978-79	Philadelphia	77	3	18	21
1979-80	St. Louis	80	6	19	25
1980-81	St. Louis	80	8	25	33
1981-82	St. Louis	71	2	20	22
	Totals	506	36	140	176

MIKE LIUT 26 6-2 180   **Goaltender**

Pivotal season ahead...Was the NHL's best goalie in 1980-81, when he was first team all-star...Slipped slightly last season along with club...Workhorse who played 64 games with 4.06 average and 28 victories...Size and stand-up style make him imposing figure...Born Jan. 7, 1956, in Weston, Ont....Attended Bowling Green University...Spent two seasons with Cincinnati in WHA...Blues claimed him in 1976 draft...Was reclaimed in 1979 expansion...Outspoken approach makes him a popular interview . . . Was backup to Washington's Mike Palmateer in Junior B hockey.

Year	Club	GP	GA	SO	Avg.
1977-78	Cincinnati (WHA)	27	86	0	4.25
1978-79	Cincinnati (WHA)	54	184	3	3.47
1979-80	St. Louis	64	194	2	3.18
1980-81	St. Louis	61	199	1	3.34
1981-82	St. Louis	64	250	2	4.06
	Totals	270	913	8	3.58

JOE MULLEN 25 5-9 180   Forward

Exploded on NHL late in 1981-82 season . . . Called up from minors, scored 25 goals, 59 points in 45 games . . . Had 18 points in 10 playoff matches . . . Big assets are quickness in the attacking zone and deadly shot . . . Short but very strong . . . Born Feb. 26, 1957, in New York . . . Father worked at Madison Square Garden . . . Played roller and street hockey as lad . . . Had 212 points in 111 games in four years at Boston College . . . Signed by Blues as free agent in 1979 . . . Had two big CHL seasons, 40-32-72 in 1979-80, 59-58-117 in 1980-81 when he was CHL Player-of-Year.

Year	Club	GP	G	A	Pts.
1981-82	St. Louis	45	25	34	59

JORGEN PETTERSSON 26 6-2 185   Forward

Signed as free agent by Blues in 1980 from Vastra Frolunda team in Sweden . . . Has scored 37 and 38 goals in first two NHL seasons . . . Deceptively fast because of long stride . . . Excellent puckhandler . . . Born July 11, 1956, in Gothenburg, Sweden . . . Was a First Division player in homeland at 16 and played 60 games for Swedish national and junior teams . . . Combines well with center Blake Dunlop . . . Made adjustment to physical NHL style very quickly . . . Fine tennis player . . . Not afraid to go into the corners and take a hit.

Year	Club	GP	G	A	Pts.
1980-81	St. Louis	62	37	36	73
1981-82	St. Louis	77	38	31	69
	Totals	139	75	67	142

BRIAN SUTTER 26 5-11 180   Forward

Eldest of four brothers in the NHL (Darryl of Chicago, Islanders' Duane and Brent) and two more (Rich, Ron) on the way . . . Had another solid season in 1981-82 with 39 goals, 75 points . . . Team captain who sets standard of hard work and dedication . . . Compensates for lack of pure skill with ambition and agressiveness . . . Smart attacker . . . Born Oct. 7, 1956, in Viking, Alberta . . . Blues' second-round pick in 1976 from Lethbridge juniors . . . Had eight goals in 10 playoff games . . . Plans to be a rancher when hockey career is over.

Year	Club	GP	G	A	Pts.
1976-77	St. Louis	35	4	10	14
1977-78	St. Louis	78	9	13	22
1978-79	St. Louis	77	41	39	80
1979-80	St. Louis	71	23	35	58
1980-81	St. Louis	78	35	34	69
1981-82	St. Louis	74	39	36	75
	Totals	413	151	167	318

PERRY TURNBULL 23 6-2 200   Forward

Has all the tools to become an all-star . . . Showed top form in flashes in first three seasons, now must add consistency to repertoire . . . Has scored 67 goals in past two seasons . . . Big, strong, fast, aggressive, strong defensively . . . Has played left wing most of career but showed well in stint at center in 1981-82 . . . Born March 9, 1959, in Bentley, Alta. . . . Played junior hockey with Portland Winterhawks . . . First-round draft pick in 1979 . . . Punishing bodychecker... Speed and abrasive approach make him effective forechecker.

Year	Club	GP	G	A	Pts.
1979-80	St. Louis	80	16	19	35
1980-81	St. Louis	75	34	22	56
1981-82	St. Louis	79	33	26	59
	Totals	234	83	67	150

ROB RAMAGE 23 6-2 200   Defenseman

Blue-chip player who had miserable season in 1981-82... Gave up Rockies' captaincy, asked to be traded... Rockies accomodated by shipping him to St. Louis... Has all-star potential with size, strength, offensive skill, sound defensive play and belligerence... Change of scene should help him... Born Jan. 11, 1959, in Byron, Ont.... Junior star with London Knights... Turned pro in 1978 with Birmingham Bulls of WHA... Was first player picked in 1979 draft... Had two sound seasons until slump last term... Member of Team Canada in 1981 world championships in Sweden... One of the NHL's strongest players because of devotion to weight-lifting program.

Year	Club	GP	G	A	Pts.
1978-79	Birmingham (WHA)	80	12	36	48
1979-80	Colorado	75	8	20	28
1980-81	Colorado	79	20	42	62
1981-82	Colorado	80	13	29	42
	Totals	314	53	127	180

COACH EMILE FRANCIS: Replaced Red Berenson as coach late in 1981-82 season, adding that title to duties as club president and general manager ... Retained job for 1982-83 season ... The Cat is a firm believer in discipline and fundamental hockey... Moved to St. Louis from New York Rangers in 1976 and saved Blues organization from extinction in 1978 when club was broke... One of the most respected men in the game ... Born Sept. 13, 1926, in North Battleford, Sask. ... Despite diminutive size (5-foot-6, 150 pounds), he had 14-season career as pro goaltender, including six NHL seasons with Chicago and Rangers ... Was general manager and often coach of the Rangers for 15 years ... Brought that team back from depths to contending status ... Was playing-manager of North Battleford Beavers semipro baseball team for many summers during playing career ... Son Bobby was leading scorer in Central League in 1981-82.

GREATEST CENTER

Perhaps to declare the Blues' greatest center a three-way tie between Red Berenson, Garry Unger and Bernie Federko indicates a lack of decisiveness or courage. However, a strong case can be made for each man, who covers a different mini-era in the team's history.

Berenson joined the team from the New York Rangers in 1967-68, its first season in the NHL, and became an important player in the Blues' becoming the most successful expansion team in the late 1960s. He was traded to Detroit in the deal that brought Unger to St. Louis, then returned to the Blues to finish his career. Berenson counted 172 goals, 412 points in 519 games as a Blue.

Unger, who holds the NHL record of playing in 914 consecutive games with Toronto, Detroit and the Blues, played 662 games in a St. Louis sweater and had 292 goals, 575 points.

Federko is a big reason why the Blues have rebounded to become a strong club in the 1980s. He has 161 goals and 449 points in 408 games.

ALL-TIME BLUE LEADERS

GOALS: Wayne Babych, 54, 1980-81
ASSISTS: Bernie Federko, 73, 1980-81
POINTS: Bernie Federko, 104, 1980-81
SHUTOUTS: Glenn Hall, 8, 1968-69

TORONTO MAPLE LEAFS

TEAM DIRECTORY: Pres.: Harold E. Ballard; Chairman: Paul McNamara; GM: Gerry McNamara; Dir. Publ.: Stan Obodiac; Coach: Mike Nykoluk. Home ice: Maple Leaf Gardens (16,307; 200' x 85'). Colors: Blue and white. Training camp: Toronto.

SCOUTING REPORT

OFFENSE: From the disaster of a 19th-place finish, right winger Rick Vaive salvaged an excellent season. He scored 54 goals to break the club record of 48, established in 1960-61 by Frank Mahovlich.

The big, hard-shooting Vaive and slick center Bill Derlago (84 points) give the Leafs some hope in the middle of reconstruction program No. 17 in the decade since Harold Ballard became the club's lone owner.

The Leafs peddled their two established attackers, center Darryl Sittler and Wilf Paiement, and will face 1982-83 with a large pack of kids. "Youth" is the word heard most from the Leafs' administration of new GM Gerry McNamara and coach Mike Nykoluk.

Vaive, Derlago and left winger John Anderson (31 goals) give the team a sound forward line around which to build their new attack.

Czech winger Miroslav Frycer, secured from Quebec for Paiement, is a superbly skilled offensive player but he suffered in his brief time with the Leafs because the team lacked a quick center to go with him. The Leafs drafted another Czech, Peter Ihnacak, who defected during the world championships, and have high hopes he'll be the man to harness Frycer's speed and ability.

Winger Terry Martin (25 goals) is a solid veteran but the remainder of the Leaf cast will be selected from untested youngsters.

DEFENSE: The 380 goals surrendered by the Leafs last season made them the worst defensive team in the NHL and they face the new season with only one established big league defenseman.

Borje Salming is that man and he had a fine season, a plus on a woeful team. He logged massive amounts of ice time and, at 31, is still one of the game's premier athletes.

The Leafs attempted something new last season when they employed three teenage defensemen and it was no surprise that they had a rough season. However, Fred Boimistruck made good progress and is a solid defensive type. Jim Benning, now all of 19, has abundant skill and should be a good one. Big Bob McGill

The steadiest of the Leafs: Defenseman Borje Salming.

can fight but he's slow and will be hard-pressed to make the club.

The Leafs' top draft choice, Gary Nylund, is a prime prospect who will move into a starting role and chaps like Bob Manno, Jim Korn, Barry Melrose, Dave Farrish and Craig Muni have a shot at jobs.

No blame could be attached to the club's goalies for the bad defensive mark. Veteran Michel Larocque and young Vincent Tremblay toiled valiantly with little support. Bob Parent, who had a good season in the minors, is in the picture, too.

MAPLE LEAF ROSTER

No.	Player	Pos.	Hgt.	Wgt.	Born	1981-82	G	A	Pts.	PIM
10	John Anderson	RW	5-11	189	3-28-57/Toronto, Ont.	Toronto	31	26	57	30
24	Normand Aubin	C	6-0	185	7-26-60/St. Leonard, Que.	Toronto	14	12	26	22
						Cincinnati	15	17	32	36
15	Jim Benning	D	6-0	185	4-29-63/Edmonton, Alta.	Toronto	7	24	31	46
11	Fred Boimistruck	D	5-11	191	1-14-62/Sudbury, Ont.	Toronto	2	11	13	32
	Bruce Boudreau	C	5-9	175	1-9-55/Toronto, Ont.	Cincinnati	42	61	103	42
19	Bill Derlago	C	5-10	190	8-25-58/Beulah, Man.	Toronto	34	50	84	42
	Slava Duris	D	6-0	175	1-5-54/Pizen, Czech.	Cincinnati	14	41	55	57
	Dave Farrish	D	6-0	188	9-1-56/Lucknow, Ont.	New Brunswick	13	24	37	80
14	Miroslav Frycer	C	5-10	185	— /Czechoslovakia	Que.-Tor.	24	23	47	78
						Fredericton	9	5	14	6
17	Stuart Gavin	LW	6-0	180	3-15-60/Ottawa, Ont.	Toronto	5	6	11	29
23	John Gibson	D	6-3	208	6-2-59/St. Catherine's, Ont.	LA-Tor.	0	2	2	85
						NH-N. Bruns.	1	2	3	30
						Cincinnati	1	2	3	30
	Ernie Godden	C	5-9	162	3-13-61/Windsor, Ont.	Toronto	1	1	2	6
						Cincinnati	32	37	69	178
16	Billy Harris	RW	6-2	194	1-29-52/Toronto, Ont.	LA-Toronto	3	3	6	10
	Peter Ihnacok									
2	Trevor Johanson	D	5-10	194	3-30-57/Thunder Bay, Ont.	LA-Toronto	4	10	14	73
	Mike Kaszycki	C	5-9	190	2-27-56/Milton, Ont.	New Brunswick	36	82	118	67
20	Jim Korn	D	6-3	210	7-28-57/Hopkins, Minn.	Det.-Toronto	2	10	12	148
	Dave Logan	D	5-10	190	7-2-54/Montreal, Que.	Cincinnati	4	12	16	199
3	Bob Manno	D	6-0	185	10-31-56/Niagara Falls, Ont.	Toronto	9	41	50	67
	Paul Marshall	LW	6-2	185	9-7-60/Toronto, Ont.	Toronto	2	2	4	2
						Cincinnati	23	29	52	61
25	Terry Martin	RW-LW	5-11	175	10-25-53/Barrie, Ont.	Toronto	25	24	49	39
4	Bob McGill	D	6-0	202	4-27-62/Edmonton, Alta.	Toronto	1	10	11	263
26	Barry Melrose	D	6-2	205	7-15-56/Kelvington, Sask.	Toronto	1	5	6	186
	Craig Muni	D	6-2	201	7-19-62/Toronto, Ont.	Toronto	0	0	0	2
	Gary Nylund	D	6-4	210	10-28-63/Vancouver, B.C.	Portland	7	59	66	267
14	Fred Perlini	C	6-2	175	4-12-62/Sault Ste. Marie, Ont.	Toronto	2	3	5	0
						Toronto (OHL)	47	64	111	75
12	Walt Poddubny	C-LW	6-1	203	2-14-60/Thunder Bay, Ont.	Wichita	35	46	81	79
						Edm.-Toronto	3	4	7	8
7	Rocky Saganiuk	RW-C	5-9	185	12-15-57/Myrnam, Alta.	Toronto	17	16	33	49
21	Borje Salming	D	6-1	185	4-17-51/Kiruna, Sweden	Toronto	12	44	56	170
	Ron Sedlbauer	LW	6-3	195	10-22-54/Burlington, Ont.	Cincinnati	27	20	47	49
	Dave Shand	D	6-0	190	8-11-56/Cold Lake, Alta.	Cincinnati	8	37	45	206
	Reg Thomas	LW	5-10	185	4-21-53/Lambeth, Ont.	Cincinnati	47	63	110	55
22	Rick Vaive	RW	6-1	190	5-14-59/Ottawa, Ont.	Toronto	54	35	89	157
8	Gary Yaremchuk	C	5-10	180	8-15-61/Edmonton, Alta.	Toronto	0	3	3	10
						Cincinnati	21	35	56	101
39	Ron Zanussi	RW	5-10	180	8-31-56/Toronto, Ont.	Toronto	0	8	8	14
						Cincinnati	12	9	21	32

No.	Player	Pos.	Hgt.	Wgt.	Born	1981-82	GP	GA	SO	Avg.
1	Michel Larocque	G	5-10	185	4-6-52/Hull, Que.	Toronto	50	207	0	4.69
	Bob Parent	G	5-9	175	2-19-58/Windsor, Ont.	Toronto	2	13	0	6.50
						Cincinnati	65	252	2	4.11
33	Curt Ridley	G	6-0	180	9-23-51/Winnipeg, Man.	Cincinnati	22	73	0	4.20
30	Vince Tremblay	G	6-1	180	10-21-59/Quebec, Que.	Toronto	40	153	1	4.52

OUTLOOK: Not great but not totally bleak. Vaive, Derlago, Anderson, Martin and Frycer give some hope for a respectable attack. Nykoluk and assistant Dan Maloney will fill the cast with the best from a fair-sized selection of youngsters.

The big problem is defense and a large amount of patience is needed to give the promising kids the chance to mature. Salming can expect another killer workload.

MAPLE LEAF PROFILES

RICK VAIVE 23 6-1 190   **Forward**
Had 54 goals in 1981-82 to break club record of 48 set in 1960-61 by Frank Mahovlich . . . Big, hard-striding winger with devastating shot . . . Key man in struggling club's hopes for the 1980s . . . Team captain . . . Joined Leafs in 1980 trade with Vancouver with center Bill Derlago for Tiger Williams and Jerry Butler . . . Counted 33 goals in 1980-81 . . . Born May 14, 1959, in Ottawa . . . Junior star with Sherbrooke Beavers . . . Turned pro early with Birmingham Bulls of WHA . . . First-round draft pick of Canucks in 1979 . . . Vancouver club gave up on him early because they felt he had a bad attitude . . . Quickly became big fan favorite in Toronto.

Year	Club	GP	G	A	Pts.
1978-79	Birmingham (WHA) ...	75	26	33	59
1979-80	Vanc.-Tor.	69	22	15	.37
1980-81	Toronto	75	33	29	62
1981-82	Toronto	77	54	35	89
	Totals	296	135	112	247

BILL DERLAGO 24 5-10 190   **Forward**
Bright spot in dismal season . . . Had 34 goals, 50 assists and play improved in all areas . . . Slick, smooth player with complete offensive skills, now solid defensively . . . Playmaking had large role in 54-goal season of winger Rick Vaive . . . Has excellent shot which he seems hesitant to use . . . Joined Leafs from Vancouver with Vaive in 1980 trade for Tiger Williams and Jerry Butler . . . Born Aug. 25, 1958, in Birtle, Man. . . . Scored 96 and 89 goals in two junior seasons with Brandon Wheat Kings . . . Canucks'

first-round draft pick in 1978...Rookie season was wrecked by knee injuries.

Year	Club	GP	G	A	Pts.
1978-79	Vancouver	9	4	4	8
1979-80	Vanc.-Tor.	77	16	27	43
1980-81	Toronto	80	35	39	74
1981-82	Toronto	75	34	50	84
	Totals	241	89	120	209

JOHN ANDERSON 25 5-11 189   Forward

Blossomed as a solid NHL winger in 1981-82 with 31 goals although play tailed off late in season...Has all the tools to be a dandy—speed, acceleration, big shot, size and strength...Work has lacked confidence until last season...Was convinced he would be traded by Leafs, went to 1981 training camp with relaxed attitude...Born in Toronto on March 28, 1957...Junior star with Toronto Marlboros...Scored 57 goals in final junior season...Leafs' first round draft choice in 1977...A budding entrepreneur, he owns and operates eight John Anderson Hamburgers restaurants...Played left wing on club's big line with Bill Derlago and Rick Vaive.

Year	Club	GP	G	A	Pts.
1977-78	Toronto	17	1	2	3
1978-79	Toronto	71	15	11	26
1979-80	Toronto	74	25	28	53
1980-81	Toronto	75	17	26	43
1981-82	Toronto	69	31	26	57
	Totals	306	89	93	182

BORJE SALMING 31 6-1 185   Defenseman

Rebounded from off season to have excellent 1981-82...Chronic sinus problem that hampered breathing was alleviated by acupuncture treatments...Because of green defense, he took heavy workload, finishing with a plus on NHL's worst defensive team...Major star since migrating from Sweden in 1973...All-star in six of nine seasons...First European-trained player to become front-line NHLer...Born April 17, 1951, in Kiruna,

Sweden . . . Played with Swedish national team . . . Superb athlete with great balance on skates, extraordinary puckhandler.

Year	Club	GP	G	A	Pts.
1973-74	Toronto	76	5	34	39
1974-75	Toronto	60	12	25	37
1975-76	Toronto	78	16	41	57
1976-77	Toronto	76	12	66	78
1977-78	Toronto	80	16	60	76
1978-79	Toronto	78	17	56	73
1979-80	Toronto	74	19	52	71
1980-81	Toronto	72	5	61	66
1981-82	Toronto	69	12	44	56
	Totals	663	113	439	553

TERRY MARTIN 27 5-11 175   Forward

Consistent, solid, two-way winger . . . His 25 goals, 49 points were his best season in NHL . . . Saw heavy duty as penalty-killer . . . Swift strong skater, good forechecker . . . Was doomed to the minors when Mike Nykoluk took over as coach halfway through 1980-81 season . . . Scored 22 goals in second half of schedule . . . Born Oct. 25, 1955, in Barrie, Ont. . . . Played junior with London Knights . . . Buffalo's third-round draft pick in 1975 . . . Part-time Sabre for four seasons . . . Claimed by Quebec in 1979 expansion draft, traded to Leafs early in 1979-80 season.

Year	Club	GP	G	A	Pts.
1975-76	Buffalo	1	0	0	0
1976-77	Buffalo	62	11	12	23
1977-78	Buffalo	21	3	2	5
1978-79	Buffalo	64	6	8	14
1979-80	Que.-Tor.	40	6	15	21
1980-81	Toronto	69	23	14	37
1981-82	Toronto	72	25	24	49
	Totals	329	74	75	149

JIM BENNING 19 6-0 185   Defenseman

Big future hope who had respectable rookie season at 18 with weak team . . . Green as grass and it often showed . . . But so did his good offensive skill, strong puckhandling, good passing . . . Defensive work improved slowly . . . Nykoluk tried to keep pressure off him . . . Needs to improve strength and, with experience, should be a good one . . . Born April 29, 1963, in Edmonton . . . Played junior hockey with Portland Winterhawks . . . Leafs' first-round draft choice in 1981... Scored 28 goals and Western League record 111 assists in final junior season.

Year	Club	GP	G	A	Pts.
1981-82	Toronto	74	7	24	31

MICHEL LAROCQUE 31 5-10 185   Goaltender

Toiled valiantly for weak club behind inexperienced defense, facing huge shot load... Solid stand-up goalie, good team man, much respected by mates... Joined Leafs late in 1980-81 from Canadiens... Was Ken Dryden's backup in Montreal for five seasons ... Born April 6, 1952, in Hull, Que.... Brilliant junior with Ottawa 67s, one of few goalies to be claimed on first round of draft... Montreal's first pick in 1972... Has shared Vezina trophy four times... Leafs' player rep to NHL Players' Association.

Year	Club	GP	GA	SO	Avg.
1973-74	Montreal	27	69	0	2.89
1974-75	Montreal	25	74	3	3.00
1975-76	Montreal	22	50	2	2.46
1976-77	Montreal	26	53	4	2.09
1977-78	Montreal	30	77	1	2.67
1978-79	Montreal	34	94	3	2.84
1979-80	Montreal	39	125	3	3.32
1980-81	Mont.-Tor.	36	122	1	3.51
1981-82	Toronto	50	207	0	4.69
	Totals	289	871	17	3.19

FRED BOIMISTRUCK 21 5-11 191   Defenseman

One of several young defensemen who must develop for club to have any future... Had solid rookie season in 1981-82 when work improved noticeably as season progressed... Missed last month with ankle injury... More solid than spectacular, good defensively, moves the puck well, not a high point producer... Finished with a plus on NHL's worst defensive team... Born Jan. 14, 1962, in Sudbury, Ont.... Played junior with Cornwall Royals, anchored two consecutive Canadian junior championship teams... Second-round draft choice by Leafs in 1980.

Year	Club	GP	G	A	Pts.
1981-82	Toronto	57	2	11	13

NORMAND AUBIN 22 6-0 185   Forward

Skilled offensive player who had 14 goals, 26 points in 43 games after midseason recall from minors...Laboring skater who has worked hard to improve, fine playmaker, and good scorer...With right wingers, he can be effective big-league player...Born July 26, 1960, in Montreal...Superb junior who had 233 goals in three junior seasons ...Third-round draft pick in 1979 from Sherbrooke Beavers...Had excellent rookie pro season in 1980-81 with New Brunswick Hawks of AHL, scoring 43 goals, 89 points.

Year	Club	GP	G	A	Pts.
1981-82	Toronto	43	14	12	26

VINCENT TREMBLAY 22 6-1 180   Goaltender

Hectic rookie season in 40 games behind weak defense...Good prospect with size, stand-up style, fine catching hand and has improved technically...Bothered by breathing problem from broken nose which was corrected by surgery in offseason...Born Oct. 21, 1959, in Quebec City...Played junior with Quebec Remparts...Drafted by Toronto in 1979...AHL all-star in 1980-81 with New Brunswick Hawks when he had 3.24 average in 46 games...Leafs feel he can be a splendid goalie with experience.

Year	Club	GP	GA	SO	Avg.
1979-80	Toronto	10	28	0	5.11
1980-81	Toronto	3	16	0	6.71
1981-82	Toronto	40	153	1	4.52
	Totals	53	197	1	4.72

COACH MIKE NYKOLUK: Easy-going, likeable man who

believes in low-key, soft-sell approach... Showed great patience with young team that is rebuilding totally with youth... Club could be youngest in NHL this season... Went from broadcast booth to head coaching post at mid-season in 1980-81 when Joe Crozier was fired... Born Dec. 11, 1934, in Toronto... Played junior hockey with Toronto and 32 games with Leafs... Was top American League center for 12 years with Hershey Bears... AHL MVP in 1966-67... Was as-

Terry Martin has scored 48 goals in last two seasons.

sistant coach under Fred Shero in Philadelphia, where team
won two Stanley Cups, and later with New York Rangers...
Color commentator on Leaf radio broadcasts in first half of
1980-81... Took over coaching job at 40-game mark and club
earned playoff spot on last night of schedule... Brother Dan was
all-star offensive lineman with Toronto Argonauts in Canadian
Football League.

GREATEST CENTER

When a team has been around as long as the Maple Leafs and
achieved as much success (not much of it in the past 15 years,
however), that its list of great centers is a long one is no major
surprise.

The men who have worked the middle for the Leafs include
Joe Primeau, Syl Apps, Teeder Kennedy, Red Kelly, Dave Keon
and Cal Gardiner. A strong case can be made for any one of them.

But the man who holds the most club records is Darryl Sittler,
a great star with the team throughout the 1970s until he was traded
to the Philadelphia Flyers late in the 1981-82 season.

In 844 games as a Leaf, Sittler scored 389 goals, had 527
assists, 916 points and produced another 65 points in 64 playoff
games. In 1976, he achieved three superb feats—10 points in one
game against the Boston Bruins, five goals in a playoff game
against the Flyers and the winning goal in overtime for Team
Canada in the first Canada Cup international tournament.

ALL-TIME MAPLE LEAF LEADERS

GOALS: Rick Vaive, 54, 1981-82
ASSISTS: Darryl Sittler, 72, 1977-78
POINTS: Darryl Sittler, 117, 1977-78
SHUTOUTS: Harry Lumley, 13, 1953-54

VANCOUVER CANUCKS

TEAM DIRECTORY: Chairman: Frank A. Griffiths; Asst. to Chairman: Arthur R. Griffiths; VP-GM: Jake Milford; Asst. GM: Jack Gordon; Dir. of Player Personnel: Larry Popein; Dir. Pub. Rel.: Norm Jewison; Coach: Roger Neilson. Home ice: Pacific Coliseum (15,613; 200′ x 85′). Colors: Black, red and yellow.

SCOUTING REPORT

OFFENSE: Only three clubs scored fewer goals than the Canucks last season but that won't worry Roger Neilson, who took over the head coaching job in time for last spring's playoff success. Neilson's teams always are defensively oriented and in selecting his players, the edge always goes to the chap who can check.

The Canucks have some quality attackers but they lack a game-breaker, a big 45-goal-plus shooter who can score on the nights when the remainder of the attack dries up and who can carry the team singlehandedly.

Center Thomas Gradin, who produced a club-record 86 points (37 goals), is one of the slickest, most skilled players in the NHL. Tough Stan Smyl (34 goals), Ivan Boldirev (33), Curt Fraser (28) and Darcy Rota (20) give some sting but much of the forward cast are low-scoring grinders—Tiger Williams, Jim Nill, Gary Lupul, Gerry Minor and Ron Delorme.

The Canucks feel that big Czech center Ivan Hlinka, who had 23 goals and 60 points in his first NHL season at 31, will be a much more potent force with a period of adjustment. Junior scoring star Moe LeMay also will get a big look.

The team has only one defenseman with much offensive potential, Kevin McCarthy, although if Rick Lanz can stay healthy, he moves the puck well.

DEFENSE: The fact that the Canucks had the fifth best defensive mark in the NHL should have been a tipoff that they would be a tough playoff team.

Playoff hero Richard Brodeur had a splendid season, too, with a 3.35 average in 52 games. He's a mature, solid goalie who thrives on a heavy workload and he's likely to receive it. Behind him, the team is thin, lacking an experienced backup. Ken Ellacott, who played 68 minor league games, and junior Wendell Young will contend for the No. 2 spot.

The Canucks have 11 bona fide contenders for employment on defense. Two of them, Lanz and Czech veteran Jiri Bubla, missed most of the season with injuries and McCarthy didn't play in the playoffs.

Harold Snepsts and Doug Halward have the edge on jobs and veterans Colin Campbell and Lars Lindgren, youngsters Andy Schleibener, Anders Eldebrink, Neil Belland and draft pick Michel Petit are in the hunt, too.

Richard Brodeur's goaltending took Canucks to finals.

CANUCK ROSTER

No.	Player	Pos.	Hgt.	Wgt.	Born	1981-82	G	A	Pts.	PIM
15	Neil Belland	D	5-11	175	4-3-61/Parry Sound, Ont.	Vancouver	3	6	9	16
						Dallas	2	20	22	18
9	Ivan Boldirev	C	6-0	190	8-15-49/Zranjanin, Yugo.	Vancouver	33	40	73	45
	Jiri Bubla	D	5-11	197	1-27-50/Ustinad Labern, Czech.	Vancouver	1	1	2	16
3	Garth Butcher	D	6-0	194	1-8-63/Regina, Sask.	Vancouver	0	0	0	9
	Jerry Butler	RW	6-0	170	2-27-51/Sarnia, Ont.	Vancouver	3	1	4	15
						Dallas	6	24	30	30
	Drew Callander	RW-C	6-2	188	8-17-56/Regina, Sask.	Dallas	40	47	87	79
5	Colin Campbell	D	5-9	190	1-28-53/London, Ont.	Vancouver	0	8	8	131
28	Marc Crawford	LW	5-11	178	2-13-61/Belland, Ont.	Vancouver	4	8	12	29
						Dallas	13	21	34	71
17	Tony Currie	C-RW	5-11	186	12-12-57/Sydney, N.S.	St. L-Van.	23	25	48	19
19	Ron Delorme	RW	6-3	182	9-3-55/Cochin, Sask.	Vancouver	9	8	17	177
10	Anders Eldebrink	D	5-11	187	12-11-60/Kalix, Swe.	Vancouver	1	8	9	21
29	Curt Fraser	LW	6-0	195	1-12-58/Winnipeg, Man.	Vancouver	28	39	67	175
23	Thomas Gradin	C	5-11	175	2-18-56/Solleftea, Swe.	Vancouver	37	49	86	32
2	Doug Halward	D	6-1	184	11-1-55/Toronto, Ont.	Dallas	8	18	26	49
						Vancouver	4	13	17	40
	Steve Hazlett	LW-C	5-9	170	12-12-57/Sarnia, Ont.	Dallas	19	34	53	48
21	Ivan Hlinka	C	6-2	219	1-26-50/Most, Czech.	Vancouver	23	37	60	16
4	Rick Lanz	D	6-1	185	9-16-61/Karluytary, Czech.	Vancouver	3	11	14	48
29	Moe Lemay	C	5-11	172	2-18-62/Saskatoon, Sask.	Vancouver	1	2	3	0
						Ottawa	68	70	138	48
13	Lars Lindgren	D	6-1	205	10-12-52/Pitea, Swe.	Vancouver	5	16	21	74
7	Gary Lupul	C	5-8	175	4-4-59/Powell River, B.C.	Vancouver	10	7	17	26
						Dallas	22	17	39	76
25	Kevin McCarthy	D	5-11	195	7-14-57/Winnipeg, Man.	Vancouver	6	39	45	84
14	Blair MacDonald	RW	5-10	180	11-17-53/Cornwall, Ont.	Vancouver	18	15	33	20
						Dallas	1	1	2	0
	Joe McDonnell	D	6-2	195	5-11-61/Kitchener, Ont.	Vancouver	0	1	1	12
						Dallas	13	24	37	46
20	Gerry Minor	C	5-8	178	10-27-58/Regina, Sask.	Vancouver	0	1	1	6
						Dallas	5	8	13	92
26	Lars Molin	C	6-0	170	12-3-58/Omskoldsvik, Swe.	Vancouver	15	31	46	10
8	Jim Nill	D	6-0	175	4-11-58/Hanna, Alta.	Vancouver	10	14	24	132
	Michel Petit	D	6-1	180	2-12-64/St. Maulo, Que.	Sherbrooke	10	39	49	106
18	Darcy Rota	LW	5-11	185	2-16-53/Prince George, B.C.	Vancouver	20	20	40	139
	Art Rutland	C	5-10	180	5-13-60/Wawa, Ont.	Dallas	35	58	93	103
	Andy Schliebener	D	6-0	190	8-16-62/Ottawa, Ont.	Vancouver	0	1	1	10
						Dallas	2	2	4	4
12	Stan Smyl	RW	5-8	190	1-28-58/Glendon, Alta.	Vancouver	34	44	78	144
27	Harold Snepsts	D	6-3	195	10-24-54/Edmonton, Alta.	Vancouver	3	14	17	153
22	Tiger Williams	LW	5-11	180	2-3-54/Weyburn, Sask.	Vancouver	17	21	38	341

No.	Player	Pos.	Hgt.	Wgt.	Born		GP	GA	SO	Avg.
35	Richard Brodeur	G	5-7	175	9-15-52/Montreal, Que.	Vancouver	52	168	2	3.35
	Ken Ellacott	G	5-9	152	3-3-59/Paris, Ont.	Dallas	68	282	1	5.52
	Wendell Young	G	5-8	178	8-1-63/Halifax, N.S.	Kitchener				

Neilson will have the team playing disciplined, dull defensive hockey and preventing goals won't be a problem.

OUTLOOK: It will be interesting to see if the Canucks, who never had won a playoff round in 12 seasons in the NHL, really did turn around their sad fortunes by advancing to the final in 1982. Was it just a freak happening, a temporary surge, or has the team finally arrived?

Neilson is an innovative, creative coach who's getting his third chance at a head job in the NHL after two years with Toronto, three at Buffalo, one as head coach.

The Canucks will play a grind-it-out style of hockey. They'll be strong defensively but in a division loaded with strong attacks, their lack of offensive sting is a handicap.

CANUCK PROFILES

THOMAS GRADIN 26 5-11 175   Forward
The master of slick, a superb skater and brilliant puckhandler . . . Set club point record with 86 in '81-82, with 37 goals, 49 assists . . . Key man in Canucks' advance to the Stanley Cup final . . . Claimed by Chicago in 1976 draft, then traded to the Canucks when Black Hawks couldn't sign him . . . Born Feb. 18, 1956, in Solleftea, Sweden . . . Spent four seasons with AIK in Sweden's First Division . . . Improved upper-body strength by working as a trash collector one summer . . . Coaches try to inspire him to shoot more but he prefers the playmaker role . . . Played for Sweden in 1981 Canada Cup . . . Has a degree in physical education and is a devoted runner and tennis player.

Year	Club	GP	G	A	Pts.
1978-79	Vancouver	76	20	31	51
1979-80	Vancouver	80	30	45	75
1980-81	Vancouver	79	21	48	69
1981-82	Vancouver	76	37	49	86
	Totals	311	108	173	281

STAN SMYL 24 5-8 190   Forward
Perhaps the team's best player in 1982 playoff success with timely scoring, strong defensive work and flat-out effort . . . No NHL

player works harder than The Steamer...One of the few practitioners of the almost lost art of the clean, open-ice bodycheck...Claimed on third round of 1978 entry draft from New Westminster (B.C.) juniors...Has improved skating and offensive skill noticeably in four NHL seasons...Born Jan. 28, 1958, in Glendon, Alta....Appears smaller than he is and foes often are surprised by his strength and impact...A big favorite with Vancouver fans because of his consistent effort...Scored a career-high 34 goals last season.

Year	Club	GP	G	A	Pts.
1978-79	Vancouver	62	14	24	38
1979-80	Vancouver	77	31	47	78
1980-81	Vancouver	80	25	38	63
1981-82	Vancouver	80	34	44	78
	Totals	299	104	153	257

IVAN BOLDIREV 33 6-0 190   Forward

Good finesse player who skates and handles the puck well...Has counted 679 points in 11 NHL seasons with five clubs...Drafted by Boston in 1969, also has played with California, Chicago and Atlanta...Traded to Canucks with Darcy Rota by Flames in 1980 for Don Lever and Brad Smith...Born Aug. 15, 1949, in Zranjanin, Yugoslavia...His family migrated to Canada when he was an infant...Very durable type who has missed only 14 games in past seven seasons...Has scored 30 or more goals in four seasons...Physical player but has the skill to avoid penalties.

Year	Club	GP	G	A	Pts.
1970-71	Boston	2	0	0	0
1971-72	Bost.-Calif.	68	16	25	41
1972-73	California	56	11	23	34
1973-74	California	78	25	31	56
1974-75	Chicago	80	24	43	67
1975-76	Chicago	78	28	34	62
1976-77	Chicago	80	24	38	62
1977-78	Chicago	80	35	45	80
1978-79	Chi.-Atl.	79	35	43	78
1979-80	Atl.-Vanc.	79	32	35	67
1980-81	Vancouver	72	26	33	59
1981-82	Vancouver	78	33	40	73
	Totals	830	289	390	679

HAROLD SNEPSTS 28 6-3 195   Defenseman

A solid backliner for seven seasons, needed showcase of playoff success to be appreciated... Strong puckhandler but he's a defensive defenseman who takes care of business in his team's zone... Bad pass gave Islanders overtime goal in first game of Cup final but he shook it off to play well... Born Oct. 24, 1954, in Edmonton... Has played in two All-Star Games... A fine tennis player who does well in celebrity tournaments... Jovial, popular player off the ice, very intense on it... Size and strength make him one of the best at keeping the front of the net clear of bodies.

Year	Club	GP	G	A	Pts.
1974-75	Vancouver	27	1	2	3
1975-76	Vancouver	78	3	15	18
1976-77	Vancouver	79	4	18	22
1977-78	Vancouver	75	4	16	20
1978-79	Vancouver	76	7	24	31
1979-80	Vancouver	79	3	20	23
1980-81	Vancouver	76	3	16	19
1981-82	Vancouver	68	3	14	17
	Totals	558	28	125	153

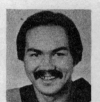

IVAN HLINKA 32 6-2 219   Forward

One of the greatest players in the history of international hockey... Counted 355 points in 269 games with the national team of Czechoslovakia, 848 points in 469 games with CHZ Litvinov in Czech major league... Joined Canucks in 1981 with defenseman Jiri Bubla through legal channels... Was claimed by Winnipeg in special draft but signed by Canucks under compensation deal... Born Jan. 26, 1950, in Most, Czech.... Big, freewheeling center who needed time to adjust to smaller NHL ice surfaces... Had 60 points and was effective on the power play... Wife Kveta is top international gymnastics coach... Studies coaching techniques at Prague University's Faculty of Sport.

Year	Club	GP	G	A	Pts.
1981-82	Vancouver	72	23	37	60

KEVIN McCARTHY 25 5-11 195   Defenseman

Missed 1982 playoffs because of a broken ankle suffered in a workout before the first series . . . Developed into a front-line rearguard last season, swift and skilled on the attack, tough defensively . . . Plagued by injuries, he missed most of 1978-79 with hip injury acquired in first Canuck game after trade from Philadelphia . . . Born July 14, 1957, in Winnipeg . . . Produced 127 points in final junior season . . . A first-round draft pick of Flyers in 1977 . . . Has played in two All-Star Games . . . An important man in the team's future if he can avoid injuries . . . Gung-ho type.

Year	Club	GP	G	A	Pts.
1977-78	Philadelphia	62	2	15	17
1978-79	Phil.-Vanc.	23	1	2	3
1979-80	Vancouver	79	15	30	45
1980-81	Vancouver	80	16	37	53
1981-82	Vancouver	71	6	39	45
	Totals	315	40	123	163

DAVE WILLIAMS 28 5-11 180   Forward

The Tiger . . . Outspoken, outrageous, a master of the put-on who's a big favorite with hockey writers . . . Describes his 1981-82 season as "dreadful" because he sagged from 35 goals to 17 . . . However, he was one of the team's strongest workers in the playoff success . . . Scored overtime goal against Calgary in first round . . . Born Feb. 3, 1954, in Weyburn, Sask. . . . Drafted by Toronto in 1974, he was a Maple Leaf favorite until he was traded to Canucks with Jerry Butler in 1980 for Rick Vaive and Bill Derlago . . . Most penalized player in NHL history with 2,485 minutes . . . Avid outdoorsman who hunts black bears with bow and arrow in the off-season.

Year	Club	GP	G	A	Pts.
1974-75	Toronto	42	10	19	29
1975-76	Toronto	78	21	19	40
1976-77	Toronto	77	18	25	43
1977-78	Toronto	78	19	31	50
1978-79	Toronto	77	19	20	39
1979-80	Tor.-Vanc.	78	30	23	53
1980-81	Vancouver	77	35	27	62
1981-82	Vancouver	77	17	21	38
	Totals	584	169	185	354

LARS LINDGREN 30 6-1 205   Defenseman

Sound, two-way defenseman... Because of injuries to three Canuck blackliners, he took heavy playoff load and excelled in march to the final... One European who revels in the heavy going and can throw a hefty bodycheck... Spent four seasons with the MoDo team in Swedish First Division... Signed by the Canucks as a free agent in 1978... Born Oct. 12, 1952, in Pitea, Sweden... Missed big part of the 1980-81 season with an assortment of injuries... Spends his summers in the north of Sweden where he's refurbishing a house that's 200 years old.

Year	Club	GP	G	A	Pts.
1978-79	Vancouver	64	2	19	21
1979-80	Vancouver	73	5	30	35
1980-81	Vancouver	52	4	18	22
1981-82	Vancouver	75	5	16	21
	Totals	264	16	83	99

RICHARD BRODEUR 31 5-7 175   Goaltender

The star of the Canucks' 1982 playoff success... Superb goaltending anchored team's advance to the final... One of the NHL's best during the season with a 3.35 average in 52 games... Compensates for small stature with strong technique and extraordinary reflexes and catching hand... Born Sept. 15, 1951, in Longueil, Quebec... Spent seven seasons in World Hockey Association with Quebec Nordiques, then was reclaimed by Islanders prior to 1979 expansion draft... Seeking depth, Canucks acquired him from Isles for a fifth-round entry draft pick... Nicknamed "Kermit"... Laid-back approach means he's not bothered by a bad goal or a bad game.

Year	Club	GP	GA	SO	Avg.
1972-73	Quebec (WHA)	24	102	0	4.75
1973-74	Quebec (WHA)	30	89	1	3.32
1974-75	Quebec (WHA)	51	188	0	3.84
1975-76	Quebec (WHA)	69	244	2	3.69
1976-77	Quebec (WHA)	53	167	2	3.45
1977-78	Quebec (WHA)	36	121	0	3.70
1978-79	Quebec (WHA)	42	126	3	3.11
1979-80	New York I.	2	6	0	4.50
1980-81	Vancouver	52	177	0	3.51
1981-82	Vancouver	52	168	2	3.35
	Totals	411	1388	10	3.59

CURT FRASER 24 6-0 195   **Forward**

Backbone of team because of solid, two-way play, hard work and aggressive approach...His 28 goals last season were high of four-year NHL career...One of the league's best fighters, seldom challenged because of prowess...Among the NHL's strongest players because of devotion to weight-lifting program...Born Jan. 12, 1958, in Cincinnati, where his father was playing hockey...Moved to Canada at an early age...Played junior hockey with Victoria (B.C.) and was a second-round draft pick in 1978...Tends to be a streak scorer...Good player on the road...Few better cornermen in the NHL.

Year	Club	GP	G	A	Pts.
1978-79	Vancouver	78	16	19	35
1979-80	Vancouver	78	17	25	42
1980-81	Vancouver	77	25	24	49
1981-82	Vancouver	79	28	39	67
	Totals	312	86	107	193

COACH ROGER NEILSON: Known as "Captain Video" for his use of videotapes as a teaching tool for hockey skills...Perhaps his new name should be "Top Towel"...His waving of a towel at referee in playoffs inspired binge of towel-flapping by Vancouver fans...Associate coach of the Canucks who took over head job when Harry Neale was suspended...Neilson promptly guided team to Stanley Cup final...Now in command as Neale moves up to GM...Fabled as an innovator plus some outrageous pranks that demonstrated loopholes in the rules...Born June 16, 1934, in Toronto...Successful junior coach of Peterborough Petes...Previously coached Toronto and Buffalo in the NHL...Much in demand as lecturer at coaching clinics...A teacher by profession with a degree in physical education from McMaster University in Hamilton, Ont....Claims he prefers being field manager in baseball to hockey coaching because the baseball man has more control over the game.

GREATEST CENTER

Until their advance to the 1982 Stanley Cup final, the Vancouver Canucks hardly had set the world on fire as a team or with great individual stars since entering the NHL in the 1970 expansion.

The finest center ever to work in the Canucks' employ was a little (5-foot-8, 165 pounds) French-Canadian, Andre Boudrias. In six seasons, Boudrias scored 121 goals and had 267 assists for 388 points.

Quick and smart, Boudrias was a master puckhandler and a skilled playmaker. He was a high-scoring junior with the Montreal Junior Canadiens, where he played on a line with another prolific little chap, Yvan Cournoyer.

Boudrias kicked around the Canadiens' organization and had a whirl with the Chicago Black Hawks before joining the Canucks.

The Canucks now have a top candidate to replace Boudrias as the top pivot in the club's history. Swedish star Thomas Gradin, who set a club record with 86 points in 1981-82, is one of the NHL's most skilled players.

ALL-TIME CANUCK LEADERS

GOALS: Ron Sedlbauer, 40, 1978-79
ASSISTS: Andre Boudrias, 62, 1974-75
POINTS: Thomas Gradin, 86, 1981-82
SHUTOUTS: Gary Smith, 6, 1974-75

WASHINGTON CAPITALS

TEAM DIRECTORY: Chairman-Pres.: Abe Polin; Acting GM: Roger Crozier; Dir. Pub. Rel.: Lou Corletto; Dir. of Player Recruitment: Jack Button; Coach: Bryan Murray. Home ice: Capital Centre (18,130; 200' × 85'). Colors: Red, white and blue. Training camp: Hershey, Pa.

SCOUTING REPORT

OFFENSE: Led by 60-goal-scorer Dennis Maruk, the Capitals have a high-powered offense. They have a talented group of young, offense-minded forwards with skating speed and vigor: Bobby Carpenter, Ryan Walter, Mike Gartner, Chris Valentine

Feisty Dennis Maruk was a 60-goal scorer last year.

and Bengt Gustaffson. The Caps ranked 11th in offense and are explosive on power plays, scoring 93 goals in a league-leading 417 manpower advantages. But their forwards need to show more discipline and checking skill in all three zones. Washington set a team record last season with 319 goals.

DEFENSE: Not enough of it, especially in the defensive zone and critical play-forming neutral zone. Darren Veitch, Rick Green and Terry Murray are the only truly reliable defensemen. The penalty-killing isn't all that bad but like most teams with many young players, too many mistakes are made in front of the net and in the slot.

"If Washington can tighten up in its own end of the ice, it can definitely improve," says Jim Devellano, the Red Wings' general manager and scouting expert.

Young goaltenders Dave Parro and Al Jensen showed promise last season but often were victimized by their teammates' mistakes. If veteran Mike Palmateer finally overcomes his physical problems and regains his form, the Capitals' goaltending will be in better shape.

OUTLOOK: Washington showed definite signs of improvement in its overall play and system of play when Bryan Murray took over as coach early last season. The Capitals will score lots of goals but they also will surrender too many goals. They never have had a winning record in eight years in the NHL, never have qualified for the playoffs, and have finished last in the Patrick Division three straight seasons. The team should escape last place in 1982-83 with the addition of the weak New Jersey Meadowlands team to their division. But unless a couple of Patrick rivals collapse, a playoff berth may be too much to ask.

Fans in Landover, Md., have grown impatient with the Capitals' failure to advance in the standings since joining the NHL in 1974. The team is losing money and owner Abe Pollin says he may sell the team. Significant improvement is a must this season for the sake of the franchise.

CAPITAL PROFILES

DENNIS MARUK 26 5-8 165   **Forward**
Affectionately nicknamed "Pee Wee" for his small stature ...
Nothing small about what he accomplished last season ...
Finished fourth in league scoring with 60 goals and 136 points

CAPITAL ROSTER

No.	Player	Pos.	Hgt.	Wgt.	Born	1981-82	G	A	Pts.	PIM
17	Timo Blomqvist	D	6-0	198	1-23-61/Helsinki, Fin.	Washington	1	11	12	62
						Hershey	0	8	8	14
29	Pierre Bouchard	D	6-2	195	2-20-48/Montreal, Que.	Washington	0	0	0	10
						Hershey	2	10	12	26
10	Bob Carpenter	C	6-0	185	7-13-63/Beverley, Mass.	Washington	32	35	67	69
	Tony Cassalato	RW	5-11	182	5-7-56/Guelph, Ont.	Washington	1	4	5	4
						Hershey	29	37	66	56
12	Glen Currie	C	6-1	174	7-18-58/Montreal, Que.	Hershey	12	12	24	6
						Washington	7	7	14	14
14	Gaetan Duchesne	LW	5-10	180	— / —	Washington	9	14	23	46
18	Lou Franceschetti	LW	6-0	172	3-28-58/Toronto, Ont.	Hershey	22	33	55	89
						Washington	2	10	12	23
11	Mike Gartner	RW	6-0	185	10-29-59/Ottawa, Ont.	Washington	35	45	80	121
	Ed Godin	RW	5-10	187	3-29-57/Donnaconna, Que.	Hershey	16	13	29	28
23	Bob Gould	RW	5-11	195	9-2-57/Petrolia, Ont.	Cal.-Wash.	21	13	34	73
						Oklahoma City	0	1	1	0
5	Rick Green	D	6-3	202	2-20-56/Belleville, Ont.	Washington	3	25	28	93
16	Bengt Gustafsson	C	6-0	185	3-23-58/Karlskoga, Swe.	Washington	26	34	60	40
	Alan Haworth	LW	5-10	188	9-11-60/Drummondville, Que.	Buffalo	21	18	39	30
						Rochester	5	12	17	10
2	Doug Hicks	D	6-0	185	5-29-55/Cold Lake, Alta.	Edmon.-Wash.	3	21	24	66
4	Randy Holt	D	5-11	185	1-15-53/Pembroke, Ont.	Cal.-Wash.	2	6	8	259
	Ken Houston	RW	6-2	200	9-15-53/Dresden, Ont.	Calgary	22	22	44	91
17	Wes Jarvis	C	5-11	185	5-30-58/Toronto, Ont.	Washington	1	12	13	18
						Hershey	31	61	92	78
	Dwayne Loudermilk	D	5-11	201	1-9-58/Barnaby, B.C.	Hershey	4	34	38	44
19	Paul MacKinnon	D	6-0	190	11-6-58/Brantford, Ont.	Washington	2	9	11	35
						Hershey	3	17	20	30
21	Dennis Maruk	C	5-8	165	11-17-55/Toronto, Ont.	Washington	60	76	136	128
4	Jim McTaggert	D	6-0	191	3-31-61/Weyburn, Sask.	Washington	2	4	6	20
						Hershey	4	12	16	190
25	Terry Murray	D	6-2	190	7-20-50/Shawville, Que.	Washington	3	22	25	60
8	Lee Norwood	D	6-0	190	2-2-60/Oakland, Calif.	Fredericton	6	13	19	74
						Que.-Wash.	7	10	17	117
	Harvey Pocza	LW	6-2	188	9-22-59/Lethbridge, Alta.	Washington	0	0	0	2
						Hershey	29	23	52	116
22	Jean Pronovost	RW	5-11	180	12-18-45/Shawinigan Falls, Que.	Hershey	35	31	66	18
						Washington	1	2	3	4
	Errol Rausse	LW	5-9	172	5-18-59/Quesnel, B.C.	Washington	0	0	0	0
						Hershey	18	25	43	6
32	Torrie Robertson	LW	5-11	184	8-2-61/Victoria, B.C.	Hershey	5	3	8	60
						Washington	8	13	21	204
24	Tom Rowe	RW	6-0	190	5-23-56/Lynn, Mass.	Hart.-Wash.	5	1	6	54
						Bing.-Hershey	21	20	41	126
	Scott Stevens	D	5-11	190	4-1-64/Kitchener, Ont.	Kitchener	6	36	42	106
20	Greg Theberge	D	5-11	195	9-3-59/Peterborough, Ont.	Washington	5	32	37	49
28	Chris Valentine	RW	6-0	190	12-6-61/Belleville, Ont.	Hershey	12	9	21	69
						Washington	30	37	67	92
6	Darren Veitch	D	6-0	195	4-24-60/Saskatoon, Sask.	Washington	9	44	53	54
						Hershey	5	10	15	16
9	Ryan Walter	C	6-0	195	4-23-58/New Westminster, B.C.	Washington	38	49	87	142

No.	Player	Pos.	Hgt.	Wgt.	Born		GP	GA	SO	Avg.
1	Rollie Boutin	G	5-9	179	11-6-57/Westlock, Alta.	Hershey	62	238	1	4.13
	Bart Hunter	G	5-10	158	10-1-59/Vancouver, B.C.	Hershey	20	76	0	4.75
35	Al Jensen	G	5-10	180	11-27-58/Hamilton, Ont.	Washington	26	81	0	3.81
						Hershey	8	24	0	3.54
29	Mike Palmateer	G	5-9	155	1-13-54/Toronto, Ont.	Washington	11	47	0	4.83
30	Dave Parro	G	5-10	165	4-30-57/Saskatoon, Sask.	Washington	52	206	1	4.20
	Pat Riggin	G	5-9	163	5-26-59/Kincardine, Ont.	Calgary	52	207	2	4.23

and still had time to show his aggressiveness with 128 penalty minutes . . . Tied for second in league with 20 power-play goals and has averaged more than one point a game in NHL career starting in 1975 with California Seals . . . "He's so small and quick that he's about as tough as anyone there is to try to check," says Ranger defenseman Andre Dore . . . Born Nov. 17, 1955, in Toronto . . . Goalies must watch him closely whenever he has the puck in the offensive zone . . . Fast-breaking center who excels at getting open for passes leading to shots on goal . . . Always a threat to break free for two-on-one rushes when opposing defense isn't careful . . . Possesses good backhand shot.

Year	Club	GP	G	A	Pts.
1975-76	California	80	30	32	62
1976-77	Cleveland	80	28	50	78
1977-78	Cleveland	76	36	35	71
1978-79	Minn.-Wash.	78	31	59	90
1979-80	Washington	27	10	17	27
1980-81	Washington	80	50	47	97
1981-82	Washington	80	60	76	136
	Totals	501	245	316	561

RYAN WALTER 24 6-0 195   Forward

Caps' captain and one of the best young team leaders in NHL . . . Had best season since joining Capitals four years ago with 38 goals, 87 points last season . . . Smooth skater with skillful offensive moves . . . A center who works hard on defense as well as offense . . . Scored on 20.8 per cent of his shots, second on team to Dennis Maruk's 22.4 shooting percentage . . . Had impressive minus-3 rating for team which allowed 19 more goals than it scored . . . Rival coaches rate him among league's best young forwards . . . Born April 23, 1958, in New Westminister, B.C. . . . Became youngest captain in NHL history when chosen to wear the "C" at 21 . . . Scored 19 power-play goals . . . Plays a physical game . . . Avid fisherman in off-season.

Year	Club	GP	G	A	Pts.
1978-79	Washington	69	28	27	55
1979-80	Washington	80	24	42	66
1980-81	Washington	80	24	45	69
1981-82	Washington	78	38	49	87
	Totals	307	114	163	277

MIKE GARTNER 23 6-0 185   Forward

A right wing with game-breaking goal-scoring capabilities... Scored five game-winning goals last season and led Capitals with 300 shots on goal... Followed 48-goal, 46-assist season in 1980–81 with 35 goals, 45 assists last year... Has the strength to fight off checks from opposing defensemen and break free from rival back-checking forwards... Born Oct. 29, 1959, in Ottawa, Ont.... Signed his first professional contract in 1978 with Cincinnati Stingers of WHA... Always seems to play his best games against strongest opponents... Has had 100 or more penalty minutes in each of last two seasons, an indication he can play with finesse or toughness equally well.

Year	Club	GP	G	A	Pts.
1978-79	Cincinnati (WHA)	78	27	25	52
1979-80	Washington	77	36	32	68
1980-81	Washington	80	48	46	94
1981-82	Washington	80	35	45	80
	Totals	315	146	148	294

BOBBY CARPENTER 19 6-0 185   Forward

"He's got a brilliant future ahead of him," says Rangers' coach Herb Brooks... Could become the first genuine American superstar in Canadian-dominated sport... Became the highest American-born draft choice in NHL history when he was the third player selected in the 1981 draft... Hailed as the greatest American-born player to enter the NHL... Starred at Massachusetts St. John's Prep, stepping directly into NHL from high school as an 18-year-old... Showed terrific offensive skills with 32 goals and 67 points in rookie season, including a four-goal game... Born July 13, 1963, in Beverly, Mass.... Still must concentrate upon upgrading his total game, especially on defense... Used both at center and left wing... Had to learn to deal with extreme media and fan pressure as a rookie... Former star Bobby Orr first recognized his skill and serves as his advisor.

Year	Club	GP	G	A	Pts.
1981-82	Washington	80	32	35	67

CHRIS VALENTINE 20 6-0 190   **Forward**

Another of the Capitals' bright, young forwards who could develop into an NHL star... A 30-goal scorer with 18 power-play scores in his rookie season... Surprised scouts from rival teams who overlooked him in early rounds of 1981 draft... Wasn't drafted until the 10th round, despite fine 65-goal season at Sorel in Quebec Major Junior League... Born Dec. 6, 1961, in Belleville, Ont.... Graceful center who shared team lead with five game-winning goals... Like most young forwards moving directly from junior hockey into NHL, he must improve his defensive play.

Year	Club	GP	G	A	Pts.
1981-82	Washington	60	30	37	67

DARREN VEITCH 22 6-0 195   **Defenseman**

Continued to develop into one of the league's most promising young defensemen in his second season in the NHL... Led Capitals' defensemen with nine goals and 44 assists and fired 203 shots on goal... Has a low, hard, accurate blue-line shot that rival goalies are learning to respect... Scored five power-play goals... Born April 24, 1960, in Saskatoon, Sask.... As a right-handed shot, he provides extra value as a defenseman... Not fast but has sufficient mobility for his size and uses his body effectively to take opposing players out of the play... Was a first-round draft choice of Washington in 1980 following outstanding season in junior hockey in which he scored 29 goals, 92 assists, 121 points for Regina... Plays an outstanding game of golf.

Year	Club	GP	G	A	Pts.
1980-81	Washington	59	4	21	25
1981-82	Washington	67	9	44	53
	Totals	126	13	65	78

TERRY MURRAY 32 6-2 190   **Defenseman**

Brother of Capitals' coach Bryan Murray... A steady but un-spectacular defensive defenseman who played a vital role last season on a team dominated by youthful players...A veteran of 13 professional seasons who has bounced around in the minor leagues since 1970...Started his NHL career in 1972–73 with old California Seals...Later played with Flyers and Red Wings...Born July 20, 1950, in Shawville, Quebec...Didn't score his first NHL goal until 1980–81 with Philadelphia, his seventh season in NHL...Tripled his career output with three goals last season.

Year	Club	GP	G	A	Pts.
1972-73	California	23	0	3	3
1973-74	California	58	0	12	12
1974-75	California	9	0	2	2
1975-76	Philadelphia	3	0	0	0
1976-77	Phil.-Det.	59	0	20	20
1978-79	Philadelphia	5	0	0	0
1980-81	Philadelphia	71	1	17	18
1981-82	Washington	74	3	22	25
	Totals	302	4	76	80

GREG THEBERGE 23 5-11 195   Defenseman

Helped strengthen a weak defense last season, his first full season in NHL since being drafted in 1979 by Capitals...Scored five goals and 37 points...Started professional career with Washington's American League farm team in Hershey, Pa....When Bryan Murray took over last season as Captial's coach, he gave Theberge a chance to play regularly...Born Sept. 3, 1959, in Peterborough, Ont....His minus-8 rating was the best among Washington defensemen who played regularly last season...Considered to be good breakout passer who sets up offensive rushes...Capitals expect big things of him this season.

Year	Club	GP	G	A	Pts.
1979-80	Washington	12	0	1	1
1980-81	Washington	1	1	0	1
1981-82	Washington	57	5	32	37
	Totals	70	6	33	39

DAVE PARRO 25 5-10 165   Goaltender

Stepped in and did a big job as Capitals' No. 1 goalie when knee injury limited veteran Mike Palmateer to only 11 games...Was in goal for 16 of Capitals' 26 wins...His 4.20 goals-against average doesn't give a true indication of how well he played for a defensively-weak team guilty of numerous mistakes and giveaways in its own zone...Born April 30, 1957, in Saskatoon, Sask....Regarded as one of Canada's best young goaltending prospects when drafted in 1977 by Boston but never got the chance he deserved with Bruins...Quebec selected him in 1979 expansion draft and traded him a few days later to Capitals.

Year	Club	GP	G	A	Pts.
1980-81	Washington	18	49	1	3.48
1981-82	Washington	52	206	1	4.20
	Totals	70	255	2	4.08

BENGT GUSTAFSSON 24 6-0 185   Forward

Former star of Swedish National Team...Has averaged 58 points in his first three seasons with Capitals...Is capable of increasing his goal and point production...His European-style play adds an extra dimension to Caps' offense...Born March 23, 1958, in Karlskoga, Sweden...Has a quick, accurate wrist shot and is an outstanding passer, skater and positional player...Although his scoring figures haven't yet been outstanding, he has earned a reputation for scoring or setting up goals in clutch situations...A fourth-round draft choice in 1978 who has shown he deserved to be drafted higher...Played soccer in his native Sweden.

Year	Club	GP	G	A	Pts.
1979-80	Washington	80	22	38	60
1980-81	Washington	72	21	34	55
1981-82	Washington	70	26	34	60
	Totals	222	69	106	175

COACH BRYAN MURRAY: Although they finished last in the Patrick Division last season, the Capitals played improved hockey with a greater sense of purpose and enthusiasm in the final 66 games of the season...The reason was Murray's coaching...An offense-minded coach with a knack for motivating younger players, Murray replaced Gary Green as coach Nov. 11, 1981, and finished his first season of NHL coaching with a 25-28-13 record . . . The older brother of Capitals' defenseman Terry Murray never played NHL hockey . . . Born Dec. 5, 1942, in Shawville, Quebec . . . Coached Regina to the Western Canada League junior championship in 1979–80 . . . Joined Capitals' organization for 1980–81 season and guided Hershey Bears of AHL to a divisional championship and their best record in 43 years . . . Named minor-league Coach of the Year for his work with Hershey in 1980–81.

GREATEST CENTER

The Minnesota North Stars have made few mistakes in trades but one player they regret dealing is Dennis Maruk.

Maruk was a 36-goal scorer for the 1977-78 Cleveland Barons, who were merged the following season with the North Stars. Believing the slightly-built Maruk was too small to be effective, the North Stars traded him to Washington for the Capitals' first-round draft choice in 1979.

It has turned out to be one of the best deals Capitals' management has made. Maruk scored 31 goals, 59 assists, 90 points in his first season with Washington. He missed 53 games with an injury in 1979-80 but exploded for 50 goals and 97 points in 1980-81 and last season was even more devastating—60 goals, 76 assists, 136 points.

"You can't take your eye off him, let down your guard, for one second or he'll do something to beat you," said Rangers' assistant coach Walt Tkaczuk, a strong two-way center during his career.

Maruk, who has slick, quick moves, was on the ice for almost half of the Capitals' goals last season. He's one of the best wrist shooters in the NHL and especially dangerous on power plays. In addition to scoring 110 goals in the last two seasons, he's scored 36 power-play goals and is regarded by opposing players as one of the most difficult, fast-breaking centers to check in the NHL.

ALL-TIME CAPITAL LEADERS

GOALS: Dennis Maruk, 60, 1981-82
ASSISTS: Dennis Maruk, 76, 1981-82
POINTS: Dennis Maruk, 136, 1981-82
SHUTOUTS: Mike Palmateer, 2, 1980-81

WINNIPEG JETS

TEAM DIRECTORY: Chairman: Bob Graham; Pres.: Michael Gobuty; VP-GM: John Ferguson; Dir. Pub. Rel. and Info.: Hartley Goldman; Dir. Player Personnel: Mike Doran; Coach: Tom Watt. Home ice: Winnipeg Arena (15,342; 200′ x 85′). Colors: Blue, red and white. Training camp: Winnipeg, Manitoba.

SCOUTING REPORT

OFFENSE: Can one man an offense make? That is, if he's not Wayne Gretzky? Dale Hawerchuk came close.

This is no attempt to say that Hawerchuk, who produced 45 goals and 103 points at 18 to win Rookie-of-the-Year honors, is another Gretzky. Although there are similarities in the way they play, especially in talent, instinct and reaction, Hawerchuk isn't the second anything. He's the first Hawerchuk.

Dale Hawerchuk shrugged off checks and won Calder Trophy.

Hawerchuk's presence was pivotal in the Jets' engineering the biggest one-season improvement, 48 points, by any club in NHL history.

However, the club is much more than a one-boy offense. They have quality attackers in Morris Lukowich (43 goals, 92 points), Dave Christian (76 points), Paul MacLean (36 goals), Willy Lindstrom (32 goals) plus defenseman Dave Babych (68 points).

There's more, too. Swedish center Thomas Steen and winger Bengt Lundholm (44 points each) are splendid prospects and so is Scott Arniel. He was Hawerchuk's winger in junior and remained in junior hockey to help Team Canada win the world junior title. The NHL portion of his season was reduced to 17 games by a badly cut hand, acquired during some horseplay in the dressing room.

Coach Tom Watt undoubtedly will be somewhat more demanding this season in his hunt for improved defensive work. But the parts are all there for a splendid attack.

DEFENSE: The acquisition of goalies Ed Staniowski and Doug Soetaert was a big move in the Jets' climb. They're solid pros in their mid-20s and that position is no problem.

Another wise move by GM John Ferguson was the acquisition of Serge Savard, the superb veteran defenseman who had retired from the Canadiens. Fergy claimed him in the waiver draft and their long friendship was a big part of Savard's return to the NHL at 36.

The wise, crafty Savard, who's slow in the feet but swift in the head, played sound defense and was invaluable in aiding the young backliners. He became the club's unofficial leader who showed the Jet kids how a classy big leaguer handles himself, on the ice and off.

Babych is a good one—big, swift, skilled and strong—who's moving slowly to all-star status. Tim Watters and Don Spring are solid kids and Craig Levie has the potential to be a good rusher. Young Moe Mantha spent much of his second pro season in the minors and now is ready for the NHL. The club's first-round draft pick, Jim Kyte, is a prime prospect.

OUTLOOK: This is a good organization that stuck to a plan through the worst season (1980-81) and it paid off. Watt, the NHL's Coach of the Year, appears certain to survive the jinx that goes with that award. He's an educator by profession, an excellent strategist who quickly earned the respect of his players.

The Jets move to the Smythe Division this season and that sector suddenly becomes one of the NHL's best because some of

JET ROSTER

No.	Player	Pos.	Hgt.	Wgt.	Born	1981-82	G	A	Pts.	PIM
11	Scott Arniel	LW	6-1	172	9-17-62/Kingston, Ont.	Winnipeg	1	8	9	14
44	Dave Babych	D	6-2	215	5-23-61/Edmonton, Alta.	Winnipeg	19	49	68	92
21	John Bethel	LW	5-11	180	1-15-57/Roxboro, Que.	Tulsa	19	51	70	83
	Rick Bowness	RW	6-1	185	1-25-55/Moncton, N.B.	Tulsa	34	53	87	201
	Dave Chartier	C	5-10	170	2-15-61/St. Lazare, Man.	Tulsa	18	17	35	126
13	Dave Christian	D-C	5-11	170	5-12-59/Warroad, Minn.	Winnipeg	25	51	76	28
16	Pat Daley	LW	6-0	176	3-27-59/Maryville, France	Fredericton	14	13	27	120
23	Lucien DeBlois	RW	5-11	200	6-21-57/Joliette, Que.	Winnipeg	25	27	52	87
28	Normand Dupont	LW	5-11	183	2-5-57/St. Michel, Que.	Winnipeg	13	25	38	22
	Murray Eaves	C	5-10	185	5-10-60/Calgary, Alta.	Winnipeg	0	0	0	0
						Tulsa	30	49	79	33
5	Danny Geoffrion	RW	5-10	185	1-21-58/Montreal, Que.	Tulsa	24	25	49	76
	Benoit Gosselin	LW	5-11	190	7-19-57/Montreal, Que.	Tulsa	31	23	54	29
10	Dale Hawerchuk	C	5-11	175	4-4-63/Toronto, Ont.	Winnipeg	45	58	103	47
	Glenn Hicks	LW	5-10	177	8-28-58/Red Deer, Alta.	Tulsa	14	34	48	103
17	Larry Hopkins	LW	6-1	205	3-17-54/Oshawa, Ont.	Winnipeg	10	15	25	22
						Tulsa	12	18	30	9
	Jim Kyte	D	6-5	205	3-21-64/Ottawa, Ont.	Cornwall	4	13	17	148
29	Doug Lecuyer	LW	5-9	179	3-10-58/Wainwright, Alta.	Tulsa	30	38	68	114
6	Barry Legge	D	6-0	186	10-22-54/Brantford, Ont.	Winnipeg	1	2	3	57
						Tulsa	0	1	1	0
	Craig Levie	D	5-11	190	8-17-59/Calgary, Alta.	Winnipeg	4	9	13	48
						Tulsa	4	7	11	17
20	Willy Lindstrom	RW	6-0	172	5-5-51/Grunns, Swe.	Winnipeg	32	27	59	33
12	Morris Lukowich	LW	5-9	167	6-1-56/Saskatoon, Sask.	Winnipeg	43	49	92	102
22	Bengt Lundholm	C	6-0	178	8-4-55/Stockholm, Swe.	Winnipeg	14	30	44	10
15	Paul MacLean	RW	6-0	190	1-15-58/Grostenquin, France	Winnipeg	36	25	61	106
19	Kris Manery	C-RW	6-0	185	9-24-54/Leamington, Ont.	Tulsa	54	35	89	60
8	Jim Mann	RW	6-0	202	4-17-59/Montreal, Que.	Winnipeg	3	2	5	79
2	Moe Mantha	D	6-2	197	1-21-61/Lakewood, Ohio	Winnipeg	0	12	12	28
						Tulsa	8	15	23	56
3	Bryan Maxwell	D	6-2	210	9-7-55/Lethbridge, Alta.	Winnipeg	1	9	10	110
18	Serge Savard	D	6-2	210	1-22-46/Montreal, Que.	Winnipeg	2	5	7	26
9	Doug Smail	LW	5-9	175	9-2-57/Moose Jaw, Sask.	Winnipeg	17	18	35	55
27	Don Spring	D	5-11	195	6-15-59/Maracaibo, Ven.	Winnipeg	0	16	16	21
25	Thomas Steen	C	5-10	195	6-8-60/Tockmark, Swe.	Winnipeg	15	29	44	42
14	Tim Trimper	LW	5-9	184	9-28-59/Windsor, Ont.	Winnipeg	8	8	16	100
7	Tim Watters	D	5-11	180	7-25-59/Kamloops, B.C.	Winnipeg	2	22	24	97
						Tulsa	1	2	3	0
24	Ron Wilson	LW	5-9	170	5-13-56/Toronto, Ont.	Winnipeg	3	13	16	49
						Tulsa	20	38	58	22

	Player	Pos.	Hgt.	Wgt.	Born		GP	GA	SO	Avg.
	Yves Dechene	G	6-2	202	1-8-59/Quebec City, Que.	Tulsa	28	112	1	4.11
34	Pierre Hamel	G	5-9	170	9-16-52/Monteal, Que.	Fredericton	29	114	1	4.35
						Tulsa	5	14	0	3.40
35	Markus Mattsson	G	6-0	180	7-30-57/Tampevé, Fin.	Tulsa	50	195	0	3.95
33	Doug Soetaert	G	6-1	180	4-21-55/Edmonton, Alta.	Winnipeg	39	155	2	4.31
31	Ed Staniowski	G	5-9	170	7-7-55/Moose Jaw, Sask.	Winnipeg	45	174	1	3.95

the finest young talent is there. The Jets have a good share of it and their climb towards the top should continue.

JET PROFILES

DALE HAWERCHUK 19 5-11 175   Forward
Extraordinary offensive player who had 45 goals, 103 points in outstanding Calder Trophy season...Comparison to Wayne Gretzky is justified because style, anticipation and skill are similar...Superb puckhandler, brilliant playmaker...His arrival was large part of club's 48-point improvement...Born in Toronto on April 4, 1963...Outstanding junior with Cornwall Royals: 286 points in two seasons, leading club to two consecutive Canadian junior titles...First player claimed in 1981 entry draft...Modest, unassuming youngster...Surprised with defensive ability...Had eight points in four playoff games.

Year	Club	GP	G	A	Pts.
1981-82	Winnipeg	80	45	58	103

MORRIS LUKOWICH 26 5-9 167   Forward
One of best three or four left wingers in NHL...Small but quick, strong and tough...Scored 43 goals last season after 35 and 33 in first two NHL terms...Owns excellent wrist shot...Born June 1, 1956, in Speers, Sask....Turned pro with Houston Aeros in WHA...Joined Jets in WHA when Houston team folded in 1978...Scored 65 goals in 1978-79...Was protected player by Jets in 1979 NHL expansion draft...Was teammate of Houston Astros' Terry Puhl in amateur baseball...Scored Jets' first goal in NHL...Team captain.

Year	Club	GP	G	A	Pts.
1976-77	Houston (WHA)	62	27	18	45
1977-78	Houston (WHA)	80	40	35	75
1978-79	Winnipeg (WHA)	80	65	34	99
1979-80	Winnipeg	78	35	39	74
1980-81	Winnipeg	80	33	34	67
1981-82	Winnipeg	77	43	49	92
	Totals	457	243	209	452

DAVE CHRISTIAN 23 5-11 170   Forward

Competent, consistent big-league forward...Has produced 71 and 76 points in his first two NHL seasons...Excellent defensive player who checks opponents' top center and kills penalties...Plays the point on power play...Played defense for the U.S. Olympic team in 1980 triumph...Born May 12, 1959, in Warroad, Minn....His family has a distinguished hockey background... Father Bill scored winning goal against USSR in 1960 Olympics' gold-medal triumph...Uncles Roger and Gord also played in Games...Joined Jets after 1980 Games and scored 18 points in 15 games.

Year	Club	GP	G	A	Pts.
1979-80	Winnipeg	15	8	10	18
1980-81	Winnipeg	80	28	43	71
1981-82	Winnipeg	80	25	51	76
	Totals	175	61	104	165

DAVE BABYCH 21 6-2 215   Defenseman

Continued rookie-season excellence and seems destined for all-star status...Has it all: size, strength, agility, puckhandling skill...Counted 44 points in first season, upped that to 68 points last term...Improved defensive play and benefitted from presence of veteran Serge Savard...Born May 23, 1961, in Edmonton ...Played Major Junior hockey at 15 with Portland Winterhawks ...Second player picked in 1980 entry draft...Good body-checker...He and brother Wayne of St. Louis Blues married twin sisters in offseason.

Year	Club	GP	G	A	Pts.
1980-81	Winnipeg	69	6	38	44
1981-82	Winnipeg	79	19	49	68
	Totals	148	25	87	112

PAUL MacLEAN 23 6-0 190   Forward

Excellent addition, acquired in summer of 1981 from St. Louis with Ed Staniowski and Bryan Maxwell for Scott Campbell and

John Markell... Produced 36 goals, 61 points in NHL rookie season... Perfect winger for center Dale Hawerchuk... Strong, aggressive in corners, good defensively, solid scorer with fine shot... Born March 9, 1959, in Grotenquin, France... Played junior hockey in Hull, Que. and was claimed by Blues on sixth round of 1978 draft... Member of the Canadian Olympic team in 1980... Spent 1979-80 season with Salt Lake in CHL, scoring 36 goals, 78 points.

Year	Club	GP	G	A	Pts.
1980-81	St. Louis	1	0	0	0
1981-82	Winnipeg	74	36	25	61
	Totals	75	36	25	61

LUCIEN DeBLOIS 25 5-11 200   Forward

Consistent two-way player... Joined team in complicated compensation deal for Ivan Hlinka, the Czech forward claimed by the Jets but signed by Vancouver... Scored 25 goals and was strong defensively... Good penalty-killer... Born June 21, 1957, in Joliette, Que.... Jets' GM John Ferguson made him a 1977 first-round draft pick of New York Rangers when he ran that team... Went from Rangers to Colorado as part of controversial 1979 deal for defenseman Barry Beck... Strong along boards and in corners... Played junior hockey in Sorel, Quebec.

Year	Club	GP	G	A	Pts.
1977-78	New York R.	71	22	8	30
1978-79	New York R.	62	11	17	28
1979-80	N.Y.R.-Col.	76	27	20	47
1980-81	Colorado	74	26	16	42
1981-82	Winnipeg	65	25	27	52
	Totals	348	111	88	199

WILLY LINDSTROM 31 6-0 172   Forward

Willy The Wisp... Smooth, slick skater with strong offensive skills who surprised with 32 goals last season... Teamed with fellow Swedes Thomas Steen and Bengt Lundholm on effective line... Born May 5, 1951, in Gruns, Sweden... Major star in

Swedish hockey, played in three world tournaments with Swedish national team... Joined the Jets in the WHA in 1975, scored 123 goals in four WHA seasons... Had 23 and 22 goals in first two NHL seasons... Among fastest skaters in league... One of the game's best practical jokers.

Year	Club	GP	G	A	Pts.
1975-76	Winnipeg (WHA)	81	23	36	59
1976-77	Winnipeg (WHA)	79	44	36	80
1977-78	Winnipeg (WHA)	77	30	30	60
1978-79	Winnipeg (WHA)	79	26	36	62
1979-80	Winnipeg	79	23	26	49
1980-81	Winnipeg	72	22	13	35
1981-82	Winnipeg	74	32	27	59
	Totals	541	200	204	404

DOUG SOETAERT 27 6-1 180   Goaltender

Important addition in 1981-82 season from New York Rangers... With another new face, Ed Staniowski, he gave team sound goaltending, a big factor in large improvement... Shuttled between Rangers and farm clubs for five seasons... Had 4.31 average in 39 games with Jets... Born in Edmonton on April 21, 1955... Junior star with Edmonton Oil Kings... Rangers' second-round pick in 1975 entry draft... Excellent stand-up goalie with good catching hand... Jets acquired him for future draft choice after Rangers gave up on him.

Year	Club	GP	GA	SO	Avg.
1975-76	New York R.	8	24	0	5.27
1976-77	New York R.	12	28	1	2.95
1977-78	New York R.	6	20	0	3.33
1978-79	New York R.	17	57	0	3.80
1979-80	New York R.	8	33	0	4.55
1980-81	New York R.	39	152	0	3.93
1981-82	Winnipeg	39	155	2	4.31
	Totals	129	469	3	4.01

ED STANIOWSKI 27 5-9 170   Goaltender

A big part of the team's 48-point improvement... Acquired from St. Louis in 1981 trade with Paul MacLean and Bryan Maxwell for Scott Campbell and John Markell... Had 20 victories and 3.95 average in 45 games... Had divided five seasons between Blues and minors... Played 39 NHL games in 1978-79... Born July

7, 1955, in Moose Jaw, Sask.... Had outstanding junior career with Regina Pats and was named Canadian junior Player of the Year in 1974-75...Second-round pick in 1975 draft... Very quick, good technically, strong competitor... Won 1979 Charlie Conacher Trophy for humanitarian efforts.

Year	Club	GP	GA	SO	Avg.
1975-76	St. Louis	11	33	0	3.19
1976-77	St. Louis	29	108	0	4.08
1977-78	St. Louis	17	57	0	3.86
1978-79	St. Louis	39	146	0	3.82
1979-80	St. Louis	22	80	0	4.33
1980-81	St. Louis	19	72	0	4.28
1981-82	Winnipeg	45	174	1	3.95
	Totals	182	670	1	3.96

SERGE SAVARD 36 6-2 210   Defenseman

Great veteran of Montreal Canadiens who became anchor of Jets' backline... Had retired at end of 1980-81 season after fine 15-season career... Jets claimed him in waiver draft and his close friend, GM John Ferguson, talked him into comeback... Played well and was invaluable working with young defensemen... Born Jan. 22, 1946, in Montreal... Survived two severely broken legs early in NHL career to become superb defenseman... Not flashy on attack but excellent defensively... Won Conn Smythe Trophy as playoff MVP in 1969... Member of eight Stanley Cup teams... Very successful businessman.

Year	Club	GP	G	A	Pts.
1966-67	Montreal	2	0	0	0
1967-68	Montreal	67	2	13	15
1968-69	Montreal	74	8	23	31
1969-70	Montreal	64	12	19	31
1970-71	Montreal	37	5	10	15
1971-72	Montreal	23	1	8	9
1972-73	Montreal	74	7	32	39
1973-74	Montreal	67	4	14	18
1974-75	Montreal	80	20	40	60
1975-76	Montreal	71	8	39	47
1976-77	Montreal	78	9	33	42
1977-78	Montreal	77	8	34	42
1978-79	Montreal	80	7	26	33
1979-80	Montreal	46	5	8	13
1980-81	Montreal	77	4	13	17
1981-82	Winnipeg	47	2	5	7
	Totals	964	102	317	419

Defenseman Dave Babych does it all for rising Jets.

COACH TOM WATT: The NHL's Coach of the Year in 1981-82, his first season in head coaching job... Guided team to 48-point improvement, the largest in NHL history... Excellent teacher of hockey skills, fine handler of young players... A teacher by profession... Earned degree and played college hockey at University of Toronto, added master's in education... Born June 17, 1935, in Toronto... Taught high school and coached hockey, football and lacrosse teams... Named coach of U. of T. Blues in 1965... Took team to 11 conference

and nine Canadian college titles in 14 seasons, building 378-96-29 won-lost-tied record... Has wide experience in international hockey... Coached Canadian national student team several times and took his Blues on a tour of China... Was a co-coach of the 1980 Canadian Olympic team... Made pro debut as assistant coach with Vancouver Canucks in 1980-81.

GREATEST CENTER

In a short length of time, there's little doubt that Dale Hawerchuk will be the greatest center in the Jets' history. He had 103 points in 1981-82 to win the Calder Trophy as the NHL's best rookie.

However, the finest center ever to wear a Jet uniform comes from the team's glory days as the finest team in the eight years of the World Hockey Association. Ulf Nilsson, one of the first great Swedish immigrants to North American hockey, built an enviable record with the Jets before he and his countryman, Anders Hedberg, the brilliant right winger, moved to the New York Rangers as free agents.

In 298 WHA games, Nilsson scored 140 goals and had 344 assists. He teamed with Hedberg and left winger Bobby Hull to form one of hockey best forward lines, an artistic combination of superbly skilled players.

Nilsson was a brilliant puckhandler and playmaker who choreographed the line's "whirling dervish" approach.

ALL-TIME JET LEADERS

GOALS: Bobby Hull, 77, 1974-75
ASSISTS: Ulf Nilsson, 94, 1974-75
POINTS: Bobby Hull, 142, 1974-75
SHUTOUTS: Joe Daley, 5, 1975-76

Official NHL Statistics

1981-82

FINAL STANDINGS

PRINCE OF WALES CONFERENCE
PATRICK DIVISION

	GP	W	L	T	GF	GA	PTS	PCT
NY Islanders	80	54	16	10	385	250	118	.738
NY Rangers	80	39	27	14	316	306	92	.575
Philadelphia	80	38	31	11	325	313	87	.544
Pittsburgh	80	31	36	13	310	337	75	.469
Washington	80	26	41	13	319	338	65	.406

ADAMS DIVISION

	GP	W	L	T	GF	GA	PTS	PCT
Montreal	80	46	17	17	360	223	109	.681
Boston	80	43	27	10	323	285	96	.600
Buffalo	80	39	26	15	307	273	93	.581
Quebec	80	33	31	16	356	345	82	.513
Hartford	80	21	41	18	264	351	60	.375

CLARENCE CAMPBELL CONFERENCE
NORRIS DIVISION

	GP	W	L	T	GF	GA	PTS	PCT
Minnesota	80	37	23	20	346	288	94	.588
Winnipeg	80	33	33	14	319	332	80	.500
St. Louis	80	32	40	8	315	349	72	.450
Chicago	80	30	38	12	332	363	72	.450
Toronto	80	20	44	16	298	380	56	.350
Detroit	80	21	47	12	270	351	54	.338

SMYTHE DIVISION

	GP	W	L	T	GF	GA	PTS	PCT
Edmonton	80	48	17	15	417	295	111	.694
Vancouver	80	30	33	17	290	286	77	.481
Calgary	80	29	34	17	334	345	75	.469
Los Angeles	80	24	41	15	314	369	63	.394
Colorado	80	18	49	13	241	362	49	.306

STANLEY CUP: NY Islanders

INDIVIDUAL LEADERS

Goals: Wayne Gretzky, Edmonton, 92.
Assists: Wayne Gretzky, Edmonton, 120.
Points: Wayne Gretzky, Edmonton, 212.
Penalty Mins.: Paul Baxter, Pittsburgh, 407.
Power-Play Goals: Paul Gardner, Pittsburgh, 21.
Shorthanded Goals: Wayne Gretzky, Edmonton, and Michel Goulet, Quebec, 6 each.
Game-Winning Goals: Wayne Gretzky, Edmonton, 12.
Three-Goal Games: Wayne Gretzky, Edmonton, 10.
Game-Tying Goals: Blaine Stoughton, Hartford, 7.
Shutouts: Denis Herron, Montreal, 3.
Goaltender Wins: Billy Smith, NY Islanders, 32.
Best Personal Goals-Against Ave.: Denis Herron, Montreal, 2.64.

INDIVIDUAL SCORING LEADERS

PLAYER	TEAM	GP	G	A	PTS	PIM	PP	SH	GW	GT
Wayne Gretzky	Edmonton	80	92	120	212	26	18	6	12	4
Mike Bossy	NY Islanders	80	64	83	147	22	17	0	10	0
Peter Stastny	Quebec	80	46	93	139	91	16	3	3	0
Dennis Maruk	Washington	80	60	76	136	128	20	2	1	1
Bryan Trottier	NY Islanders	80	50	79	129	88	18	2	10	2
Denis Savard	Chicago	80	32	87	119	82	8	0	4	1
Marcel Dionne	Los Angeles	78	50	67	117	50	17	1	5	4
Bobby Smith	Minnesota	80	43	71	114	84	20	0	4	3
Dino Ciccarelli	Minnesota	76	55	52	107	138	20	0	4	5
Dave Taylor	Los Angeles	78	39	67	106	130	13	0	3	0
Glenn Anderson	Edmonton	80	38	67	105	71	9	0	8	2
Dale Hawerchuk	Winnipeg	80	45	58	103	47	12	0	2	2
Mike Rogers	NY Rangers	80	38	65	103	43	6	1	2	0

PLAYERS BY TEAM

PLAYER	TEAM	GP	G	A	PTS	PIM	PP	SH	GW	GT
Rick Middleton	Boston	75	51	43	94	12	19	1	9	3
Barry Pederson	Boston	80	44	48	92	53	13	4	7	0
Peter McNab	Boston	80	36	40	76	19	11	1	5	2
Ray Bourque	Boston	65	17	49	66	51	4	0	2	2
Brad Park	Boston	75	14	42	56	82	8	0	1	1
Terry O'Reilly	Boston	70	22	30	52	213	0	1	3	1
Steve Kasper	Boston	73	20	31	51	72	1	3	3	0
Keith Crowder	Boston	71	23	21	44	101	0	0	1	1
Wayne Cashman	Boston	64	12	31	43	59	3	0	1	0
Tom Fergus	Boston	61	15	24	39	12	2	0	2	0
Mike O'Connell	Boston	80	5	34	39	75	1	0	0	0
Don Marcotte	Boston	69	13	22	35	14	0	0	3	0
Normand Leveille	Boston	65	14	19	33	49	1	0	4	0
Bruce Crowder	Boston	63	16	11	27	31	1	0	1	0
Stan Jonathan	Boston	67	6	17	23	57	1	0	0	0
Mike Gillis	Boston	53	9	8	17	54	0	0	0	0
Mike Milbury	Boston	51	2	10	12	71	0	0	1	0
Brad McCrimmon	Boston	79	1	8	9	83	0	0	0	0
Randy Hillier	Boston	25	0	8	8	29	0	0	0	0
Larry Melnyk	Boston	48	0	8	8	84	0	0	0	0
Mike Krushelnyski	Boston	17	3	3	6	2	0	1	0	0
Marco Baron	Boston	44	0	2	2	35	0	0	0	0
Craig Mactavish	Boston	2	0	1	1	0	0	0	0	0
Rogie Vachon	Boston	38	0	1	1	0	0	0	0	0
David Barr	Boston	2	0	0	0	0	0	0	0	0
Doug Morrison	Boston	3	0	0	0	0	0	0	0	0
Dick Redmond	Boston	17	0	0	0	4	0	0	0	0

Chicago's Denis Savard was the NHL's sixth-leading scorer.

PLAYER	TEAM	GP	G	A	PTS	PIM	PPG	SHG	GW	GT
Mike Foligno	Detroit	26	13	13	26	28	3	0	0	0
	Buffalo	56	20	31	51	149	4	0	6	0
	Total	82	33	44	77	177	7	0	6	0
Gilbert Perreault	Buffalo	62	31	42	73	40	2	0	4	0
Dale McCourt	Detroit	26	13	14	27	6	6	0	0	0
	Buffalo	52	20	22	42	12	4	1	2	1
	Total	78	33	36	69	18	10	1	2	1
John Van Boxmeer	Buffalo	69	14	54	68	62	7	0	1	1
Yvon Lambert	Buffalo	77	25	39	64	38	14	0	4	2
Jean F. Sauve	Buffalo	69	19	36	55	46	5	0	1	0
Tony McKegney	Buffalo	73	23	29	52	41	8	0	0	1
Craig Ramsay	Buffalo	80	16	35	51	8	0	1	2	1
Lindy Ruff	Buffalo	79	16	32	48	194	3	0	6	1
Ric Seiling	Buffalo	57	22	25	47	58	7	1	3	1
Alan Haworth	Buffalo	57	21	18	39	30	3	0	1	2
Andre Savard	Buffalo	62	18	20	38	24	2	1	3	0
Mike Ramsey	Buffalo	80	7	23	30	56	2	0	0	0
Richie Dunn	Buffalo	72	7	19	26	73	0	0	1	1
Steve Patrick	Buffalo	41	8	8	16	64	0	0	0	0
Larry Playfair	Buffalo	77	6	10	16	258	0	0	0	3
Brent Peterson	Detroit	15	1	0	1	6	0	0	0	0
	Buffalo	46	9	5	14	43	0	0	0	0
	Total	61	10	5	15	49	0	0	0	0
Bill Hajt	Buffalo	65	2	9	11	44	0	0	0	0
Robert Mongrain	Buffalo	24	6	4	10	6	0	0	2	0
Gilles Hamel	Buffalo	16	2	7	9	2	0	0	1	0
Bob Hess	Buffalo	33	0	8	8	14	0	0	0	0
Ron Fischer	Buffalo	15	0	7	7	6	0	0	0	0
Randy Cunneyworth	Buffalo	20	2	4	6	47	0	0	0	0
Don Edwards	Buffalo	62	0	2	2	2	0	0	0	0
Haanu Virta	Buffalo	3	0	1	1	4	0	0	0	0
Sean McKenna	Buffalo	3	0	1	1	2	0	0	0	0
Jim Walsh	Buffalo	4	0	1	1	4	0	0	0	0
Jeff Eatough	Buffalo	1	0	0	0	0	0	0	0	0
Kai Suikkanen	Buffalo	1	0	0	0	0	0	0	0	0
Valmore James	Buffalo	7	0	0	0	16	0	0	0	0
Mike Moller	Buffalo	9	0	0	0	0	0	0	0	0
Paul Harrison	Pittsburgh	13	0	0	0	0	0	0	0	0
	Buffalo	6	0	0	0	2	0	0	0	0
	Total	19	0	0	0	2	0	0	0	0
Mel Bridgman	Philadelphia	9	7	5	12	47	3	0	1	0
	Calgary	63	26	49	75	94	6	2	3	0
	Total	72	33	54	87	141	9	2	4	0
Lanny McDonald	Colorado	15	6	9	15	20	0	0	1	1
	Calgary	55	34	33	67	37	10	1	3	0
	Total	71	40	42	82	57	10	1	4	1
Guy Chouinard	Calgary	64	23	57	80	12	13	0	4	1
Pekka Rautakallio	Calgary	80	17	51	68	40	5	0	3	3
Jim Peplinski	Calgary	74	30	37	67	115	3	3	5	4
Kevin Lavallee	Calgary	75	32	29	61	30	6	0	3	2
Paul Reinhart	Calgary	62	13	48	61	17	8	0	0	0
Willi Plett	Calgary	78	21	36	57	288	5	0	2	2
Kent Nilsson	Calgary	41	26	29	55	8	13	0	0	2

After joining Calgary, Lanny McDonald got 34 goals.

PLAYER	TEAM	GP	G	A	PTS	PIM	PPG	SHG	GW	GT
Ken Houston	Calgary	70	22	22	44	91	3	0	0	0
Jamie Hislop	Calgary	80	16	25	41	35	0	2	1	2
Phil Russell	Calgary	71	4	25	29	110	0	0	0	0
Gary McAdam	Calgary	46	12	15	27	18	0	0	1	1
Denis Cyr	Calgary	45	12	10	22	13	2	0	2	0
Dan Labraaten	Calgary	43	10	12	22	6	1	0	0	0
Bob Murdoch	Calgary	73	3	17	20	76	0	0	0	2
Stephen Konroyd	Calgary	63	3	14	17	78	0	0	1	0
Bill Clement	Calgary	69	4	12	16	28	0	0	0	0
Charles Bourgeois	Calgary	54	2	13	15	112	0	0	0	0
Pat Riggin	Calgary	52	0	5	5	4	0	0	0	0
Dave Hindmarch	Calgary	9	3	0	3	0	0	0	0	0
Pat Ribble	Washington	12	1	2	3	14	0	0	0	0
	Calgary	3	0	0	0	2	0	0	0	0
	Total	15	1	2	3	16	0	0	0	0
Ed Beers	Calgary	5	1	1	2	21	0	0	0	0
Mike Dwyer	Calgary	5	0	2	2	0	0	0	0	0
Gord Waffle	Calgary	11	1	0	1	6	0	0	0	0
Carl Mokosak	Calgary	1	0	1	1	0	0	0	0	0
Rejean Lemelin	Calgary	34	0	1	1	0	0	0	0	0
Randy Turnbull	Calgary	1	0	0	0	2	0	0	0	0
Bruce Eakin	Calgary	1	0	0	0	0	0	0	0	0
Bobby Lalonde	Calgary	1	0	0	0	0	0	0	0	0
Allan MacInnis	Calgary	2	0	0	0	0	0	0	0	0
Tim Hunter	Calgary	2	0	0	0	9	0	0	0	0
Denis Savard	Chicago	80	32	87	119	82	8	0	4	1
Doug Wilson	Chicago	76	39	46	85	54	14	1	3	3
Tom Lysiak	Chicago	71	32	50	82	84	10	2	4	2
Al Secord	Chicago	80	44	31	75	303	14	0	6	0
Tim Higgins	Chicago	74	20	30	50	85	6	0	2	1
Grant Mulvey	Chicago	73	30	19	49	141	3	0	3	0
Rich Preston	Chicago	75	15	28	43	30	1	1	1	1
Doug Crossman	Chicago	70	12	28	40	24	7	0	1	1
Reg Kerr	Chicago	59	11	28	39	39	1	0	1	1
Terry Ruskowski	Chicago	60	7	30	37	120	2	0	0	0
Darryl Sutter	Chicago	40	23	12	35	31	4	3	0	2
Ted Bulley	Chicago	59	12	18	30	120	2	0	2	0
Bob Murray	Chicago	45	8	22	30	48	3	1	0	0
Peter Marsh	Chicago	57	10	18	28	47	0	0	0	1
Keith Brown	Chicago	33	4	20	24	26	2	0	0	0
Bill Gardner	Chicago	69	8	15	23	20	1	4	0	0
Dave Hutchison	Chicago	66	5	18	23	246	0	1	0	0
Greg Fox	Chicago	79	2	19	21	137	0	0	0	0
Glen Sharpley	Chicago	36	9	7	16	11	0	0	2	0
Rick Paterson	Chicago	48	4	7	11	8	0	0	1	0
Jerry Dupont	Chicago	34	0	4	4	51	0	0	0	0
Steve Ludzik	Chicago	8	2	1	3	2	0	0	0	0
Florent Robidoux	Chicago	4	1	2	3	0	0	0	0	0
Miles Zaharko	Chicago	15	1	2	3	18	0	0	0	0
Dave Feamster	Chicago	29	0	2	2	29	0	0	0	0
Tony Esposito	Chicago	52	0	2	2	0	0	0	0	0
John Marks	Chicago	13	1	0	1	7	0	0	0	0
Murray Bannerman	Chicago	29	0	1	1	0	0	0	0	0

PLAYER	TEAM	GP	G	A	PTS	PIM	PPG	SHG	GW	GT
Troy Murray	Chicago	1	0	0	0	0	0	0	0	0
Tony Tanti	Chicago	2	0	0	0	0	0	0	0	0
Steve Larmer	Chicago	3	0	0	0	0	0	0	0	0
Don Lever	Calgary	23	8	11	19	6	1	0	0	0
	Colorado	59	22	28	50	20	3	0	1	1
	Total	82	30	39	69	26	4	0	1	1
Bob MacMillan	Calgary	23	4	7	11	14	1	0	0	0
	Colorado	57	18	32	50	27	3	0	1	2
	Total	80	22	39	61	41	4	0	1	2
Brent Ashton	Colorado	80	24	36	60	26	3	0	4	1
Steve Tambellini	Colorado	79	29	30	59	14	9	0	0	1
Rob Ramage	Colorado	80	13	29	42	201	6	0	0	1
Merlin Malinowski	Colorado	69	13	28	41	32	0	1	0	1
Aaron Broten	Colorado	58	15	24	39	6	5	1	5	2
Dwight Foster	Colorado	70	12	19	31	41	1	1	0	1
Bob Miller	Colorado	56	11	20	31	27	1	0	2	1
Dave Cameron	Colorado	66	11	12	23	103	0	1	0	0
Paul Gagne	Colorado	59	10	12	22	17	2	0	0	0
Tapio Levo	Colorado	34	9	13	22	14	3	0	0	0
Joe Micheletti	St. Louis	20	3	11	14	28	2	0	0	0
	Colorado	21	2	6	8	4	0	0	0	0
	Total	41	5	17	22	32	2	0	0	1
Stan Weir	Edmonton	51	3	13	16	13	1	0	1	0
	Colorado	10	2	3	5	10	0	0	1	0
	Total	61	5	16	21	23	1	0	2	0
Bob Lorimer	Colorado	79	5	15	20	68	1	0	0	0
Joe Cirella	Colorado	65	7	12	19	52	2	0	1	0
Kevin Maxwell	Minnesota	12	1	4	5	8	0	0	0	0
	Colorado	34	5	5	10	44	0	0	1	0
	Total	46	6	9	15	52	0	0	1	0
Joel Quenneville	Colorado	64	5	10	15	55	0	0	0	0
Veli Pekka Ketola	Colorado	44	9	5	14	4	4	0	1	1
Graeme Nicolson	Colorado	41	2	7	9	51	0	0	0	0
Mike Kitchen	Colorado	63	1	8	9	60	0	0	0	0
John Wensink	Colorado	57	5	3	8	152	1	0	0	0
Jukka Porvari	Colorado	31	2	6	8	0	0	0	0	0
Yvon Vautour	Colorado	14	1	2	3	18	1	0	0	0
Paul Miller	Colorado	3	0	3	3	0	0	0	0	0
Jeff Larmer	Colorado	8	1	1	2	8	0	0	0	0
Phil Myre	Colorado	24	0	2	2	0	0	0	0	0
Glenn Resch	Colorado	61	0	2	2	8	0	0	0	0
Ed Cooper	Colorado	2	1	0	1	0	0	0	0	0
Richard Chernomaz	Colorado	2	0	0	0	0	0	0	0	0
Peter Gustavsson	Colorado	2	0	0	0	0	0	0	0	0
Christer Kellgren	Colorado	5	0	0	0	0	0	0	0	0
Randy Pierce	Colorado	5	0	0	0	4	0	0	0	0
John Hughes	Colorado	8	0	0	0	13	0	0	0	0
Jim Dobson	Minnesota	6	0	0	0	4	0	0	0	0
	Colorado	3	0	0	0	2	0	0	0	0
	Total	9	0	0	0	6	0	0	0	0
Mark Osborne	Detroit	80	26	41	67	61	5	0	3	0
Reed Larson	Detroit	80	21	39	60	112	4	2	2	1

PLAYER	TEAM	GP	G	A	PTS	PIM	PPG	SHG	GW	GT
Mike Blaisdell	Detroit	80	23	32	55	48	4	0	3	2
Walt McKechnie	Detroit	74	18	37	55	28	2	0	3	1
John Ogrodnick	Detroit	80	28	26	54	28	3	2	3	3
Willie Huber	Detroit	74	15	30	45	98	5	0	2	0
Danny Gare	Buffalo	22	7	14	21	25	2	0	1	0
	Detroit	37	13	10	23	74	2	1	0	0
	Total	59	20	24	44	99	4	1	1	0
Mark Kirton	Detroit	74	14	28	42	62	0	1	0	1
Vaclav Nedomansky	Detroit	68	12	28	40	22	1	0	0	0
Greg Smith	Detroit	69	10	22	32	79	2	0	1	0
Eric Vail	Calgary	6	4	1	5	0	1	0	0	0
	Detroit	52	10	14	24	35	3	0	0	1
	Total	58	14	15	29	35	4	0	0	1
Paul Woods	Detroit	75	10	17	27	48	0	1	1	0
Derek Smith	Buffalo	12	3	1	4	2	0	0	0	1
	Detroit	49	6	14	20	10	0	0	0	0
	Total	61	9	15	24	12	0	0	0	1
Don Murdoch	Detroit	49	9	13	22	23	1	0	1	1
Jim Schoenfeld	Buffalo	13	3	2	5	30	0	0	1	0
	Detroit	39	5	9	14	69	0	0	0	1
	Total	52	8	11	19	99	0	0	1	1
Jody Gage	Detroit	31	9	9	18	2	0	0	1	0
Theodore Nolan	Detroit	41	4	13	17	43	0	2	0	0
John Barrett	Detroit	69	1	12	13	93	0	0	0	0
Mark Lofthouse	Detroit	12	3	4	7	13	0	0	0	0
Greg Joly	Detroit	37	1	5	6	30	0	1	0	0
Brad Smith	Detroit	33	2	0	2	80	0	0	1	0
Claude Loiselle	Detroit	4	1	0	1	2	1	0	0	0
Claude Legris	Detroit	1	0	1	1	0	0	0	0	0
Rejean Cloutier	Detroit	2	0	1	1	2	0	0	0	0
Joe Paterson	Detroit	3	0	0	0	0	0	0	0	0
Corrado Micalef	Detroit	18	0	0	0	9	0	0	0	0
Gilles Gilbert	Detroit	27	0	0	0	2	0	0	0	0
Bob Sauve	Buffalo	14	0	0	0	2	0	0	0	0
	Detroit	41	0	0	0	0	0	0	0	0
	Total	55	0	0	0	2	0	0	0	0
Wayne Gretzky	Edmonton	80	92	120	212	26	18	6	12	4
Glenn Anderson	Edmonton	80	38	67	105	71	9	0	8	2
Paul Coffey	Edmonton	80	29	60	89	106	13	0	1	0
Mark Messier	Edmonton	78	50	38	88	119	10	0	3	2
Jari Kurri	Edmonton	71	32	54	86	32	6	1	5	1
Dave Lumley	Edmonton	66	32	42	74	96	4	1	6	3
Risto Siltanen	Edmonton	63	15	48	63	24	6	0	1	0
Matti Hagman	Edmonton	72	21	38	59	18	5	0	2	0
Pat Hughes	Edmonton	68	24	22	46	99	4	2	0	1
Kevin Lowe	Edmonton	80	9	31	40	63	1	1	2	0
Dave Hunter	Edmonton	63	16	22	38	63	0	0	3	1
Laurie Boschman	Toronto	54	9	19	28	150	1	0	1	1
	Edmonton	11	2	3	5	37	0	0	0	0
	Total	65	11	22	33	187	1	0	1	1
Lee Fogolin	Edmonton	80	4	25	29	154	0	0	0	0
Brett Callighen	Edmonton	46	8	19	27	28	3	0	1	0
Dave Semenko	Edmonton	59	12	12	24	194	4	0	1	0

PLAYER	TEAM	GP	G	A	PTS	PIM	PPG	SHG	GW	GT
Garry Lariviere	Edmonton	62	1	21	22	41	0	0	0	0
Garry Unger	Edmonton	46	7	13	20	69	0	0	2	0
Charlie Huddy	Edmonton	41	4	11	15	48	0	0	0	1
Tom Roulston	Edmonton	35	11	3	14	22	0	1	0	0
Mike Forbes	Edmonton	16	1	7	8	26	0	0	0	0
Grant Fuhr	Edmonton	48	0	6	6	6	0	0	0	0
Ken Berry	Edmonton	15	2	3	5	9	0	0	0	0
Marc Habscheid	Edmonton	7	1	3	4	2	1	0	0	0
Lance Nethery	NY Rangers	5	0	0	0	0	0	0	0	0
	Edmonton	3	0	2	2	2	0	0	0	0
	Total	8	0	2	2	2	0	0	0	0
Curt Brackenbury	Edmonton	14	0	2	2	12	0	0	0	0
Andy Moog	Edmonton	8	0	1	1	2	0	0	0	0
Todd Strueby	Edmonton	3	0	0	0	0	0	0	0	0
Don Jackson	Edmonton	8	0	0	0	18	0	0	0	0
Ron Low	Edmonton	29	0	0	0	2	0	0	0	0
Blaine Stoughton	Hartford	80	52	39	91	57	13	1	4	7
Pierre Larouche	Montreal	22	9	12	21	0	3	0	0	0
	Hartford	45	25	25	50	12	11	1	1	1
	Total	67	34	37	71	12	14	1	1	1
Doug Sulliman	Hartford	77	29	40	69	39	5	0	4	1
Ron Francis	Hartford	59	25	43	68	51	12	0	1	1
Mark Howe	Hartford	76	8	45	53	18	3	0	1	0
Garry Howatt	Hartford	80	18	32	50	242	1	0	2	0
Rick Meagher	Hartford	65	24	19	43	51	2	1	2	3
Chris Kotsopoulos	Hartford	68	13	20	33	147	5	0	1	1
Blake Wesley	Hartford	78	9	18	27	123	3	0	1	0
Don Nachbaur	Hartford	77	5	21	26	117	0	0	0	0
Warren Miller	Hartford	74	10	12	22	68	1	1	0	2
Dave Keon	Hartford	78	8	11	19	6	0	1	1	0
Mark Renaud	Hartford	48	1	17	18	39	0	0	0	0
Jordy Douglas	Hartford	30	10	7	17	44	4	0	2	1
George Lyle	Detroit	11	1	2	3	4	0	0	0	0
	Hartford	14	2	12	14	9	1	0	0	0
	Total	25	3	14	17	13	1	0	0	0
Dan Bourbonnais	Hartford	24	3	9	12	11	0	0	0	0
Paul Shmyr	Hartford	66	1	11	12	134	0	0	0	0
Ray Neufeld	Hartford	19	4	3	7	4	1	0	0	0
Mickey Volcan	Hartford	26	1	5	6	29	1	0	0	0
Jack McIlhargey	Hartford	50	1	5	6	60	0	0	0	0
Norm Barnes	Hartford	20	1	4	5	19	0	0	0	1
Don Gillen	Hartford	34	1	4	5	22	0	0	0	0
Russ Anderson	Pittsburgh	31	0	1	1	98	0	0	0	0
	Hartford	25	1	3	4	85	0	0	1	0
	Total	56	1	4	5	183	0	0	1	0
Greg Millen	Hartford	55	0	5	5	2	0	0	0	0
Marty Howe	Hartford	13	0	4	4	2	0	0	0	0
Stuart Smith	Hartford	17	0	3	3	15	0	0	0	0
Randy MacGregor	Hartford	2	1	1	2	2	0	0	0	0
Paul MacDermid	Hartford	3	1	0	1	2	0	0	0	0
Gilles Lupien	Hartford	1	0	1	1	2	0	0	0	0
Mike Fidler	Hartford	2	0	1	1	0	0	0	0	0
Dan Fridgen	Hartford	2	0	1	1	0	0	0	0	0
Jeff Brownschidle	Hartford	3	0	1	1	2	0	0	0	0

PLAYER	TEAM	GP	G	A	PTS	PIM	PPG	SHG	GW	GT
Mike Veisor	Hartford	13	0	1	1	0	0	0	0	0
Mike McDougal	Hartford	3	0	0	0	0	0	0	0	0
Dave McDonald	Hartford	3	0	0	0	0	0	0	0	0
Glenn Merkosky	Hartford	7	0	0	0	2	0	0	0	0
Michel Galarneau	Hartford	10	0	0	0	4	0	0	0	0
Marcel Dionne	Los Angeles	78	50	67	117	50	17	1	5	4
Dave Taylor	Los Angeles	78	39	67	106	130	13	0	3	0
Jim Fox	Los Angeles	77	30	38	68	23	5	1	0	4
Larry Murphy	Los Angeles	79	22	44	66	95	8	1	2	4
Steve Bozek	Los Angeles	71	33	23	56	68	10	0	5	1
Mark Hardy	Los Angeles	77	6	39	45	130	1	0	0	1
Charlie Simmer	Los Angeles	50	15	24	39	42	3	0	2	1
Greg Terrion	Los Angeles	61	15	22	37	23	1	0	3	0
Dan Bonar	Los Angeles	79	13	23	36	111	1	0	0	0
Bernie Nicholls	Los Angeles	22	14	18	32	27	8	1	1	0
Doug Smith	Los Angeles	80	16	14	30	64	1	0	1	0
Ian Turnbull	Toronto	12	0	2	2	8	0	0	0	0
	Los Angeles	42	11	15	26	81	1	0	1	0
Steve Jensen	Los Angeles	45	8	19	27	19	1	0	1	0
John Kelly	Los Angeles	70	12	11	23	100	0	0	0	0
Jerry Korab	Los Angeles	50	5	13	18	91	3	0	0	0
Mike Murphy	Los Angeles	28	5	10	15	20	0	2	0	0
Dean Hopkins	Los Angeles	41	2	13	15	102	0	0	0	0
Paul Mulvey	Pittsburgh	27	1	7	8	76	0	0	0	0
	Los Angeles	11	0	7	7	50	0	0	0	0
	Total	38	1	14	15	126	0	0	0	0
Dave Lewis	Los Angeles	64	1	13	14	75	0	0	0	0
Alan Hangsleben	Washington	17	1	1	2	19	0	0	0	0
	Los Angeles	18	2	6	8	65	0	0	0	0
	Total	35	3	7	10	84	0	0	0	0
Rich Chartraw	Los Angeles	33	2	8	10	56	1	0	0	0
Jay Wells	Los Angeles	60	1	8	9	145	0	0	0	0
Daryl Evans	Los Agneles	14	2	6	8	2	0	0	0	0
Rick Martin	Los Angeles	3	1	3	4	2	1	0	0	0
Scott Gruhl	Los Angeles	7	2	1	3	2	0	0	0	0
Al Sims	Los Angeles	8	1	1	2	16	0	0	0	0
Warren Holmes	Los Angeles	3	0	2	2	0	0	0	0	0
Rob Palmer	Los Angeles	5	0	2	2	0	0	0	0	0
Mario Lessard	Los Angeles	52	0	2	2	6	0	0	0	0
Glen Goldup	Los Angeles	2	0	0	0	2	0	0	0	0
Bobby Sheehan	Los Angeles	4	0	0	0	2	0	0	0	0
Dave Morrison	Los Angeles	4	0	0	0	0	0	0	0	0
Bobby Smith	Minnesota	80	43	71	114	84	20	0	4	3
Dino Ciccarelli	Minnesota	76	55	52	107	138	20	0	4	5
Neal Broten	Minnesota	73	38	59	97	42	7	2	4	0
Steve Payne	Minnesota	74	33	44	77	76	11	0	3	2
Craig Hartsburg	Minnesota	76	17	60	77	115	5	0	2	2
Al MacAdam	Minnesota	79	18	43	61	37	5	2	4	3
Steve Christoff	Minnesota	69	26	30	56	14	4	0	1	0
Brad Palmer	Minnesota	72	22	23	45	18	7	0	3	0
Tom McCarthy	Minnesota	40	12	30	42	36	3	0	1	0
Tim Young	Minnesota	49	10	31	41	67	1	0	1	1

Minnesota's Bobby Smith led his team in points with 114.

PLAYER	TEAM	GP	G	A	PTS	PIM	PPG	SHG	GW	GT
Gordie Roberts	Minnesota	79	4	30	34	119	0	0	0	0
Brad Maxwell	Minnesota	51	10	21	31	96	0	1	1	1
Mark Johnson	Pittsburgh	46	10	11	21	30	1	1	0	0
	Minnesota	10	2	2	4	10	1	0	0	0
	Total	56	12	13	25	40	2	1	0	0
Mike Eaves	Minnesota	25	11	10	21	0	2	0	1	0
K. E. Andersson	Minnesota	70	9	12	21	18	0	0	2	1
Anders Hakansson	Minnesota	72	12	4	16	29	0	4	1	0
Fred Barrett	Minnesota	69	1	15	16	89	0	0	0	0
Curt Giles	Minnesota	74	3	12	15	87	0	0	1	0
Jack Carlson	Minnesota	57	8	4	12	103	1	0	1	0
Bill Nyrop	Minnesota	42	4	8	12	35	0	1	1	0
Ken Solheim	Minnesota	29	4	5	9	4	2	0	2	0
Gary Sargent	Minnesota	15	0	5	5	18	0	0	0	0
Murray Brumwell	Minnesota	21	0	3	3	18	0	0	0	0
Dan Poulin	Minnesota	3	1	1	2	2	0	0	0	0
Ron Meighan	Minnesota	7	1	1	2	2	0	0	0	0
Gilles Meloche	Minnesota	51	0	1	1	6	0	0	0	0
Warren Young	Minnesota	1	0	0	0	0	0	0	0	0
Udo Kiessling	Minnesota	1	0	0	0	2	0	0	0	0
Archie Henderson	Minnesota	1	0	0	0	0	0	0	0	0
Peter Hayek	Minnesota	1	0	0	0	0	0	0	0	0
Roger Melin	Minnesota	2	0	0	0	0	0	0	0	0
Mike Antonovich	Minnesota	2	0	0	0	0	0	0	0	0
Dave Richter	Minnesota	3	0	0	0	11	0	0	0	0
Ron Friest	Minnesota	10	0	0	0	31	0	0	0	0
Don Beaupre	Minnesota	29	0	0	0	19	0	0	0	0
Keith Acton	Montreal	78	36	52	88	88	10	0	5	3
Guy Lafleur	Montreal	66	27	57	84	24	9	0	3	1
Mark Napier	Montreal	80	40	41	81	14	9	0	5	5
Mario Tremblay	Montreal	80	33	40	73	66	7	0	4	2
Pierre Mondou	Montreal	73	35	33	68	57	8	2	4	3
Larry Robinson	Montreal	71	12	47	59	41	5	1	0	0
Steve Shutt	Montreal	57	31	24	55	40	5	0	3	1
Doug Jarvis	Montreal	80	20	28	48	20	1	0	4	0
Bob Gainey	Montreal	79	21	24	45	24	1	3	1	1
Rejean Houle	Montreal	51	11	32	43	34	2	1	1	0
Rod Langway	Montreal	66	5	34	39	116	1	0	1	0
Doug Wickenheiser	Montreal	56	12	23	35	43	1	0	3	0
Doug Risebrough	Montreal	59	15	18	33	116	2	2	2	1
Brian Engblom	Montreal	76	4	29	33	76	1	0	0	0
Mark Hunter	Montreal	71	18	11	29	143	0	0	5	0
Robert Picard	Montreal	62	2	26	28	106	2	0	0	0
Gaston Gingras	Montreal	34	6	18	24	28	3	0	3	0
Craig Laughlin	Montreal	36	12	11	23	33	2	0	1	0
Chris Nilan	Montreal	49	7	4	11	204	0	0	1	0
Gilbert Delorme	Montreal	60	3	8	11	55	0	0	0	0
Rick Wamsley	Montreal	38	0	2	2	4	0	0	0	0
Jeff Brubaker	Montreal	3	0	1	1	32	0	0	0	0
Dave Orleski	Montreal	1	0	0	0	0	0	0	0	0
Bill Kitchen	Montreal	1	0	0	0	7	0	0	0	0
Richard Sevigny	Montreal	19	0	0	0	10	0	0	0	0
Denis Herron	Montreal	27	0	0	0	4	0	0	0	0

PLAYER	TEAM	GP	G	A	PTS	PIM	PPG	SHG	GW	GT
Mike Bossy	NY Islanders	80	64	83	147	22	17	0	10	0
Bryan Trottier	NY Islanders	80	50	79	129	88	18	2	10	2
John Tonelli	NY Islanders	80	35	58	93	57	5	0	5	2
Clark Gillies	NY Islanders	79	38	39	77	75	8	0	5	1
Denis Potvin	NY Islanders	60	24	37	61	83	11	1	4	0
Bob Bourne	NY Islanders	76	27	26	53	77	5	2	2	1
Duane Sutter	NY Islanders	77	18	35	53	100	4	0	0	0
Mike McEwen	NY Islanders	73	10	39	49	50	1	0	1	0
Bob Nystrom	NY Islanders	74	22	25	47	103	0	0	4	0
Brent Sutter	NY Islanders	43	21	22	43	114	3	0	1	0
Stefan Persson	NY Islanders	70	6	37	43	99	3	0	2	1
Anders Kallur	NY Islanders	58	18	22	40	18	2	3	3	2
Wayne Merrick	NY Islanders	68	12	27	39	20	1	0	3	0
Tomas Jonsson	NY Islanders	70	9	25	34	51	0	0	1	1
Butch Goring	NY Islanders	67	15	17	32	10	1	5	1	0
Billy Carroll	NY Islanders	72	9	20	29	32	0	3	1	0
Dave Langevin	NY Islanders	73	1	20	21	82	0	0	0	0
Ken Morrow	NY Islanders	75	1	18	19	56	0	0	0	0
Hector Marini	NY Islanders	30	4	9	13	53	1	0	1	0
Gord Lane	NY Islanders	51	0	13	13	98	0	0	0	0
Greg Gilbert	NY Islanders	1	1	0	1	0	0	0	0	0
Bill Smith	NY Islanders	46	0	1	1	24	0	0	0	0
Neil Hawryliw	NY Islanders	1	0	0	0	0	0	0	0	0
Paul Boutilier	NY Islanders	1	0	0	0	0	0	0	0	0
Roland Melanson	NY Islanders	36	0	0	0	14	0	0	0	0
Mike Rogers	NY Rangers	80	38	65	103	43	6	1	2	0
Ron Duguay	NY Rangers	72	40	36	76	82	10	1	3	2
Mark Pavelich	NY Rangers	79	33	43	76	67	12	3	3	3
Ed Johnstone	NY Rangers	68	30	28	58	57	4	0	3	3
Don Maloney	NY Rangers	54	22	36	58	73	6	1	5	0
Reijo Routsalainen	NY Rangers	78	18	38	56	27	7	0	3	0
Dave Maloney	NY Rangers	64	13	36	49	105	6	1	3	2
Robbie Ftorek	Quebec	19	1	8	9	4	0	0	0	0
	NY Rangers	30	8	25	33	24	2	0	2	0
	Total	49	9	33	42	28	2	0	2	0
Barry Beck	NY Rangers	60	9	29	38	111	5	0	0	1
Dave Silk	NY Rangers	64	15	20	35	39	1	0	0	1
Mikko Leinonen	NY Rangers	53	11	19	30	18	2	0	3	0
Mike Allison	NY Rangers	48	7	15	22	74	0	0	0	0
Tom Laidlaw	NY Rangers	79	3	18	21	104	0	0	0	0
Steve Vickers	NY Rangers	34	9	11	20	13	2	0	2	0
Andre Dore	NY Rangers	56	4	16	20	64	0	0	0	1
Nick Fotiu	NY Rangers	70	8	10	18	151	0	0	1	0
Rob McClanahan	Hartford	17	0	3	3	11	0	0	0	0
	NY Rangers	22	5	9	14	10	0	0	1	1
	Total	39	5	12	17	21	0	0	1	1
Ron Greschner	NY Rangers	29	5	11	16	16	0	0	0	0
Dean Talafous	NY Rangers	29	6	7	13	8	1	0	2	0
Carol Vadnais	NY Rangers	50	5	6	11	45	1	0	0	0
Ed Hospodar	NY Rangers	41	3	8	11	152	0	0	0	0
Peter Wallin	NY Rangers	40	2	9	11	12	0	0	1	0
Tom Younghans	Minnesota	3	1	0	1	0	0	1	0	1
	NY Rangers	47	3	5	8	17	0	0	0	0
	Total	50	4	5	8	17	0	1	0	1

PLAYER	TEAM	GP	G	A	PTS	PIM	PPG	SHG	GW	GT
Tim Bothwell	NY Rangers	13	0	3	3	10	0	0	0	0
Steve Weeks	NY Rangers	49	0	3	3	0	0	0	0	0
Mark Morrison	NY Rangers	9	1	1	2	0	0	0	1	0
Mike Backman	NY Rangers	3	0	2	2	4	0	0	0	0
Anders Hedberg	NY Rangers	4	0	1	1	0	0	0	0	0
John Davidson	NY Rangers	1	0	0	0	2	0	0	0	0
Ed Mio	NY Rangers	25	0	0	0	4	0	0	0	0
Kenny Linseman	Philadelphia	79	24	68	92	275	2	3	0	0
Brian Propp	Philadelphia	80	44	47	91	117	13	0	6	2
Bill Barber	Philadelphia	80	45	44	89	85	13	4	6	1
Ron Flockhart	Philadelphia	72	33	39	72	44	10	0	2	1
Darryl Sittler	Toronto	38	18	20	38	24	5	2	0	2
	Philadelphia	35	14	18	32	50	5	1	2	2
	Total	73	32	38	70	74	10	3	2	4
Bobby Clarke	Philadelphia	62	17	46	63	154	2	1	3	1
Ray Allison	Philadelphia	51	17	37	54	104	5	0	2	1
Tim Kerr	Philadelphia	61	21	30	51	138	7	0	2	0
Reggie Leach	Philadelphia	66	26	21	47	18	5	0	5	0
Ilkka Sinisalo	Philadelphia	66	15	22	37	22	1	0	0	1
Behn Wilson	Philadelphia	59	13	23	36	135	5	0	3	0
Paul Holmgren	Philadelphia	41	9	22	31	183	4	0	3	0
Bob Hoffmeyer	Philadelphia	57	7	20	27	142	4	0	0	0
Brad Marsh	Calgary	17	0	1	1	10	0	0	0	0
	Philadelphia	66	2	22	24	106	0	0	1	0
	Total	83	2	23	25	116	0	0	1	0
Al Hill	Philadelphia	41	6	13	19	58	0	0	0	1
Greg Adams	Philadelphia	33	4	15	19	105	0	0	0	0
Glen Cochrane	Philadelphia	63	6	12	18	329	0	1	0	1
Mark Botell	Philadelphia	32	4	10	14	31	0	0	1	0
Tom Gorence	Philadelphia	66	5	8	13	8	0	1	0	0
Jimmy Watson	Philadelphia	76	3	9	12	99	0	0	1	0
Fred Arthur	Philadelphia	74	1	7	8	47	0	0	0	0
Bob Dailey	Philadelphia	12	1	5	6	22	0	0	0	0
Frank Bathe	Philadelphia	28	1	3	4	68	0	0	0	0
Steve Smith	Philadelphia	8	0	1	1	0	0	0	0	0
Lindsay Carson	Philadelphia	18	0	1	1	32	0	0	0	0
Rick St. Croix	Philadelphia	29	0	1	1	2	0	0	0	0
Pete Peeters	Philadelphia	44	0	1	1	19	0	0	0	0
Dave Michayluk	Philadelphia	1	0	0	0	0	0	0	0	0
Thomas Eriksson	Philadelphia	1	0	0	0	4	0	0	0	0
Gordie Williams	Philadelphia	1	0	0	0	2	0	0	0	0
Mark Taylor	Philadelphia	2	0	0	0	0	0	0	0	0
Gary Morrison	Philadelphia	7	0	0	0	2	0	0	0	0
Reid Bailey	Philadelphia	10	0	0	0	23	0	0	0	0
Rick Kehoe	Pittsburgh	71	33	52	85	8	17	0	1	3
Randy Carlyle	Pittsburgh	73	11	64	75	131	7	1	0	0
Pat Boutette	Pittsburgh	30	23	51	74	230	14	1	2	2
Paul Gardner	Pittsburgh	59	36	33	69	28	21	0	2	2
Mike Bullard	Pittsburgh	75	37	27	64	91	10	0	5	0
George Ferguson	Pittsburgh	71	22	31	53	45	4	3	0	3

PLAYER	TEAM	GP	G	A	PTS	PIM	PPG	SHG	GW	GT
Rick MacLeish	Hartford	34	6	16	22	16	4	0	0	0
	Pittsburgh	40	13	12	25	28	2	2	1	0
	Total	74	19	28	47	44	6	2	1	0
Paul Baxter	Pittsburgh	76	9	34	43	407	4	0	2	0
Greg Malone	Pittsburgh	78	15	24	39	125	3	0	2	2
Pat Price	Pittsburgh	77	7	31	38	322	2	0	0	0
Peter Lee	Pittsburgh	74	18	16	34	98	2	0	3	1
Doug Shedden	Pittsburgh	38	10	15	25	12	4	0	2	0
Gregg Sheppard	Pittsburgh	58	11	10	21	35	0	0	1	0
Ron Stackhouse	Pittsburgh	76	2	19	21	102	0	0	0	0
Rod Schutt	Pittsburgh	35	8	12	20	42	0	0	3	0
Andre St. Laurent	Los Angeles	16	2	4	6	28	0	1	0	0
	Pittsburgh	18	8	5	13	4	1	0	1	0
	Total	34	10	9	19	32	1	1	1	0
Bobby Simpson	Pittsburgh	26	9	9	18	4	0	0	1	0
Steve Gatzos	Pittsburgh	16	6	9	15	14	1	0	0	0
Pat Graham	Pittsburgh	42	6	8	14	55	0	0	1	0
Mario Faubert	Pittsburgh	14	4	8	12	14	4	0	2	0
Greg Hotham	Toronto	3	0	0	0	0	0	0	0	0
	Pittsburgh	25	4	6	10	16	2	0	0	0
	Total	28	4	6	10	16	2	0	0	0
Jim Hamilton	Pittsburgh	11	5	3	8	2	0	0	1	0
Marc Chorney	Pittsburgh	60	1	6	7	63	0	0	1	0
Kevin McClelland	Pittsburgh	10	1	4	5	4	0	0	0	0
Randy Boyd	Pittsburgh	23	0	2	2	49	0	0	0	0
Michel Dion	Pittsburgh	62	0	1	1	4	0	0	0	0
David Hannan	Pittsburgh	1	0	0	0	0	0	0	0	0
Bennett Wolf	Pittsburgh	1	0	0	0	2	0	0	0	0
Tony Feltrin	Pittsburgh	4	0	0	0	4	0	0	0	0
Gary Edwards	Pittsburgh	6	0	0	0	2	0	0	0	0
Gary Rissling	Pittsburgh	16	0	0	0	55	0	0	0	0
Peter Stastny	Quebec	80	46	93	139	91	16	3	3	0
Real Cloutier	Quebec	67	37	60	97	34	8	0	5	2
Marian Stastny	Quebec	74	35	54	89	27	13	0	3	1
Michel Goulet	Quebec	80	42	42	84	48	7	6	3	5
Anton Stastny	Quebec	68	26	46	72	16	10	0	4	1
Dale Hunter	Quebec	80	22	50	72	272	0	2	1	2
Wilf Paiement	Toronto	69	18	40	58	203	6	1	1	2
	Quebec	8	7	6	13	18	3	2	1	0
	Total	77	25	46	71	221	9	3	2	2
Marc Tardif	Quebec	75	39	31	70	55	14	0	3	2
Mario Marois	Quebec	71	11	32	43	161	2	0	0	0
Jacques Richard	Quebec	59	15	26	41	77	1	3	1	0
Dave Pichette	Quebec	67	7	30	37	152	3	0	0	0
Alain Cote	Quebec	79	15	16	31	82	0	0	1	2
Pat Hickey	Toronto	1	0	0	0	0	0	0	0	0
	NY Rangers	53	15	14	29	32	3	0	3	0
	Quebec	7	0	1	1	4	0	0	0	0
	Total	61	15	15	30	36	3	0	3	0
Pierre Lacroix	Quebec	68	4	23	27	74	1	0	0	1
Pierre Aubry	Quebec	62	10	13	23	27	0	1	1	0
Normand Rochefort	Quebec	72	4	14	18	115	0	0	1	0

PLAYER	TEAM	GP	G	A	PTS	PIM	PPG	SHG	GW	GT
Andre Dupont	Quebec	60	4	12	16	100	0	0	2	0
Jere Gillis	NY Rangers	26	3	9	12	16	0	0	1	0
	Quebec	12	2	1	3	0	0	0	1	0
	Total	38	5	10	15	16	0	0	2	0
Wally Weir	Quebec	62	3	5	8	173	0	0	0	0
Basil McRae	Quebec	20	4	3	7	69	0	0	0	0
Jean Hamel	Quebec	40	1	6	7	32	0	0	1	0
Gaston Therrien	Quebec	14	0	7	7	6	0	0	0	0
Dale Hoganson	Quebec	30	0	6	6	16	0	0	0	0
Dan Bouchard	Quebec	60	0	3	3	36	0	0	0	0
Richard David	Quebec	5	1	1	2	4	0	0	0	0
Terry Johnson	Quebec	6	0	1	1	5	0	0	0	0
Michel Plasse	Quebec	8	0	1	1	0	0	0	0	0
John Garrett	Hartford	16	0	1	1	2	0	0	0	0
	Quebec	12	0	0	0	0	0	0	0	0
	Total	28	0	1	1	2	0	0	0	0
Christian Tanguay	Quebec	2	0	0	0	0	0	0	0	0
Michel Bolduc	Quebec	3	0	0	0	0	0	0	0	0
Louis Sleigher	Quebec	8	0	0	0	0	0	0	0	0
Bernie Federko	St. Louis	74	30	62	92	70	11	0	6	2
Blake Dunlop	St. Louis	77	25	53	78	32	10	1	1	0
Brian Sutter	St. Louis	74	39	36	75	239	14	0	3	1
Jorgen Pettersson	St. Louis	77	38	31	69	28	8	0	2	0
Perry Turnbull	St. Louis	79	33	26	59	161	2	0	2	0
Joe Mullen	St. Louis	45	25	34	59	4	10	0	3	0
Mike Zuke	St. Louis	76	13	40	53	41	1	1	2	0
Wayne Babych	St. Louis	51	19	25	44	51	4	0	3	2
Jack Brownschidle	St. Louis	80	5	33	38	26	3	0	1	1
Mike Crombeen	St. Louis	71	19	8	27	32	0	1	1	0
Larry Patey	St. Louis	70	14	12	26	97	1	4	2	0
Guy Lapointe	Montreal	47	1	19	20	72	0	0	0	0
	St. Louis	8	0	6	6	4	0	0	0	0
	Total	55	1	25	26	76	0	0	0	0
Rick LaPointe	St. Louis	71	2	20	22	127	0	0	0	0
Rick Wilson	St. Louis	48	3	18	21	24	1	0	1	0
Blair Chapman	St. Louis	18	6	11	17	8	2	0	0	0
Ed Kea	St. Louis	78	2	14	16	62	0	0	0	0
Kari Eloranta	Calgary	19	0	5	5	14	0	0	0	0
	St. Louis	12	1	7	8	6	1	0	1	0
	Total	31	1	12	13	20	1	0	1	0
Bill Baker	Colorado	14	0	3	3	17	0	0	0	0
	St. Louis	35	3	5	8	50	1	0	0	0
	Total	49	3	8	11	67	1	0	0	0
Jim Pavese	St. Louis	42	2	9	11	101	0	0	1	0
Ralph Klassen	St. Louis	45	3	7	10	6	0	1	1	0
Bill Stewart	St. Louis	22	0	5	5	25	0	0	0	0
Mark Reeds	St. Louis	9	1	3	4	0	0	0	0	0
Perry Anderson	St. Louis	5	1	2	3	0	0	0	0	0
Alain Vigneault	St. Louis	14	1	2	3	43	0	0	0	0
Richie Hansen	St. Louis	2	0	2	2	0	0	0	0	0
Mike Liut	St. Louis	64	0	2	2	2	0	0	0	0
Alain Lemieux	St. Louis	3	0	1	1	0	0	0	0	0
Bob Crawford	St. Louis	3	0	1	1	0	0	0	0	0

PLAYER	TEAM	GP	G	A	PTS	PIM	PPG	SHG	GW	GT
Gary Edwards	St. Louis	10	0	1	1	0	0	0	0	0
Gerry Hart	St. Louis	35	0	1	1	100	0	0	0	0
Scott Campbell	St. Louis	3	0	0	0	52	0	0	0	0
Neil Labatte	St. Louis	4	0	0	0	6	0	0	0	0
Glen Hanlon	Vancouver	28	0	0	0	22	0	0	0	0
	St. Louis	2	0	0	0	0	0	0	0	0
	Total	30	0	0	0	22	0	0	0	0
Rick Vaive	Toronto	77	54	35	89	157	12	5	6	3
Bill Derlago	Toronto	75	34	50	84	42	6	0	2	0
John Anderson	Toronto	69	31	26	57	30	7	0	3	3
Borje Salming	Toronto	69	12	44	56	170	1	0	0	0
Bob Manno	Toronto	72	9	41	50	67	3	1	0	2
Terry Martin	Toronto	72	25	24	49	39	4	0	1	1
Miroslav Frycer	Quebec	49	20	17	37	47	5	0	2	0
	Toronto	10	4	6	10	31	1	0	2	0
	Total	59	24	23	47	78	6	0	4	0
Rene Robert	Toronto	55	13	24	37	37	2	0	1	1
Rocky Saganiuk	Toronto	65	17	16	33	49	0	0	1	0
Jim Benning	Toronto	74	7	24	31	46	2	0	0	0
Normand Aubin	Toronto	43	14	12	26	22	3	0	1	0
Dan Maloney	Toronto	44	8	7	15	71	1	0	0	1
Trevor Johansen	Los Angeles	46	3	7	10	69	0	0	0	0
	Toronto	13	1	3	4	4	0	0	0	0
	Total	59	4	10	14	73	0	0	0	0
Fred Boimistruck	Toronto	57	2	11	13	32	0	0	1	0
Jim Korn	Detroit	59	1	7	8	104	0	0	0	1
	Toronto	11	1	3	4	44	0	0	0	0
	Total	70	2	10	12	148	0	0	0	1
Stewart Gavin	Toronto	38	5	6	11	29	1	0	0	0
Robert McGill	Toronto	68	1	10	11	263	0	0	0	0
Don Luce	Toronto	39	4	4	8	32	0	1	0	0
Ron Zanussi	Toronto	43	0	8	8	14	0	0	0	0
Walt Poddubny	Edmonton	4	0	0	0	0	0	0	0	0
	Toronto	11	3	4	7	8	1	0	0	0
	Total	15	3	4	7	8	1	0	0	0
Billy Harris	Los Angeles	16	1	3	4	6	0	0	0	0
	Toronto	20	2	0	2	4	0	0	0	0
	Total	36	3	3	6	10	0	0	0	0
Barry Melrose	Toronto	64	1	5	6	186	0	0	0	0
Fred Perlini	Toronto	7	2	3	5	10	1	0	0	0
Paul Marshall	Toronto	10	2	2	4	2	1	0	0	0
Gary Yaremchuk	Toronto	18	0	3	3	10	0	0	0	0
Michel Larocque	Toronto	50	0	3	3	2	0	0	0	0
Ernie Godden	Toronto	5	1	1	2	6	0	0	0	0
Bruce Boudreau	Toronto	12	0	2	2	6	0	0	0	0
John Gibson	Los Angeles	6	0	0	0	18	0	0	0	0
	Toronto	27	0	2	2	67	0	0	0	0
	Total	33	0	2	2	85	0	0	0	0
Vincent Tremblay	Toronto	40	0	2	2	2	0	0	0	0
Darwin McCutcheon	Toronto	1	0	0	0	2	0	0	0	0
Paul Higgins	Toronto	3	0	0	0	17	0	0	0	0
Craig Muni	Toronto	3	0	0	0	2	0	0	0	0

PLAYER	TEAM	GP	G	A	PTS	PIM	PPG	SHG	GW	GT
Thomas Gradin	Vancouver	76	37	49	86	32	6	3	4	1
Stan Smyl	Vancouver	80	34	44	78	144	10	2	5	1
Ivan Boldirev	Vancouver	78	33	40	73	45	10	0	4	3
Curt Fraser	Vancouver	79	28	39	67	175	11	0	5	1
Ivan Hlinka	Vancouver	72	23	37	60	16	7	0	2	2
Tony Currie	St. Louis	48	18	22	40	17	4	0	2	1
	Vancouver	12	5	3	8	2	2	0	0	0
	Total	60	23	25	48	19	6	0	2	1
Lars Molin	Vancouver	72	15	31	46	10	1	1	4	1
Kevin McCarthy	Vancouver	71	6	39	45	84	1	0	0	0
Darcy Rota	Vancouver	51	20	20	40	139	2	0	0	1
Dave Williams	Vancouver	77	17	21	38	341	5	1	1	2
Blair MacDonald	Vancouver	59	18	15	33	20	4	0	2	0
Jim Nill	St. Louis	61	9	12	21	127	1	2	0	0
	Vancouver	8	1	2	3	5	0	0	1	0
	Total	69	10	14	24	132	1	2	1	0
Lars Lindgren	Vancouver	75	5	16	21	74	0	0	1	0
Per-Olov Brasar	Vancouver	53	6	12	18	6	0	0	1	1
Gary Lupul	Vancouver	41	10	7	17	26	0	1	0	3
Ron Delorme	Vancouver	59	9	8	17	177	0	0	0	0
Doug Halward	Vancouver	37	4	13	17	40	1	0	0	0
Harold Snepsts	Vancouver	68	3	14	17	153	0	0	0	0
Rick Lanz	Vancouver	39	3	11	14	48	2	0	0	0
Marc Crawford	Vancouver	40	4	8	12	29	0	0	0	0
Neil Belland	Vancouver	28	3	6	9	16	1	0	0	1
Anders Eldebrink	Vancouver	38	1	8	9	21	0	0	0	0
Colin Campbell	Vancouver	47	0	8	8	131	0	0	0	0
Jerry Butler	Vancouver	25	3	1	4	15	0	0	0	0
Moe Lemay	Vancouver	5	1	2	3	0	1	0	0	0
Jiri Bubla	Vancouver	23	1	1	2	16	0	0	0	0
Richard Brodeur	Vancouver	52	0	2	2	0	0	0	0	0
Joe McDonnell	Vancouver	7	0	1	1	12	0	0	0	0
Gerry Minor	Vancouver	13	0	1	1	6	0	0	0	0
Andy Schliebener	Vancouver	22	0	1	1	10	0	0	0	0
Garth Butcher	Vancouver	5	0	0	0	9	0	0	0	0
Dennis Maruk	Washington	80	60	76	136	128	20	2	1	1
Ryan Walter	Washington	78	38	49	87	142	19	1	3	1
Mike Gartner	Washington	80	35	45	80	121	5	2	5	0
Bobby Carpenter	Washington	80	32	35	67	69	7	1	3	2
Chris Valentine	Washington	60	30	37	67	92	18	0	5	2
Bengt Gustafsson	Washington	70	26	34	60	40	3	0	2	3
Darren Veitch	Washington	67	9	44	53	54	5	0	1	2
Greg Theberge	Washington	57	5	32	37	49	2	0	0	0
Bobby Gould	Calgary	16	3	0	3	4	0	0	1	0
	Washington	60	18	13	31	69	1	0	1	1
	Total	76	21	13	34	73	1	0	2	1
Rick Green	Washington	65	3	25	28	93	1	0	0	1
Terry Murray	Washington	74	3	22	25	60	0	0	0	0
Doug Hicks	Edmonton	49	3	20	23	44	1	0	0	0
	Washington	12	0	1	1	11	0	0	0	0
	Total	61	3	21	24	66	1	0	0	0
Gaetan Duchesne	Washington	74	9	14	23	46	0	0	1	0
Torrie Robertson	Washington	54	8	13	21	204	3	0	0	0

PLAYER	TEAM	GP	G	A	PTS	PIM	PPG	SHG	GW	GT
Lee Norwood	Quebec	2	0	0	0	2	0	0	0	0
	Washington	26	7	10	17	115	3	0	1	0
	Total	28	7	10	17	117	3	0	1	0
Tim Tookey	Washington	28	8	8	16	35	5	0	0	0
Glen Currie	Washington	43	7	7	14	14	0	1	0	0
Wes Jarvis	Washington	26	1	12	13	18	0	0	0	0
Lou Franceschetti	Washington	30	2	10	12	23	0	0	1	0
Timo Blomqvist	Washington	44	1	11	12	62	0	0	0	0
Paul MacKinnon	Washington	39	2	9	11	35	0	0	0	0
Randy Holt	Calgary	8	0	0	0	9	0	0	0	0
	Washington	53	2	6	8	250	0	0	0	0
	Total	61	2	6	8	259	0	0	0	0
Tom Rowe	Hartford	21	4	0	4	36	1	1	0	0
	Washington	6	1	1	2	18	0	0	0	0
	Total	27	5	1	6	54	1	1	0	0
Jim McTaggart	Washington	19	2	4	6	20	0	1	1	0
Tony Cassolato	Washington	12	1	4	5	4	0	0	0	0
Roland Stoltz	Washington	14	2	2	4	14	0	0	0	0
Bob Kelly	Washington	16	0	4	4	12	0	0	0	0
Richard Bidner	Washington	12	2	1	3	7	0	0	1	0
Jean Pronovost	Washington	10	1	2	3	4	0	0	0	0
Howard Walker	Washington	16	0	2	2	26	0	0	0	0
Al Jensen	Washington	26	0	2	2	6	0	0	0	0
Mike Siltala	Washington	3	1	0	1	2	0	0	0	0
Orest Kindrachuk	Washington	4	1	0	1	2	1	0	0	0
Mike Palmateer	Washington	11	0	1	1	6	0	0	0	0
Dave Parro	Washington	52	0	1	1	4	0	0	0	0
Eric Calder	Washington	1	0	0	0	0	0	0	0	0
Pierre Bouchard	Washington	1	0	0	0	10	0	0	0	0
Errol Rausse	Washington	2	0	0	0	0	0	0	0	0
Harvie Pocza	Washington	2	0	0	0	2	0	0	0	0
Tony Camazzola	Washington	3	0	0	0	4	0	0	0	0
Jim McGeough	Washington	4	0	0	0	0	0	0	0	0
Jay Johnston	Washington	6	0	0	0	4	0	0	0	0
Dale Hawerchuk	Winnipeg	80	45	58	103	47	12	0	2	2
Morris Lukowich	Winnipeg	77	43	49	92	102	13	0	6	3
Dave Christian	Winnipeg	80	25	51	76	28	6	1	3	1
David Babych	Winnipeg	79	19	49	68	92	11	0	2	3
Paul MacLean	Winnipeg	74	36	25	61	106	12	0	1	1
Willy Lindstrom	Winnipeg	74	32	27	59	33	5	0	5	0
Lucien DeBlois	Winnipeg	65	25	27	52	87	1	1	2	2
Thomas Steen	Winnipeg	73	15	29	44	42	4	0	1	0
Bengt Lundholm	Winnipeg	66	14	30	44	10	3	0	3	1
Normand Dupont	Winnipeg	62	13	25	38	22	4	0	2	0
Doug Smail	Winnipeg	72	17	18	35	55	2	1	1	0
Larry Hopkins	Winnipeg	41	10	15	24	22	0	0	3	0
Tim Watters	Winnipeg	69	2	22	24	97	0	0	0	0
Tim Trimper	Winnipeg	74	8	8	16	100	0	1	0	1
Ron Wilson	Winnipeg	39	3	13	16	49	0	0	0	0
Don Spring	Winnipeg	78	0	16	16	21	0	0	0	0
Craig Levie	Winnipeg	40	4	9	13	48	0	0	1	0
Moe Mantha	Winnipeg	25	0	12	12	28	0	0	0	0
Bryan Maxwell	Winnipeg	45	1	9	10	110	0	0	0	0

PLAYER	TEAM	GP	G	A	PTS	PIM	PPG	SHG	GW	GT
Scott Arniel	Winnipeg	17	1	8	9	14	1	0	0	0
Serge Savard	Winnipeg	47	2	5	7	26	0	0	1	0
Jimmy Mann	Winnipeg	37	3	2	5	79	0	0	0	0
Ed Staniowski	Winnipeg	45	0	5	5	4	0	0	0	0
Barry Legge	Winnipeg	38	1	2	3	57	0	0	0	0
Barry Long	Winnipeg	5	0	2	2	4	0	0	0	0
Doug Soetaert	Winnipeg	39	0	2	2	14	0	0	0	0
Dan Geoffrion	Winnipeg	1	0	0	0	5	0	0	0	0
Murray Eaves	Winnipeg	2	0	0	0	0	0	0	0	0

Eddie Mio helped trigger Ranger revival.

GOALTENDERS' RECORDS

ALL GOALS AGAINST A TEAM IN ANY GAME ARE CHARGED TO THE INDIVIDUAL GOALTENDER OF THAT GAME FOR PURPOSES OF AWARDING THE BILL JENNINGS TROPHY.

CODE: GPI—GAMES PLAYED IN. MINS—MINUTES PLAYED. GA—GOALS AGAINST. SO—SHUTOUTS. AVE—60-MINUTE AVERAGE. EN—EMPTY NET GOALS (NOT COUNTED IN PERSONAL AVERAGES BUT INCLUDED IN TEAM TOTALS).

WON-LOST-TIED RECORD BASED ON WHICH GOALTENDER WAS PLAYING WHEN WINNING OR TYING GOAL WAS SCORED.

GOALTENDERS	TEAM	GPI	MINS	GA	EN	SO	AVE	W	L	T
Mark Holden	Montreal	1	20	0	0	0	.00	0	0	0
Denis Herron	Montreal	27	1547	68	0	3	2.64	12	6	8
Rick Wamsley	Montreal	38	2206	101	0	2	2.75	23	7	7
Richard Sevigny	Montreal	19	1027	53	1	0	3.10	11	4	2
Herron/Sevigny	Montreal					1				
MONTREAL	**TOTAL**	80	4800	223		6	2.79	46	17	17

(Herron & Sevigny shared shutout against Colorado, Nov. 11, 1981)

Bill Smith	NY Islanders	46	2685	133	0	0	2.97	32	9	4
Roland Melanson	NY Islanders	36	2115	114	3	0	3.23	22	7	6
NY ISLANDERS	**TOTAL**	30	4800	250		0	3.13	54	16	10

Jacques Cloutier	Buffalo	7	311	13	1	0	2.51	5	1	0
Bob Sauve	Buffalo	14	760	35	1	0	2.76	6	1	5
Don Edwards	Buffalo	62	3500	205	3	0	3.51	26	23	9
Paul Harrison	Buffalo	6	229	14	1	0	3.67	2	1	1
BUFFALO	**TOTAL**	80	4800	273		0	3.41	39	26	15

Mike Moffat	Boston	2	120	6	0	0	3.00	2	0	0
Marco Baron	Boston	44	2515	144	3	1	3.44	22	16	4
Rogie Vachon	Boston	38	2165	132	0	1	3.66	19	11	6
BOSTON	**TOTAL**	80	4800	285		2	3.56	43	27	10

Rick Heinz	Vancouver	3	180	9	0	1	3.00	2	1	0
Richard Brodeur	Vancouver	52	3010	168	2	2	3.35	20	18	12
Glen Hanlon	Vancouver	28	1610	106	1	1	3.95	8	14	5
VANCOUVER	**TOTAL**	80	4800	286		4	3.58	30	33	17

L. Middlebrook	Minnesota	3	140	7	0	0	3.00	0	0	2
Gilles Meloche	Minnesota	51	3026	175	2	1	3.47	26	15	9
Don Beaupre	Minnesota	29	1634	101	3	0	3.71	11	8	9
MINNESOTA	**TOTAL**	80	4800	288		1	3.60	37	23	20

Grant Fuhr	Edmonton	48	2847	157	2	0	3.31	28	5	14
Ron Low	Edmonton	29	1554	100	2	0	3.86	17	7	1
Andy Moog	Edmonton	8	399	32	2	0	4.81	3	5	0
EDMONTON	**TOTAL**	80	4800	295		0	3.69	48	17	15

John Davidson	NY Rangers	1	60	1	0	0	1.00	1	0	0
John Vanbiesbrouck	NY Rangers	1	60	1	0	0	1.00	1	0	0
Ed Mio	NY Rangers	25	1500	89	0	0	3.56	13	6	5

GOALTENDERS	TEAM	GPI	MINS	GA	EN	SO	AVE	W	L	T
Steve Weeks	NY Rangers	49	2852	179	3	1	3.77	23	16	9
Steve Baker	NY Rangers	6	328	33	0	0	6.04	1	5	0
NY RANGERS	**TOTAL**	80	4800	306		1	3.83	39	27	14
Pete Peeters	Philadelphia	44	2591	160	3	0	3.71	23	18	3
Rick St. Croix	Philadelphia	29	1729	112	3	0	3.89	13	9	6
Pelle Lindbergh	Philadelphia	8	480	35	0	0	4.38	2	4	2
PHILADELPHIA	**TOTAL**	80	4800	313		0	3.91	38	31	11
Ed Staniowski	Winnipeg	45	2643	174	2	1	3.95	20	19	6
Doug Soetaert	Winnipeg	39	2157	155	1	2	4.31	13	14	8
WINNIPEG	**TOTAL**	80	4800	332		3	4.15	33	33	14
Gary Edwards	Pittsburgh	6	360	22	0	1	3.67	3	2	1
Michel Dion	Pittsburgh	62	3580	226	8	0	3.79	25	24	12
Nick Ricci	Pittsburgh	3	160	14	2	0	5.25	0	3	0
Paul Harrison	Pittsburgh	13	700	64	1	0	5.49	3	7	0
PITTSBURGH	**TOTAL**	80	4800	337		1	4.21	31	36	13
Al Jensen	Washington	26	1274	81	0	0	3.81	8	8	4
Dave Parro	Washington	52	2942	206	4	1	4.20	16	26	7
Mike Palmateer	Washington	11	584	47	0	0	4.83	2	7	2
WASHINGTON	**TOTAL**	80	4800	338		1	4.23	26	41	13
Dan Bouchard	Quebec	60	3572	230	2	1	3.86	27	22	11
John Garrett	Quebec	12	720	62	0	0	5.17	4	5	3
Michel Plasse	Quebec	8	388	35	1	0	5.41	2	3	1
Clint Malarchuk	Quebec	2	120	14	0	0	7.00	0	1	1
QUEBEC	**TOTAL**	80	4800	344		1	4.30	33	31	16
Pat Riggin	Calgary	52	2934	207	1	2	4.23	19	19	11
Rejean Lemelin	Calgary	34	1866	135	2	0	4.34	10	15	6
CALGARY	**TOTAL**	80	4800	345		2	4.31	29	34	17
Paul Skidmore	St. Louis	2	120	6	0	0	3.00	1	1	0
Mike Liut	St. Louis	64	3691	250	3	2	4.06	28	28	7
Rick Heinz	St. Louis	9	433	35	2	0	4.85	2	5	0
Gary Edwards	St. Louis	10	480	45	0	0	5.63	1	5	1
Glen Hanlon	St. Louis	2	76	8	0	0	6.32	0	1	0
ST. LOUIS	**TOTAL**	80	4800	349		2	4.36	32	40	8
Claude Legris	Detroit	1	28	0	0	0	.00	0	0	1
Bob Sauve	Detroit	41	2365	165	5	0	4.19	11	25	4
Gilles Gilbert	Detroit	27	1478	105	2	0	4.26	6	10	6
Corrado Micalef	Detroit	18	809	63	1	0	4.67	4	10	1
Greg Stefan	Detroit	2	120	10	0	0	5.00	0	2	0
DETROIT	**TOTAL**	80	4800	351		0	4.39	21	47	12
John Garrett	Hartford	16	898	63	1	0	4.21	5	6	4
Greg Millen	Hartford	55	3201	229	5	0	4.29	11	30	12
Mike Veisor	Hartford	13	701	53	0	0	4.54	5	5	2
HARTFORD	**TOTAL**	80	4800	351		0	4.39	21	41	18

GOALTENDERS	TEAM	GPI	MINS	GA	EN	SO	AVE	W	L	T
Richard Laferriere	Colorado	1	20	1	0	0	3.00	0	0	0
Glenn Resch	Colorado	61	3424	230	5	0	4.03	16	31	11
Phil Myre	Colorado	24	1256	112	1	0	5.35	2	17	2
Steve Janaszak	Colorado	2	100	13	0	0	7.80	0	1	0
COLORADO	**TOTAL**	80	4800	362		0	4.53	18	49	13
Murray Bannerman	Chicago	29	1671	116	2	1	4.17	11	12	4
Tony Esposito	Chicago	52	3069	231	8	1	4.52	19	25	8
Warren Skorodenski	Chicago	1	60	5	1	0	5.00	0	1	0
CHICAGO	**TOTAL**	80	4800	363		2	4.54	30	38	12
Mike Blake	Los Angeles	2	51	2	0	0	2.35	0	0	0
Doug Keans	Los Angeles	31	1436	103	5	0	4.30	8	10	7
Mario Lessard	Los Angeles	52	2933	213	3	2	4.36	13	28	8
Jim Rutherford	Los Angeles	7	380	43	0	0	6.79	3	3	0
LOS ANGELES	**TOTAL**	80	4800	369		2	4.61	24	41	15
Vincent Tremblay	Toronto	40	2033	153	3	1	4.52	10	18	8
Michel Larocque	Toronto	50	2647	207	4	0	4.69	10	24	8
Bob Parent	Toronto	2	120	13	0	0	6.50	0	2	0
TORONTO	**TOTAL**	80	4800	380		1	4.75	20	44	16

All-Time NHL Records

Game

MOST GOALS: 7, Joe Malone, Quebec Bulldogs, Jan. 31, 1920 vs. Toronto St. Pats; (Modern) 6, Syd Howe, Detroit Red Wings, Feb. 3, 1944 vs. New York Rangers; 6, Red Berenson, St. Louis Blues, Nov. 7, 1968 vs. Philadelphia Flyers; 6, Darryl Sittler, Toronto Maple Leafs, Feb. 7, 1976 vs. Boston Bruins

MOST ASSISTS: 7, Bill Taylor, Detroit Red Wings, Mar. 16, 1947 vs. Chicago Black Hawks

MOST POINTS: 10, Darryl Sittler, Toronto Maple Leafs, Feb. 7, 1976 vs. Boston Bruins (six goals, four assists)

MOST PENALTY MINUTES: 67, Randy Holt, Los Angeles Kings, Mar. 11, 1979 vs. Philadelphia Flyers

Season

MOST GOALS: 92, Wayne Gretzky, Edmonton Oilers, 1981-82

MOST ASSISTS: 120, Wayne Gretzky, Edmonton Oilers, 1981-82

MOST POINTS: 212, Wayne Gretzky, Edmonton Oilers, 1981-82

MOST SHUTOUTS: 22, George Hainsworth, Montreal Canadiens, 1928-29; (Modern) 15, Tony Esposito, Chicago Black Hawks, 1969-70

MOST PENALTY MINUTES: 472, Dave Schultz, Philadelphia Flyers, 1974-75

MOST POINTS BY A ROOKIE: 103, Dale Hawerchuk, Winnipeg, 1981-82

MOST ASSISTS BY A GOALIE: 8, Mike Palmateer, Washington Capitals, 1980-81

Career

MOST SEASONS: 26, Gordie Howe, Detroit Red Wings, Hartford Whalers, 1946-47 to 1970-71, 1979-80

MOST GAMES: 1,767, Gordie Howe, Detroit Red Wings, Hartford Whalers

MOST GOALS: 801, Gordie Howe, Detroit Red Wings, Hartford Whalers

MOST POINTS: 1,850, Gordie Howe, Detroit Red Wings, Hartford Whalers

MOST PENALTY MINUTES: 2,485, Dave Williams, Toronto, Vancouver, 1974-82

MOST SHUTOUTS: 103, Terry Sawchuk, Detroit, Boston, Toronto, Los Angeles, New York Rangers

MOST CONSECUTIVE GAMES: 914, Garry Unger, Toronto, Detroit, St. Louis, Atlanta, Feb. 4, 1968 through Dec. 15, 1979

Joe Malone, Montreal and Quebec: Seven goals in one game.

NHL Trophy Winners

HART MEMORIAL TROPHY

Awarded to the league's Most Valuable Player. Selected in a vote of hockey writers and broadcasters in each of the 21 NHL cities. The award was presented by the National Hockey League in 1960 after the original Hart Trophy was retired to the Hockey Hall of Fame. The original Hart Trophy was donated in 1923 by Dr. David A. Hart, father of Cecil Hart, former manager-coach of the Montreal Canadiens.

1923-24 Frank Nighbor, Ottawa	1953-54 Al Rollins, Chicago
1924-25 Billy Burch, Hamilton	1954-55 Ted Kennedy, Toronto
1925-26 Nels Stewart, Montreal M.	1955-56 Jean Beliveau, Montreal
1926-27 Herb Gardiner, Montreal C.	1956-57 Gordie Howe, Detroit
1927-28 Howie Morenz, Montreal C.	1957-58 Gordie Howe, Detroit
1928-29 Roy Worters, New York A.	1958-59 Andy Bathgate, New York R.
1929-30 Nels Stewart, Montreal M.	1959-60 Gordie Howe, Detroit
1930-31 Howie Morenz, Montreal C.	1960-61 Bernie Geoffrion, Montreal
1931-32 Howie Morenz, Montreal C.	1961-62 Jacques Plante, Montreal
1932-33 Eddie Shore, Boston	1962-63 Gordie Howe, Detroit
1933-34 Aurel Joliat, Montreal C.	1963-64 Jean Beliveau, Montreal
1934-35 Eddie Shore, Boston	1964-65 Bobby Hull, Chicago
1935-36 Eddie Shore, Boston	1965-66 Bobby Hull, Chicago
1936-37 Babe Siebert, Montreal C.	1966-67 Stan Mikita, Chicago
1937-38 Eddie Shore, Boston	1967-68 Stan Mikita, Chicago
1938-39 Toe Blake, Montreal C.	1968-69 Phil Esposito, Boston
1939-40 Eddie Goodfellow, Detroit	1969-70 Bobby Orr, Boston
1940-41 Bill Cowley, Boston	1970-71 Bobby Orr, Boston
1941-42 Tommy Anderson, New York A.	1971-72 Bobby Orr, Boston
1942-43 Bill Cowley, Boston	1972-73 Bobby Clarke, Philadelphia
1943-44 Babe Pratt, Toronto	1973-74 Phil Esposito, Boston
1944-45 Elmer Lach, Montreal C.	1974-75 Bobby Clarke, Philadelphia
1945-46 Max Bentley, Chicago	1975-76 Bobby Clarke, Philadelphia
1946-47 Maurice Richard, Montreal	1976-77 Guy Lafleur, Montreal
1947-48 Buddy O'Conner, New York R.	1977-78 Guy Lafleur, Montreal
1948-49 Sid Abel, Detroit	1978-79 Bryan Trottier, New York I.
1949-50 Charlie Rayner, New York R.	1979-80 Wayne Gretzky, Edmonton
1950-51 Milt Schmidt, Boston	1980-81 Wayne Gretzky, Edmonton
1951-52 Gordie Howe, Detroit	1981-82 Wayne Gretzky, Edmonton
1952-53 Gordie Howe, Detroit	

The Bruins' Eddie Shore won the Hart four times.

VEZINA TROPHY

Awarded to the goalie voted most valuable by the Professional Hockey Writers' Association. Up until the 1981-82 season, the trophy was awarded to the goalie or goalies for the team which gives up the fewest goals during the regular season.

The trophy was presented to the NHL in 1926-27 by the owners of the Montreal Canadiens in memory of Georges Vezina, former Canadien goalie.

1926-27 George Hainsworth, Montreal C.	1961-62 Jacques Plante, Montreal
1927-28 George Hainsworth, Montreal C.	1962-63 Glenn Hall, Chicago
1928-29 George Hainsworth, Montreal C.	1963-64 Charlie Hodge, Montreal
1929-30 Tiny Thompson, Boston	1964-65 Terry Sawchuk, Toronto
1930-31 Roy Worters, New York A.	Johnny Bower, Toronto
1931-32 Charlie Gardiner, Chicago	1965-66 Lorne Worsley, Montreal
1932-33 Tiny Thompson, Boston	Charlie Hodge, Montreal
1933-34 Charlie Gardiner, Chicago	1966-67 Glenn Hall, Chicago
1934-35 Lorne Chabot, Chicago	Denis DeJordy, Chicago
1935-36 Tiny Thompson, Boston	1967-68 Lorne Worsley, Montreal
1936-37 Normie Smith, Detroit	Rogatien Vachon, Montreal
1937-38 Tiny Thompson, Boston	1968-69 Glenn Hall, St. Louis
1938-39 Frank Brimsek, Boston	Jacques Plante, St. Louis
1939-40 Davey Kerr, New York R.	1969-70 Tony Esposito, Chicago
1940-41 Turk Broda, Toronto	1970-71 Ed Giacomin, New York R.
1941-42 Frank Brimsek, Boston	Gilles Villemure, New York R.
1942-43 Johnny Mowers, Detroit	1971-72 Tony Esposito, Chicago
1943-44 Bill Durnan, Montreal	Gary Smith, Chicago
1944-45 Bill Durnan, Montreal	1972-73 Ken Dryden, Montreal
1945-46 Bill Durnan, Montreal	1973-74 Bernie Parent, Philadelphia
1946-47 Bill Durnan, Montreal	Tony Esposito, Chicago
1947-48 Turk Broda, Toronto	1974-75 Bernie Parent, Philadelphia
1948-49 Bill Durnan, Montreal	1975-76 Ken Dryden, Montreal
1949-50 Bill Durnan, Montreal	1976-77 Ken Dryden, Montreal
1950-51 Al Rollins, Toronto	Michel Larocque, Montreal
1951-52 Terry Sawchuk, Detroit	1977-78 Ken Dryden, Montreal
1952-53 Terry Sawchuk, Detroit	Michel Larocque, Montreal
1953-54 Harry Lumley, Toronto	1978-79 Ken Dryden, Montreal
1954-55 Terry Sawchuk, Detroit	Michel Larocque, Montreal
1955-56 Jacques Plante, Montreal	1979-80 Bob Sauve, Buffalo
1956-57 Jacques Plante, Montreal	Don Edwards, Buffalo
1957-58 Jacques Plante, Montreal	1980-81 Richard Sevigny, Montreal
1958-59 Jacques Plante, Montreal	Denis Herron, Montreal
1959-60 Jacques Plante, Montreal	Michel Larocque, Montreal
1960-61 Johnny Bower, Toronto	1981-82 Bill Smith, New York I.

Islander Billy Smith was 1981-82 Vezina Trophy winner.

ART ROSS TROPHY

Awarded to the player who compiles the highest number of scoring points during the regular season.

If players are tied for the lead, the trophy is awarded to the one with the most goals. If still tied, it is given to the player with the fewer number of games played. If these do not break the deadlock, the trophy is presented to the player who scored his first goal of the season at the earliest date.

The trophy was presented by Art Ross, the former manager-coach of the Boston Bruins, to the NHL in 1947.

Season	Player and Clubs	Games Played	Goals	Assists	Points
1917-18	Joe Malone, Mtl. Canadiens	20	44	–	44
1918-19	Newsy Lalonde, Mtl. Canadiens	17	23	9	32
1919-20	Joe Malone, Quebec	24	39	9	48
1920-21	Newsy Lalonde, Mtl. Canadiens	24	33	8	41
1921-22	Punch Broadbent, Ottawa	24	32	14	46
1922-23	Babe Dye, Toronto	22	26	11	37
1923-24	Cy Denneny, Ottawa	21	22	1	23
1924-25	Babe Dye, Toronto	29	38	6	44
1925-26	Nels Stewart, Montreal	36	34	8	42
1926-27	Bill Cook, N.Y. Rangers	44	33	4	37
1927-28	Howie Morenz, Mtl. Canadiens	43	33	18	51
1928-29	Ace Bailey, Toronto	44	22	10	32
1929-30	Cooney Weiland, Boston	44	43	30	73
1930-31	Howie Morenz, Mtl. Canadiens	39	28	23	51
1931-32	Harvey Jackson, Toronto	48	28	25	53
1932-33	Bill Cook, N.Y. Rangers	48	28	22	50
1933-34	Charlie Conacher, Toronto	42	32	20	52
1934-35	Charlie Conacher, Toronto	48	36	21	57
1935-36	Dave Schriner, N.Y. Americans	48	19	26	45
1936-37	Dave Schriner, N.Y. Americans	48	21	25	46
1937-38	Gordie Drillon, Toronto	48	26	26	52
1938-39	Toe Blake, Mtl. Canadiens	48	24	23	47
1939-40	Milt Schmidt, Boston	48	22	30	52
1940-41	Bill Cowley, Boston	46	17	45	62
1941-42	Bryan Hextall, N.Y. Rangers	48	24	32	56
1942-43	Doug Bentley, Chicago	50	33	40	73
1943-44	Herbie Cain, Boston	48	36	46	82
1944-45	Elmer Lach, Montreal	50	26	54	80
1945-46	Max Bentley, Chicago	47	31	30	61
1946-47	Max Bentley, Chicago	60	29	43	72
1947-48	Elmer Lach, Montreal	60	30	31	61
1948-49	Roy Conacher, Chicago	60	26	42	68
1949-50	Ted Lindsay, Detroit	69	23	55	78
1950-51	Gordie Howe, Detroit	70	43	43	86
1951-52	Gordie Howe, Detroit	70	47	39	86

The Rangers' Bill Cook twice captured the Ross Trophy.

Season	Player and Clubs	Games Played	Goals	Assists	Points
1952-53	Gordie Howe, Detroit	70	49	46	95
1953-54	Gordie Howe, Detroit	70	33	48	81
1954-55	Bernie Geoffrion, Montreal	70	38	37	75
1955-56	Jean Beliveau, Montreal	70	47	41	88
1956-57	Gordie Howe, Detroit	70	44	45	89
1957-58	Dickie Moore, Montreal	70	36	48	84
1958-59	Dickie Moore, Montreal	70	41	55	96
1959-60	Bobby Hull, Chicago	70	39	42	81
1960-61	Bernie Geoffrion, Montreal	64	50	45	95
1961-62	Bobby Hull, Chicago	70	50	34	84
1962-63	Gordie Howe, Detroit	70	38	48	86
1963-64	Stan Mikita, Chicago	70	39	50	89
1964-65	Stan Mikita, Chicago	70	28	59	87
1965-66	Bobby Hull, Chicago	65	54	43	97
1966-67	Stan Mikita, Chicago	70	35	62	97
1967-68	Stan Mikita, Chicago	72	40	47	87
1968-69	Phil Esposito, Boston	74	49	77	126
1969-70	Bobby Orr, Boston	76	33	87	120
1970-71	Phil Esposito, Boston	76	76	76	152
1971-72	Phil Esposito, Boston	76	66	67	133
1972-73	Phil Esposito, Boston	78	55	75	130
1973-74	Phil Esposito, Boston	78	68	77	145
1974-75	Bobby Orr, Boston	80	46	89	135
1975-76	Guy Lafleur, Montreal	80	56	69	125
1976-77	Guy Lafleur, Montreal	80	56	80	136
1977-78	Guy Lafleur, Montreal	78	60	72	132
1978-79	Bryan Trottier, New York I.	76	47	87	134
1979-80	Marcel Dionne, Los Angeles	80	53	84	137
1980-81	Wayne Gretzky, Edmonton	80	55	109	164
1981-82	Wayne Gretzky, Edmonton	80	92	120	212

FRANK J. SELKE TROPHY

Awarded to the forward "who best excels in the defensive aspects of the game."

The trophy was presented to the NHL in 1977 by the Board of Governors in honor of Frank J. Selke, a "Builder" member of the Hall of Fame who spent more than 60 years in the game as coach, manager and front-office executive.

1977-78 Bob Gainey, Montreal
1978-79 Bob Gainey, Montreal
1979-80 Bob Gainey, Montreal

1980-81 Bob Gainey, Montreal
1981-82 Steve Kasper, Boston

WILLIAM M. JENNINGS AWARD

Awarded to the goalie or goalies for the team which gives up the fewest goals during the regular season. To be eligible, a goalie must play at least 25 games.

The trophy was presented to the NHL in 1982 in memory of William M. Jennings, an architect of the league's expansion from six teams to the present 21.

1981-82 Denis Herron, Montreal
　　　　 Rick Wamsley, Montreal

BILL MASTERTON TROPHY

Awarded by the Professional Hockey Writers' Association to "the NHL player who exemplifies the qualities of perseverance, sportsmanship and dedication to hockey." Named for the late Minnesota North Star player.

1967-68 Claude Provost, Montreal
1968-69 Ted Hampson, Oakland
1969-70 Pit Martin, Chicago
1970-71 Jean Ratelle, New York R.
1971-72 Bobby Clarke, Philadelphia
1972-73 Lowell MacDonald, Pittsburgh
1973-74 Henri Richard, Montreal
1974-75 Don Luce, Buffalo

1975-76 Rod Gilbert, New York R.
1976-77 Ed Westfall, New York I.
1977-78 Butch Goring, Los Angeles
1978-79 Serge Savard, Montreal
1979-80 Al MacAdam, Minnesota
1980-81 Blake Dunlop, St. Louis
1981-82 Glenn Resch, Colorado

JAMES NORRIS MEMORIAL TROPHY

Awarded to the league's best defenseman. Selected by a vote of hockey writers and broadcasters in each of the 21 NHL cities.

It was presented in 1953 by the four children of the late James Norris Sr., in memory of the former owner-president of the Detroit Red Wings.

1953-54 Red Kelly, Detroit	1967-68 Bobby Orr, Boston
1954-55 Doug Harvey, Montreal	1968-69 Bobby Orr, Boston
1955-56 Doug Harvey, Montreal	1969-70 Bobby Orr, Boston
1956-57 Doug Harvey, Montreal	1970-71 Bobby Orr, Boston
1957-58 Doug Harvey, Montreal	1971-72 Bobby Orr, Boston
1958-59 Tom Johnson, Montreal	1972-73 Bobby Orr, Boston
1959-60 Doug Harvey, Montreal	1973-74 Bobby Orr, Boston
1960-61 Doug Harvey, Montreal	1974-75 Bobby Orr, Boston
1961-62 Doug Harvey, New York R.	1975-76 Denis Potvin, New York I.
1962-63 Pierre Pilote, Chicago	1976-77 Larry Robinson, Montreal
1963-64 Pierre Pilote, Chicago	1977-78 Denis Potvin, New York I.
1964-65 Pierre Pilote, Chicago	1978-79 Denis Potvin, New York I.
1965-66 Jacques Laperriere, Montreal	1978-80 Larry Robinson, Montreal
1966-67 Harry Howell, New York R.	1980-81 Randy Carlyle, Pittsburgh
	1981-82 Doug Wilson, Chicago

CONN SMYTHE TROPHY

Awarded to the Most Valuable Player in the Stanley Cup Playoffs. Selected in a vote of the League Governors.

The trophy was presented by Maple Leaf Gardens Ltd. in 1964 to honor the former coach, manager, president and owner of the Toronto Maple Leafs.

1964-65 Jean Beliveau, Montreal	1973-74 Bernie Parent, Philadelphia
1965-66 Roger Crozier, Detroit	1974-75 Bernie Parent, Philadelphia
1966-67 Dave Keon, Toronto	1975-76 Reggie Leach, Philadelphia
1967-68 Glenn Hall, St. Louis	1976-77 Guy Lafleur, Montreal
1968-69 Serge Savard, Montreal	1977-78 Larry Robinson, Montreal
1969-70 Bobby Orr, Boston	1978-79 Bob Gainey, Montreal
1970-71 Ken Dryden, Montreal	1979-80 Bryan Trottier, New York I.
1971-72 Bobby Orr, Boston	1980-81 Butch Goring, New York I.
1972-73 Yvan Cournoyer, Montreal	1981-82 Mike Bossy, New York I.

Detroit's Red Kelly was first winner of the Norris Trophy.

CALDER MEMORIAL TROPHY

Awarded to the league's outstanding rookie. Selected by a vote of hockey writers and broadcasters in each of the 21 NHL cities. It was originated in 1937 by Frank Calder, first president of the NHL. After his death in 1943, the league presented the Calder Memorial Trophy in his memory.

To be eligible to receive the trophy, a player cannot have participated in more than 20 games in any preceding season or in six or more games in each of any two preceding seasons.

The top rookies (from 1932-33 to 1936-37 they were named but no trophy was presented):

1932-33 Carl Voss, Detroit
1933-34 Russ Blinco, Montreal M.
1934-35 Dave Schriner, New York A.
1935-36 Mike Karakas, Chicago
1936-37 Syl Apps, Toronto
1937-38 Cully Dahlstrom, Chicago
1938-39 Frank Brimsek, Boston
1939-40 Kilby MacDonald, New York R.
1940-41 Johnny Quilty, Montreal C.
1941-42 Grant Warwick, New York R.
1942-43 Gaye Stewart, Toronto
1943-44 Gus Bodnar, Toronto
1944-45 Frank McCool, Toronto
1945-46 Edgar Laprade, New York R.
1946-47 Howie Meeker, Toronto
1947-48 Jim McFadden, Detroit
1948-49 Pentti Lund, New York R.
1949-50 Jack Gelineau, Boston
1950-51 Terry Sawchuk, Detroit
1951-52 Bernie Geoffrion, Montreal
1952-53 Lorne Worsley, New York R.
1953-54 Camille Henry, New York R.
1954-55 Ed Litzenberger, Chicago
1955-56 Glenn Hall, Detroit
1956-57 Larry Regan, Boston

1957-58 Frank Mahovlich, Toronto
1958-59 Ralph Backstrom, Montreal
1959-60 Bill Hay, Chicago
1960-61 Dave Keon, Toronto
1961-62 Bobby Rousseau, Montreal
1962-63 Kent Douglas, Toronto
1963-64 Jacques Laperriere, Montreal
1964-65 Roger Crozier, Detroit
1965-66 Brit Selby, Toronto
1966-67 Bobby Orr, Boston
1967-68 Derek Sanderson, Boston
1968-69 Danny Grant, Minnesota
1969-70 Tony Esposito, Chicago
1970-71 Gil Perreault, Buffalo
1971-72 Ken Dryden, Montreal
1972-73 Steve Vickers, New York R.
1973-74 Denis Potvin, New York I.
1974-75 Eric Vail, Atlanta
1975-76 Bryan Trottier, New York I.
1976-77 Willi Plett, Atlanta
1977-78 Mike Bossy, New York I.
1978-79 Bobby Smith, Minnesota
1979-80 Ray Bourque, Boston
1980-81 Peter Stastny, Quebec
1981-82 Dale Hawerchuk, Winnipeg

A Bruin rookie named Bobby Orr won the Calder in 1967.

LADY BYNG TROPHY

Awarded to the player combining the highest type of sportsmanship and gentlemanly conduct plus a high standard of playing ability. Selected by a vote of hockey writers and broadcasters in the 21 NHL cities.

Lady Byng, the wife of the Governor-General of Canada in 1925, presented the trophy to the NHL during that year.

1924-25 Frank Nighbor, Ottawa	1953-54 Red Kelly, Detroit
1925-26 Frank Nighbor, Ottawa	1954-55 Sid Smith, Toronto
1926-27 Billy Burch, New York A.	1955-56 Earl Reibel, Detroit
1927-28 Frank Boucher, New York R.	1956-57 Andy Hebenton, New York R.
1928-29 Frank Boucher, New York R.	1957-58 Camille Henry, New York R.
1929-30 Frank Boucher, New York R.	1958-59 Alex Delvecchio, Detroit
1930-31 Frank Boucher, New York R.	1959-60 Don McKenney, Boston
1931-32 Joe Primeau, Toronto	1960-61 Red Kelly, Toronto
1932-33 Frank Boucher, New York R.	1961-62 Dave Keon, Toronto
1933-34 Frank Boucher, New York R.	1962-63 Dave Keon, Toronto
1934-35 Frank Boucher, New York R.	1963-64 Ken Wharram, Chicago
1935-36 Doc Romnes, Chicago	1964-65 Bobby Hull, Chicago
1936-37 Marty Barry, Detroit	1965-66 Alex Delvecchio, Detroit
1937-38 Gordie Drillon, Toronto	1966-67 Stan Mikita, Chicago
1938-39 Clint Smith, New York R.	1967-68 Stan Mikita, Chicago
1939-40 Bobby Bauer, Boston	1968-69 Alex Delvecchio, Detroit
1940-41 Bobby Bauer, Boston	1969-70 Phil Goyette, St. Louis
1941-42 Syl Apps, Toronto	1970-71 Johnny Bucyk, Boston
1942-43 Max Bentley, Chicago	1971-72 Jean Ratelle, New York R.
1943-44 Clint Smith, Chicago	1972-73 Gil Perreault, Buffalo
1944-45 Bill Mosienko, Chicago	1973-74 John Bucyk, Boston
1945-46 Toe Blake, Montreal	1974-75 Marcel Dionne, Detroit
1946-47 Bobby Bauer, Boston	1975-76 Jean Ratelle, NYR.-Boston
1947-48 Buddy O'Connor, New York R.	1976-77 Marcel Dionne, Los Angeles
1948-49 Bill Quackenbush, Detroit	1977-78 Butch Goring, Los Angeles
1949-50 Edgar Laprade, New York R.	1978-79 Bob MacMillan, Atlanta
1950-51 Red Kelly, Detroit	1979-80 Wayne Gretzky, Edmonton
1951-52 Sid Smith, Toronto	1980-81 Rick Kehoe, Pittsburgh
1952-53 Red Kelly, Detroit	1981-82 Rick Middleton, Boston

Butch Goring won Lady Byng when he was with the Kings.

STANLEY CUP WINNERS

	Season	Champions	Coach
	1892-93	Montreal A.A.A.	
	1894-95	Montreal Victorias	Mike Grant*
	1895-96	Winnipeg Victorias	
	1896-97	Montreal Victorias	Mike Grant*
	1897-98	Montreal Victorias	F. Richardson
	1898-99	Montreal Shamrocks	H. J. Trihey*
	1899-1900	Montreal Shamrocks	H. J. Trihey*
	1900-01	Winnipeg Victorias	
	1901-02	Montreal A.A.A.	R. R. Boon*
	1902-03	Ottawa Silver Seven	A. T. Smith
	1903-04	Ottawa Silver Seven	A. T. Smith
	1904-05	Ottawa Silver Seven	A. T. Smith
	1905-06	Montreal Wanderers	
	1906-07	Kenora Thistles (January)	Tommy Phillips*
	1906-07	Montreal Wanderers (March)	Cecil Blachford
	1907-08	Montreal Wanderers	Cecil Blachford
	1908-09	Ottawa Senators	Bruce Stuart*
	1909-10	Montreal Wanderers	Pud Glass*
	1910-11	Ottawa Senators	Bruce Stuart*
	1911-12	Quebec Bulldogs	C. Nolan
**	1912-13	Quebec Bulldogs	Joe Marlowe*
	1913-14	Toronto Blue Shirts	Scotty Davidson*
	1914-15	Vancouver Millionaires	Frank Patrick
	1915-16	Montreal Canadiens	George Kennedy
	1916-17	Seattle Metropolitans	Pete Muldoon
	1917-18	Toronto Arenas	Dick Carroll
***	1918-19	No decision.	
	1919-20	Ottawa Senators	Pete Green
	1920-21	Ottawa Senators	Pete Green
	1921-22	Toronto St. Pats	Eddie Powers
	1922-23	Ottawa Senators	Pete Green
	1923-24	Montreal Canadiens	Leo Dandurand
	1924-25	Victoria Cougars	Lester Patrick
	1925-26	Montreal Maroons	Eddie Gerard
	1926-27	Ottawa Senators	Dave Gill
	1927-28	New York Rangers	Lester Patrick
	1928-29	Boston Bruins	Cy Denneny
	1929-30	Montreal Canadiens	Cecil Hart
	1930-31	Montreal Canadiens	Cecil Hart
	1931-32	Toronto Maple Leafs	Dick Irvin
	1932-33	New York Rangers	Lester Patrick
	1933-34	Chicago Black Hawks	Tommy Gorman
	1934-35	Montreal Maroons	Tommy Gorman
	1935-36	Detroit Red Wings	Jack Adams
	1936-37	Detroit Red Wings	Jack Adams
	1937-38	Chicago Black Hawks	Bill Stewart
	1938-39	Boston Bruins	Art Ross

Nels Stewart paced the Montreal Maroons to Cup in 1925-26.

Boston went all the way in 1938-39.

1939-40	New York Rangers	Frank Boucher
1940-41	Boston Bruins	Cooney Weiland
1941-42	Toronto Maple Leafs	Hap Day
1942-43	Detroit Red Wings	Jack Adams
1943-44	Montreal Canadiens	Dick Irvin
1944-45	Toronto Maple Leafs	Hap Day
1945-46	Montreal Canadiens	Dick Irvin
1946-47	Toronto Maple Leafs	Hap Day
1947-48	Toronto Maple Leafs	Hap Day
1948-49	Toronto Maple Leafs	Hap Day
1949-50	Detroit Red Wings	Tommy Ivan
1950-51	Toronto Maple Leafs	Joe Primeau
1951-52	Detroit Red Wings	Tommy Ivan
1952-53	Montreal Canadiens	Dick Irvin
1953-54	Detroit Red Wings	Tommy Ivan
1954-55	Detroit Red Wings	Jimmy Skinner
1955-56	Montreal Canadiens	Toe Blake
1956-57	Montreal Canadiens	Toe Blake
1957-58	Montreal Canadiens	Toe Blake
1958-59	Montreal Canadiens	Toe Blake
1959-60	Montreal Canadiens	Toe Blake
1960-61	Chicago Black Hawks	Rudy Pilous
1961-62	Toronto Maple Leafs	Punch Imlach
1962-63	Toronto Maple Leafs	Punch Imlach
1963-64	Toronto Maple Leafs	Punch Imlach
1964-65	Montreal Canadiens	Toe Blake
1965-66	Montreal Canadiens	Toe Blake
1966-67	Toronto Maple Leafs	Punch Imlach
1967-68	Montreal Canadiens	Toe Blake
1968-69	Montreal Canadiens	Claude Ruel
1969-70	Boston Bruins	Harry Sinden
1970-71	Montreal Canadiens	Al MacNeil
1971-72	Boston Bruins	Tom Johnson
1972-73	Montreal Canadiens	Scotty Bowman
1973-74	Philadelphia Flyers	Fred Shero
1974-75	Philadelphia Flyers	Fred Shero
1975-76	Montreal Canadiens	Scotty Bowman
1976-77	Montreal Canadiens	Scotty Bowman
1977-78	Montreal Canadiens	Scotty Bowman
1978-79	Montreal Canadiens	Scotty Bowman
1979-80	New York Islanders	Al Arbour
1980-81	New York Islanders	Al Arbour
1981-82	New York Islanders	Al Arbour

* In the early years the teams were frequently run by the Captain.

** Victoria defeated Quebec in challenge series. No official recognition.

*** In the spring of 1919 the Montreal Canadiens traveled to Seattle to meet Seattle, PCHL champions. After five games had been played—teams were tied at 2 wins each and 1 tie—the series was called off by the local Department of Health because of the influenza epidemic and the death from influenza of Joe Hall.

NHL TV/Radio Roundup

The USA Cable Network will carry 33 regular-season games, with emphasis on Monday nights, plus the All-Star Game, Stanley Cup conference championships and finals and selected divisional playoff games. Al Trautwig is the host and Dan Kelly the play-by-play announcer.

BOSTON BRUINS
Bruins' games are carried on WSBK-TV (Channel 38) with Fred Cusick and John Peirson at the mikes. Bob Wilson and John Bucyk handle the radio side on WITS (1510).

BUFFALO SABRES
Ted Darling handles telecasts on WGR-TV (Channel 2) with Pat Hannigan providing color commmentary. Darling and Hannigan also work together on the Cable TV Productions. Rick Jeanneret does play-by-play on WGR Radio (550 AM).

CALGARY FLAMES
The Flames can be found on CFAC-TV (Channels 2 and 7), with Ed Whalen and Jim Van Horne describing the action. Peter Maher and Doug Barley are their radio counterparts for CHQR (810).

CHICAGO BLACK HAWKS
Pat Foley is the voice of the Black Hawks on WIND radio (560). He also handles TV on SportsVision cable.

DETROIT RED WINGS
Bruce Martyn does the play-by-play and Sid Abel provides the color for the Red Wings on WJR radio (760) and WKBD-TV (Channel 50).

EDMONTON OILERS
CFRN (1260) broadcasts all the Oiler games, with Rod Phillips and Ken Brown describing the action. The television outlet is CITV (Channel 13).

HARTFORD WHALERS
Chuck Kaiton handles the radio chores for WTIC (1080) and Scott Wahle is the TV voice of the Whalers on WVIT-TV (Channel 30).

Canuck Harold Snepsts cross-checks Islander John Tonelli.

LOS ANGELES KINGS

Kings' games are carried on KHJ-TV (Channel 9) and KPRZ radio (1150), with Bob Miller and Nick Nickson describing the action.

MINNESOTA NORTH STARS

Bob Kurtz and Tom Reid man the mikes for telecasts on KMSP-TV (Channel 9). On radio it's Al Shaver and Ted Robinson over KSTP (1500).

MONTREAL CANADIENS

The Canadiens are covered in English on CBMT (Channel 6) and French on CBFT (Channel 2). Danny Gallivan and Dick Irvin handle telecasts in English while Lionel Duval, Rene Lecavalier and Gilles Tremblay say it in French. English language radio broadcasts are carried on CBM (940) and CFCF (600) with Irvin and Ron Reusch, and Richard Garneau teams with Duval to provide French radio coverage on CBF (690).

NEW JERSEY

TV and radio arrangements were incomplete at press time.

NEW YORK ISLANDERS

WOR-TV (Channel 9), with Jiggs McDonald and Eddie Westfall, and WMCA radio (570), with Barry Landers and Jean Potvin, are the outlets for the defending champions.

NEW YORK RANGERS

Jim Gordon does play-by-play and Phil Esposito and Mike Eruzione the color on WOR-TV (Channel 9), while Marv Albert and Sal Messina call the shots on WNEW radio (1130).

PHILADELPHIA FLYERS

Gene Hart and Bobby Taylor cover the Flyers on WIP radio (610) and WTAF-TV (Channel 29).

PITTSBURGH PENGUINS

Penguin games can be heard on KQV (1410) and seen on WPGH-TV (Channel 53) with Mike Lange and Terry Schiffhauer describing the action.

QUEBEC NORDIQUES

Nordique action is on radio CKCV (1280), with Andre Cote and Michel Villeneuve behind the mike, and on CFCM-TV (Channel 4), with Claude Bedard and Francois Lacombe doing the honors.

ST. LOUIS BLUES

Dan Kelly and Gus Kyle work the radio side on KMOX (1120). TV Arrangements were not complete at press time.

TORONTO MAPLE LEAFS

Bill Hewitt, Bob Cole and Ron Hewat cover the Maple Leafs on CBLT-TV (Channel 5) and CHCH-TV (Channel 11) as well as radio network HEWPEX.

VANCOUVER CANUCKS

All games are carried on CKNW radio (980) with Jim Robson doing play-by-play. BCTV televises Wednesday night games while CBS (Channel 2) carries "Hockey Night in Canada" games.

WASHINGTON CAPITALS

Ron Weber covers Capital games on WTOP radio (1500), Jim West and Yvon Labre are the TV voices on WDCA (Channel 20).

WINNIPEG JETS

Jet games are carried on CJOB radio (680) and CKND-TV (Channel 9). Ken Nicholson and Curt Keilback do the radio and Brian Swain amd Dave Richardson are the TV announcers.

Official 1982–83 NHL Schedule

SUBJECT TO CHANGE   *Afternoon Game

Tue Oct 5
NY at Van
Pitt at NJ
Calg at Edm

Wed Oct 6
Hart at Mont
Que at Buff
Wash at NYR
Tor at Chi
StL at Det
Minn at Winn
Van at LA

Thu Oct 7
Mont at Bos
Que at Phil
NYI at Calg
Tor at StL

Fri Oct 8
NYI at Edm
NYR at NJ
Det at Minn

Sat Oct 9
Bos at Hart
Buff at Que
Chi at Mont
NYR at Pitt
Phil at Wash
NJ at Tor
Winn at Det
Minn at StL
Calg at LA
Edm at Van

Sun Oct 10
Pitt at Bos
Hart at Buff
Wash at Phil
Winn at Chi

Mon Oct 11
Mont at Que
NYI at NYR

Tue Oct 12
Bos at NJ

Van at Pitt
LA at Winn
Edm at Calg

Wed Oct 13
Phil at NYR
Wash at Tor
StL at Chi

Thu Oct 14
Van at Bos
Edm at Hart
Buff at Phil
Mont at NJ
LA at Que
Pitt at NYI
Tor at Minn
Det at Calg
Winn at StL

Sat Oct 16
Edm at Bos
Van at Hart
Buff at Wash
NYR at Mont
Phil at Que
LA at NYI
NJ at Pitt
Chi at Tor
Det at StL
Calg at Minn

Sun Oct 17
Edm at Buff
LA at NYR
Det at Chi
Calg at Winn

Mon Oct 18
Phil at NJ
StL at Minn

Tue Oct 19
Bos at Calg
Van at NYI

Wed Oct 20
Hart at Edm
Buff at Chi

Mont at Wash
Que at Det
Van at NYR
StL at Pitt
NJ at LA
Minn at Tor

Thu Oct 21
Bos at Edm
Hart at Calg
Mont at Phil
Pitt at Que
Wash at NYI

Fri Oct 22
NJ at Winn

Sat Oct 23
Bos at Van
Hart at LA
Buff at Det
Que at Mont
NYR at NYI
Phil at Pitt
Minn at Wash
Calg at Tor
Chi at StL

Sun Oct 24
Bos at LA
StL at Buff
NYI at Chi
Minn at NYR
Det at Phil
Edm at Winn

Tue Oct 26
Hart at Van
Buff at Mont
Tor at Que
Calg at NYI
Minn at NJ

Wed Oct 27
Bos at Tor
Calg at NYR
Wash at Pitt
StL at Det
Chi at Edm
LA at Winn

Thu Oct 28
NYI at NJ
Pitt at Phil
Det at Minn

Fri Oct 29
Chi at Van
LA at Edm

Sat Oct 30
Bos at Mont
Det at Hart
Buff at Tor
NYR at Que
NJ at NYI
Phil at Minn
Calg at Pitt
Wash at StL
Chi at LA

Sun Oct 31
Mont at Buff
Pitt at NYR
Phil at Winn
*Van at Edm

Mon Nov 1
Calg at NJ

Tue Nov 2
Minn at Hart
NJ at Mont
Van at Que
Pitt at NYI
Det at StL

Wed Nov 3
Bos at Buff
NYI at Det
Wash at Chi
Tor at LA
Winn at Edm

Thu Nov 4
Hart at Bos
Minn at Mont
Van at Phil
Pitt at NJ
Winn at Calg

Fri Nov 5
NYR at Edm
StL at Wash

Sat Nov 6
Buff at Hart
Van at Mont
Minn at Que
Phil at NYI
NYR at Calg
Pitt at LA
NJ at Det
Tor at StL

Sun Nov 7
Det at Bos
Hart at Wash
Van at Buff
NYI at Phil
Tor at Chi
Calg at Winn

Mon Nov 8
Edm at Que
Wash at NJ

Tue Nov 9
Mont at Minn
StL at NYI
LA at Calg

Wed Nov 10
Que at Hart
Phil at Buff
Mont at Chi
StL at NYR
Edm at Pitt
NJ at Wash
Det at Tor
LA at Van

Thu Nov 11
Que at Bos
NYI at Minn
NYR at Phil
Edm at NJ

Sat Nov 13
Buff at Bos

StL at Hart
Mont at LA
NJ at Que
NYI at Wash
Edm at Phil
Calg at Pitt
Minn at Tor
Chi at Det
Van at Winn

Sun Nov 14
StL at Bos
Pitt at Buff
Edm at NYR
Minn at Chi
Van at Winn

Tue Nov 16
Bos at Que
Mont at Hart
Edm at NYI
Calg at Wash
NJ at StL
Det at Van
Minn at LA

Wed Nov 17
Hart at Pitt
Buff at Winn
Tor at NYR
NJ at Chi

Thu Nov 18
Bos at NYI
Buff at Minn
Que at Mont
Calg at Phil
Det at LA

Fri Nov 19
Wash at Winn

Sat Nov 20
Bos at Pitt
Calg at Hart
Buff at LA
Phil at Mont
Chi at NYI
NYR at Tor
NJ at Minn
Det at StL
Van at Edm

Sun Nov 21
Calg at Bos
Que at Edm
NYI at NYR
StL at Phil.
Wash at Van
Det at Chi

Tue Nov 23
Mont at StL
Que at Van
Minn at NYI
Wash at Calg

Wed Nov 24
Bos at Phil
Buff at Hart
Mont at Det
Minn at NYR
Tor at Pitt
Wash at Edm
NJ at LA
Chi at Winn

Thu Nov 25
NYI at Bos
Que at Calg

Fri Nov 26
Chi at Hart
StL at Buff
Pitt at Minn
Tor at Wash
NJ at Van
Edm at Winn

Sat Nov 27
*Hart at Bos
Det at Mont
Chi at Que
NYR at NYI
Phil at LA
Pitt at StL
NJ at Calg
Winn at Tor

Sun Nov 28
NYR at Buff
NYI at Wash
Phil at Van
Edm at Det

Mon Nov 29
Winn at Mont
Chi at NJ
Calg at Minn

Tue Nov 30
Winn at Que
NYI at StL
LA at Van

Wed Dec 1
Hart at NYR
Mont at Buff
Phil at Edm
Chi at Pitt
Tor at NJ
Minn at Det
Calg at LA

Thu Dec 2
Que at Bos
Pitt at Wash
Minn at StL

Fri Dec 3
Hart at NJ

NYI at Winn
Calg at Van

Sat Dec 4
Bos at Mont
NYR at Hart
Buff at Que
NYI at Tor
Phil at Pitt
Chi at Wash
NJ at Det
*StL at LA
Winn at Minn
Calg at Edm

Sun Dec 5
Phil at Bos
Chi at Buff
Tor at NYR
StL at Van
LA at Edm

Mon Dec 6
Hart at Mont
Winn at NJ

Tue Dec 7
Bos at Que
Tor at NYI
Winn at Wash
StL at Edm
LA at Calg

Wed Dec 8
Mont at Hart
Buff at Pitt
NYI at Det
NYR at Chi
Van at Tor

Thu Dec 9
Mont at Bos
Que at Phil
Wash at NJ
StL at Calg
Van at Minn
Edm at LA

Fri Dec 10
NYR at Wash
Calg at Winn

Sat Dec 11
*Chi at Bos
Phil at Hart
Buff at Mont
Que at Pitt
NJ at NYI
Det at Tor
Van at StL
Edm at Minn
LA at Winn

Sun Dec 12
Bos at Wash

Hart at Buff
Que at Chi
NJ at NYR
Pitt at Phil
Calg at Det

Tue Dec 14
Hart at Minn
Buff at NYI
Tor at Que
LA at Wash
Winn at StL

Wed Dec 15
Mont at Van
LA at NYR
Det at Pitt
StL at Tor
Winn at Chi

Thu Dec 16
Buff at Bos
Det at Phil
Wash at Minn
Van at Calg

Fri Dec 17
Hart at Winn
NYI at NYR
NJ at Edm

Sat Dec 18
*LA at Bos
Hart at StL
Buff at Que
Mont at Calg
Phil at NYI
NYR at Det
Wash at Pitt
Chi at Tor
Minn at Van

Sun Dec 19
Que at Buff
Mont at Edm
Wash at Phil
NJ at Winn
LA at Chi

Mon Dec 20
Pitt at NYR

Tue Dec 21
Pitt at Hart
NYR at Que
StL at Det
Minn at Calg
Winn at LA

Wed Dec 22
Buff at NYR
Phil at NJ
Tor at Chi
Minn at Edm

Thu Dec 23
Bos at Hart
Mont at Que
Wash at NYI
Pitt at Det
Tor at StL
Calg at Van
Edm at LA

Sun Dec 26
NJ at Bos
NYI at Hart
Det at Buff
Que at Mont
NYR at Pitt
Phil at Wash
StL at Chi
Minn at Winn
Edm at Calg
Van at LA

Mon Dec 27
Phil at Det

Tue Dec 28
Bos at StL
Hart at Que
Tor at Mont
Pitt at Wash
Chi at Calg
Winn at Van

Wed Dec 29
Mont at Tor
StL at Pitt
Det at Minn
Chi at Edm
Winn at LA

Thu Dec 30
Wash at Hart
NYR at NJ
Phil at Calg

Fri Dec 31
Bos at Minn
NYI at Buff
Chi at Det
Edm at Van

Sat Jan 1
Hart at Tor
NYI at Pitt
*NYR at Wash
Phil at StL
Winn at Edm

Sun Jan 2
Bos at Winn
Hart at Buff
Pitt at Mont
Wash at Que
Phil at Chi
Van at NJ
Det at Tor

Mon Jan 3
Det at NYR

Tue Jan 4
Buff at NYI
Mont at Que
Van at Phil
Chi at StL
Edm at Calg

Wed Jan 5
Bos at Chi
Buff at NYR
Wash at Det
Tor at NJ
StL at Minn
Edm at Winn

Thu Jan 6
Van at Hart
LA at Mont
Tor at Wash
Winn at Calg

Fri Jan 7
Bos at NJ
Van at Buff
Que at NYR
Pitt at Edm

Sat Jan 8
Bos at Mont
Phil at Hart
Que at NYI
Wash at StL
Det at Calg
Chi at Minn

Sun Jan 9
Hart at Phil
LA at Buff
NJ at NYR
Pitt at Winn
Det at Edm
Minn at Chi

Mon Jan 10
Que at NJ

Tue Jan 11
Hart at Mont
Winn at NYI
LA at Wash
Edm at StL

Wed Jan 12
Bos at Tor
Que at Buff
Winn at NYR
Minn at Pitt
Edm at Chi
Calg at Van

Thu Jan 13
Que at Bos
Mont at Hart
NYI at NJ
Pitt at Phil
Tor at Minn
LA at Det
Van at Calg

Fri Jan 14
Wash at Buff
StL at Winn

Sat Jan 15
*NYR at Bos
NJ at Hart
Buff at Wash
Mont at Pitt
Calg at Que
LA at NYI
*Chi at Phil
Tor at Det
Edm at Minn

Sun Jan 16
Phil at NYR
LA at NJ
Det at Chi
Winn at Van

Mon Jan 17
Minn at Bos
StL at Tor

Tue Jan 18
Hart at NYI
Calg at Mont
StL at Que
NYR at Van
Phil at Wash
Edm at LA

Wed Jan 19
NJ at Pitt
Wash at Chi
Tor at Winn
Det at Minn
Van at Edm

Thu Jan 20
Buff at Bos
Hart at LA
NYI at Mont
Calg at Phil
StL at NJ

Fri Jan 21
Que at Wash
NYR at Winn

Sat Jan 22
Bos at Det
Hart at Minn
Buff at Mont
Que at Pitt

Phil at NYI
Chi at Tor
Calg at StL
Edm at Van

Sun Jan 23
Hart at Chi
Winn at Buff
NYR at Phil
*NJ at Wash
LA at Edm

Mon Jan 24
Bos at NYR
Pitt at Tor

Tue Jan 25
Winn at Que
NJ at Phil
Van at Det
Minn at StL
Calg at LA

Wed Jan 26
Mont at Buff
Wash at Pitt
Tor at Edm
Van at Chi

Thu Jan 27
Que at Hart
Mont at NYR
NYI at LA
Winn at Phil
Tor at Calg
StL at Minn

Fri Jan 28
Chi at Buff
Pitt at Wash

Sat Jan 29
*Det at Bos
Winn at Hart
Buff at Tor
Wash at Mont
NJ at Que
NYI at Van
NYR at Pitt
Phil at Minn
LA at StL
Calg at Edm

Sun Jan 30
NYI at Edm
Chi at NYR

Mon Jan 31
Winn at Bos
Pitt at NJ
Minn at Tor

Tue Feb 1
Hart at Que

Mont at Van
NYI at Calg
NYR at LA
Det at Wash
Chi at StL

Wed Feb 2
Hart at Tor
Minn at Buff
Phil at Winn
Pitt at Chi
StL at Det

Thu Feb 3
Que at Bos
Mont at Calg
NYI at NJ
Minn at Wash
LA at Edm

Fri Feb 4
Mont at Edm
Pitt at Winn

Sat Feb 5
*Hart at Bos
*Buff at Que
Minn at NYI
NYR at StL
*Phil at LA
Pitt at Calg
NJ at Wash
Van at Tor
Chi at Det

Sun Feb 6
Bos at Buff
*Mont at Winn
Wash at Que
*NYR at Chi
Van at NJ
Tor at Det

Tue Feb 8
All-Star Game
   at Long Island

Wed Feb 9
Det at Hart
Van at Pitt
NJ at Chi

Thu Feb 10
Pitt at Bos
Buff at LA
Winn at Mont
Que at Calg
Wash at NYI
NYR at Minn
StL at Phil

Fri Feb 11
Que at Edm
Van at Wash

Sat Feb 12
*Tor at Bos
Hart at NYI
Buff at Calg
NYR at Mont
LA at Pitt
NJ at StL
*Winn at Det
Chi at Minn

Sun Feb 13
*Van at Bos
*Tor at Hart
*Que at Chi
LA at Phil
*Winn at Wash

Mon Feb 14
Buff at StL
Edm at Mont

Tue Feb 15
LA at Hart
NYI at Que
Det at Pitt
Minn at NJ
Van at Winn

Wed Feb 16
Bos at Buff
Wash at NYR
StL at Tor
Calg at Chi

Thu Feb 17
Que at Minn
Pitt at NYI
Edm at Phil
Tor at StL
LA at Det
Mont at Hart

Fri Feb 18
Bos at Winn
Calg at Buff
Wash at Van

Sat Feb 19
Bos at Minn
Chi at Hart
Mont at NYI
Que at StL
*NYR at Phil
Edm at Pitt
Wash at LA
Calg at Tor

Sun Feb 20
Hart at Det
Edm at Buff
Winn at NYR
NJ at Phil
LA at Van